Anytime

Anytime

Edited by Cynthia C. Davidson

Anyone Corporation
New York, New York

The MIT Press
Cambridge, Massachusetts
London, England

Editor
Cynthia C. Davidson

Associate Editor
Paul Henninger

Copy Editor
Miranda Robbins

Design
2x4

Anytime is the eighth in a series of eleven planned volumes documenting the annual international, cross-disciplinary conferences being sponsored by the Anyone Corporation to investigate the condition of architecture at the end of the millennium.

Printed and bound in the United States of America.

Library of Congress Catalog Card Number: 99-63030

ISBN: 0-262-54102-5

Anyone Corporation is a not-for-profit corporation in the State of New York with editorial and business offices at 41 West 25th Street, 11th floor, New York, New York 10010.
Email: anyone@anycorp.com

Photo Credits
Photos by Ryuji Miyamoto: pages 76–79.

Photos by Hisao Suzuki: page 82.

Photos by Jacqueline Salmon: pages 84–89.

TABLE OF CONTENTS

Acknowledgments

One of the most potent aspects of the Anyone project is its cross-cultural base. At each Any conference, individuals from different nations gather in one room for three days of face-to-face discussions. In the energy and spontaneity of these conversations, it is easy to be misunderstood because of cultural differences. While these moments can be dislocating and uncomfortable, it is also one of the Anyone philosophies that misunderstanding and dislocation are highly productive forms. Not easy, but productive nonetheless. They crack open cultural repressions and allow us to ask new questions and to learn from one another. For example, the "mid-Anatolian time" of Ankara, as Anytime conference organizer Haluk Pamir called it, ran head-on into Anyone's "New York time" with thought-provoking repercussions. The results, which continue to churn up unanswered questions, begin to appear in the following pages. The story of how these pages came to be, the "real time" of Anytime, began in Geneva, Switzerland, in 1995, with Suha Özkan, the worldly secretary general of the Aga Khan Award for Architecture. After discussing the Any conferences in Geneva, Suha, Peter Eisenman, and I traveled to Ankara in 1996, where the important introduction was made to Haluk Pamir, an architect and professor at Middle East Technical University. Under Suha's and Haluk's steady and determined guidance, a constituency began to build to bring Anytime to Ankara in June 1998. Two important parties came forward: the Architects Association of Turkey, 1927, who agreed to organize the event, and Tepe Construction, Turkey's largest builder, who offered to sponsor the meeting. To plan the conference, dedicated teams were formed, including Tansel Korkmas, Erkin Aytaç, Güven Sargin, Fatih Öz, Zeynep Aktüre, AA officers Abdi Güzer and Haldun Ertekin, and Tepe Managing Director Hasan Barutçu, as well as METU students. The new Çankaya Municipality Contemporary Arts Gallery opened its one-day-old auditorium and galleries for Anytime and for an international architecture exhibition, the first in Ankara since it became the capital of Turkey 75 years ago. When the conference adjourned, work on the book began in both Ankara and New York. Zeynep Aktüre was an extraordinary help with translations and the Turkish newslines found in these pages; Edwin Gunn, Miranda Robbins, interns Benjamin Prosky and Brad Samuels, and associate editor Paul Henninger poured over the texts, and 2x4, Inc., produced the striking and "timely" design of this eighth volume in the Anyone series of conference books. The continuity of the Anyone project has always relied on an international community. Suha Özkan, Haluk Pamir, and Tepe Construction made possible the Anytime conference and this book; even more importantly, Shimizu Corporation in Tokyo has made possible the entire 10-year Anyone project. This is one cross-cultural collaboration about which there is no misunderstanding; indeed, there is deep and lasting gratitude. – C. C. D.

Introduction: Whose Time is It, Anyway? Cynthia C. Davidson

1 Jason Goodwin, *Lords of the Horizons: A History of the Ottoman Empire* (New York: Henry Holt & Company, Inc., 1999). All references to Goodwin in this essay are from this volume.

In his discursive history of the Ottoman Empire, *Lords of the Horizons*, British author Jason Goodwin writes about its later years, "As the empire opened itself up to reform it began erecting public clocks, in an effort to graft on what was punctilious and punctual about the successful West."[1] Built mostly by Armenian Christians and often near the minarets that had dominated the skyline of the overwhelmingly Islamic empire, the clocks were the public acknowledgment of another time, and another way of life, than that kept by the Ottomans. Goodwin continues, "The harder the empire tried to secularize time – to bring it up to date, and make it open and available to all – the more absolutely ordinary it became." Once the formidable empire looked outward for its future rather than inward, once it adopted the time of another society, its very foundations began to weaken.

Though the mechanical clock had been present in Ottoman Turkey at least since the 16th century, its presence in a society that kept its own, "natural" time presented what Ugur Tanyeli calls here a "crisis of the clock." Because the position of the sun had determined the rhythms of Ottoman Islamic society, the clock proved to be "the first 'absolute' substitute for a natural reality in all of history," Tanyeli writes, and it "gradually put the sun 'out of order.'" It is likely that a century passed between the invention of the mechanical clock in Europe and its arrival in the Ottoman Empire, but this machine whose sole function is to measure time "became a sign bearing new meanings in Ottoman Turkey, from the beginning of [the empire's] history until its collapse in the early 20th century."

Over the centuries those meanings changed for the Ottoman Empire. Regarded simply as a sign of prestige and prosperity, the clock was initially viewed as a collector's item, something to be treasured and not necessarily used. It simply was not needed for telling time. When hundreds of years later the public clock towers started to appear, clock time was becoming fully integrated in Ottoman society. J.F. Fraser observed in 1906: "Oh, the Turkish time! . . . The day begins with sunrise. That is 12 o'clock. But the sun does not rise at the same time every day. So the Turk . . . is constantly twiddling the lever of his cheap Austrian watch to keep it right. Nobody is ever sure of the time."[2]

The uncertainty of the hour led to a further unraveling of the magnificent but declining empire, to a "loss of cohesion, and the rise of the private man and institution." This splintering of time from social space and the resulting confusion could be sorted out, Goodwin says, by consulting the *Almanach à l'Usage du Levant*, which chronicled the different times now extant in the empire in order to weave them together for some kind of social efficiency. On December 9, 1898, for example, the British counsel in Istanbul consulted the almanac, Goodwin writes, only to find "that the Greeks were lagging a fortnight behind, and believed it to be 27 November. The Bulgars and Armenians agreed with the Greeks, but the Jews were well into their fifth millennium, and Muslims were living in the fourteenth century and the Ottoman government too, although broadly quattrocentro followed a calendar which seemed two years out of date."

When the Ottoman Empire was challenged militarily in the early 20th century and finally disassembled by the Allies after Germany's defeat in World War I, Atatürk led the 1919 National Movement to unseat the Allies' occupation of Ottoman Turkey. After the declaration of the Turkish Republic in 1923, Atatürk, elected its first president, began a modernization program in Turkey unlike any other in history. Over the next several years, sweeping changes were made in modes of dress, the language, and the alphabet, and Ankara, a town of only 20,000, was made the new capital. In declaring Turkey a secularized nation rather than one under Islamic law, Atatürk in effect severed the country from the time(s) of its past, literally and figuratively, and created a tabula rasa condition

2 Fraser is cited by Goodwin in *Lords of the Horizons*.

of extraordinary scale. The hour, however, was no longer in question. This was a time of modernization over the time of the mullahs, of the mechanical clock over the hour of the prayer.

In 1998, Ankara, now a city of 2.5 million, was host to the Anytime conference. Importantly, the thematic of the event reintroduced the question of time to Turkey, this time in the context of the space and time of architecture. Although Atatürk had defused the debate between the secular time of the clock tower and the religious time of the minaret, he never cultivated an architecture symbolic of the new republic. At the Anytime conference, the idea of indeterminate time, or times, that questions the time of history, of acceleration and collapse, of trajectories and futures, was posed by architecture at this pivotal moment of the millennium.

Setting a conference about space and time in Turkey makes one aware of the considerable differences in the concepts of time and space among Anatolia, Western Europe, and the United States. The approaching end of the 20th century and beginning of the 21st, and more significantly, the end of the second millennium and beginning of the third, have raised Western public consciousness of time to a fin de siècle fervor. Public digital clocks calibrated to the millisecond count down the minutes left in the millennium; the *New York Times* lists the number of days left in 1999 in a daily page-one paid advertisement and the Eiffel Tower displays them in lights, while luxury hotels have been taking 1999 New Year's Eve reservations for the past two or three years. This intensive focus on a moment of change in the Roman calendar suggests that we now live by a homogeneous time that has a global reach. The Any conferences themselves are framed by the end of the millennium, but the annual nomadic movement of Any from hemisphere to hemisphere has introduced not only a cross-cultural discussion but also the idea of cross-cultural times. The very multiplicity, or indeterminacy, of time that seemed to undermine the inner strength of the Ottoman Empire is perhaps today what enables multiple societies to thrive within the monolithic structure of homogenizing globalization and global capital. As Jale Erzen points out here, the same clock that was introduced to give order to the uncontrollable can also be seen as the "any," or the indefinite, which acquires meaning only when there are limits.

In ancient Anatolia, the nomad wandering westward to avoid the limitations imposed by the laws and social time of developing settlements kept to no time but his own. Today, precisely to keep pace with the dominant time of global capital, we are again nomads, roaming the globe on airplanes and pitching our "tents" in Hiltons and Hyatts. The cell phones and laptop computers that have become essential equipment for participating in the global economy also allow us to plug in or out of multiple systems at our own, personal rate, rather than follow customary social rhythms. This is not the "natural" time of the ancient nomad, whose days and nights were determined simply by sunrise and sunset, but an accelerated global time, a 24-hour workday that has necessitated the time of the individual who, through these new "mechanical" devices, fights the clock to create his or her own "natural" time, however stolen it might be.

The time of globalization, or its many times, is something Saskia Sassen prefers to call temporalities, or periods of duration. For her, these different temporalities reflect the different rates of acceleration at which various economic activities occur. Those same degrees of acceleration can be understood as the differences between the time of information and the time of experience, which occur over different periods and are ultimately reflected in the physical development of cities and their services.

In her essay here Sassen names two distinct temporalities, "the collapsing temporality of the national state as a historic institution, and master temporality often thought of as historic time . . . [and] the new temporality of economic globalization." While these conceptual constructs enable Sassen to the look at the global economy, they also introduce spatial questions. For example, the new cross-border geography of the global economy, she writes, "emerges from the juxtaposition of two different trajectories and temporalities – those of the nation state and those of globalization"; in other words, a new topography of space and time is being generated, one that poses new questions and conditions for architecture.

Despite this provocation, the actual debate about architecture at Anytime coalesced around old dialectical pairings like generic/specific and narrative/nonnarrative, familiar constructs that only begin to approach the idea of how degrees of acceleration effect architecture and cities. In Ankara, for example, there is no such concept of speed as the "New York minute," and the image of progress so necessary to political futures is not an experimental Millennium Dome but a new contemporary arts center that, to a New York eye, appears rooted in an "earlier" style (that is, time) of postmodernism. (For more on the "progress" of modernization, see Fredric Jameson's essay here.) These differences, themselves reflections of degrees of acceleration, failed to propel a discussion on possible architectural topographies; rather, as if unnoticed, they returned architecture to familiar (although perhaps no longer safe) ground.

The now often quoted line from *Hamlet*, "Time is out of joint," which Jacques Derrida used to describe the condition of current thought, clearly describes the so-called familiar condition of architecture today. The question is, is it in fact so familiar? With the accelerating speed of media and the virtual time and space of the Internet, the time of information has become displaced from the time of experience. When the time of information and the time of experience were one, the Gothic cathedrals, with their soaring spaces and religious icons, were the dominant media. But with the development of the printing press and later the photograph (that is, the accelerated economies of mass production), information began to be separated from experience. In an effort to regain its time, experience transformed substance into image. In architecture, this can first be seen in the pastiche facades of "postmodernism." Now the "wish you were here" picture postcard image is becoming architecture's equivalent of the media sound bite. It is one of the crises posed by the new topography of space and time that Sassen addresses.

At this crossroads in time, architecture seems to have two choices: one, as Fred Jameson suggests here, is to forget about time and to talk about space; the other is to forget the time of information and image and to return to the time of architecture's space. This is not to suggest a return to the past, to Gothic or baroque space. Rather, it might mean a move away from language, away from hardened semiotic space to a space of the body, mind, and eye – to an affective space. A second, corollary condition of this space could be to leave the symbolic function of the image to media. This does not mean a return to a space where information and experience are one, but rather, where the space of experience can be separated from the dictates of the time of experience.

If architecture, like the Ottoman Empire, opens itself up to "reform" by modeling its future on the time of information, it can only expect the same fate; confusion, ordinariness, and utter collapse as a discipline. Perhaps, as Jameson suggests, it is too late to talk about time. Or, perhaps the lesson in the undecidability of Anytime is to rethink time before it's too late for space.

Anytime in Anatolia Suha Özkan

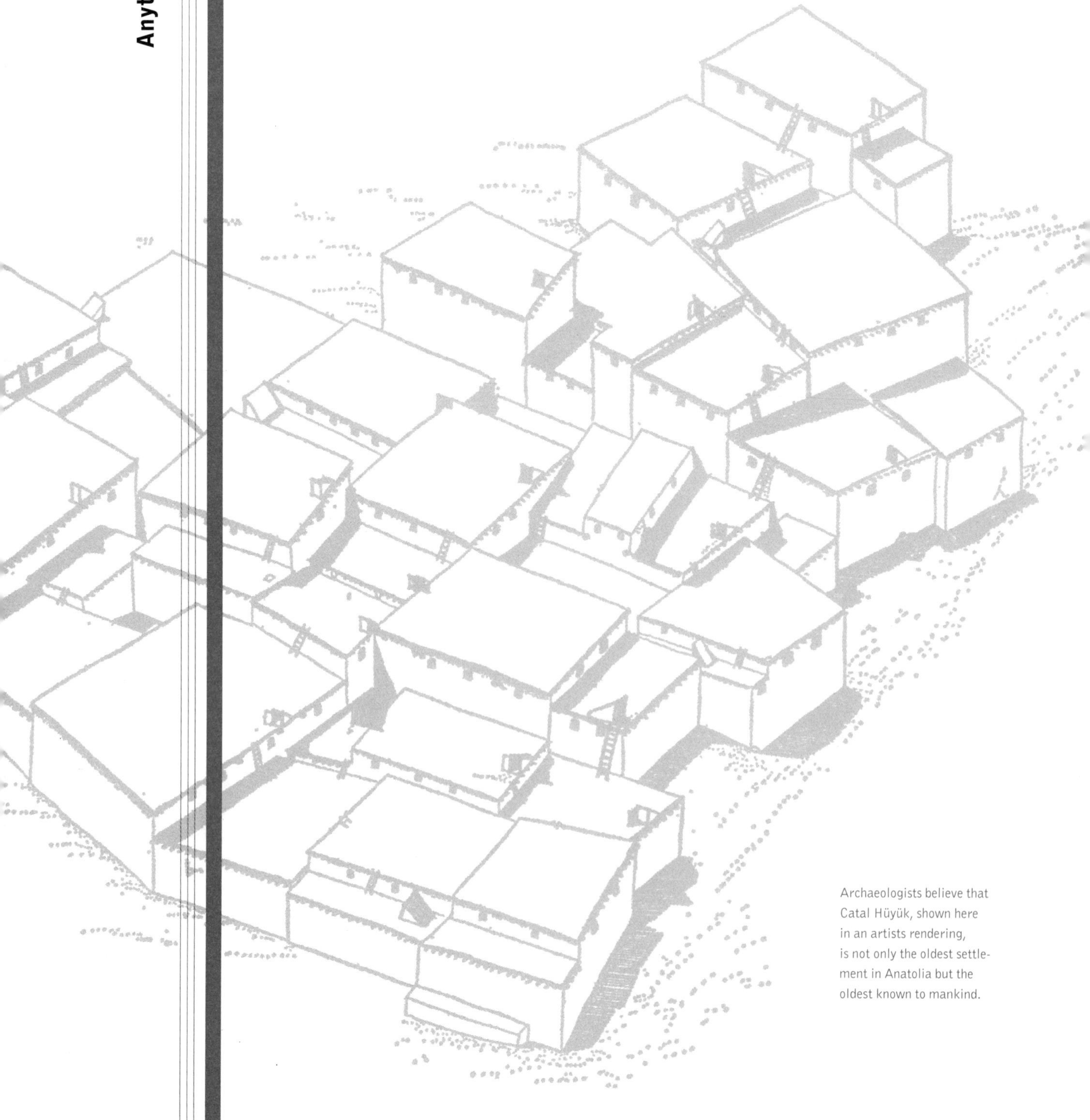

Archaeologists believe that
Catal Hüyük, shown here
in an artists rendering,
is not only the oldest settlement in Anatolia but the
oldest known to mankind.

I am hard-pressed to think of a place better than Turkey for holding the Anytime Conference. The name *Turkey* mainly represents the post-1923 Turkish Republic, however, thus it may be more appropriate and, in terms of time, more embracing if we refer to this place as Anatolia, often referred to as "the cradle of civilizations." Anatolia is the melting pot of many past and present civilizations that span over nine millennia.

"Time" in history, time in culture, time in music or in architecture refer to different aspects of this abstract concept, which in fact structure and determine our thinking and perceptions. When we speak of the relativity of perceptions and experiences, we basically refer to them in time. Perhaps that is why we so readily accepted the fourth dimension as described by Albert Einstein as a self-evident fact. Though he was referring to one important aspect of time in physics, the abstraction of relativity made so much sense in all fields of human experience that it became a major philosophical instrument in every realm.

In poetry, T. S. Eliot referred to time more in reference to happenings and place:

> Because I know that time is always time
> And place is always and only place
> And what is actual is actual only for one time
> And only for one place

In music, George Frideric Handel conceived of time as the process of validation of eternal values. One of his earliest pieces, composed during his stay in Italy, was the dramatic oratorio *Il Trionfo del Tempo e del Disinganno* (The triumph of time and truth) (1707), in which he staged the everlasting contradiction of life between "beauty and pleasure," which represent ephemeral joys and experiences and the lasting values borne out by "time and truth," which in the end are victorious. The story tells of the ultimate polarity of earthly experience

and heavenly values. Time and truth become the qualities of eternity, as time, standing by the side of lasting values, yields the ultimate "truth."

In 1724 Handel composed the historic opera *Tamerlano*, in which he stages the 1402 battle between two Turkish emperors, Tamerlane and Bayazit I, which took place on the steppes of Ankara, almost where the Ankara airport is today. Anatolian and Turkish culture have been a source of inspiration and mystery for many Western artists. Both Mozart and Beethoven composed marches to honor the Turks and used the motifs of Ottoman music to enrich their own musical expressions. Works such as *Marcia Turca* and *Abduction from the Seraglio*, among others, project Turkish time and cultural history into timelessness, to be heard by the ears of generations to come.

In order to appreciate the rich culture and the almost endless continuity of time in Turkey, it is more rewarding to consider the geographic cultural context of Anatolia than the political entity known as Turkey. Turks have ruled Anatolia since 1071, following the victory of the Seljuks over the Byzantine Empire; thus in the long historical continuum of this land, the Turks are rather recent inhabitants. Only 927 years have passed since Alpaslan of the Great Seljuk Empire defeated Romanos Diogenes of Byzantium. In Anatolia's long history, even that can be considered a very short time.

One can make the best sense of Anatolian time and its rich cultural history by viewing it as an overlay of successive histories and cultures. It is one of civilization's most complex palimpsests.

To understand the region's cultural wealth, one must taste the traditional wheat pudding, called *Asure* (say *a-SHOO-reh*) and learn the biblical legend that goes with it, relating to when the Great Flood had subsided and Noah's Ark landed on Mount Ararat. (The remnants of the Ark are still believed to be there and were photographed by the renowned Turkish artist Ara Güler for *Life* in the early 1960s.) According to legend, Noah asked each survivor to bring him whatever food they could. This was then boiled into a thick paste and distributed to all who were hungry. Today, the legendary, even ceremonial dessert tastes different in every part of the country, and even from home to home, but it is still the much beloved traditional Asure. It contains the best of every nut, fruit, or spice that the household possesses, and it is still cooked with the same spirit in a certain month of the year. Asure is not only a culinary delight but also a symbol of the cultural continuity of Anatolia, served in a cup.

A few broad sketches such as this legend may help to remind us where Anatolia stands in the universal continuity of time.

The archaeologist James Mellaart, in *Catal Hüyük: A Neolithic Town in Anatolia*, unearths not only the oldest settlement pattern in Anatolia but also of mankind (6500 BC). He persuasively describes how the houses were clustered for mutual protection in a rural setting. The cellular pattern of Catal Hüyük, without streets or walkways,' was an ingenious architectural solution to protect a community from human or animal attacks. The houses and shrines were built in an additive manner, wall to wall, and were only accessible via terraces and ladders. This formed an urban pattern for a defensible social existence without ramparts and moats. In Catal Hüyük and in another settlement, Hacilar, the history of human civilization can be traced back nine millennia.

Almost since the beginning of the field of archaeology itself, archaeological campaigns have uncovered and verified that Anatolia has been inhabited for thousands of years by many different cultures in continual succession, either through capture or changing modes of production or communication. Indeed, the cultural entities that have existed in Anatolia are a representative microcosm of the history of world civilization.

During the height of Pharaonic Egypt, the Hittites lived in Central Anatolia. Because they did not have the agricultural prosperity of the Nile, the Hittites formed a more modest but no less sophisticated civilization. When challenged by the troops of Rameses II, they did not yield. Eventually the two civilizations signed the first known peace accord, in Kadesh. The sophistication of the Hittite culture is reflected in their archives. The cuneiform tablets discovered in Hattusas revealed substantial information about the daily life of the Hittites. They recorded not only ceremonial documents but also documents for business and trade transactions.

The location, climate, and properties of Anatolia have helped to make it the crossroads of civilization, for there is no major empire in history that has not conquered Anatolia or at least aspired to do so. In 4th century BC, the Persian emperor Darius went through Anatolia and across the Dardanelles to challenge Alexander the Great. Both the Greeks and the Romans built their best temples in Anatolia. Beautiful Helen was an inhabitant of Troy (Canakkale) and Heredotus hailed from Halicarnasus (Bodrum). The rational, rectilinear subdivision of land, which generated the orderly plans of such classical cities as Miletus, Pergamum, and Priene, became, as Sibylle Moholy-Nagy noted, the generic urban patterns of the cities of the 20th century. Today one can find almost intact archaeological sites side by side with contemporary settlements. It is as if time has stood still.

Legend recounts that in the vicinity of Ankara, near Polatli, Alexander the Great was presented with the impossible puzzle of the Gordion knot, a series of complicated knots on a rope. He dismantled the so-called insoluable knot with a stroke of his sword, which showed his commitment to power as the unique solution for any problem, including the legendary knot of Gordion. Symbolically, the solution also opened the gates of the East to Alexander.

Anatolia has always been the routes between the East and West, the North and South. Whoever captured land and dwelled here has faced the overwhelming responsibility of keeping the territory. Throughout history this has never been an easy task for any ruler, for it did not simply require care and dedication to be its custodian.

Saint Paul began his first missions by going north from Palestine through Antioch, and he accompanied the Virgin Mary, who spent her last days in Anatolia near Ephesus. Christianity grew, despite the oppressive Roman regime, and developed a sophisticated subterranean architecture in the cities of Cappadocia, allowing contemporary Roman rule above ground to coexist with expanding Christianity underground. The Christian cities of Cappadocia were the literal expression of one of history's first underground movements.

When one experiences the natural settings of Central Asia it is not difficult to understand why the Turks became so strongly attached to Anatolia. Every aspect of it is similar to their original land, only better and richer. While the Seljuk Empire in Iran and Iraq declined, the Seljuks of Anatolia prospered and sowed the seeds of a bigger empire, the Ottoman, which was comparable to the Roman or British empires.

The Seljuks were artistic and imaginative and imported to Anatolia the best of their culture from the land between the rivers Amu-Derya and Syr-Derya. They were also pragmatic, however, and they paid more attention to trade and industry than anything else. All of their major buildings were functional types like caravanserais, which were the essential nodal points along the trade routes.

As the custodians of Anatolia, Seljuks faced the tremendous task of blocking the Crusaders' access to the Holy Land from the 12th century onward, perhaps history's most dramatic and enduring encounter between East and West. One still finds evidence of the impact of this encounter, both architectural and anthropological. As the civilizations succeeded one another, the cultural sediment of architectural relics of the times lived began to build. It is the great richness of this land and should be protected and cherished.

The Ottomans, who developed trade and communication patterns, also developed a rather sophisticated pattern of political management. Compared to the Persian empire and that of Alexander the Great, they survived the longest on this land, which was the heart of the Ottoman Empire. At its peak, the empire stretched from Yemen to the Crimea, from Algeria to the Persian Gulf. The Ottomans further developed the Seljuk pattern of horseback and caravan methods of communication and granted the autonomy of faith, culture, and language to its new territories. The colonized lands retained a freedom far greater than that granted by most of history's colonial regimes.

The Seljuks and the successor principalities who governed Anatolia between the 11th and 14th centuries brought their own architecture with them, which was simple, functional, and somehow austere, but it needed to be adapted to the conditions of Anatolia. The Ottomans, however, had the opportunity to interact with Byzantium (or the Eastern Roman Empire). They were pluralists, not only politically but also in their cultural expressions. They were interested in synthesizing styles and methods developed by different cultures, and made good use of the best of every culture that they politically dominated. Whether in architecture, music, painting or culinary expertise, the historically existing cultural expressions were richly accommodated within what was now called Ottoman.

Ottoman architecture evolved from a single-cell, simple mosque in Bilecik to the masterpiece of Selimiye Mosque in Edirne (1569–74). The long process of learning and absorbing the multitudes of Anatolia's cultural resources took more than two centuries. When studied comparatively, it is hard to disagree that Anatolia possessed a sophisticated culture and artistry that paralleled the Italian Renaissance. It is intriguing to speculate, given the history, what the architectural result would have been had Pope Pius VI employed Sinan to design the dome of St. Peter's in Rome, and Suleyman the Magnificent had employed Michelangelo for Suleimaniye Mosque in Istanbul. Both were the distinguished talents of the same epoch, despite their obvious differences, and both were commissioned to create their best work for powerful patrons.

In the later years of the empire, the Ottoman Royal Court was conversant with aestheic developments in the West. The baroque, rococo, and empire styles, and, later, art nouveau, found sympathetic clientele among the Ottoman court and nobility. In the 10th century, Sultan Abdülmecit employed the Forsatti brothers, from the Swiss Canton of Ticino, to research and uncover the Byzantine mosaic murals in Hagia Sophia that the Ottomans had covered when the church was converted to a mosque. As Gaspar Forsatti removed precious tiles and scraped away the adhesive stucco, he discovered several masterpieces of Byzantine art, including a magnificent portrait of the Virgin Mary (who is equally respected as the holiest of the saints by Muslims and is called *Meryem Ana* – Mother Mary – in Turkish.) On the day of his discovery Gaspar demanded an audience with the sultan and requested to be excused and decommissioned. When the sultan asked him why, Forsatti said that as he uncovered one work of art he was destroying another, and his "architect heart" would bear the pain and confront the responsibility. In short, the Ottomans respected the heritage that they inherited and treated it with care.

The movement on the part of the East to take part in the Western world started with the Ottomans. It is continued by present-day Turkey, not only politically but also culturally and with an even stronger emphasis. The observable difference between the two eras is that when the Ottomans used the European styles that they fancied, such as the baroque or art nouveau, they were committed to interpreting and adapting it for their own context. In present-day Turkey, however, this attitude has diminished. Therefore, while we can speak about Turkish baroque or art nouveau as having an inherent quality, Turkish modern architecture is more temporal and stylistic than it is an exercise with intrinsic value and quality.

In the first decade of the Turkish Republic, architects trained in the West struggled to define an architectural identity that would be Ottoman, Turkish, or Anatolian, which was perceived as the most legitimate architectural approach and the idiom of the time. Architects like Kemalettin, Vedat, Hasip, and their Western colleagues like Giulio Mongeri, found the new state a sympathetic client that implicitly wished to continue the Ottoman palace tradition in architecture. The major buildings erected in Istanbul, Ankara, and the provinces were not based on the neoclassical templates of J.N.L. Durand but were the products of a genuine exploration of both Turkey's heritage and Western modes of construction.

In the mid-1930s, significant opposition arose against this tradition, which was later called the "First National Architecture" movement. The opponents of the heritage-based development of identity claimed that the virtue of the Turkish revolution that culminated in the Turkish Republic was the denial of whatever pertains to past, particularly Ottoman, traditions. The mission of the second generation of architects, led by Seyfettin Arkan, Abidin Mortas, and Sevki Balmumcu, and to an extent Sedat Eldem, was one of uncompromising Western modernity. Turkey's close ties with Germany, the education available there, and the

apparent simplicity of less labor-intensive work, quickly changed the whole climate of architectural discourse and education. This change was so aggressive that even professors like Vedat Tek and Giulio Mongeri found themselves outside the Academy of Fine Arts as their studios were ordered closed.

The unconditional acceptance of modernity dominated the architecture of Turkey, where the major client was the state itself. In the years preceding and during World War II, a major influx of European dissidents was welcomed to Turkey and absorbed in all areas of academia and practice. Architecture was no exception. Bruno Taut, Paul Bonatz, Hans Poelzig, and Clemens Holzmeister were among the many who contributed to architecture education and practice. Two lines of architecture were visible then. One was the heavy, stone-clad, Germanic approach of Holzmeister; the other, that of Bonatz and Eldem, was equally monumental but embellished by local motifs. Since Turkey did not enter World War II, the country was more insular, and the latter approach, later called the "Second National Architecture" movement, again experimented with refining a Turkish identity in architecture.

The postwar years brought real democracy to Turkey in the form of a multiparty government. Between the 1940s and late-1970s, modernism as practiced in the West was the uncontested architectural lingua franca that no one dared to question. Architectural schools produced graduates with modernist values and aims. Middle East Technical University was established in Ankara in order to challenge this development, but it soon became more committed to modernism in a more conscious way, for it was the only institution using the Bauhaus basic course.

Turkey's three schools of architecture in the early 1960s proliferated to a dozen by the mid-1970s and have now been consolidated in some twenty schools nationwide. The problem is that each school has imported some Western-based curriculum structure in imitation of the European model. Ironically, the schools end up imitating one another.

When more relaxed architectural ethics were sought, postmodernism became a way out for Turkish architecture, especially where clients wanted the architects to provide for their own "taste." What was seen as unethical according to the tenets of modernism could now be accommodated and defended under the rubric of Western postmodernism. Popular taste found financing and support in newly developed capitalism and petty enterprises.

In the 1980s Turkey became one of the bigger players in the global arena. This eventually attracted foreign capital and know-how in every field. Architecture was no exception. In this process, local architects who wanted to be effective without taking too many risks transformed Turkey into a playground of imported architecture, which was mainly slightly better derivatives of their own design philosophy. It is sad to observe how little Turkish architecture has been published abroad. The winners of the Aga Khan Award for Architecture and the work of Sedat Eldem and Turgut Cansever are the rare exceptions.

In essence, Turkey has always been a self-validating society. It has looked to the West as a model, but it has achieved primarily what was possible within its own limitations. Today, when we look back at our predecessors, we do not see any major modernist architectural achievement. This often takes Western observers by surprise. In a special issue of *The Economist*, one author shared his disappointment in not finding any remarkable "world class" modern architecture in Turkey except for the elegant and symbolic Bosphorous Bridge that connects Asia and Europe.

For validation in every field we look to the West, predominantly to Europe. Architecture is no exception. Turkish architects never

"copy" immediately, perhaps because living at the crossroads of all time we are inherently suspicious; everything new may not necessarily be good. Therefore, about a decade elapses between the current architecture in the West and what is being practiced or accepted in Turkey. For anyone conversant with worldwide developments, it is frustrating to observe that influences subsiding in the West find new life in Turkey.

Among the one million qualified architects in the world today, twenty-five thousand are in Turkey (to be precise 25,246 in 1998), or 2.5 percent. Among these, 8,700 are employed in architectural offices and construction; 1,000 in academia; 4,800 in central and local government institutions; 6,000 work in other fields; and 4,500 are lost somewhere in the process and eventually in the records. Perhaps, as in many other countries, this distribution shows that the schools of architecture cultivate many other talents as well, for only one out of three graduates works directly in building design and practice.

Architectural publishing here is vivid and lively. *Yapi*, *Mimarlik*, *Arredamento-Mimarlik*, *Mimar*, and *Tasarim* are predominantly architectural journals. Each is more than fifteen years old, and the circulations range from five to fifteen thousand. Other journals published by large media enterprises are mainly dedicated to interiors and lifestyles, although architecture too is covered substantially. In addition, association and academic scholarly and research journals reflect the quality of research and thinking in Turkey. The quality and diversity of Turkish architectural media can compete with that of many Western countries; when compared with the architectural journalism in the East and South, Turkish publishing is unrivaled. This is basically due to the strong construction industry, which is also the locomotive of the Turkish economy. The intellectual commitment of Turks to communicate almost exclusively in Turkish must also be taken into account. But perhaps the most important aspect is the self-confidence gained from looking back at one's own society. In this respect Turkish architectural intelligentsia and media can be compared to that of Italy, Spain, and perhaps Indonesia.

Indeed, the architectural media, which are well-represented here, will communicate the transactions, voice the diverging, converging, and opposing points of view, and capture *Anytime* in 1998 and in Ankara for all time and for this place.

SUHA ÖZKAN IS THE SECRETARY GENERAL OF THE AGA KHAN AWARD FOR ARCHITECTURE IN GENEVA AND A FORMER VICE PRESIDENT OF MIDDLE EAST TECHNICAL UNIVERSITY IN ANKARA.

EMEL AKÖZER

NEVZAT SAYIN

MARK GOULTHORPE

HAN TÜMERTEKIN

CAN BILSEL

AKRAM ABU HAMDAN

SERHAN ADA

CAN ÇINICI

WINY MAAS

RAHUL MEHROTRA

ZEYNEP MENNAN

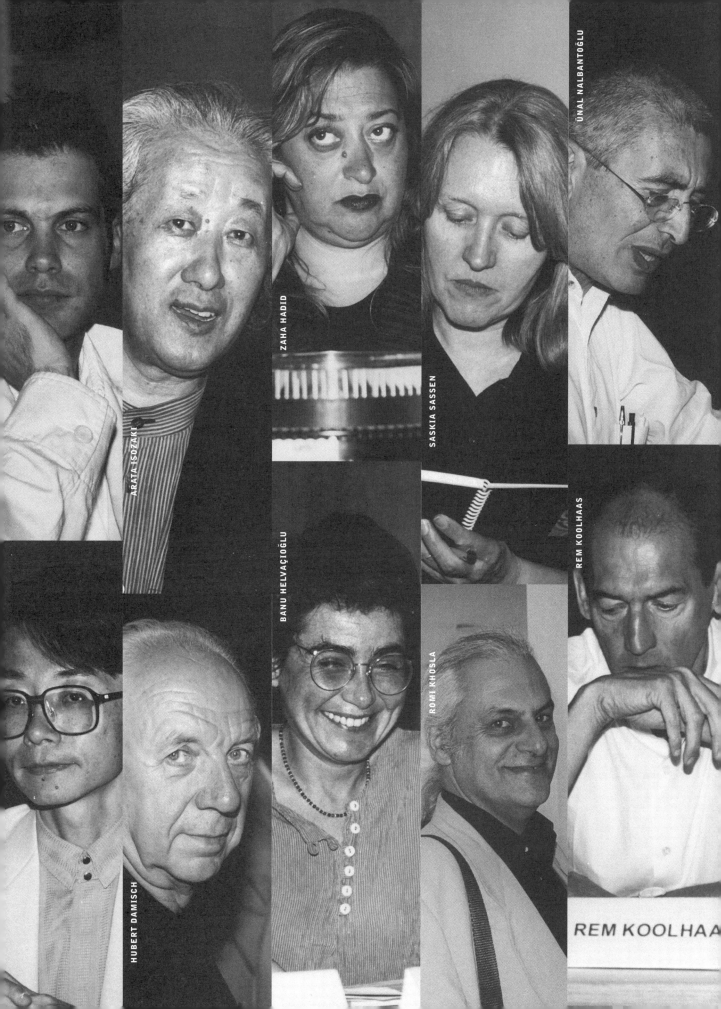

ARATA ISOZAKI

ZAHA HADID

SASKIA SASSEN

ÜNAL NALBANTOĞLU

BANU HELVACIOĞLU

ROMI KHOSLA

REM KOOLHAAS

HUBERT DAMISCH

REM KOOLHAA

JOHN RAJCHMAN

BERNARD TSCHUMI

BRUCE MAU

JALE ERZEN

MICHAEL SORKIN

UĞUR TANYELİ

CHARLES JENCKS

FREDRIC JAMESON

İLHAN TEKELİ

PETER EISENMAN

AHMET İNAM

SUHA ÖZKAN

ABDI GÜZER

HALDUN ERTEKIN

AHMET İNAM

CYNTHIA DAVIDSON

PHYLLIS LAMBERT

HALUK PAMIR

HASAN BARUTÇU

GLU

Beginnings Ten young architects present projects and conceptual work that pertain to origins or beginnings, that deal with breaking away, rupture, change, movement, with architecture as the seed of interdisciplinary concepts.

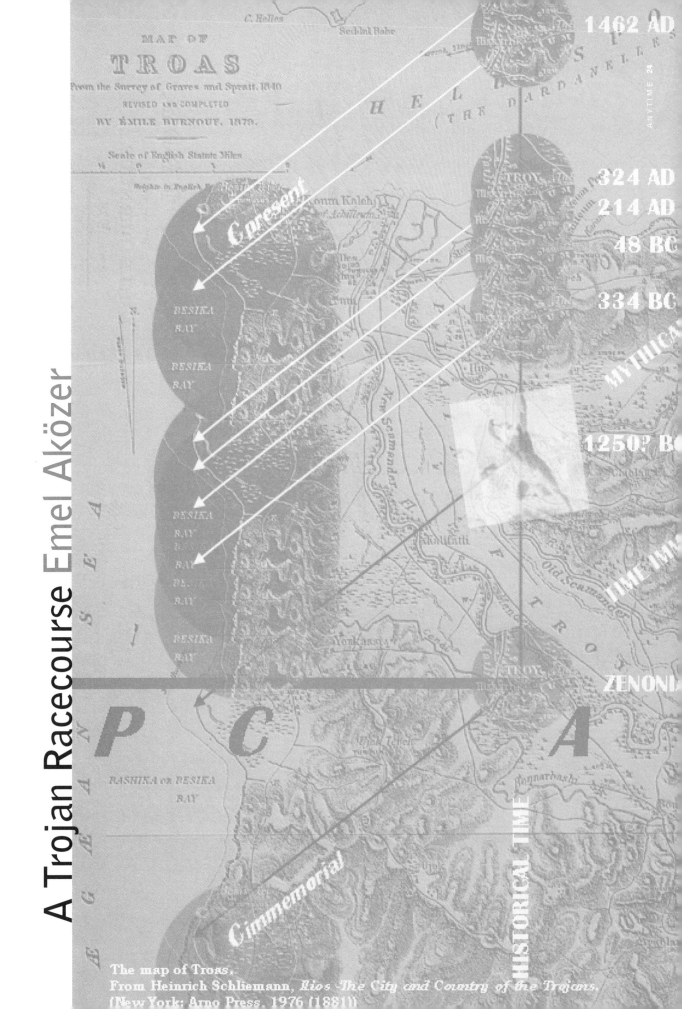

A Trojan Racecourse Emel Aközer

MAP OF

TROAS

From the Survey of Graves and Spratt, 1840

REVISED AND COMPLETED

BY ÉMILE BURNOUF, 1879.

Scale of English Statute Miles

1462 AD

324 AD
214 AD

48 BC

334 BC

1250? BC

MYTHICA

Present

TIME IMM

ZENONI

Cimmemorial

HISTORICAL TIME

The map of Troas.
From Heinrich Schliemann, *Ilios -The City and Country of the Trojans.*
(New York: Arno Press, 1976 [1881])

Take a racecourse, *AB*, of indefinitely great length.
Let Achilles [the "fastest runner" as a term in Zeno's Paradox]
be placed at *A*; let the tortoise
[the "slowest" as the other term in Zeno's Paradox,
symbolizing "immortality" beyond the reach of Achilles] . . .
be placed at any point C between *A* and B;
and at t let Achilles and the tortoise each begin to move towards B.

[And also let Aias, Odysseus, and Antilochus
who ran the first Trojan Race
during the funeral contests for Patroclus,
set forth by the swift-footed Achilles in mythical time,
and the classical and postclassical war lords
re-enacting Achilles in historical time,
Alexander the Great, the Macedonian,
Julius Caesar, Augustus, Hadrian, Caracalla, the Romans,
and Mehmet II the Ottoman, and others,
and the "deconstructive Achilles" as well,
join a "hermeneutic race" from the point A,
while from the point C, on the other hand,
twelve Trojan children, sons of noble Trojans
slain by Achilles and thrown upon the pyre about dead Patroclus,
and all the other children who have fallen victim to the war lords,
and the immortal brain children of the nobility of logocentrism,
accompany the tortoise with the same pace.]

Suppose that Achilles does catch up with the tortoise;
i.e., that there is some point P on *AB* such that at some time t' after t
both Achilles and the tortoise are at P.
Since the tortoise has been moving towards B, P is between C and B, thus:
It follows that "the pursuer must first get to where the pursued started from";
i.e., that at some time between t and t' Achilles is at C.
Now when Achilles is at C, the tortoise is at some point, C1, between C and B;
but clearly Achilles must reach C1 before t';
and when he is at C1, the tortoise is already ahead, at C2, between C1 and B.
And in general, if Achilles is at C_i,
the tortoise is already at C_{i+1}, one step ahead of him.
Thus 'it is necessary that the slower should always be some distance ahead',
and Achilles can never catch the tortoise.

[Achilles' followers can never catch up
with those whom they chase after.][1]

1 Jonathan Barnes, *The Presocratic Philosophers* (London: Routledge and Kegan Paul, 1982), 273–74.

Fit the racecourse to Troas.
Let it start from the ruins of Troia.
Let the slopes of Besik Tepe,
the mound known as the tomb of Achilles,
correspond to C . . .

Let the racecourse slope down
to a stage of infinite transformations
where the past and the present,
the fictional and the real
incessantly meet and break apart,
a place grounded in a peaceful landscape
of olive trees and oaks and cotton fields.

The beginning of the Trojan race is, like most beginnings, in the world of myth. It was sung by the Bronze Age bards as a fragment of an epic that unfolded throughout centuries, before it was immortalized in written texts called the *Iliad*, a first version of which was compiled and written down, according to an ancient tradition, in the sixth century BC during the reign of the Athenian tyrant Peisistratos.[2]

We do not know whether the epic imitated reality or reality imitated the epic in different times and places. Nor do we know whether Homer of Chios or Smyrna was a poet of genius who "began the weaving of the web"[3] and was later imitated by the *Homeridae*, or if he was a poetic character with whom the Bronze Age poets ecstatically identified themselves during the Bronze Age festivities (*Homeros* means hostage). We may guess, however, that there have been many Homers, many *Iliads*, many Troias, and many Trojan races, both fictional and real, or rather, neither fictional nor real.

The legend itself hints at the possibility of Trojan races that preceded the one it delineates so vividly. The old mythical warrior Nestor makes known a manifest sign in the landscape of war that had perhaps been "the turning-post of a race in days of men of old," a dry stump between two white stones, then chosen by Achilles as his turning-post.[4] The race known to the mythical consciousness and sung by the Bronze Age bards was set forth by the *swift-footed* Achilles for his friend Patroclus's honor in mythical time, in the tenth year of the legendary Trojan War. The mythical heroes Aias, Odysseus, and Antilochus ran it.

According to the epic, after he avenged his beloved companion Patroclus's death by killing Hector and defiling his corpse, and made a funeral feast and cut the throats of twelve glorious sons of the noble Trojans before Patroclus's pyre, and burned the corpses, the *man-slaying* Achilles, *swift of foot*, gathered Achaians and "brought forth prizes; cauldrons and tripods and horses and mules and strong oxen and fair-girdled women and grey iron"[5] for the funeral contests. He offered the best prize for fleetness of foot:

> [A] mixingbowl of silver, richly wrought; six measures it held, and in beauty it was far the goodliest in all the earth, seeing that Sidonians, well skilled in deft handiwork, had wrought it cunningly, and men of the Phoenicians brought it over the murky deep, and landed it in harbour, and gave it as a gift to Thoas; and as a ransom for Lycaon, son of Priam, Jason's son Euneos gave it to the warrior Patroclus. This bowl did Achilles set forth as a prize in honour of his comrade, even for him who so should prove fleetest in speed of foot.[6]

Odysseus *of many wiles* came first in the race with the help of Pallas Athene, and won the mixingbowl. And yet, Antilochus, Nestor's son, gave glory to Achilles by saying that "hard were he [Odysseus] for any other Achaean to contend with in running, save only for Achilles."[7]

Supposedly a thousand years after the epic race, which was believed to have taken place on the plain of Troia, Alexander the Great, the Macedonian, paid homage, on his way to conquests, to his legendary ancestor Achilles (the Mycenaean?) by running a great distance as an athlete from Ilion to his tomb (to the mound called Besik Tepe, at the northern edge of Besika Bay), where he laid a wreath in 334 BC.[8] His companion Hephaestion, in whose honor he was to set forth funeral games in his later life, laid another wreath at the tomb of Patroclus.[9] Alexander the Great declared the city of Novum Ilion free, exempted it from tribute, and enriched the temple of Athene Ilias, before departing to confront his own Hector, Darius, the Persian king.

Alexander the Great reenacted Achilles's part in the legend in the historical world. He "designed his life as a project," and intentionally crafted his own image by imitating and emulating and striving to surpass his heroic model, and weaving history with the

2 Michael Wood, *In Search of the Trojan War* (New York: Facts on File Publications, 1985), 126; Gregory Nagy, "An Evolutionary Model for the Making of Homeric Poetry: Comparative Perspectives," in Jane B. Carter and Sarah P. Morris, eds., *The Ages of Homer* (Austin: University of Texas Press, 1995), 163–79.

3 Ibid., 126.

4 Homeros, *Iliad*, 23: 325–33. In Gregory R. Crane, ed., *The Perseus Project* (http://www.perseus.tufts.edu, May 1997).

5 Ibid., 23: 740–95.

6 Ibid., 23: 740–50.

7 Ibid., 23: 790–95.

8 Wood, *In Search of the Trojan War*, 30, 168.

9 Cornelius C. Vermeule III, "Neon Ilion and Ilium Novum: Kings, Soldiers, Citizens, and Tourists at Classical Troy," in Jane B. Carter and Sarah P. Morris, eds., *The Ages of Homer* (Austin: University of Texas Press, 1995), 467–82; Ada Cohen, "Alexander and Achilles – Macedonians and 'Mycenaeans,'" in *The Ages of Homer*, 483–505.

10 Cohen, "Alexander and Achilles – Macedonians and 'Mycenaeans,'" 483ff.

Iliad, which he kept beneath his pillow while sleeping.[10] His deeds inspired Roman emperors who sought to revive his empire.

In 48 BC Julius Caesar visited Ilium Novum to honor his own legendary ancestor, the Trojan Aeneas. He drew inspiration not only from the Trojan hero but also from Alexander the Great, and followed in his footsteps. He promised to rebuild Troia, where "even the ruins were destroyed," as the Roman capital, "reroofing their ancestral home," as it was told by Horace in the *Odes*,[11] and made the Roman engineers renew the temple of Athene built by King Lysimachus. Augustus restored the temple before the end of the millennium.[12]

11 Wood, In Search of the Trojan War, 50.
12 Vermeule, "Neon Ilion and Ilium Novum," 470f

The ancient coast road that ran from Abydos through Ilium, Alexandria, Troas, Assos, and Elaea to Cyme and Smyrna was repaired before the arrival of Hadrian in AD 124, and in AD 214 it was renewed for Septimius Severus's son Caracalla. The latter, who believed that Achilles was his ancestor through his mother Julia Donna of Syrian nobility, enacted the part of a new Alexander the Great on his passage to the East:

> Caracalla sacrificed at the tomb of Achilles, ran his troops in arms around it, and erected a bronze statue of Achilles. The emperor also cremated his literary freedman and favourite, Festus, on a great pyre in imitation of the funeral rites of Patroclus and buried him in the largest tomb (Üçek Tepe) in the Troad.[13]

13 Ibid., 476.

In the fourth century AD Constantine the Great dreamed of founding the new Rome at Ilium. In the 18th century the travellers reported that they saw the remains of gates at the harbor, started and then abandoned by the emperor.[14]

14 Ibid., 477; Wood, In Search of the Trojan War, 31

In 1462 Mehmet II, who believed that by conquering Constantinople he avenged Troia and the people of Asia, visited the city, walked around it and "made offerings at the tomb of Achilles with his friend Cyriac of Ancona, the peripatetic early Renaissance antiquary."[15] Cyriac, the first archaeologist, used to wander among the Mediterranean ruins expecting that the ancient world might be revived by the descendants of the Greeks and of the Trojans – the Turks, as well.[16]

15 Ibid., 37f.
16 Ibid., 37; Vermeule, "Neon Ilion and Ilium Novum," 477f.

During World War I, young men who had first discovered the Iliad and Achilles in their school books dreamed of proving Achilles's valor on their way to Gallipoli and, believing in the historicity of the myth, brought it into reality once again, in a battle "No Hector nor Achilles ever knew."[17]

17 Maurice Baring quoted in Wood, In Search of the Trojan War, 34.

* * *

18 Vadim Linetski, "Nabakov and Swift, Achilles and the Tortoise: Sublime Innocence, or the Uncanny Return of the Referent in Poststructuralist Theory Along the Lines of Zeno's Paradox," in *Sarah Zupko's Cultural Studies Center* (http://www.mes.net/zupko/bakhtin/nat.htm, December 1996).

An essentially different interpretation of the Trojan race was offered still in the fifth century BC in the work of Zeno of Elea, the Greek philosopher and mathematician, and the inventor of dialectic (as he was introduced by Aristotle of Stageira, who became the tutor of Alexander the Great after having set up a school of philosophy in Assos). Zeno imagines an Achilles who is a two-dimensional, fast runner and then a race between him and the tortoise. Although he was born of a goddess, Achilles was mortal. Zeno shows that the tortoise, which represents immortality, always wins.

The paradox of Achilles and the tortoise has been reinterpreted and elaborated in structuralist and poststructuralist attempts to challenge logocentrism.[18] In the herme-neutic race between logocentrism and poststructuralism, the latter seems to expect "deconstructive Achilles's final overtaking" of the tortoise, the logocentric tradition, "by means of (non-mimetic) identification."[19]

19 Ibid., 5.

This project offers a reinterpretation of the Trojan race and of the hermeneutic race that is so intimately woven with the former. It follows in the footsteps of Zeno of Elea, the dialectician and the inventor of paradoxes.

EMEL AKÖZER TEACHES DESIGN AND THEORY AT MIDDLE EAST TECHNICAL UNIVERSITY. SHE IS CURRENTLY CONDUCTING RESEARCH ON THE ARCHITECTURE OF PALLIATIVE CARE IN TURKEY.

Thematic Architecture: Significance + Urban Interaction

Akram Abu Hamdan

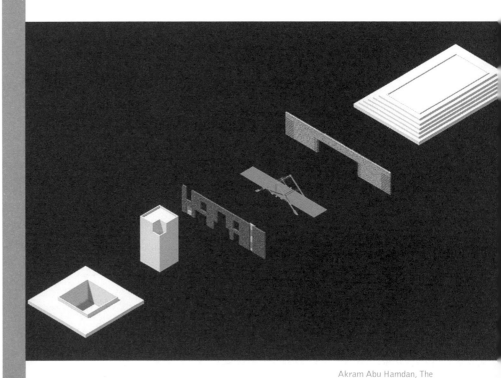

Akram Abu Hamdan, The Royal Academy for Civilization Research, 1984.

As the developing world rapidly equips itself with advanced forms of abstract technology, it remains far from reaching its fulfillment in basic technology. In its aspiration to rub shoulders with the developed world and its slick urban imagery, the developing world positions itself on the receiving end of architectural concepts and construction technologies that cannot be maintained or read as part of a natural, evolutionary process.

Mimicking industrialized world culture allows developing societies to accelerate the image of their own progress, while attempting to diminish the gap between the lifestyles of the two worlds. This raises the question as to how the developing world should react in the age of the exponential and ultrarapid growth of technology, which inherently alters the development of architecture.

In their quest for architectural identity, architects in the developing world have been paradoxically charged both to reproduce the vernacular and to abandon it for a commodified Western imagery. This abnegation of identity and assumption of the identity of another are manifest in other fields as well, including art and fashion. At the same time, nationalistic pride has resulted in the emergence of ethnic styles as manifestations of political statements. To investigate the diverse relationships of space within societies, histories, and cultural associations, a typological appraisal might be useful. Such an analysis would specify the innate characteristics rooted in historical contexts, and could eventually be expanded to encompass

technological growth. By desynchronizing the inherent factors of regional characteristics in order to develop a system in keeping with the social and pragmatic requirements and functions, a building could be treated as a typology determined by local conventions, even within the context of abstract representation.

Architecture in this case is not oriented toward stylistic representation but comes about as a result of the process unfolding itself. However, the intention is not to create an artificial excitement: the individual is invited to move freely and to develop his own feelings and state of mind. It is a process unconcerned with external appearances and image, yet fulfilling the requirements of space for a stage for human interaction and engagement while carrying out its pragmatic functions.

On the whole, this work is concerned with buildings that generate urban space and buildings that are in and of themselves urban spaces. This is conducted with the conviction that the issue of human interaction with architecture is much more valid than that of aesthetics, and that style, trends, and treatments pertaining to artistic expression should emerge as by-products of this interaction and not be at the core of it.

In addition, it is the intention that this work bears a direct relationship to its region, responding to its environment, to practiced methods and materials, while adopting a language that is pure and basic. The unassuming imagery is partly a reaction to an environment that has witnessed misguided and superfluous construction over the last twenty years or so: proposing the continuing trend of abstraction into the realm of architecture, but within the limitations of the particular region.

PROJECTS: THE ROYAL ACADEMY FOR ISLAMIC CIVILIZATION RESEARCH, 1984

The specific requirements of the program initiated an urbanistic approach aimed at uniting the project's elements in one integral framework while retaining the identity and character of each component. Here, the Muslim belief in the Oneness of God is reflected in the adoption of a prominent element acting as the unifying base for the whole composition, thereby avoiding breaking up the project into a less formal, domestic configuration.

The main components of the project include a library, museum, auditorium, conference center, computer department, printing press, workshops, cafeteria, prayer hall, and temporary living quarters for visiting scholars.

The proposed 20,000-square-meter building was to be located on a hilly five-acre site on the outskirts of Amman. The design concept was inspired by the strong imagery of the old city of Jerusalem, which can be seen on the hills to the west. From a distance, the old city walls seem to become a podium that elevates the low-energy activity of the city. This calmness is represented by the refined buildings, towers, and trees, which radiate the image of the city from the podium surface. In contrast, the high-energy activity of the city takes place out of sight, within the podium itself. While the lower part of the podium is shaped by the substantial slope of the site, its upper deck is a clean-cut surface of extreme horizontality.

In the same spirit, the design for the research center promotes the adoption of certain freestanding architectural elements, each selected to heighten the interaction between the user and the space. The podium deck provides ceremonial, multidirectional access to the cultural and religious functions that tower over it. It also supports the housing quarter on its eastern front and acts as a large stage for social interaction, fused with an arrangement of freestanding vertical elements that act as stage sets. These elements include a clock tower, which gives the podium deck a town square feel, a communication tower, a water tower, trees, and flagpoles. The movement of the sun casts ever-changing shadows that impart a dynamic feel to the otherwise static urban space.

The podium itself is a building block of three floors. The lowest floor accommodates the highest energy activities, such as the printing press and workshops and a service tunnel. The middle two levels house the conference center, auditorium, computer department, cafeteria, and administration offices. These levels also include the lower service sections for the library and the museum. Light and ventilation enter through sunken courtyards within the podium body, which on the podium deck read as "holes in the ground."

The main access to the academy is through a single entry at a high point on the site along the south facade of the podium. The podium is faced with alternate courses of two shades of limestone. This treatment emphasizes the horizontality of the podium block as a base, in contrast with the vertical elements that tower above it.

Akram Abu Hamdan, The Royal Academy for Civilization Research, model and precedents, 1984.

The Jordan Pavilion for Expo 2000 in Hannover is an example of architecture whose raison d'être is solely communicative or representational. It attempts to be an architectural event that transports the spectator to a realm of mental images pertaining to Jordan. The specificity of the images is derived from the stratification of active forces that molded Jordan into its present state. Only through archaeology can one decipher its different layers and gain insight into its essence rather than mere appearances.

The architecture of the pavilion itself is a direct communicative medium in which the human subject becomes a functional component in the process of interpretation. Rather than "forming" itself around the basic spatial functions dictated by its users, here architecture only functions or operates through the cerebral activity of the subject. For this reason the spatial typology of an archaeological dig is proposed as a reservoir for an exploded mosaic. This redefines the familiar modes of understanding public spaces and their uses

by providing a landscape of abstract imagery that engages the public in an active process of reading. The imagery is governed by a rigorous grid system whose components are arbitrarily manifested in the third dimension in blocks of varying heights and volumes. The autonomy of each block is accentuated by the message it emits. The diversity of these messages in both content and form is heightened by commissioning various Jordanian artists to produce the mosaic according to a predetermined composition.

The collective participation of artists, craftsmen, and designers in the process of forming the mosaic is intended to promote a democratic microclimate of artistic expression.

The morphology of public space in this project presents itself as an entity that fuses multiple layers of reading with a highly charged visual context. The simultaneity of the readings and their visual density uproot the spectator from familiar notions of time and space and place him or her in a metaphysical realm suspended between communication and contemplation.

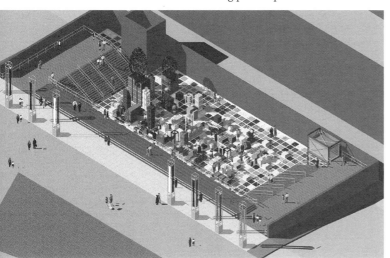

AKRAM ABU HAMDAN IS
AN ARCHITECT PRACTICING
IN AMMAN, JORDAN.

How to Make a Shuttle with Dust and Wind

Nevzat Sayin and Serhan Ada

THREE FORMS AND A VOID

A void inside a leather goods factory is bound to be seen as functional. It can be explained as giving depth to the third dimension, as increasing the height of the space, as providing for important air circulation. Its size and location are due to these reasons as well. But its form cannot be explained by these functions. We scroll back from the end to the beginning in order to seek out the facts of beginning, which almost invent themselves during the process, even though they are so clear they cannot be seen to be anything else. – N.S.

NEVZAT SAYIN IS AN
ARCHITECT IN ISTANBUL.
HE TEACHES AT ISTANBUL
TECHNICAL UNIVERSITY
AND MIDDLE EAST TECH-
NICAL UNIVERSITY IN
ANKARA AND IS A CON-
TRIBUTING EDITOR OF THE
CULTURE MAGAZINE **FOL**.

Because he was undecided
he taught us to decipher the dust
And because he is undecided
a cloud from the thirstiness
of the generations born from his fire
passed above our seas
— from Adonis, The Songs of
Mihyar, The Damascene

Doing is somehow like starting on a journey with dust. It is not possible to predict the dust, its cloudiness or its muddiness. One doesn't know, nor can one know, its when and how. Only that dust exists. As it is not possible to embark with nothing, one embarks with dust. Departing is only possible with encouragement from dust. However, encouragement is not a type of energy. Energy is generated by the wind, the direction, speed, and smell of which directly determines the act of doing. The wind that drags, carries, and leaves the dust is the creator of doing. Where there is dust, one can start to build – to write. In the beginning dust is; in reality dust is not.

The idea, whatever it targets, evolves from chaos and nullity and can only progress with dualities. Plato separates the realm of Being (the forms or ideas) and the realm of becoming (time, existence). Many, many years later Martin Heidegger dedicates almost all of his work to the same duality.

In the building Nevzat Sayin completed in the Gaziosmanpasha municipality of Istanbul there is a shuttle. In trying not to understand but at least to explain this shuttle, we have to analyze the shuttle's relationships in language(s).

A shuttle is literally the instrument used by the weaver or fabric maker to weave thread into fabric. It is also part of a sewing machine, where it serves the same purpose. The Turkish dictionary does not illuminate an explanation with metaphors. In French, however, shuttle is *navette*, a word that opens a number of doors at the same time. Navette is derived from *nef* (nave). Nef is the main part of the church, extending from the choir to the main entrance. Nef itself derives from *navis*, meaning ship; thus the form of the nef in a church is nothing other than a reversed body of a vessel. Navis in a way is synonymous with the Latin *navigium*. Starting a journey, navigating, sailing, and guiding all come from the same root. Another French word close to navette is *navet* (beetroot). When one visualizes the shape of the root, it becomes self evident that the affinity of words can be explained by the similarities of forms. Shuttle, nef, and beetroot. Given that nef was also the name given to Ottoman ships in the Middle Ages, we can easily imagine that we are in a realm of forms rather than a realm of things.

The vessel is the indisputable form of horizontal movement, but it is also a metaphor for many other things. The rainbow over Noah's Ark is a sign for peace, and in the Ancient Egyptian *The Book of the Dead*, as well as in ancient Chinese legends, sea voyages end peacefully. The nef form itself was conceptualized as a celestial dream ship. In the *Bhagavad-Gita* the boat is a metaphor for knowledge and a symbol of the solar system. The crescent is also identified with a boat. In the Sumerians, the Moon-God navigator of the skies is none other than the son of the supreme God. Peace transposed from the seas to the heavens becomes a promise for inner rest and paradise.

The shuttle form of the vessel as it moves across the horizontal sea parallels the form of the cypress as it reaches from the earth to the sky. Passing from the horizontal movement of the vessel to the vertical stillness of the cypress, does something change? This tall and sober tree is one of the integral forms of the Mediterranean Basin and the southern belt of Europe. The root of the Turkish word for cypress – *servi* – comes from the Persian *serv*. The secondary and figurative meaning is "to announce or herald with surprise," from which another series of old adjective-noun combinations is derived. These combinations, found in Divan poetry in the Aruz style[1] – where *serv* means "the stance of a lover" – can be almost endlessly multiplied. For example, *Serv-i azad* is an ordinary but very tall cypress and *Serv-i nâz*, a tall lover; *Serv-i revân*, a walking cypress; *Serv-i çeman*, the lover walking elegantly and graciously.

1 Divan poetry, inspired by Persian rhyme and meter, was produced by the literary school of the Ottomans.

Throughout the Mediterranean, cypresses serve as headstones, as guardians of the dead. The ancient Greeks and Romans associated the cypress with the deities of hell. In Japan, the Hinoki cypress held a significant place in Shinto rituals. The ritual fire was sparked by rubbing together two pieces of Hinoki, making the cypress a metaphor for energy. In its stillness (or is it movement?), the cypress comes from the earth and reaches to the sky, taking its place in the center of space with its energy.

The vessel and the cypress, two different metaphors for the same form, diverge at the very place they coincide: in language. In the symbolic combination of Divan poetry, *serv-i simin* (silver Cypress) is the luminous path the moonlight creates on the sea.

* * *

Dust is the beginning of a journey. It is enough. But to continue, wind is necessary. In the building Nevzat Sayin designed, dust is the vessel and the cypress. The vessel, a metaphor for time, is always closely related to the wind, the creator of movement and the traveling companion of the vessel through the ages. The cypress, on the other hand, is an armor against the wind. Cypresses surround cemeteries and fields of crops to protect the land from the eroding effects of the wind. They guarantee quiet for the dead and protection for the crops. The surprisingly contradictory yet close relationship of the cypress and the vessel with the wind is evocative of the dualities inherent in ideas.

Which wind dragged the shuttle that recalls these forms into the building in Gaziosmanpasha? During the project the shuttle was present as dust, but in which phase did it (really) materialize? In the middle of building? At which undecided phase of construction was the shuttle stretched by steel cables? Maybe no one, including the architect, knows the answer. At the very most we can try to decipher it.

Einstein said that time in itself is nothing, that is, there is no time: time is only the result of events happening in it. Space too, Einstein held, is in itself nothing, there is no absolute space. It exists only because of the energy it contains. And according to Heidegger, time is initially encountered in those entities that are changeable; change is in time. These aspects of time and space are found in the shuttle.

The shuttle is a hole in reality, between floors and throughout the building; a volume sensed not by its presence but by its absence; a form perceivable only as an abstraction; its emptiness brings in air, light, and all that happens outside. The shuttle has both horizontal and vertical positions and functions, like the vessel and the cypress. On each floor it is perceived and constructed as having a horizontal position, yet through its vertical repetition it is an axis for the whole building. It is not meaningless

that it suddenly appeared while attempting to solve the problem of insufficient floor heights. The wind to which it owes its existence (or its absence) is implied in the dynamics of the building itself. Apart from its position, the shuttle breaks through the limited floor height to visually interrelate the floors and take in the natural light and air. The forms of the vessel and the cypress disappear, abstracted in the shuttle's concrete functions. This hole/shuttle, stretched with steel cables and placed at the center of the building, is somehow like parentheses between the past and the future. Heidegger defines past and future as "not an absolute nullity but rather something present which lacks something. This lack is named with the 'no longer now' and 'not yet now.'" The emptiness of the shuttle's form is a being between past and future, living in today.

From whence comes the wind? Where does it reach? And where does it end? The wind can only be understood in the present tense. Its direction, its speed, its smell can only be sensed. The wind itself is a function of time, its past and its future part of the language of representation. — S.A.

SERHAN ADA HEADS THE DEPARTMENT OF PERFORMING ARTS MANAGEMENT AT ISTANBUL BILGI UNIVERSITY. HE CONTRIBUTES TO THE CULTURE MAGAZINE FOL AND TO RADIKAL NEWSPAPER, AND IS AUTHOR OF DECLARATION OF POETRY, A BOOK OF POEMS.

Hystera Protera Mark Goulthorpe

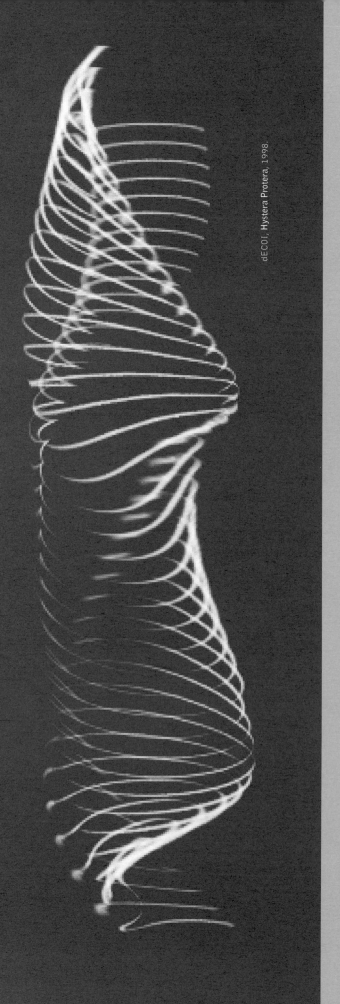

dECOI, Hystera Protera, 1998.

When we received the invitation to present a project on the theme of origins it came at a curious moment; we were already thinking about the origins of *bibliotheke* and of the book and writing in general; of the establishment of a system of knowledge in light of the apparent shift from print to electronic media. This is evidently a paradigm shift, not only in our telematic archive but in our entire mnemonic practice – our ability to fix time and space in lineage, in memory.

I can't really say where this began; it just emerged from a general background and has begun to separate itself into definable, if elusive, form – a form of process, perhaps. Maybe it began with the history of bibliotheke, and perhaps with a history of writing, both of which divide and disappear at specific points, and both of which seem important in any discussion of origin. The vanished Library of Alexandria, for instance – ultimate origin and prototype of a historic form, born out of Ptolomy's dream of total knowledge. The Great Library in fact exists nowhere; it is suspended between archaeology and literature, its trace ambiguous and contingent.

Curiously, it is a literary slip that accounts for this absence, a reference to bibliotheke – literally receptacle of books (i.e., bookshelf) – that was translated as "library," conjuring all that is expected of a historic type-form. There is a sense in which the library does exist as the hollow shell of the *Museion*, the palace whose walls, we now believe, contained recesses (shelves) which held scrolls, the library existing within the thickness of those walls, within the absence of a doubled presence.

The Great Library therefore appears contingent, implicated within another structure – a curious gap opened within a prototypical form. This, it seems, was not merely a local error but is an integral part of the foundation of a system of knowledge, the *différance* opened at any origin, here in quite physical terms.

Just as the library doubles implicitly in the doubt of its physical trace, it doubles explicitly in the guise of its other and rival: the library at Pergamum, a sort of allegorical counterpart and shadow within which developed an equal and opposite academism. It is as if at the

moment of an attempted foundation (of totality, veracity, and rationality – these were Alexandria's aims), a rival tendency emerged that opened a gap to all manner of uncertainty and forgery, which gave birth to a counterfeit culture. The two libraries, in their struggle to outdo one another, acquired numerous fakes, many becoming quite notorious, despite their evident inauthenticity, as Pergamum reveled in disturbing Alexandria's self-righteous certitude. Even the attempt to repress this irrational and dangerous other by severely limiting the export of papyrus simply created a technical development. Pergamum exploited parchment and developed the bound codice, which would eclipse the scroll.

Long before Caesar's fire consumed the Great Library (the fire itself is a historic fact of dubious veracity and perhaps a misinterpretation of historic texts), the bibliotheke was already consumed by division, différance appearing everywhere within the original form, a sort of conditional self-immolation of a form of presence. But one might allow that Caesar's uncertain conflagration marked the last rites of a hieroglyphics, buried by the articulate form of an alphabetic codice. Egyptian mental tactility narrowed to the visual-phonetic logic of the Greco-Roman world.

The privileging of the eye and ear that alphabetics implies conjures the image of a prior writing, of the necessary priority of writing, which implicates the question of memory, of mnemonics, of the medium of temporal retention.

Maurice Blanchot writes in "The Absence of the Book":

> Apparently we only read because the writing is already there, laid out before our eyes. Apparently. But the first person who ever wrote, who cut into stone and wood under ancient skies, was far from responding to the demands of a view that required a reference point and gave it meaning. . . . What he left behind him was not something more, something added to other things; it was not even something less – a subtraction of matter, a hollow in relation to the relief. Then what was it? A hole in the universe: nothing that was visible, nothing that was invisible. "I suppose the first reader was engulfed by that non-absent absence, but without knowing

anything about it, and there was no second reader because reading was from then on understood to be the vision of an immediately visible – that is, intelligible – presence, was affirmed for the very purpose of making this disappearance into the absence of the book impossible.

"Making this disappearance into . . . absence . . . impossible" is the tendency that underlies all of our strategies of presence, of the linearity, visuality, and temporality that those words imply.

Perhaps we can take Blanchot's insight as an introduction to how everything changes without anything having changed, a shift in cognition that allows us to see originality in terms other than those of presence; to see the absence of presence with neither affirmation nor negation.

Jacques Derrida, in his seminal "Différance," rigorously accounts for this:

> An interval must separate the present from what it is not in order for the present to be itself. . . . In constituting itself, in dividing itself dynamically, this interval is what might be called spacing, the becoming-space of time or the becoming-time of space (temporization). And it is this constitution of the present, as an "originary" and irreducibly nonsimple synthesis of marks, or traces of retensions and protensions (and therefore, stricto sensu nonoriginary) . . . that I propose to call archi-writing, archi-trace, or différance. Which (is) (simultaneously) spacing (and) temporization.

It is this division, or gap (the absence) – the inevitable introduction of an interval, a time-delay at the origin that compromises the presence of any beginning – that makes it necessarily double. The division allows us to think the history of writing as a history of spacing and temporization and to think this absence of the book, which then disappears in the indeterminate bibliotheke.

This is abstract but crucial, since this is the point at which time is implicated; to establish an origin is to determine something as a point of presence, which implies immediately that it is separated from that which it is not – a difference is established, both temporal and spatial. Generally, our patterns of thought have forgotten this in our desire for the certitude offered by presence, but this initial différance continually surfaces to remind us of the inherent

incertitude of origins that allows a certain slippage, or play – a momentary reversal of temporal and spatial priority.

This brings us to the pertinence of Blanchot's question and the point of departure for our speculation: "What summons us to write, when the time of the book determined by the beginning-end relation, and the space of the book determined from a center, cease to impose themselves?" Perhaps as we engage a new paradigm of writing – the new electronic surface of inscription – it is this absence that reappears and is articulated in space. This new paradigm summons us to write (differently). A writing as the condition of a writing, which wraps and unwraps its own presence/absence?

So here we began a form of nonoriginary writing, a temporal trapping, or electronic decora(c)tion. The resulting figure takes on the form of a disappearing eye (a double trace of a compromised visuality, since it is indeed visuality that is eclipsed here). The process produces traces, series upon series of glyphic rather than graphic forms (no content, no destination) suspended in space, just as we are somehow suspended before them. A species of electronic hieroglyphics that restores an enigma that was lost when those of the Egyptians became readable, lost their occult status, became writing; lost their absent presence.

Ammon, the king of Egypt, dismissed the god Theuth's legendary invention of writing as an unnatural aid to living memory, a suspension of living presence. This surfaces again in Plato's diatribe against writing's falsity, its absence. With Moses, writing becomes a means of clarifying and completing presence; in his stammering double reading of the oral and written Torah – the writing of God – each reinforces the other, as if they were somehow complimentary properties of a basic mnemonic sense.

Both traditions, though, are careful to separate image from writing: Plato celebrates an image-based, idolatrous mnemonics against the abstraction of writing; Moses, forbidding images, displays an iconoclastic preference for the word. Both denied différance, the spatial-temporal absence at the heart of presence.

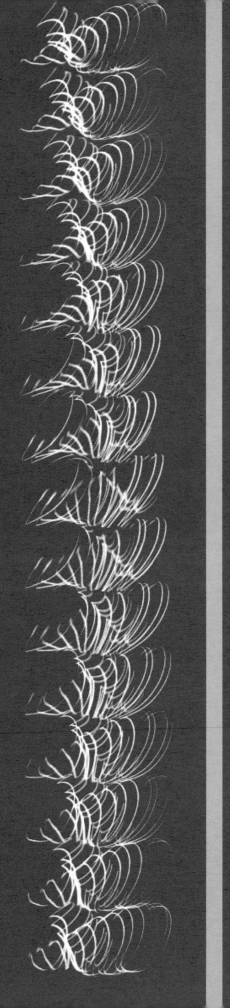

7

6

5

4

3

2

1

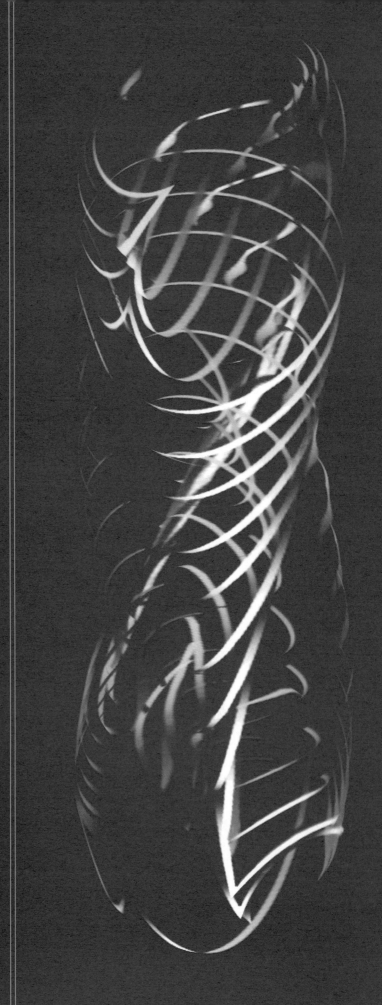

The hieroglyphs offer a different model, their tripartite structure both a writing and an imagery, an icon-elastic medium, a complex and ambiguous suspension that addresses the full range of the mental sensorium, stimulates a sort of tactile and multiple mentality, which lives this différance. The privileging of the distant and idealizing senses – sight and hearing – that occurs in an alphabetic (visual-phonetic) code demands a strict separation of effects, which the multiform hieroglyphs collapse. In the curious synaesthesia of electronics one might well look back to the hieroglyphic effect, not as a fixed point of origin but as an originary play that suggests a bodily comprehension and temporality.

Here, a writing is image, but image as a repetition, a spatial and temporal transformation that suggests a sort of unmotivated or endlessly-first reading. It is the trace of an absence, of a locus that has vanished: a trace of difference and deferral. It is a transformational process (which carries the operations of translation, rotation, reflection). It assumes no fundamental dimension, is scaleless. It produces an effect rather than a reading, a disturbance of the optical field, an opti-kinetics generated by the repetition of a dissimilar series.

Our project oscillates between grammar and geometry. It is a pattern of repetition and difference, a form of rhythm that laps and overlaps cyclically as process, as flow, as a blinking device. By repeating the history of writing in the circle of its historic possibility, we introduce a vertigo or double-invagination into our familiar patterns of thought. The field-frame is folded into the noncenter of itself, endlessly revealing the absence of its presence. This bibliotheke of ornament, this nonplace contingent on a writing of absence, no longer contains or enframes; it circulates. A suspension of spatial and temporal certitude, a space-time involution, or *hysteron proteron*, or "a suspension of natural or logical sequence." Or in deference to Luce Irigaray, *Hystera Protera*, a move away from the linear logics of the eye and ear to the temporal rhythms of the body, to a chemics rather than an optics.

Hystera translates as cave, but also as womb, which here seems a suitably poignant ambiguity in our discourse on origins: a fluid and cyclical process of cave-womb-writing. A condition of origin: a sort of nonphysical model of différance, of the process of originality. Not so much an architecture as a model for the possibility of architecture.

This a decora(c)tive circuit that oscillates between center and margin, between decoration and structure, and traces a displaced psychology. It reveals an endlessly displaced creative locus, the liquification of determinism. This is perhaps the most crucial aspect of the model: in its processural or microprocessural meanderings, as in its suspension of referent (i.e., its spatial and temporal dislocation), it disenfranchises all presence. There are, as Derrida reminds us, no kingdoms of différance .

This project is a meditation on origins, or the changed nature – specifically, of writing, of origins, of books, and bibliotheke – that seem to have come to the electronic surface. We are simply repeating, in a literal sense, the history of those originary forms: the formlessness of the great bibliotheke couched within the thickness of a writing, a scrollwork, suspending that origin over- or within-itself. The point being, perhaps, that once our attitude toward origins shifts, the entire temporal schema in which they are implicated is dislocated, which causes massive disturbance across the conceptual terrain.

MARK GOULTHORPE IS THE FOUNDER AND CREATOR OF DECOI, A RESEARCH-BASED ARCHITECTURAL ATELIER IN PARIS. DECOI RECENTLY WON A COMPETITION FOR AN ARCHITECTURAL ART INSTALLATION FOR THE REFURBISHED BIRMINGHAM HIPPODROME THEATRE.

Winding Ankara Can Çinici / Aslıhan Demirtaş

Wind (wəind), v.[1] Pa. t. and pple. **wound** (wound). [OE. *windan* :— OTeut. **wendan*, related to **wand-* in WANDER v., WEND v.] †1. intr. To go on one's way, take oneself; to proceed, go — 1608 2. trans. To wield (a weapon, an implement). Obs. or dial. OE. 3. intr. To turn this way and that; to writhe. Obs. exc. dial. OE. †4. trans. To put into a curved or twisted form or state; to bend — 1624. b. intr. To take or have a bent form; now only dial. or techn. of a board, door, etc., to be twisted. late ME. 5a. refl. = 6a, b. arch. ME. b. trans. To turn; to cause to move in a curve. arch. ME. 6a. intr. To move in a curve; to turn, esp. in a specified direction. Obs. exc. as in b, c. late ME. b. To move along in a sinuous course; to go or travel along, up, down, etc. a path or road which turns this way and that — 1682. c. transf. Of a line, road, or the like: To have a curved (esp. a sinuous) course; to lie or extend in a curve or succession of curves — 1555. d. with advb. acc., or trans. with obj. (one's or its) way, etc. — 1667. e. trans. To traverse in a curved or sinuous course. arch. — 1648. 7. Naut. a. intr. Of a ship: To turn in some direction, e.g. to swing round when at anchor; to lie with her head towards a particular point of the compass. b. trans. To turn (a vessel) about, or in some particular direction — 1613. 8. To turn or deflect in a particular direction; esp. to turn or lead (a person) according to one's will; also to turn and w. Now rare or Obs. late ME. †b. To draw, bring, or involve (a person) in, attract into, by alluring or enticing methods — 1655. 9. intr. To pursue a devious, circuitous, or intricate course in argument, statement, or conduct; to use circumlocution or subtle terms of argument, arch. late ME. 10. intr. and refl. †a. With out: To extricate or disentangle oneself from a state of confinement or embarassment — 1667. b. With in, into: To insinuate oneself — 1548. 11. trans. To turn or pass (something) around something else so as to encircle or enclose it and be in contact with it; to turn, twist, or wrap (something) about, round, or upon something else ME. 12. To put (thread, tape, or the like) in coils or convolutions around something, as a reel, or upon itself, so as to form it into a compact mass (hank, skein, ball, etc). Also with from or off, to undo the coils of (thread, etc.) by rotating the object on which they are wound; to unwind. ME. 13. To encircle with or enclose in something passed round and in contact; now only of binding a thing round with tape, wire, or the like ME. b. spec. To wrap (a corpse) in a shroud or winding-sheet; to shroud. Obs. exc. dial. ME. c. Chiefly in pa. pple. and fig.: To involve, entangle ME. 14. intr. To turn so as to encircle and lie in contact with something else; to twist or coil about, around, or upon something. So to w. off, to unwind. 1575. †15. trans. To plait, wreathe, weave — 1601. 16. To haul or hoist by turning a winch, windlass, or the like, around which a rope or chain is passed. a. gen. late ME. b. Naut. To move or warp (the ship), by hauling, as on a capstan or windlass. Also absol. or intr. 1515. c. Mining. To hoist (coal, etc.) to the surface — 1883. 17. To set (a watch, clock, or other mechanism) in order for going by turning an axis with a key or other device so as to coil the spring tighter or draw up the weights 1601. b. fig. To exalt or 'screw up' to a certain pitch — 1635.

1. But winde away, bee gone I say SHAKS. 6b. The lowing herd wids slowly o'er the lea GRAY. d. He .. windes .. his oblique way Amongst innumerable Starrs MILT. 8. He can w. the proud Earl to his will SCOTT. 9. Merch. v.i.i. 154. 10b. Of your having .. wound yourself .. almost into his confidence DICKENS. 11. To w. (a person, etc.) round one's (little) finger, to make him do anything. 13. Her twinbrother couldn't w. up a top for his life DICKENS. b. She had winded a many of them in her time 1860.

W. up: a. trans. To draw up or hoist with a winch or the like. †b. fig. To involve, implicate. c. †(a) To coil, roll, or fold up; to furl; (b) to coil (thread, etc.) into a compact mass: chiefly in phr. †to w. up a bottom, one's bottoms, usu. fig. to sum up, conclude. d. †(a) To sum up; (b) to bring to a close ot conclusion; to form the conclusion of, be the final event in; (c) to bring (an affair) to a final settlement; spec. to arrange and adjust the affairs of (a company or business concern) on its dissolution; (d) absol. or intr. to bring the proceeding to a close; to conclude with something e. = 17a. f. fig. To set in readiness for action; to raise (feeling) to a high degree; now usu., to put into a state of tension or intensity of feeling, etc.; to excite.

Architectural design requires temporary and unstable idealizations, which underlie its durability over time and transformation, right after its affirmation. Ankara is a city based on an unconditional modernist ideal. Atatürk set out, in the early 1920s, to found an entirely new capital for Turkey. During the years of its foundation, the city was developed according to the ideas of the German urbanist Hermann Jansen. His thinking was greatly influenced by the Garden City movement and by the regressive ideas of Camillo Sitte. The castle and plan of the old quarters of Ankara were preserved and a new center built, which was later embodied, at least symbolically, by the Mausoleum of Atatürk on a site not too far away from the old center. Thus Ankara was reborn as a double-centered capital. As it turns out, this is only one of a series of dualisms that we have encountered in the process of Turkish modernization.

At present, Ankara houses the powerful civic institutions of a capital city, and yet it has become impotent when it comes to transforming and manifesting itself urbanistically and architecturally. The city only remembers and recalls; it represses its desires and intentions. Ankara is trapped in the nostalgia of the early Republican period. Or, we might call it a *nostalgia for nostalgia*, since even the reality of Ankara is based on pre-modern ideals. This is apparent in housing projects executed in early periods, which are based on rural schemes and rural ways of life.

Turkish modernism's attitude toward "the old" is not destruction but isolation. This attitude, however, is paradoxical in the sense that the isolated itself is glorified obsessively. The old, never replaced or transformed by the new, exists in a deadly state of isolation. This gives rise to several dualisms. Old center versus new center, Ankara versus Istanbul, old buildings left to their fates beside new ones. Anitkabir (Atatürk's Mausoleum) and the Citadel are traces of the past that have become elements of obsession, disconnected from any real reference to time. This can be interpreted as a memory loss, which is evidence of an inability to cope with the present tense. The reality of Ankara is thereby repressed in order to avoid a confrontation with the present.

Time in Ankara has not progressed since the time of excitement and ambition that surrounded its reconstruction in the 1920s. Its assertions, representations, and materializations have stood still since that time. The two projects shown here agitate and distract the architecture of the city. They depart from the idea of what the city "really is" and attempt to remove the *fog of time* caused by regressive idealizations of Ankara and its architecture.

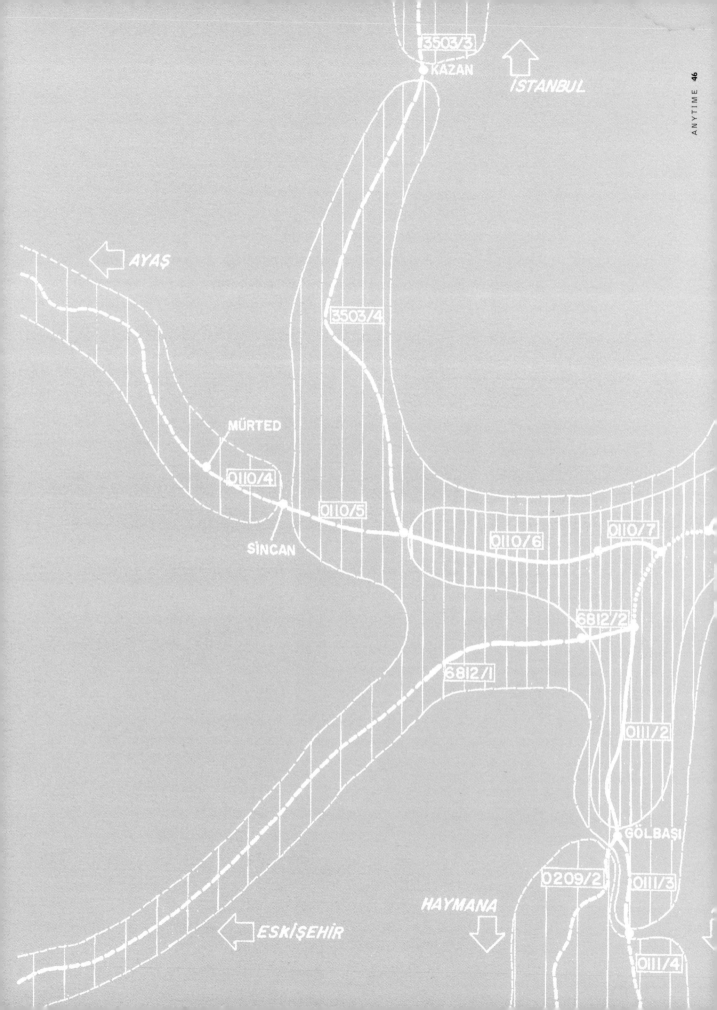

As in most urban areas, the network of roads in and around Ankara homogenizes the relationship between dwelling space and territory. Ankara has developed almost exclusively along highways. Specifically, the city is characterized by a star-shaped network of intercity roads. This snakelike road structure winds its way along the groves and gentle hills of the typical mid-Anatolian landscape. It spreads over the topography like an independent layer.

The conventional view of the city as a *house* or *dwelling* has historically suggested the possibility of *gateways*. But as Ankara grows and entrances and exits to the highways proliferate, the city entrance problem can no longer be reduced to the glorification of particular locations in the land.

Paradoxically, Turkish culture under modernization has considered roads to be corrupt spatial mechanisms. The road is the other of architecture. It is for this reason that the problem of entrance is resolved here as a new architectural type wherein the Ankara-Istanbul highway forms a knot.

Here, the road's essential desire – to be as fast and as short as possible – is violated through the construction of the *road as building* and *building as road*. The building is a product of the destruction of the instrumental properties of the road. It is not bound to place and can be located anywhere along the highway.

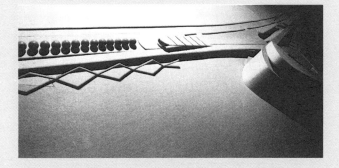

"E LA NAVE VA": PROJECT BY CAN ÇINICI AND ASLIHAN DEMIRTAŞ

The second project is a new Public Relations Building within the Turkish Grand National Assembly Campus. The site lies at the periphery of the administrative quarter of Ankara, which is triangular in plan.

Our project can be seen as an unconditional engagement with "the real"; that is, the actual desires and intentions of a political body and public realm. The emergence of the ideal of participatory democracy in Turkey in the 1990s necessitates the breaking of the closed boundaries of the campus. Rather than belonging to the campus, our proposal belongs to the city, to the *outside*. Although the scale of the building is not colossal in its context, its massive appearance seems to violate and overflow the boundaries of the site.

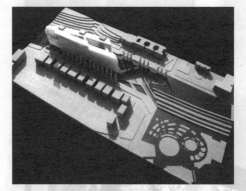

Our aim was to interpret the existing massive wall on the site, which is normally used to repel the public outside. We created an elliptical "enclave" defined by a similar wall that *embraces* people coming from the park nearby while functioning as the actual periphery of the building at street level. The entrance and the mezzanine levels are for security controls, waiting areas, and restaurants. The above floors are all office space grouped around two major atria.

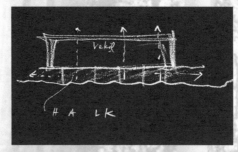

These projects date from 1990 and 1997 respectively. Neither was realized, but had they been, they would have been built in five to ten years of "Turkish time," which represents a significant delay between inception and realization.

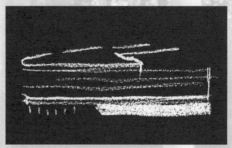

All architecture by its very nature *arrives late*, contains within it a sense of *time lapse*. It requires both a projection and an idealization. Architectural projection abstracts the time in which it operates. Consequently, the most vital architecture comes from the courage to "always begin" and from a devotion to an unconditional and non-idealized search for the "present." Beginnings should always be devoid of idealizations, however, endings are inseparable from them.

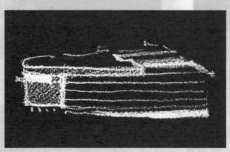

CAN ÇINICI AND ASLIHAN DEMIRTAŞ PRACTICE ARCHITECTURE IN ANKARA.

Beginning; Zero Han Tümertekin

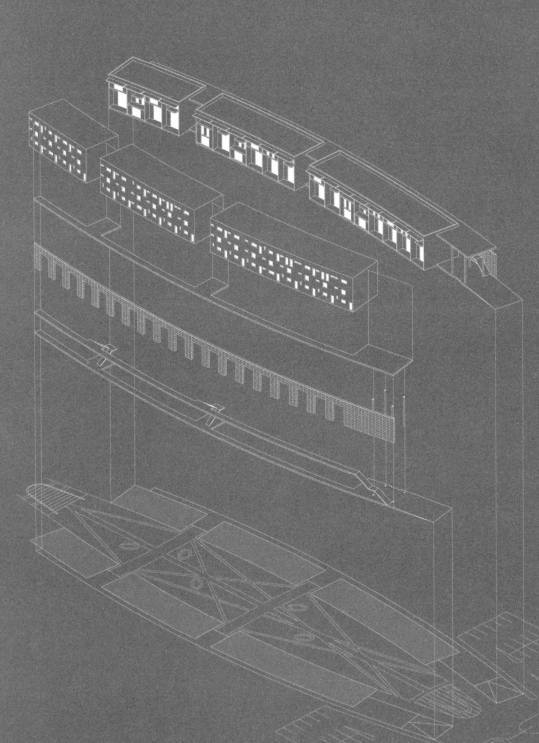

Mimarlar Tasarim Ve Manismanlik Hizmetleri, ATK Housing, Exploded axonometric, 1998.

Every design seeks its own Zero Point, which entails a complete loss of memory.

The architect should start with problems, not solutions.

The problem is to establish a relation with the Other.

The stronger the relation with the Other, the clearer the context of design becomes.

The architect should design the event within the space, before constructing the space itself.

By designing a merely visual banquet or an object to be looked at, architecture is revealed to be an activity of constructing not only space but the life within that space.

All evaluations of a design lack perspective regarding the architect's past, present, and projected future.

Without an architect, there cannot be a structure with a complete temporality. Design without an architect is nothing but the bringing together of various spatial elements.

The architect makes use of spatial elements as instruments of his intended acts and words.

The temporality of a design is completely different from the temporality of "what-is-perceived-as-real."

The temporality of the "what-is-perceived-as-real" depends on the perceiver.

The senses register movement, enhancing the temporality of perception.

A sensorial movement could be made by extending perception with the use of permeable spatial elements.

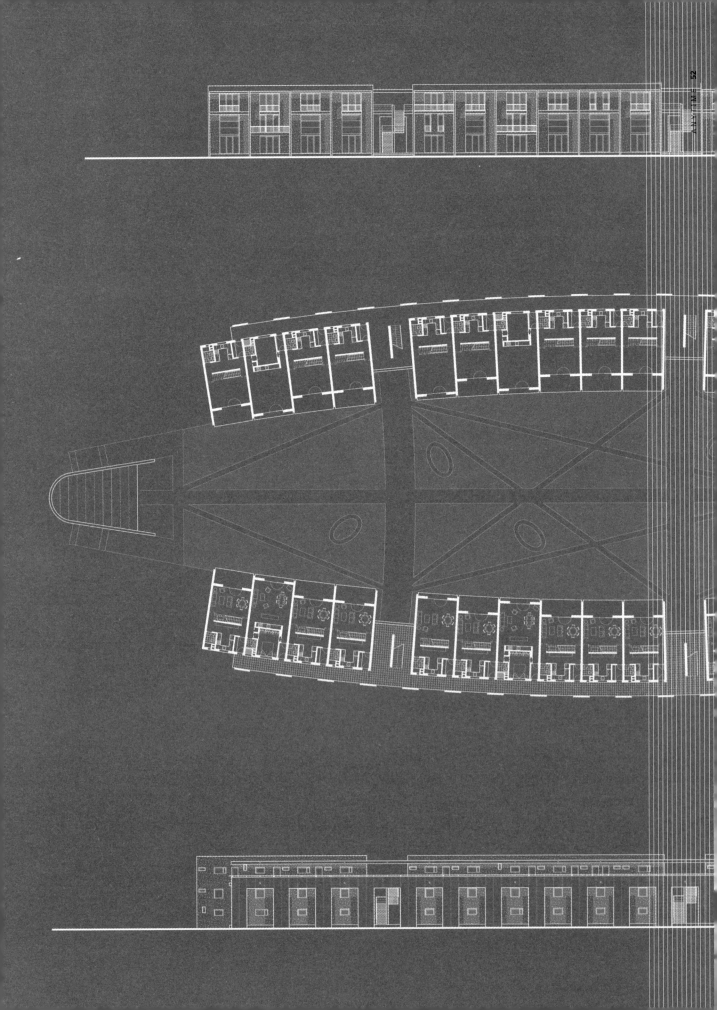

The temporality of a building originates in movement and takes the form of the individual's momentary experiences during that movement.

Experience is the ultimate form of data collected from the environment and processed through a personal filter.

The quality of space constructed by the architect has a direct effect on the process of data collection.

The architect can create neither event nor experience but can only determine the conditions that in turn would create this very experience.

Design is the untouchable, unperceivable discourse of the architect.

The architect transfers his design over himself by building, by constructing a specific living upon this very design.

The design is only apparent to the architect.

Living, which is undertaken on the basis of the ultimate product of design process, is a space of metaphor and formalization. This transforms raw materials collected by the perception from sensual space into formalized space.

Living constructs access to space. The actualization of spatial potential and processes of spatialization is achieved through movement, continuity of perception, and sense-object relationships.

Being-seen is space dependent. Being unable to assert an absolute is in being-seen's own nature. Everything is subjective, is obtained and abolished through experience.

Building is the reality that is constructed, perceived, and lived where and when one actually is.

HAN TÜMERTEKIN
ESTABLISHED HIS ARCHI-
TECTURAL FIRM IN 1986.
HE HAS BEEN NOMINATED
TWICE FOR THE AGA
KHAN AWARD FOR ARCHI-
TECTURE, AND RECEIVED
THE TURKISH NATIONAL
ARCHITECTURAL AWARD
FOR HIS A.T.K. HOUSING
PROJECT IN ISTANBUL.

Mimarlar Tasarim Ve Manismanlik Hizmetleri; ATK Housing, Plan and elevations; 1998.

LIGHTNESS

Beginning Winy Maas

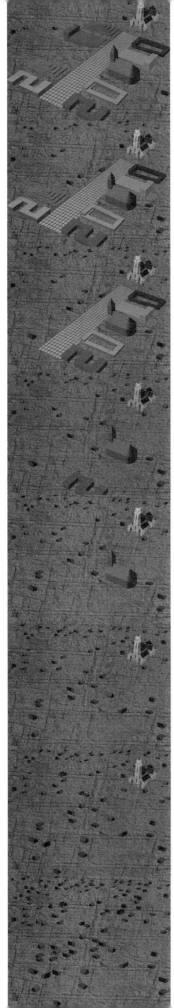

MVRDV, Town planning study for the manifestation of "Rotterdam 2045," 1995.

55 MAAS > BEGINNING

CHAMELEONS

One of the remarkable tendencies within current culture is the adaptability of the "new." One can see this in a concentrated manner within this Any group, its very initiators have shown an incredible capacity for beginning and beginning again, to such an extent that every project could be interpreted to be about beginning and thus celebrating a desperate hope for eternal youth.

This *rebirthing* has shown the importance of direct absorption of the current, of any beginning, of any newness.

It is a chameleonic approach that has proven to be an incredible tool of power and control. It challenges any prospect, any start. It sets a standard for the intelligence of a new generation, of a next beginning.

"Classical" techniques of beginning, such as brutality or frivolity, can thus be excluded from the battlefield.

ULTIMATE EXTRAVAGANZA / MASSIVE UNIQUENESS

This technique of "swallowing" flourishes at the very same moment that architecture has been swallowed by overwhelming urban conditions in which massive building production leads to a "tapestry" of built matter. This enormous production, the accelerating techniques, and the enormous internalization lead to a situation in which everything can be made and every object seems to be buildable. Nothing seems weird or extravagant anymore. What should be made under these circumstances? Does one still aspire to the extravaganza? Or are we suffering from an *object fatigue*, a consequence of

the multitude of objects competing for everyone's attention, all these buildings clamoring to say something?

In the search for the one-off, in a slew of the unique, the expression of *the* individual object seems to become ridiculous. In a massive *sea of uniqueness*, the individual object simply ceases to exist. It is swallowed by mediocrity.

The "obligation" of the architectural avant-garde of the 1990s to put "everything" into one building, into one design, as an "echo" or "mirror" of the current pluriformity and chaos seems highly unworkable. It overestimates the power of architecture, a sincere act of vanity. And anyway, why should we make chaos when we are already surrounded by it?

How to conceive a beginning or, better, an *emerging project*, under these circumstances? Should there be "agendas" that enable one to respond to this complex situation and to almost systematically research the current pluriformity?

These agendas, supported by a series of projects — both research and realization — seem to be necessary if we are to imagine a potential future and construct a possible argument amidst this vagueness, this pluriformity, this massivity.

LANDSCAPE

Several methods have been used recently to explore this phenomenon: the continuous plan, for example, that has become popular in recent architecture and has led to an architecture of "grottos." Though its very aim seems to be to explore the new by the investigation of the plurigeometrical, it still seems to literally cover the studied complexity with a *blanket of unity*. It therefore denies its aim more then exploring and revealing it. Although this approach at times makes use of parameters, it seems to be more form-driven then content-driven. One can start to speak of a *neo-Jugendstil*.

This movement has taken to using the word *landscape*. Indeed, landscape is in; it pops up in architectural debate even more frequently than Americans say "fuck." What are we to make of this?

Landscape refers to innocence: the landscape architect has always been the one who personifies the pastoral, the harmonic, and the environmentally correct: all morally very "good" and "noble" tasks. This is a highly politically correct approach, a highly effective tool used to seduce, convince, and build.

Any project based solely on that strategy is highly suspect.

Landscape is about overview. It is one of the professions that has the power to oversee the panorama of differences, a potential that has an obligation to study and criticize morality.

PARAMETERS

How can landscape be explored?

If progress is still the main aim of research, hypothesis remains the way to deal with it.

A parameter-driven approach therefore still seems to be the best escape from the mythical hideaway that is the recent complexity 'n' chaos applications in architecture. A parameter-driven approach could enhance the complexity studies with a step-by-step method, in which a series of projects can be used to develop an agenda as mentioned above.

What parameters should be investigated? What agenda can develop further knowledge about this context of banality?

BANALITY

Is there still a role for banality from which to acquire this knowledge? Since the majority of building production deals with banal issues, why are we still aspiring for the extravaganza? Why are we not interested in the banal? Are we afraid of banality?

In our avant-garde desires this issue stands for an absorbing en masse, the prescribed experience.

It has become the emblem of what is not totally full-fledged anymore, a vivid illustration of the very 20th- century dilemma: in our search for the unique, we all find the same; desiring the authentic and exceptional, we make it all banal.

When we look to this phenomenon of banality ironically, we deny the humanity in it. We look down on it the way the Victorian bourgeois looked down on the workers; it is a view with contempt, mixed with shame. Just like then, a Dickensian architecture is needed to give back to banality that human, useful face.

BIFURCATION

In a sea of banality, architecture seems to bifurcate. On the one hand, it becomes synonymous with urbanism, on the other, the role of the interior grows.

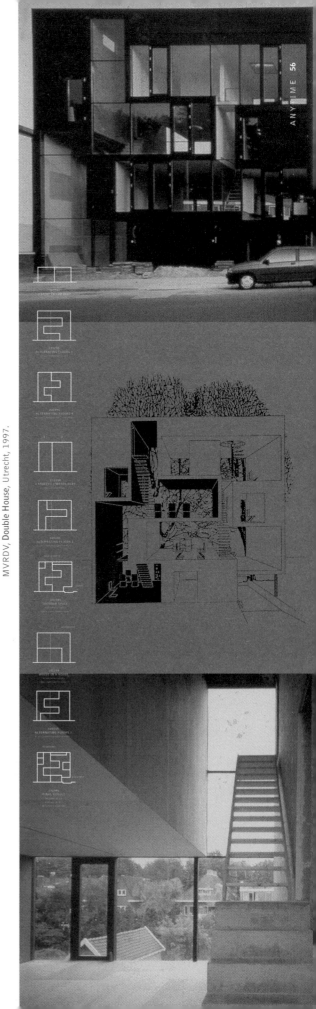

MVRDV, **Double House**, Utrecht, 1997.

INTERIOR

Because of the proximity of buildings and the bigness of objects, the role of the interior has been enlarged.

The in-between, the public space, has become more and more interiorized because of its overdesign: benches, lampposts, and plants seem to domesticate public space.

This goes hand in hand with the way in which the public domain has been enlarged into other domains. Private life has been mixed with public space. Private love confessions are shown on television, private phone calls are held on zebra paths.

Public space extends until it is seemingly endless and shapeless. It cannot be studied in terms of form or geometry or composition, but in terms of observation and statistics.

URBANISM

When architecture becomes urbanism, it enters the realm of quantities and infrastructure as a tool for organization; it enters the domain of time and relativism. A realm where things come, things go.

LITENESS AND TEMPORARINESS

How can we adopt the technique of "change" more literally within the realm of urbanism and architecture? Can we find an environment that can be broken down or cleared more easily, so that we can change our urbanistic goals within a certain time? Can we imagine a lighter urbanism that questions the permanence of the town? Should all existing urban fabric be permanent? Are all our buildings so beautiful or valuable

that we have to work with them as though they are all monuments? Can this heavy and fixed approach be replaced by a lighter form of urbanism in which we make space for experiment and imagination?

If we consider the economic value of the built environment, the life of a new computer is two to three years and a car, six years. A *house* has an economical value of about thirty years and an *office building* a value of forty years. That suggests that enormous parts of our environment could "rebegin." Since most of our recent developments have an economical value of forty to fifty years, incredible voids and multiple fantasies should occur within thirty years. Enormous parts of our towns could be redesigned in which the monuments appear as Mont St. Michels on a plain of liteness. Existing towns find the opportunity to dissolve themselves into the landscape. Extreme melanges of programs become imaginable: from living on a farm to farming within the town.

An equation of settlements, agriculture, and nature could be proposed again, an echo of Frank Lloyd Wright's Broadacre City.

This lite exploitation of (parts of) our territories could be compared with the Middle Ages farming system, where the land was divided into three equal parts. In the first year, one third was used for cattle, one third for crops, and one third was kept empty. One year later, all the parts changed their uses, so that one third could regain its biological potential, etc.

"Change" thus finds its position within urbanism. It defines space for the "unpredictable."

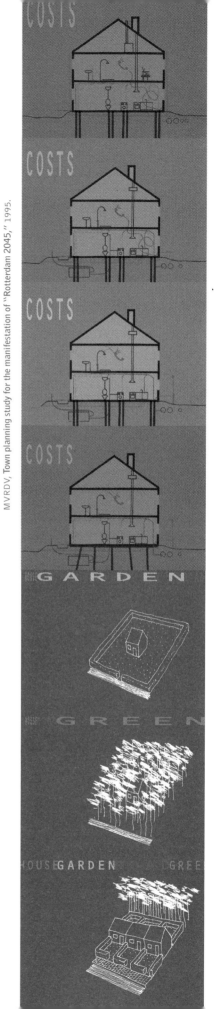

MVRDV, Town planning study for the manifestation of "Rotterdam 2045," 1995.

This lite form of urbanism can be accelerated within the current mass production of buildings by reducing the economic value of expensive parts of urbanization: grass roads instead of asphalt, ecological pools instead of sewage pipes, electricity instead of gas pipes for heating, mobile phones instead of phone wires, wooden piles instead of sand foundations, minibuses or buses-on-demand instead of expensive metrolines.

This economy can create exciting possibilities: within the same budget we can develop big gardens around the houses, or a communal forest could be planted. For a relatively low price, a villa-like environment can be made.

Economy thus obtains a connection with ecology. It delivers the paradoxical feeling that ecological durability has been translated into liteness and temporariness.

DATASCAPE

In this urban field, events occur or take place in apparently unorganized patterns, the very chaos of which possesses hidden logics. This allows "gravities" to emerge from this endless tapestry of objects.

These gravities reveal when they are sublimated beneath certain assumed, maximized constraints.

Maximization or extremization leads by definition to extremes, edges that are defined by *resistances*. This evocation of resistance seems to be the moment in which society reveals its face, the very limits of our civilization: the norms, the rules, the morals.

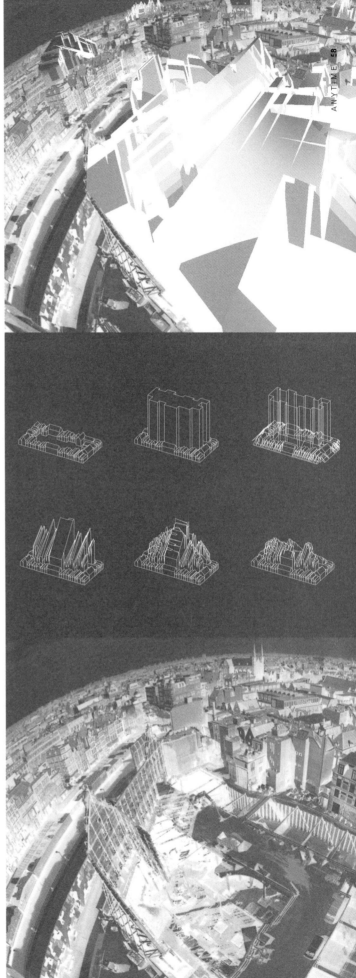

MVRDV, Gothics, 1996.

Under maximized circumstances, every demand, rule, or norm manifests itself in pure and unexpected forms that go beyond artistic intuition or known geometry and replace it with *research*.

Form becomes the result of that extrapolation, a *datascape* of the demands behind it. It balances between ridiculization and criticism, making pragmatics sublime, connecting moral with norm. The possibility might be found to criticize the norm and the moral behind it. As we replace artistic intuition with an argument, we develop hypotheses that observe, extrapolate, analyze, and criticize our contemporary behavior, thus imagining "progress" and opening up perspectives.

This might be understood as a project of acceleration. And one could even call it apocalyptic.

FARMAX

One way to resolve these gravities in space is with pressure and density. Density, which mainly occurs where more important investments are made, is still a taboo in the welfare states of Western Europe. This fear is expressed in laws, by-laws, and building codes. The light adagio of the modern movement, for instance, was sublimated in building codes at the beginning of the 20th century, and has limited European density, now one third that of Manhattan or Hong Kong.

This paradigm of concentration leads to a seemingly endless list of datascapes. Without a narrative they could be conceived as a *New Neufert*. These datascapes drive the work in our office: social resistances are revealed

in the Double House in Utrecht; light rules in the VPRO building; monumental regulations have led to the suspended housing in Amsterdam and the urban *shadow plan* for Bergen op Zoom.

E-SCAPE: BEGINNING

These datascapes, as both studies and realizations, might address William Gibson, who believed that the greater achievements of the 20th century can be found in its structures of information, rather than in buildings. Brett Steel, in a text on datascapes, points to the crucial difference between datascapes and the "normal" production of space:

A provisional answer can be read into the very term "datascape" itself: namely in the double reading of the word: data as a form of "landscape," and the project itself as a form of data-escape. It is this dual notation, a task of giving an "appearance" to information while at the same time constructing a sense of "escape" from the very tyranny of such an image qua task, that one might begin to address both Fred Jameson's instinct to historicize the appearance of datascapes and Barthes' desire to find in them the possibility of new meanings. [1]

1 Brett Steel, *Data e scape*, Architectural Association, London, 1998.

WINY MAAS IS A PARTNER IN THE ROTTERDAM FIRM MVRDV AND CO-EDITOR WITH JACOB VAN RIJS AND RICHARD KOEK OF **FARMAX: EXCURSIONS ON DENSITY.**

PLAN

WINDOW

LARGE GLASS PANEL

ENTRA

CONCRETE WAL

STAIR

De la nature morte vivante:
An Architecture of Standstill Can Bilsel

NAGIRA APARATA

APERTURE

INTERIOR PERSPECTIVE

1 Barbara Lesák, "Visionary of the European Theatre," in *Frederick Kiesler*, ed. Lisa Phillips (New York: Whitney Museum of American Art, 1989), 40. See also Barbara Lesák, "Elektromechanische Bühnenbilder," *Die Kulisse explodiert: Friedrich Kiesler's Theaterexperimente und Architekturprojekte 1923–1925*, (Vienna: Löcker Verlag, 1988); R. L. Held, *Endless Innovations: Frederick Kiesler's Theory and Scenic Design* (Ann Arbor, Michigan: UMI Research Press, 1982).

2 Kiesler later claimed to be the first designer who used moving pictures in a theater installation. See Kiesler, "Utilisation du cinéma en 1922, dans R.U.R., de Karel Capek," in *Frederick Kiesler, Artiste-architecte* (Paris: Centre Georges Pompidou, 1996) 42–3.

3 Kiesler, "Kiesler's Pursuit of an Idea," *Progressive Architecture* (July 1961), 109.

4 Kiesler, "Débâcle des Theaters," *Die Internationale Ausstellung neuer Theatertechnik* (Vienna: Neue Freie Presse, 1924).

Figure 1. Can Bilsel, The "electromechanical" set reframed.

Since the first decades of the 20th century, when the photographic image was theorized, the camera eye has constituted the paradigm of an innovative concept of a transient moment of experiencing. The apparatus not only gives access to a larger scopic field, extending human vision, but also introduces a different experience of temporality. The instant proper to photography is not the immediate and transient moment of experience. It is a reproduced, objectified, and archived moment, one that exists in the traces that it leaves. The following project reflects on this photographic instant.

It was just such an instant that Frederick Kiesler captured in 1923 in his design for the theater set of the R.U.R. by Karel Capek, in Berlin. Capek's play represents an inhuman future, which finds its expression in the events that take place in a robot factory. Finding a particular attraction to the mechanized setting of the science fiction play, Kiesler was able to experiment with audiovisual devices and with a language of constructivist, abstract forms.

For the stage of the R.U.R. Kiesler took the challenge of designing an "electromechanical" panel, instead of providing a theater set in the conventional sense. Kiesler's design consisted of a large collage of mechanical devices, an aperture, a *tanagra aparata*, a megaphone, a seismograph, and a lightbulb fixed on the surface of a wall in bas-relief.[1] A large mechanical eye in the form of a camera diaphragm constituted the most imposing feature of the collage. Kiesler projected motion pictures onto the screen placed in the middle of the aperture, implying that the images were concealed within the depth of a mechanical eye.[2] The other dominant feature of the panel was a viewing device, which Kiesler subsequently called "television."[3] The television was, in fact, an application of tanagra aparata, an optical device used at the turn of the century in puppet theaters and marionette shows. The tanagra itself consisted of a miniature scene on which appear images of the actors standing behind the panel. With a configuration of mirrors, the device reduced the live images of the actors and presented them on the screen. The "electromechanical" set, in other words, served *not* as a fixed background against which the action takes place, but as an intermediary apparatus which reproduces and presents the images of the actors in real time and space.

Kiesler's design was noteworthy among the avant-garde projects of the 1920s because it reversed the conventional spatial relation between stage and audience. In the catalogue of the *Internationale Ausstellung neuer Theatertechnik*, Kiesler argued against a theater of illusion in which the stage was treated as a picture, a two-dimensional representation of theatrical space. Instead, he called for the development of the real space of the stage, in all its plenitude, as an integral part of the performance. The only way to convey the spatially lived moment on stage "with optical precision," he insisted, lay in the metamorphosis of movement in space.[4] Thus, Kiesler undertook the project of translating the theatrical movement of the performance into an architecture that he called, "de la nature morte vivante." This was an architecture conceived as a "synthesis of immobility and movement," consisting of an apparatus that was constantly transformed in time.

Yet, how did the architect conceive and design this translation of movement into space? Was the architecture of the stage composed of stills, each corresponding to a privileged moment, a terminal instant of the performance? An architecture designed frame by frame? Or was this architecture composed of accidental snapshots, immobile sections of constant, uninterrupted movement?[5] Anticipating a temporality fragmented by cinematic frames, Kiesler's "electromechanical" set operated with a succession of stills creating its own rhythm, which could be slowed down or accelerated as the events of the performance proceeded. This architecture of the stage was more cinematic than theatrical. Yet, unlike film, this architectural apparatus produced and reproduced itself in the real space of the theater. In the way it reconstituted movement on stage, Kiesler's architecture seems to have created a linear sequence of temporality, one that is parallel to, yet different from, "real time." The architectural apparatus produced its own mechanical, abstract time.

Given the innovative experiment with temporality offered by the R.U.R. set, the question remains how to reconsider this architectural apparatus with respect to its own historicity and with respect to our present condition. The project presented here is an attempt to reframe and reproduce the electromechanical set. It begins with the realization that the figures of the panel, the recording apparatuses, acquired a new significance over time. In his search for the architecture of a robot factory, one that belongs to a dehumanized future, Kiesler seems to have captured a new language. What Kiesler produced in a single panel was a vocabulary of abstract yet, at the same time, iconographic forms, a repository of referents to what, through Walter Benjamin, we came to recognize as "the age of mechanical reproducibility."

It is precisely for this reason that a reconstruction of the R.U.R. panel is impossible. The very act of reconstruction assumes a temporal distance from the once-upon-a-time of a work. It attempts to rebuild the work anew "as it really was." The intention here is not to reconstruct. The real challenge that the electromechanical set offers today is the possibility of reproducing the apparatuses in the form of a ruin or a redundancy that does not refer to an original work but brings the R.U.R. into the present of a here and now.

The project flattens out the machines of the R.U.R. and prepares them for re-embodiment in the fossilized form of a large glass. This panel is placed in a cameralike container, a space that admits little light. This is an interior whose boundaries are defined to the extent that light is projected on the recording apparatuses. The project on display is neither an original work of art nor its identical reproduction. The panel, insofar as it embodies the machine parts, defines both the object as well as the architectural frame of experience. This reframing of the R.U.R. explores the architectural condition of an inner landscape, in which time is not defined as succession, progression, or evolution but as a discontinuous fragment written in the void of space.

Figure 2. Frederick Kiesler. Detail of the stage set for Karel Capek's **R.U.R.**, Theater am Kurfürstendamm, Berlin 1923 (Harvard Theater Collection, Cambridge, Masschusetts).

5 These questions are particularly relevant in Kiesler's stage design for Eugene O'Neill's *Emperor Jones* in Berlin, 1924. Following its performance, Kiesler published six images taken at different moments during the play and then connected them to one another as cinematic frames. With this montage, Kiesler gave the impression that a continuous change of scenery took place throughout the performance and that the transformation of the space was mechanically coordinated within a time sequence. An accelerating drum beat indicated the passage of time during the play. In a later interview, Kiesler recalled that what was important to him "was the translation of the beats of the drums into a continuous flow of light, moving scenery and color; . . . time merges into space." See Kiesler, "Kiesler's Pursuit of an Idea," *Progressive Architecture* (July 1961), 111.

CAN BILSEL HAS WORKED AS AN ARCHITECT IN PARIS AND AT ATELIER BILSEL IN ANKARA. HE HAS ALSO DONE RESEARCH IN URBAN PRESERVATION FOR THE AGA KHAN FOUNDATION.

Working in Bombay: The City as Generator of Practice
Rahul Mehrotra

As we move into the next century, we will witness a predominantly "Urban India" and "Urban Asia." Cities like Bombay, Hyderabad, Kuala Lumpur, Bangkok, and Shanghai are expected to become some of the largest urban conglomerates in the world.

Architects and designers working in these urban contexts are now dealing with an entire gamut of social, cultural, and economic issues and problems that are often alien to their professions. In conventional praxis the professional architect does not engage in this wider set of issues but rather chooses to operate with the specificity of a site, in the process often becoming disconnected from the larger context of practice. Unprecedented urban growth is challenging design practitioners to redefine their role in society.

Our approach to working in Bombay has been actually to use the city as a generator of practice, thereby not only attempting, as designers, to contribute in some way to this larger urbanization issue, but more impor-

tantly to evolve an approach and architectural vocabulary nourished by the powerful phenomena of urban evolution. In fact, Bombay is a laboratory from which our practice has extracted lessons. We have been involved with a wide range of activities in the city, and these experiences in turn have been consistently woven into our design approach. Our work with urban issues in Bombay has enabled us to generate a vocabulary that connects spatial and architectural elements from the past with a contemporary approach to urban building.

Working in Bombay is different from working in other regional centers in India. Elsewhere, the imposition of a region-specific cultural agenda often demands that architects demonstrate their ethnic credentials. Bombay, on the other hand, in many ways guarantees a certain degree of conceptual freedom, permitting a modulation of the traditional and the contemporary in whatever permutation one thinks is appropriate. This intertwining of times, of attitudes, of the coming together

and moving apart of past and present, has historically created Bombay's urban kaleidoscope. It is an urban phenomenon that does not lend itself to simplistic readings of its form, which is pluralistic in nature and does not make explicit its origins, intentions, or rationale.

Indeed, the urban phenomenon of Bombay was unintended, for it was built by the British expressly for trade links with India and perhaps was never expected to become a large town. As with other settlements that are not expected to grow, Bombay was not planned. Instead it came into being through impulsive and incremental growth. Its form expressed the idea of the city as a field of human enterprise. This had some shortcomings. The lack of a master plan or clear overall design resulted in a city that was always ill-prepared for growth. Yet it also made for some flexibility. Every addition or intervention was an opportunity to compensate for deficiencies or to reinforce positive attributes of the existing

physical structure, which allowed the city to renew its physical expression in response to contemporary aspirations – to the time.

As a result, Bombay was never conceived as or built in a singular image. In fact, its evolution consistently makes evident a series of dualities, a phenomenon in which many worlds, many ideas and interests, have influenced the city's growth. Besides an incredibly rich and varied building stock, Bombay also inherited a colonial urban diagram that survived until the 1950s. The dual city configuration created two worlds: first, the separation between the British and Indians, and second, between rich and poor. By the 1960s, however, these separate worlds and spaces had gently slipped into each other, creating one space that accommodates two worlds. This change was accelerated, as in most Asian cities, by massive demographic shifts. Waves of distress migration from the hinterlands inundated the city and irreversibly altered its very structure, both physically and socially.

The images that emerged throughout Asia were of sharp dualities: of rich and poor; of Western cities juxtaposed with traditional ones; of temporary cities of impermanent materials nestled around cities of reinforced concrete and steel. In Bombay the most emblematic of these dualities is the *Bazaar* housed in the Victorian arcades in the historic city center. Here the chaotic informal sector that comprises the Bazaar has inserted itself within the disciplined arcades that characterize Bombay's Victorian core. These extreme manifestations of urban form are physically compressed to create an incredible set of images. They symbolize the emerging pluralism in the built environments of most Indian and Asian cities. It is in this environment charged with duality, where "many times" coexist simultaneously – compressed, layered, and juxtaposed with one another – that the "beginning" of our practice lies.

We spent a greater part of the first three years of our now nine-year-old practice unscrambling the patterns that make up the environment of this schizophrenic space and time capsule. Research became our predominant activity and mechanism for understanding Bombay. We looked at architecture and urban history. We documented historic areas as well as contemporary urban centers and architecture. We worked with conservation legislation, interacted with local historical societies, worked on policies for recycling city land, and took on an entire gamut of activities that engaged us with the city. All of this exposed us to the different worlds that existed in Bombay and the different "times" that created these varied worlds. To cut across these differences while respecting their integrity and aspirations became something of an obsession. How do we as architects work for the city's many worlds? Do we respond simultaneously to the past, present,

Rahul Mehrotra Associates, Laxmi Machine Works, Corporate Headquarters. ANYTIME 68

and future? How do we do this when all these times exist simultaneously? Can we design with a divided mind?

It was in this frenzy of experimentation that we rediscovered the logic of modernism, which had gallantly addressed a broad range of issues relevant to our society. Modernism stood out as resilient, robust, and withstanding the test of time. Over the years, through practice, we became further committed to the relevance of the modernist ethos. It has had a great impact on contemporary India and Asia, both in terms of its rigor and in terms of its ability to cut across cultural differences and the historical past, an omnipresent force in most regions in Asia. Distinct from both postmodernism's facile image-grabbing and advanced capitalism's oversimplification of modernism into a bag of aesthetic tricks, modernism in Asia – India through China – is still linked intrinsically to a social agenda, economic rationale, and political ideology. It was for these very reasons that countries in Asia

first embraced modernism in their transition from colonial domination. The architectural identity of postcolonial India, for example, is one entirely founded on modernism.

Besides modernism's historic antecedents, for us, the relevance of this ethos also lies its capacity to adjust, adapt, and absorb a particular locale's architectural milieu. In a country as steeped in tradition as India, to view one's culture afresh, as modernism permits, is important. However, our research on the city revealed that a misunderstood form of modernism often perpetuated the tabula rasa mind-set of the preceding generation of architects – the sort of attitude that states, "I have seen the future and it works!" In response to this situation, our practice is committed to addressing not only issues in the contemporary urban landscape but also to identifying aspects of India's historic cities that have continuing relevance for emerging postcolonial urbanism. We are active in urban conservation projects in Bombay and seek to

RAHUL MEHROTRA IS PRIN-
CIPAL AT RAHUL MEHROTRA
ASSOCIATES IN BOMBAY.
HE IS CO-AUTHOR WITH
SHARADA DWIVEDI OF **THE
CITIES WITHIN**. HIS PRO-
JECTS INCLUDE THE CORPO-
RATE HEADQUARTERS FOR
LAXMI MACHINE WORKS IN
COIMBATORE, INDIA.

facilitate the gentle transition from historic
city to the contemporary urban milieu.

For our building conservation projects in
Bombay, we emphasize a "creative conservation," in which we develop a critical dialogue
between the old and new. We view the
revitalization of a building through patterns
of contemporary use as the generator of the
conservation process. As designers, we can
see opportunities in the reorganization of a
historic building. In addition, we have learned
a great deal about design from conservation,
which in turn informs all of our work. The
design of a good modern building and the
process of conserving a historic one are not
really different practices.

In historic buildings, our approach has
often been to strip the space down to its
bare architecture and confront it on those
terms. We thus see interiors work as spatial
and architectural rather than decorative. In
Bombay, as in many large cities, the greater
bulk of work for young practices involves

interior renovation, additions, alteration, and
new interventions. Through these smaller
projects, we have evolved a vocabulary that
informs our architecture. Layering space to
create illusions of size, creating devices for
greater flexibility, and experimenting with
materials and textures are all techniques that
have found their way into our projects. In
that sense, the architecture of the interior and
exterior become contiguous. We apply the
same set of values and approaches to both
types of work.

Our approach has been to abstract and
interpret spatial arrangements and building
elements to generate a contemporary sensibility and building vocabulary. We combine
materials, juxtapose conventional craftsman-
ship with industrial materials, and contrast
traditional spatial arrangements with contemporary spatial organization. In short, we strive
to give expression to the multiple worlds,
pluralism, and dualities that so vividly characterize the Asian cityscape.

title:

Zeynep Mennan / Mehmet Kütükçüoğlu / Kerem Yazgan

The full stop marks the end/beginning of a sentence, secures the syntactic/semantic consistency of either side. The security in the presence of the sentence is ruptured by the space of the full stop. Each full stop represents and embodies moments of rupture within a text, threatening its consistency and orientation.

The full stop is exiled from the space of the sentence. Its entry into this space would correspond to a rupture *within* the sentence. But that rupture is represented by the dash, which is incorporated into the presence of the sentence. The anxiety that draws the full stop away from the sentence is overcome by the lightness of the dash.

TITLE: Delayed

The frivolous autonomy of the dash that renders it immune to either side of a sentence is the principle of *anacoluthon*.

Anacoluthon [LL, fr. LGk *anakolouthon* inconsistency in logic, fr. Gk, neut. of *anakolouthos*, inconsistent, fr. *an-* + *akolouthos* following, fr. *ha-*, *a-* together + *keleuthos* path] (ca. 1706): syntactical inconsistency or incoherence within a sentence; *esp*: the shift from one construction to another (as in "you really ought – well, do it your own way") – From *Webster's Ninth New Collegiate Dictionary* (Springfield, Massachusetts: Merriam Webster, Inc., 1990).

Anacoluthon is "a grammatical interruption or lack of implied sequence within a sentence. That is, beginning a sentence in a way that implies a certain logical resolution, but concluding it differently than the grammar leads one to expect. Anacoluthon can be either a grammatical fault or a stylistic virtue, depending on its use. In either case, it is an interruption or a verbal lack of symmetry. Anacoluthon is characteristic of spoken language or interior thought, and thus suggests those linguistic domains when it occurs in writing." – http://humanities.byu.edu/rhetoric/anacolut.htm

Basically a shift from one construction to another, as in the sentence "You really ought – well, do it your own way," an anacoluthon breaks into the original sentence and transforms it in an unexpected way, or in a way that is not implied logically. The given sentence never reaches a logical resolution. Attention shifts from the two parts of the sentence to something third that is as yet unknown and is represented by a void – the dash. The dash, which signals the moment of absence when the sentence is interrupted or collapses, has a cryptic meaning. This emerging third condition absorbs all of the creative energy of the sentence.

If the two parts of the sentence are understood as states, one can see that they are neighboring but nonsequential, brought into proximity, but not necessarily into a new sequence, by the help of an agent, the anacoluthon. The anacoluthon gathers at least two nonsequential states with a culmination point,

anacoluthon can be defined as an agent between one state and the other, one construct and the other one activity and the other, one idea/Idea and the other . . .

amounting to a rupture between them: the anacoluthic moment.©

The anacoluthic moment is a moment of absence, of discontinuity that acts as a joint between two incompatible structures.

The anacoluthon is a rhetorical device

DASH

Any culture produces a system of delays.

any discipline produces a system of delays

This system secures the integrity of a culture, which by definition builds upon a set of procedural and behavioral codes that transform it into a machine for delay.

Television companies use machines for delay to censor unexpected unacceptable occurrences during live broadcasts, which are aired with a delay of one to five seconds.

Cultural delay machines censor the immediacy of alien customs that are deferred through its codes. Likewise, urban space is a delay mechanism; indeed, any built environment constructs a system of delays through hierarchically organized spaces of confrontation.

Delay is a cultural production that has a psychic counterpart: an ever-growing obsession with speed: speed of production, of consumption, of reflection, of innovation.

This text uniquely refers to the dictionary as a quick referencing system. It is deliberately "Websterian" as an exercise that attempts to unload both the content and format of scholarly referencing and footnoting systems for a fresh new orientation.

This is a psychology of intolerance; intolerance of any loss of speed, that is, of delay.

Delay is a condition linked to the assumption of an origin and a telos. For delay to occur at least two states need to exist: A and B, a beginning and an end placed in a sequence. B is delayed with respect to A. The notion of delay becomes intelligible and acquires both significance and commensurability within sequential series.

The commensurability of delay derives from the scaling of time. Scale is a mental construct that time inhabits. The temporal scale is a selective one. It sifts through the activities to which it gives measure. Through this we arrive at different times: the time of reflection, of perception, of conception, of production, of cognition, of rationalization: the times of a work.

This multiplicity of times indicates that in the construction of time, anachronism is built-in.

Time is built, anachronism is built-in.

The desire for speed today is based upon the will to undo the built-in anachronism that occurs between the multiple times of a work. A common obsession among architects is to achieve a linear process, a clear itinerary from the beginning (*A*) to the end (*B*) of a work. Any point along this line is a delay in relation to point B. The architect's preoccupation with speed focuses mainly on reconciling the discrepancies (or delays) that occur between the different velocities of the modalities of a work.

The ultimate goal of this linear process is to develop a secure link to a superdiscourse, i.e., to a specific culture. Notions of speed and delay are intimately bound to the concept of culture. The striking paradox of a cultural machine of delay is its promotion of speed.

No speed can overcome delay.

Speed and delay belong to a vicious cycle of mutual promotion. The itinerary of a work in this vicious cycle gradually exhausts its creative energies and settles into a state of entropy.

Entropy: The degradation of the matter and energy in the universe to an ultimate state of inert uniformity. – *Webster's Ninth New Collegiate Dictionary*

The anacoluthon can be reintroduced as an agent of inter-ruption, breaking up the vicious cycle of speed and delay and disturbing the entropic itinerary. The anacoluthic moment is an instant when any affiliation to a culture, any reliance on a safe foundation, is made at the cost of anxiety and insecurity.

An anacoluthic moment marks the end of one state and the beginning of another. This leap from one state to another is a moment of lightness in which the heavy, cumbersome, and repetitious uniformity of the first state is discharged. Leaving a state behind then takes the form of a conscious disorientation, misorientation, or rupture.

an anacoluthic moment is a moment of failure; failure of syntactical symmetry, meaning, orientation, logic, time . . .

An anacoluthic moment is a singular moment in which what follows cannot be predetermined; it can disintegrate into chaos or leap to a different level of order or construction. As a point of mediation, an anacoluthic moment is represented by the dash, which creates an anxious, problematic moment with respect to both sides, an oscillation on the edge, a state of alert that opens a cursory look into a behavior nearing an unstable equilibrium. This is a state of immediacy (of noncognition, of no time, of nonsense). The anacoluthic leap is a diversion toward the immediate.

This diversion from an assumed wholeness is an accident. The accident is a condition of discontinuity, lightness, and immediacy. Loaded with unknown and unexpected possibilities, the immediacy of the anacoluthic moment raises both anxiety and amusement, which await release.

Diversion: 1. The act or instance of diverting from a course, activity or use: DEVIATION. 2. Something that diverts or amuses: PASTIME. – *Webster's Ninth New Collegiate Dictionary*

The anacoluthic moment is the creative moment.

It is a moment of relief: relief from the urge for consistent and logical constructions and orientations, relief from the vicious cycle that perpetuates our obsessive concern with such notions as speed, delay, and anachronism.

Indeed, an anacoluthic moment forgets these concerns. At this moment of absence they lose their significance and existence, and immediately commensuration dissolves.

The anacoluthic moment is incommensurable.

Delay dissolves and the speed of innovation is acquired in the dissolution of delay.

Time collapses.

This temporary loss of commensuration occurs in the void of the anacoluthic shift, or the act of creation. This void, which juxtaposes absence and presence, is the space of a beginning.

The nondurational, instantaneous nature of the anacoluthic moment forces us to settle into a second state, a state of recognition, with a new momentum: This is the beginning of a new construct, a new ground, which also recovers a consciousness of the former.

The totality of this process constitutes the lifetime of a creative work. The anacoluthon is the agent of its production and research.

ZEYNEP MENNAN IS A LECTURER AND DESIGN CRITIC AT MIDDLE EAST TECHNICAL UNIVERSITY IN ANKARA.

MEHMET KÜTÜKÇÜOGLU AND **KAREM YAZGAN** ARE PARTNERS OF THE FIRM TEGET MIMARL, AND BOTH TEACH AT MIDDLE EAST TECHNICAL UNIVERSITY.

15.06.98 LAGOS: NIGERIA'S NEW MILITARY LEADERSHIP ORDERS THE RELEASE OF NINE OF THE COUNTRY'S MOST PROMINENT POLITICAL PRISONERS.

Trajectories If history provides a set of grounds, assumptions, and methods that guide not only the practices of design and building but also those of conceptualization, then how does history, bound to the past, produce movement, transitions, becomings? How does history move us into a future that is grounded in history but also involves an unpredictable leap beyond it? How can the time of history produce the time of the new? How does the new alter our view of the past?

Simulated Origin, Simulated End

Arata Isozaki / Akira Asada

Time is what a clock measures. — Albert Einstein

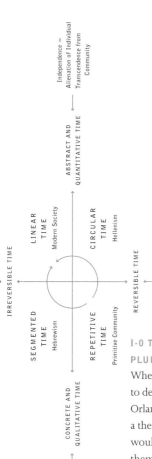

I-0 THE RELATIVITY AND PLURALITY OF TIME

When Disney commissioned me to design their headquarters in Orlando, Florida, they requested a thematical architecture that would be consistent with the theme park. Based on this requirement, the Team Disney Building came to embody "time." Located within Disney World, the headquarters has a north/south axis and straddles a large, artificial pond. There is a circular courtyard with a huge, cone-shaped wall built around it, assuming the form of a gigantic sundial. Using the sundial, one can read solar time, which is different from local time. The difference between the time indicated by each worker's wristwatch and that designated by the sundial tells us that time is a plural being and is ultimately an artificial construct.

Plates inscribed with propositions concerning time – from East to West, past to present – are planted in the pebble-covered floor of the courtyard. They include Einstein's famous words, "Time is what a clock measures." It is common knowledge that the chronometers and watches people use do not necessarily indicate one and the same time. The fact that time is indicated only by imprecise clocks points very simply to the fact that time is relative.

In the East, and especially in Japan, until the mid-19th century, the time of daily life was divided into twelve segments: six sections from dawn to dusk and six sections from dusk to dawn. As a result, the length of the time unit – *ikkoku* – varied from day to day. Naturally, only on the vernal and autumn equinoxes were the lengths of night and day equal. In the 16th century, when the modern Western clock was introduced into Japan, it was of no use until a craftsman developed a device that enabled the time on the Western clock to be indicated in the Japanese way. The device became obsolete when Japan began to follow Greenwich Mean Time, but was an example of how different social conventions can necessitate a system of translation; time is essentially relative. And in architecture as well, time has always appeared differently.

A-1

Let me begin by touching upon "a brief history of time," not that of Stephen Hawking's bestselling book, but the one presented in Yusuke Maki's book, *A Comparative Sociology of Time* (*Jikan no hikaku shakaigaku* [Iwanami Shoten, 1981]). It schematizes a history of time as follows.

1. In primitive communities, time was qualitative and repetitive. For instance, this year's festival was not situated between last year's and next year's, but rather was motivated by a repetition of the same time.
2. In ancient Greek culture, time, with the development of the commodity economy, came to be considered quantitative. Thus the advent of continuous circular time.
3. In Judaic culture, linear time was constituted as a qualitative segment bounded by an origin and an end.
4. Finally, synthesizing points two and three, as it were, a quantitative linear time without beginning or end was established and became dominant in modern society.

Using Maki's simple schematization as a premise, I would like to further illustrate the inherent peculiarity of time in modern society. The modern age, after all, is an age of capitalism generated by unlimited quantitative accumulation. That is, capitalism does not have a qualitative end; rather, it moves forward by indefinitely deferring the negative end: crisis. (Of course the most suitable political expression of the deferment is the nuclear deterrence that seeks to maintain temporary order by indefinitely deferring another negative end: nuclear war.)

The structure of endless time in modern society can be elucidated using a ubiquitous example: paper money. How can this thing, which is itself totally valueless, be valuable? For payment, a person accepts paper money only upon the assumption that another person will accept it tomorrow. If the end of the world – doomsday – is determined, however, we could at least say that nobody would accept any paper money on that day. And it follows that nobody would accept it on the day before. By way of backward induction, even today we could stop accepting it. In other words, it is only because Judgment Day is constantly deferred as an unsettled account that the system of currency – capitalism – can function. (Even if the state seeks to regulate the system by legislating currency, instances of hyperinflation reveal that legislation alone cannot totally assure the "general acceptability" of a currency that has lost credit.)

The same logic can be applied to the so-called "Prisoner's Dilemma," which is a paradigm for the (im)possibility of cooperation in individualist society. In this scenario, a pair of suspects in a crime are questioned separately. Each is encouraged to reveal the other's role in exchange for a lighter punishment, even though both would be better off if they tacitly collaborated and refused to reveal anything incriminating about the other. In the end, both lose because each chooses, in a rational individualist calculation, to betray the other for the sake of him or herself. This is a case of what Amartya Sen has called "rational fools." However, if this scenario were repeated indefinitely, the rational calculation of the cumulative result would make everyone better off. (For instance, the "tit-for-tat" strategy – to refuse to cooperate only after the other betrayed in the previous stage – proves beneficial to both sides.) However, what if there is a last game that is strategically equivalent to a one-shot game, one in which each side inexorably chooses to save itself? If so, then the game before will follow the same pattern. And, by backward induction, both sides from the beginning will have to choose not to collaborate with their partners-in-crime. These examples show how modern capitalist society is literally driven by an endless time structure and how it functions only by indefinitely deferring the telos.

Shifting our concern to the cultural domain, we realize that the movement of the avant-garde that advances by way of "denial for the sake of denial" unexpectedly corresponds to the movement of modern capitalism. In the age of classicism, the goal was to achieve an ideal image beyond time. The avant-garde movement began as the destruction of the norm and sought to continue to repeat this gesture of denial, because reaching a certain destination would mean the death of the movement. The division of avant-garde and arrière-garde, left wing and right wing, has been mapped along the axis of forward linear movement. (I could have used the term *modernism* here instead of *avant-garde* since modernism was the relative counterpart with respect to classicism. But, as exemplified by Arthur Rimbaud's declaration, "Il fault être absolument moderne" [we must be absolutely modern], modernism tends toward "absolute modernity" in order to compete with traditionalism. High modernist work is precisely such a case. In *The Sense of an Ending* [1967], Frank Kermode uses the oxymoron "traditionalist modernism" to describe James Joyce's *Ulysses* as an attempt to eternalize a pedestrian dimension of events in a single, randomly chosen day by superimposing a mythological dimension. In the work of William Burroughs, on the other hand, he sees a malignant example of avant-garde art and detects an obstinate self-destructive drive provoked by an apocalyptic nihilism. In the context of visual art, Michael Fried, in his essay "Art and Objecthood" [1967], sees an

"instantaneousness" in the work of the high modernists that presences all at once – that which enables an "absorption" of an audience beyond time – while in minimalism he detects an impure "theatricality" deployed by the element of time. Because the term *modernism* has been used in this reactionary sense, I decided to use *avant-garde*, a more straightforward term.)

In the domain of architecture, too, avant-garde movements have moved forward through the denial of denial. First, they propose a manifesto in order to deny the past and then attempt to produce a new architecture according to the manifesto. But no sooner is it formulated than the new architecture becomes an object of denial. As I have already stated, the forward movement is isomorphic to that of modern capitalism. In architecture in particular, when the avant-garde inclines toward functionalism and productivism, it ends up being assimilated into the movement of capital itself. Looking back at what has happened in Japan in the recent past, we can consider the metabolism of the 1960s as the last avant-garde – metabolism not in a biological sense but as an "ism" in architecture and urbanism. It intended to be an indefinitely transforming and growing architecture/urbanism. Then the task of radicalism – neither avant-garde nor modernist – was to sever the movement of avant-garde/modern capitalism. How was the task posed and what was achieved from it? It is time to summon one of the main proponents of radicalism at that time: Arata Isozaki.

1 Michel Foucault, Language, Counter-Memory, Practice, ed. Donald F. Bouchard (Ithaca: Cornell University Press, 1977), 194.

I-1 PROCESS AND ITS SEVERANCE

The organic model has been introduced into architecture time and again since ancient times. The most typical example, anthropomorphism, assumed a static model of time because it was only concerned with projecting the human shape into the architectural order. Anthropomorphism begins with classicism's understanding of the human body as an ideal architectural proportion and results in Le Corbusier's Radiant City, where the municipal center is figured as the human brain, the industrial area as the body, the factory zones as limbs, and the traffic network as the circulation system. This distribution of the body in urban space belongs to the same line of thinking that adopted the holy crucifix as the ideal plan for churches.

The metabolist movement of the 1960s sought to make the biomorphic model something more dynamic, based on a model of cellular metabolism. Observed from a macro viewpoint, the city is in a process of constant transformation. The metabolists made a technical proposal to systematically connect the long transformation cycles (roads and transportation systems) and the short transformation cycles (buildings). Accordingly, they proposed an image of a future city: a megastructure that operates over a long period of time, with shorter duration capsules plugged in and out. This was modeled on the way the human form as a whole is sustained by the constant regeneration of cells.

Around the same time, and from an understanding of the conjuncture similar to the metabolists, I began to pay attention to the biological model of ontogeny. In the process of the genesis and growth of a life form, emergent properties come into existence from uniform cells and grow in various directions. Different organs for different functions are generated as a metamorphosis of the same cells. Following this model, I thought that an architecture could be developed that encapsulated various constitutive elements for institutions, similar to the way that organs are generated. Today we can easily simulate this process with computer graphics; at that time, we had to schematize it in primitive diagrams on the drawing board.

In metabolism's generational models — as well as Archigram's — growth and transformation are considered only on the axis of linear time. The future city is proposed as a straightforward extension of the present city. Both movements assumed that the state of the future could be automatically visualized through the use of technology. Even if we can simulate the process of transformation, in order to transpose it onto the conventional blueprint, a static image has to be extracted by terminating the transformation. An instant in the process of transformation has to be chosen, that is, a decision must be made, though there is no objective standard for this decision. Hence the subject intervenes in the flux of the transforming image and freezes it by subjective judgment. I call this *severance*.

At the moment the decision is made, the time that is supposed to flow in linear continuity is erased and replaced by an alternative time. The intervention of the subject, as in decision-making, for example, produces a singular time. The intervention of selective decision-making into the generative process of ontogeny, namely, the severance of the biological process, I called *process planning* (1962).

In order to explicitly present the fact that the image in the process of becoming or metamorphosis is frozen, a form extending in a tubelike continuum was literally cut to expose the section. As different times are bundled to form a reality, there are innumerable lines of decision; none of them are definite, however. If a decision is made at all, it is only by way of blind intervention. What is actually happening in contemporary cities is not the result of a predetermined order but of a chain of contingent accidents. In each accident, one time is terminated and an alternative time is generated. Is it at all possible to predict a future in such a state of affairs? It is almost fraudulent to speak of this undecidable state as utopia. If so, honestly speaking, our future is nothing but a ruin. Or more precisely, we can speak of the future only as a ruin. I arrived at this understanding of time by paying attention to the intervention-qua-severance of the organic process.

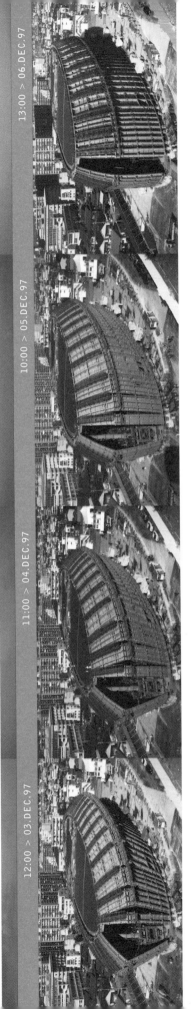

A-2

The severing of chronological time – what Friedrich Hölderlin called the *caesura* – reveals the time outside the chronological axis as vertical as opposed to horizontal time. This should also be distinguished from *kairos*, an eternal instant filled with transcendental meaning (as opposed to *kronos*, the passage of time). Following Gilles Deleuze, it is *aeon* (as opposed to *kronos*) that indicates the tense of the pure event, which is neither past nor present nor future, but infinitive. It is not a point on the chronological time axis, but rather an "inframince" split in the Duchampian sense, a split which infinitely divides itself.

Let me quote a breathtaking passage from Michel Foucault's "Theatrum Philosophicum":

> We can trace this schism to its limits, but we will never find the indivisible atom that ultimately serves as the minutely present unity of time.... On both sides of the wound, we invariably find that the schism has already happened (and that it had already taken place, and that it had already happened that it had already taken place) and that it will happen again (and in the future, it will happen again): it is less a cut than a constant fibrillation. What repeats itself is time; and the present – split by this arrow of the future that carries it forward by always causing its swerving on both sides – endlessly recurs.[1]

In this precise sense, *aeon*, the time of pure event, is also the time of repetition and return. The return in this context is nevertheless that which dislocates circular time; it is time being "out of joint," the turn of the eccentric wheel. Deleuze's interpretation of Nietzsche's eternal return – the culmination of the philosophy of time in our age – was exactly this. When our postmetabolist Isozaki says that he has discovered the time in which ruins eternally return in a section of linear time, it should mean the same.

I have just invoked a line of Western thought, and it is not impossible to cite a similar line in Eastern thinking. For instance, Dogen, a Japanese Zen monk from the 13th century (1200–1253), posed the concept of *uji* (being time) in his *Shobogenzo* (The eye and treasury of true law). According to his formulation (which may be a bit coercive grammatically), "uji X, uji Y" should not be read as "sometimes X, sometimes Y" but as "exists time X, exists time Y"; It does not mean that X time and Y time come and go one after another, sequentially, but that each time is, exists fully as an absolute present – as outside the time axis or as a severance of the time axis. In fact, a 20th-century Japanese philosopher, Tanabe Gen, likened Dogen's concept of time to Richard Dedekind's "cut" in mathematics.

However, one always has to be cautious when invoking Eastern concepts in comparison to Western ones. The ancient Eastern concept of time has an exotic attraction even for us contemporary Asians. But if it is understood as a return to the origin or an escape toward eternity, as a reaction to the time of modern capitalism, there can be no potential in the comparison or invocation. In any case, we have to think in the schism between East and West, past and present – and future. Now Arata Isozaki is going to show how he has been tackling that task.

I-2 THE SIMULATED ORIGIN

A tea room I designed was named Uji An, after Dogen's concept of *uji*. I basically followed the custom by which tea rooms were often named after phrases found in the classics; yet this was also a reminder that old tea masters considered the tea ceremony as the only encounter in a lifetime – "one time, one encounter" (*ichigo ichie*). Sharing tea allows participants to share the moment. Such an event intervenes in the flow of time, transferring the consciousness of the participants to the interiority of time. Time is that which, according to Dogen, "comes flying." In other words, an intervention in one instant draws the plural times flowing from different origins into one place. The time and place of encounter – this is the essence of the tea room. The architecture of the tea room should stimulate the senses with subtle movement, transformation, and transition within tranquillity. The architectonic is devised as a detector of the subtle movements within a micro-space. Therein, participants encounter the instant. Uji An was designed as a contemporary version of such a device.

Tea rooms thus embody an encounter with time without origin. In many cultural zones, including those of the West, origin has been represented by monuments that materialize the will to eternal duration. The favored material for these has been stone, because of its slow weathering and decay. Eternity is considered guaranteed in a form that sustains its identity against the transition of moments. In Japan, where the technique of carving stones has

not been fully developed, a totally different way of dealing with time has been devised.

The best example is the way the Ise Shrine has been systematically renovated every 20 years for nearly thirteen centuries. It has two totally identical sites with identical buildings, between which the sacred domain is alternately transposed. After the renovation of one site has been completed at the end of a 20-year interval, a ritual of transference of God from the old to the new site takes place. After the ritual, the old buildings are demolished. The holes of the central columns – believed to host God – are maintained and the old sites (*kodenchi*) covered with pebbles. Thus an empty lot remains in the deep forest.

This ritual of transference repeats the first ritual that took place in the year 692 A.D. Also reproduced are the stored ecclesiastical items; they are a few thousand in number, and the craftsmen who make them pass on the same techniques they inherited over the given amount of time. Furthermore, the procedure of the ritual totally repeats the utterance of the traditional words. The first instance of the total repetition of the origin after 20 years – the *arché* – is simulated again and again. The architecture of Ise Shrine persists in the will to sustain the event of arché, not only in form but also in technique.

Although the fragility of the simple pillars and thatched roof must be acknowledged as architectonically weak – especially after the techniques of adding stone bases and roof tiling were introduced to Japan from China in the 7th century –

the native techniques have been deliberately preserved at Ise. From the beginning, durability was never taken into consideration. A 20-year duration was considered sufficient. There is no belief in the eternity of material. Instead, eternity is guaranteed by repetition.

It should be noted that this ritual that simulates the arché was initiated in the late-7th century. It was also around this time that the name of the nation, Japan, was coined. Constantly threatened by the invasion of continental forces from China and Korea, Japan, relying on a legislative system imported from China, constituted itself as a nation-state. Around this time, the Japanese writing system was also devised through the transformation of the Chinese alphabet. By simplifying Chinese ideograms (*mana*), the Japanese kana syllabary was made, which was eventually considered essential and original to Japanese culture. Culture (*bunka*) – meaning literally "literation" in the Sino-cultural sphere – was first introduced from China. It was only later that a culture unique to Japan was fabricated. In architecture, too, especially the temple and shrine architecture under the overwhelming influence of the continental Buddhist culture, Japanese elements had to be extracted and polished to counterpose the foreign elements. In that context, Ise Shrine was established deliberately to express Japanese uniqueness. Simple pillars and thatched roofs were chosen as aesthetic and ritual elements, irrespective of rational considerations of stability and durability. The method of sustaining a style came to be a social system of the vicennial reconstruction cycle. Such an obsessive return was possible only in Japan, an insular nation. The organized return of the arché is, at the deeper level, consistent with Kokugaku, the Edo-period discipline of nationalist scholarship that skillfully told and retold the story of Japan's pure origin, a form of nationalism that always appeals to the return of the old glory, and the Tenno system that continues to be an invisible sovereign. What they have in common is the simulation of arché rendered as a method to reactivate the duration of energy, which naturally tends toward decline. Finally, again, we encounter another biological model: life, death, and rebirth, namely, succession by reproduction. Even architecture is involved in the life cycle; after weathering and decay, it is rebuilt to reproduce identical features. In the case of cellular reproduction, mutations occur in the process of succession. In the history of Ise Shrine there were also a number of tendencies to mutate. On each occasion, however, a certain force

of restoration intervened and pushed it back to its original pure form, which in fact is just a romantically imagined archetype. This is a radical movement to retrovert the flow of time anachronically; but inasmuch as it is a simulation of the arché, it is similar to the movement of radical oxygen in cells, which is nothing but a tendency to self-destruct.

In Ise Shrine, the real historical origin is veiled, paradoxically, in the guise of repetition. In fact, the shrine was simply a symbolic representation fabricated by the state at a time when it faced the crisis of external pressure in the late-7th century. Ise was built to enforce cultural centripetalism. The performance is repeated every 20 years to invoke the fiction of the repressed origin, which in reality did not exist. Is it possible then to analyze the social mechanism of retrogressing time in order to reveal the true historical origin of the repeated arché? Is it possible to revert the vector of retrogressing historicity? What is at stake now is the moment of reversion.

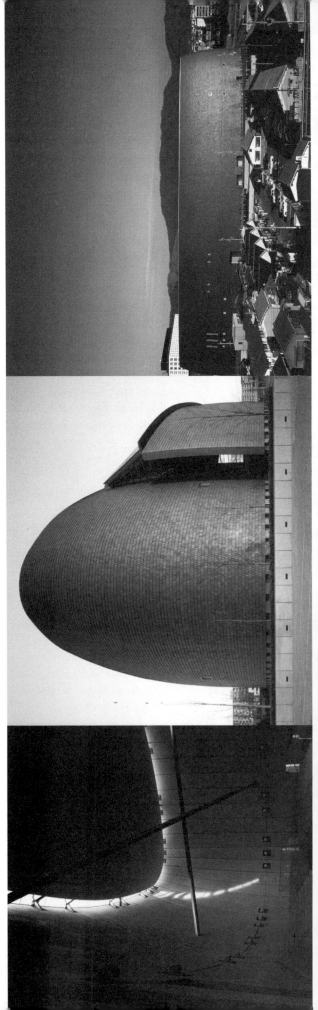

83 ASADA / ISOZAKI > SIMULATED ORIGIN, SIMULATED END

Arata Isozaki & Associates, Nara Centennial Hall. Completed October 1998 in Nara, Japan.

AKIRA ASADA TEACHES AT
THE KYOTO INSTITUTE OF
ECONOMIC RESEARCH AND
IS THE EDITOR OF THE JOUR-
NAL *CRITICAL SPACE*. HE IS
THE AUTHOR OF *KOZOTO
CHIKARA* (STRUCTURE AND
POWER) AND *HERUMESU NO
ONGAKU* (MUSIC AND
HERMES).

ARATA ISOZAKI IS AN ARCHI-
TECT IN TOKYO. HIS MANY
PROJECTS INCLUDE THE
MUSEUM OF CONTEMPORARY
ART IN LOS ANGELES, THE
KYOTO CONCERT HALL,
AND LA CASA DEL HOMBRE
IN LA CORUÑA.

THIS ESSAY WAS TRANS-
LATED FROM THE JAPANESE
BY SABU KOHSO.

A-3

The movement of modern capitalism has been accelerating
faster and faster. Since the collapse of the second world (the
previous socialist bloc) and
the third world, modern capitalism has begun to cover the
whole globe, supported by the
development of the cyber network. On a worldwide scale,
uneven development – overpro-
duction on the one hand and
impoverishment on the other –
has spread; surplus capital is
moving everywhere around the
globe, blowing and bursting
bubbles. The scenes of "delirious Tokyo" and even more
delirious Asian cities, which fas-
cinate our Dutch postcolonialist,
have been just transitory phenomena in which we could see
a nightmare of metabolism,
enlarged and intensified beyond
the expectations of its inventors.

On the other hand, the anxiety provoked by the acceleration
is producing a desire for the
apocalypse that intensifies as
we approach the end of the
millennium. Not the real apocalypse but a parody of the apocalypse. It is epitomized by the
Aum Supreme Truth Cult that
engaged in terrorism by
spreading sarin gas in Japan in
1995. For the cult it was not
enough to prophesy the apocalypse, they had to act upon it.
(Strictly speaking, their apocalypse was not the coming of an
"end," but more like pushing a
reset button. Reinterpreting
the idea of the transmigration
of souls with their sensibility
nurtured in the age of virtual
reality, Aum considered killing
people as their salvation –
enabling them to start from a
better position in the next

"stage" before having committed more sins in this "stage."
Of course, it has nothing to do
with virtual reality but was
simply a delusion of "possible
worlds.") As opposed to the
majority of religions, this
group was not at all interested
in symbolic expressions of
space; they built and left only
temporary barracks. For those
who believe that the end is
near, what is the meaning of
architecture?

All in all, what is at stake now
is neither an acceleration of
modern capitalism nor an anticipation and acting out of the
simulated ending. The avant-
garde has repeated its manifestos
such as "X is over, cheers to Y"
and "Y is dead, long live Z" long
enough. What we are con-
fronting is a conjuncture in
which the end itself is over, as it
were. Here we have to be very
careful. Interpreted in a simplistic way, "the end of the end"
might lead us to an easy version
of postmodernism: now that
history is over, we can indulge
in an endless game of citation
and eclecticism . . . However, as
its self-referential form suggests,
"the end of the end" is a convoluted phenomenon. It leads us
not to the end (fin) nor to the
endless nirvana of posthistory
but to the "closure without end"
(clôture sans fin) of Jacques Derrida. We have to place ourselves
in that convoluted space-time in
order to continue radical speculation and experimentation,
because paradoxically that is the
only chance for new beginnings.

But it is useless to repeat
the by-now-classical credo of
deconstruction. Now Arata
Isozaki will speak about "under
construction."

I-3 UNDER CONSTRUCTION

Let me introduce another biological model, the Nara Centennial
Hall, now "under construction."
It has one continuous wall that
is a closoid curve (25 meters
high) surrounding an oval plan
(136 meters long by 42 meters
wide). In order to raise its units
of precast concrete enforced
with steel plates, we employed
a special lifting technique called
the "Panta Dome Method." In
the process of incubation,
certain life forms go through
metamorphoses. Like the
moment of hatching or blooming, this architecture was
erected all at once by pushing
up the elements that had been
hinged (to become walls and
ceiling) and folded on the
ground. Raising all of the architectural elements arranged on
the ground involved lifting as
much as five thousand tons to
construct a huge internal space,
without columns, and without
construction scaffolding.
The process of hatching and
blooming follows with the
progression of time. Construction of architecture also faces
the future, for it too follows
the progression of time. The
construction of the Nara Centennial Hall as a singular event
was intentionally a performance to be seen and enjoyed
by all citizens, not simply the
successful erection of a building. Process itself is always and
already a construction. In this
sense, everything in our world
is under construction.

Three Minus Two, Two Plus One: Architecture and the Fabric of Time

Hubert Damisch

As far as space and time are concerned, Hegel has a way of classifying the arts that is paradoxical inasmuch as it is simultaneously generative and subtractive – generativity depending in this case on subtraction, and even proceeding from it. Architecture and sculpture come first in this classification because they take place and operate in the three dimensions of

the objective world. Next comes painting, the concept of which implies the elimination of one dimension – that is, three minus one; painting develops itself up to the point of being converted into a pure magic of color that is nevertheless still of a spatial character, bound as it is to the two dimensions of the

wall or the picture plane on which the interior self, the "subject" as we call it, projects itself in the guise of permanent configurations of forms and color. Last comes music, in its seemingly linear, one-dimensional, and ephemeral mode of manifestation – that is, three minus two; music, as Hegel writes in his *Lessons on Aesthetics*, does not proceed so much from the disappearance or subtraction of one more dimension of space than it does from the suppression of spatiality in general. The main task of music is to make manifest the most intimate self, the deepest subjectivity, the ideal soul, resounding, finding an echo, in the pure and permanently flowing element of time.

Architecture and music thus correspond to two opposite poles, traditionally referred to as the arts of space (architecture, sculpture, painting), and the arts of time (music and poetry). Far from assigning it the first rank in the hierarchy of the arts, Hegel considers architecture the most incomplete of all, claiming that it is unable to adequately express the spiritual through the use of materials concerned mostly with obeying the laws of gravity and therefore reduced to providing an external environment with only symbolic significance. Music, on the other hand, is thought to be the "romantic" art par excellence, because it deals with a material as insubstantial as sound – a material which, in turn, implies a double negation of exteriority; space is nullified by the way in which the body reacts to a mere vibration, which is thereby converted into a mode of expression of pure interiority.

The strictly conceptual opposition of space, as the element of exteriority and objectivity, and time or duration, as the element of interiority and subjectivity, is contradicted by the reality of movement. Movement is defined in terms of space and time, or perhaps it is space and time that are defined in terms of movement. Form in music is related to movement, just as movement is related to form. This calls for further investigations into the fabric of time, a fabric that, in spite of its alleged "linearity," allows music to reflect itself in the mirror of form and structure and thereby recognize the spatial image of its development, its construction, and its architecture. But if, according to Friedrich Schelling's famous metaphor, architecture is nothing but "frozen music" (*eine erstarrte Musik*), how are we to define music? As "defrosted architecture?"

In the *Story of Amphion* as told by Paul Valéry (who used it as an argument for a "melo-drama," set to music by Arthur Honegger), a temple is built through the agency of music. Having received the lyre from Apollo, the mortal Amphion gives birth both to music and architecture when he begins to play it. The stones move and assemble themselves into a temple. Hence the challenge for the composer, who refrains from making use of all the resources of his art until they are developed in Valéry's story under Amphion's touch. The same is true for architecture, which, at first, was to be presented more as a simple exercise of movements and combinations than of structure or composition. In the same way that music retrospectively reflects itself in its own architecture, architecture projects itself in its own generative, not to say musical, process. But its relation to time and to its fabric goes deeper than a succession of choices and displacements, a mere succession of moves, as in a game or a play; it involves – or relies on – a kind of movement or dynamic inherent to its own fabric and which requires, in order to become visible, an approach other than metaphor, an approach that involves the medium of images, according to their own movement, their own circulation, and their own dynamics.

Painting was for a long time associated with architecture. With the Renaissance, linear perspective became a common basis for both arts and provided architects and painters with an instrument that allowed them to commute freely between the actual three-dimensional space of architecture and the two-dimensional plane on which it was represented. This seemed to exclude any consideration of time or dura-tion, except for the representation of ruins and decay or of the building process itself. The transformations that could take place within the frame of perspective all implied, in one way or another, a displacement that could be treated according to the same geometrical

lines on which the comparison between archi-tecture and music relied; any attempt to make room for the representation or expression of movement and its dynamics had to conform either to the rules of proportion or to the principles of harmony.

This state of affairs was radically altered by the discovery of photography and the invention of the cinematograph. According to Walter Benjamin, not only did photography change the very notion of art by replacing the question of photography as art with the notion of art as photography (that is to say, mechanically reproducible), it also called for a transformation of the whole Hegelian system of the arts. Benjamin, among others, noted that photography provided a better hold on an image, a work of art, and especially a building, than could be obtained from dealing with the object itself. But this not only derives, as he thought, from the reductive aspect of photography and its greater mastery over a three-dimensional object (especially architecture) by the elimination of one dimension. What photography and, moreover, film reveal is that architecture cannot be considered only as an art of space; room has to be made, in its practice as well as in its concepts, for time and movement.

Hegel's lessons left no room for photography and film. He was still free to consider architecture and music as the two opposite poles of art – one static, related to the laws of gravity as they operate in space, and the other dynamic, corresponding to the movement of sounds as they take place in time. Painting, as it eventually developed into a magic of color, emancipated itself from the reign of matter only to enter the field of appearances. As far as movement was concerned (and, according to Aby Warburg, it was of great concern to Renaissance art), painting succeeded in evoking, representing, or "expressing" it in a more or less illusionistic way but did not succeed in actually producing, or even "imitating," it. For movement, as Gilles Deleuze later put it, does not only take place in space, as something that occurs between objects; it expresses duration, in the Bergsonian sense, as something that, in opposition to time, cannot be divided into parts. The same applies to music, the movements of which actually take place in measurable, divisible time, in such a way that one can deal with it in terms of composition, of structure, of architecture. But the movement of sounds – their *tempo*, even their color, and, most of all, their rhythm, as they echo, according to Hegel, the rhythms of the heart and the soul – are more a *matter* of duration than of time: a matter of duration, as Henri Bergson describes in *Matter and Memory*.

The discovery of photography dramatically altered the classification system of the arts. For photography, from the very beginning, has been related to both space and time. It relates to space as the element in which the project is actually taking place and that allows for the reduction of the "view," the object, or the model to the two dimensions of the photographic image. And it is related to time as well, as the inescapable condition for imprinting the image on the sensitized plate or paper. It is related to time but not to duration, since the time of exposure implies the elimination of movement ("Stand still!" "Ne bougez plus!"). The subsequent development that led to the "snapshot," or the *instantané*, allowed photography to deal with movement, but only by fixing it, having it "frozen." For a long time, photography was thus torn between two poles of attraction: on the one hand, the analysis of movement as it could be caught and represented through a succession of snapshots, and on the other, the image of stability. Here, of course, the paragon was architecture, which resists the ravages of time and surpasses the living model or still life in its ability to stand still in front of the camera.

The arrival of film disposed of the alleged opposition between the arts of space and the arts of time on which the traditional classification of the arts had relied. A new turn was given to the notion of "projection," which, since the Renaissance, had been a component of the arts of *disegno* – architecture, sculpture, and painting. Projection was no longer considered merely a geometric process related to the two dimensions of the plane, but a dynamic one involving a third dimension, the dimension of time, inseparable from the mechanism of the camera and the running of the film. With regard to architecture, the move was of great consequence, for the cinematographic approach meant dealing with architecture in terms not only of time but also of movement and, through it, of duration.

In a 1932 lecture on the *Story of Amphion*, Valéry referred to duration as the equivalent of memory and the equivalent of form: "*duration*, that is to say memory, that is to say form." If when listening to music we supposedly have to memorize its developments in order to "understand" it, in the same way that we supposedly have to memorize the first words of a sentence in order for it to make sense in our mind when completed, it doesn't mean that musical form is to be thought of in terms of space, as something we can only access in retrospect. Projection plays its role in the process, in a dynamic and prospective way; for form is present, form is perceived, form is at work, on the move, for the listener, from the very beginning of the execution of a sonata as well as for the uttering of a sentence.

But what about architecture? What are we to learn about it from or through photography? What are we to learn about it from or through film? And, no less important, does film outdate photography, make it irrelevant, with regard to architecture? I recently raised this issue in a short book that I worked on with the French photographer Jacqueline Salmon, on Robert Mallet-Stevens's Villa Noailles in Hyères, one of the *incunabula* of modern architecture. The issue was all the more relevant in that Mallet-Stevens himself first worked as a set designer for the film industry (he designed, along with Fernand Léger, the sets for Marcel L'Herbier's *L'Inhumaine*, a film that was conceived and received as a manifesto in support of modern architecture). The tension between film and architecture was also at stake in a film on the villa that was commissioned of Man Ray by the Noailles in 1928, *Les Mystères du château du dé* (The mysteries of the castle of dice).

In looking at Salmon's photographs and at Man Ray's film, one must be attentive not only to day passing into night, as reflected in the photographs, but also to the analogies and the differences between the two approaches to the building, analogies and differences that culminate in Man Ray's rhetorical figures of movement (Man Ray being, first of all, the great photographer we all know). His film starts with a wide-angle, 360-degree pan of the terrace, with its openings on the outside, and then ignores the Mediterranean landscape (just as Salmon will, 70 years later) to shuffle into the house, through its corridors, staircases, and tunnels, and raise the eye toward the stained-glass grid that corresponds to the sky of the great salon. Here the handheld camera slowly slides over the metallic

grids on which the collection of paintings was stored and, turning upside down, finally ends up back on the terrace. It is a dramatic circular move that echoes the pan of the terrace and also turns the building upside down. I find it to be a good introduction to the notion of "defrosted architecture" inspired by Schelling, as well as to the relations between architecture and what I called the fabric of time, its texture and, by the same token, its relation to space. It is a good introduction to the way in which architecture addresses the eye and the body through the movement of the camera, just as music addresses the ear and the body through the movement of sound.

HUBERT DAMISCH IS THE DIRECTOR OF STUDIES AT L'ECOLE DES HAUTES ETUDES EN SCIENCES SOCIALES IN PARIS, AND AUTHOR OF MANY BOOKS, INCLUDING **THE ORIGIN OF PERSPECTIVE**.

The Ambition of the New
Zaha Hadid

I understand Anytime to be an investigation of the temporal logic of cultural progress and change. Primary to the notion of time is an examination of the dialectical relationship of the new and what came before it and an investigation of the process by which the new is produced and innovation is achieved. I would like to address these issues of time, of oscillation and the ambition of the new, in terms of my own trajectory and the influence of the notion of time on my own work, not only in terms of its conceptual significance but also in terms of the chronological development of my projects over the past twenty years.

Time is crucial in the sense that one has to respond to the moment. My own work actually started in the mid-1970s when the notion of history was at its highest since the modernist tabula rasa, and the idea of newness was being considered in terms of postmodernity. For me, this led to how ideas of rupture and fragmentation could liberate the plan, which led to ideas of abstraction and fluidity and a kind of oscillational process in which one could move back and forth in time. Ultimately, these ideas and methods of operating led me to new ideas about spatiality.

I will start with a very early work, Malevich's Tektonik (1976–77), my graduation project at the Architectural Association. This project explored the "mutation" factor of the programmatic requirements of a 14-level hotel on the Hungerford Bridge over the Thames. The horizontal "tektonik" conforms to and makes use of the apparently random composition of suprematist forms to meet the demands of the program and site. The 14 levels systematically adhere to the tektonik, turning all conceivable constraints into new possibilities for space.

With this joining of Malevich's tektonik and a hotel program came the idea that one could return to a previous moment in time – in this case the early part of the 20th century – to investigate the issues of that time and what they could imply in terms of change and newness. From the superimposition of this displaced condition on London came ideas of rupture and the discovery of the diagonal – a discovery that the diagonal could imply many different degrees upon many different degrees. This was, I think, very important.

We realized that dealing with the ideas of the modern no longer necessarily meant the obliteration of an existing context. The idea of juxtaposing two "times" created a superimposition and, eventually, a hybridization. Things that had occurred at different times could now happen simultaneously. We developed a kind of X-ray method of operation, a kind of archaeology that allows for many layers occurring simultaneously. The drawing not only conveys a frozen moment in time, it also shows ideas of movement, which allowed us to generate a different kind of spatiality. This idea of projection also became very critical to the work.

Two things began to occur. Within the idea of projection and the spatial organization there also existed an idea of rupture or explosion. The combination of fragmentation and explosion with the antigravitational nature of Malevich's tektoniks led to a certain liberty from the ground, or a freedom of the plan, which also led to ideas of organizational fluidity. The organization of the plan and the idea of the projection and its distortions began to be framed in one moment that became like a storyboard, in which many sequences over a period of time are compressed into one image. Fluidity and compression were possible in the same space.

These ideas of projection and spatiality were very strong in the drawings for the Hong Kong Peak project (1982–83). Projection, which was just a method for presenting work, became a way to relate the project to ideas of distortion, fluidity, and curvature, as well as a way to capture a whole day in the life of the building. The site, high on a hill above the city, demanded a certain programmatic inventiveness as well as an overwhelming significance to, and relief from, the congestion of the city itself. Looking at the topography and scale of the city led to certain ideas of spatiality, including the idea of a large room in the city. The projection became a larger story than the actual building. The boundaries of the project were the city itself, thus the projection also dealt with an urbanscape and how the idea of a compressed skyline could have an influence on the space of the city.

In the Peak project the strategy of projection was realized through a process of excavation and transplantation. To accentuate the dramatic visual conditions and natural arterial features of the site, constructive elements of various materials are thrust onto the hill, vertically and horizontally, in a kind of suprematist geology. We proposed to remove granite from the area of the site south of the Crown Land. The excavated rock is then polished and reintroduced into various parts of the site to create a polished man-made mountain. The excavated segment, extending into the hill, then becomes the locus for a series of programmatic superimpositions layered horizontally in a series of architectural beams that peer over the mountainside. These geological ideas for landscape, the difference between rock and solid, transparent and fluid, and ideas of landscaping and quarrying, began to imply a degree of transience and fluidity within the organization of the plan.

15.06.98 ANKARA: PRIME MINISTER AND MOTHERLAND PARTY CHAIRMAN MESUT YILMAZ AND REPUBLICAN PEOPLE'S PARTY CHAIRMAN DENIZ BAYKAL SIGN A PROTOCOL THAT CONFIRMS THEIR AGREEMENT ON AN EARLY ELECTION.

15.06.98 ANKARA: KAZAKY PRESIDENT NURSULTAN NAZARBAYEV ANNOUNCES THAT TRADE BETWEEN TURKEY AND KAZAKHSTAN SHOULD BE INCREASED TO $1 BILLION AS A RESULT OF A 10-YEAR PLAN TO ACHIEVE THAT GOAL.

95 HADID > THE AMBITION OF THE NEW

A severe landscape was also an issue in one of our most recent projects, the Museum of Islamic Art in Qatar (1998). The fact that there was no strong precedent for an institution of this kind, combined with the museum's rather strange collection, allowed us to develop an original typology that is rooted in the Islamic predilection for repetitive patterns with moments of difference.

As in the earlier projects, the connection between abstraction and landscape was investigated first through drawing. The site, in the city of Doha, is dry and sandy, and faces the corniche along the Doha harbor. To really get a map of the site we made the almost flat terrain into a little mountain range in order to see how different kinds of spaces could shift from being very large and high to a kind of multiple space for overlapping programs. In addition to using the strategies of superimposition and projection, rotational drawings, like in calligraphy, were made as a way to engage ideas of fluid space and movement. These ideas of calligraphy and fluidity served as a way to engage the material diversity of the museum's collection. The scheme is laid out as several fields of influence which share a common form. The whole building acts as a container for programmatic "objects" – a notion which is echoed in the gallery spaces: an extensive terracing of horizontal and sloped plates which house the spectrum of artifacts.

I should also address the dialectic relationship of the building with respect to the landscape. The notion of a natural tectonic, the layers of the ground over a period of time, all of them geologically dealing with the idea of sand, became very important. The building is not only surrounded by new landscape but also incorporates the characteristics of the landscape within its architectonic, thus fusing it with its context. Topiary, paths, and various soft ground surface treatments are proposed from the corniche boundary to the edge of the building in one continuous design. This area formally slopes into the main lobby space, creating both an inviting open entrance feature to the museum as well as transforming the main lobby into a landscape of terraced plateaus leading to the gallery spaces.

All of these ideas, from the ideas of abstraction, which led to ideas of topography and fluidity, to the ideas of rupture, of explosion and antigravitational forces that imply a degree of liberty from the ground, are obviously very important. All of the different superimposed topographies show how over time very small changes occur. How you deal with the ground, how pushing and raising it can imply different ideas of spatiality, how the diagonal, or cut, through a building implies a different organization altogether; these all liberate space and allow us to move through it differently.

ZAHA HADID IS A LONDON-BASED ARCHITECT. SHE HAS TAUGHT AT THE ARCHITECTURAL ASSOCIATION, LONDON, AND IN THE HARVARD AND COLUMBIA GRADUATE PROGRAMS. CURRENT PROJECTS INCLUDE AN INSTALLATION AT THE MILLENNIUM DOME, LONDON, AND THE CONTEMPORARY ARTS CENTER, CINCINNATI, OHIO.

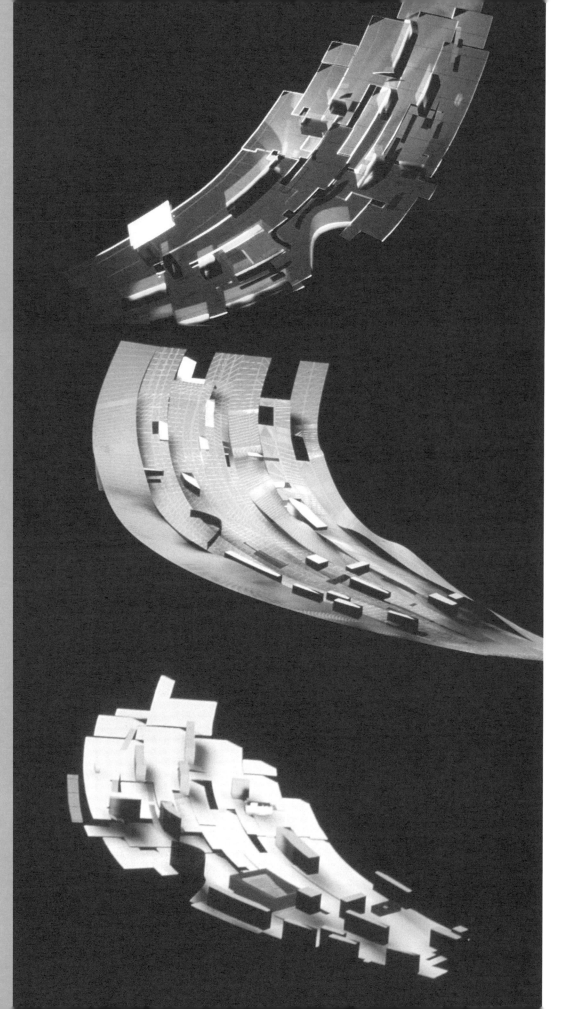

HADID > THE AMBITION OF THE NEW   15.06.98 NEW YORK CITY: THE DOW JONES INDUSTRIAL AVERAGE SUFFERS ITS 5TH LARGEST POINT LOSS IN HISTORY, OFF MORE THAN 5 PERCENT, DOWN 207.01 POINTS TO 8627.93. THE NIKKEI INDEX DRIFTS DOWNWARD IN RESPONSE. EUROPEAN MARKETS, LED BY LONDON AND FRANKFURT, HOLD FIRM.

An Ankara Chronicle: Fidelity to an Impossibility
Banu Helvacioğlu

Entrance to the new Çankaya Municipality Contemporary Arts Gallery in Ankara, June 15, 1998.

1 Walter Benjamin, "A Berlin Chronicle," in One-Way Street and Other Writings, trans. Edmund Joseph and Kingsley Shorter (London: Verso, 1985), 316.

2 Hannah Arendt, Introduction in Illuminations, by Walter Benjamin, trans. Harry Zohn (New York: Schocken Books, 1969), 13.

If there were a text to this talk, it would have been called "An Ankara Chronicle," mimicking a certain Jew in Berlin in 1932 who, aware of his own will to death but unaware of the future death toll and destruction, reminisced about his childhood and youth by walking us through the city. "Here," writes Walter Benjamin in "A Berlin Chronicle," "I am talking of a space, of moments and discontinuities."[1] The space contains transparent images, the vista of the city, and the temporality of the present filled with experiences, new articulations as well as memories.

Here in Ankara, on June 15, 1998, I am in an auditorium in an art gallery that stands on the site of a now demolished water depository. According to my father's account, the water depository was built in the 1940s. Across the street, where the American Embassy stands, there used to be a bus stop. On the way back from school my father would get off the bus at that stop and walk home through gardens and fruit trees. To get to his house he had to jump over a stream and walk uphill. I was born after the stream had dried out, but I remember this neighborhood being filled with fruit trees. My grand-mother used to live across from the American Embassy. Each time we visited her, there it was: the mysterious place called the water depository. Since it did not have windows, I was always curious as to what was inside the gray building. People lived in buildings; water was too abstract a being for me to comprehend. One day, having tried the patience of all the adults in my grandmother's house, my grandmother took me to the kitchen, turned on the tap, and said, "There, you see, this is what is inside the water depository." Water coming from the tap astonished me even more, but right then and there I learned my lesson and decided not to ask archaeological questions. What is inside anything is a flow that cannot be seized, grasped, or understood but can be glanced at, sensed, used, or wasted.

So here I am, in the water depository of my childhood turned into an art gallery. God knows what it will turn into in the future. I cannot help but be amazed by the fact that I am obliged to talk about beginnings, history, past, and future in this concrete space. If it were possible to address all the questions posed by this panel on beginnings, movements, and becoming, the response would have to be allegorical. For just as time itself is an allegory, the notions of beginning and becoming are allegorical. Reflecting on Benjamin's writing, Hanna Arendt argues that "allegory always pro-ceeds from an abstract notion and then invents something palpable to represent it almost at will."[2]

Like Benjamin, I too think of time as both a knowable entity and the space of the unknown. In exploring the site of the present as made up of moments of both continuity and discontinuity, however, I "invent" something different from Benjamin's concept of Messianic time. Call it a fidelity to an impossibility; I wish to explore the intersection of time as a knowable entity and time that contains the unknown in the miracle of the moment. Needless to say, this is not an original invention. Poets and philosophers have contemplated the miracle of the moment for centuries. My fidelity goes to Helene Cixous, who deconstructs the will to death in her "thirst for the instant."

At the outset, then, what is being called into question is the concept of the beginning, the original moment, which is always identified with the notion of return. Between the inseparable pair of beginning and return there is a vista of the unknown where the metaphysics of spirits, ghosts, medusas, Adams and Eves, messiahs, and other beings dance with abstract conceptions of time, temporality, and periodization. Personal and political memories, reminiscences, loyalties, and yearnings have no immunity from this rich metaphysical terrain. Schooled in different versions of this metaphysical thinking and disciplined in the universal tradition of phallocentric living, we always associate the notion of time with death, loss, separation, and with unceasing efforts to control, to delay, and to postpone the end. From this perspective it is not surprising that we are continuously bombarded by themes like "the rise and fall of civilizations," founded on the principles of original beginnings and ends, "the clash of civilizations," founded on the premise that each civilization returns to its origins, and other variations of fin de siècle scenarios in aesthetics, philosophy, and politics, all of which are accompanied by mood swings between progress and Armageddon.

In investigating the pervasive logic that identifies the beginning with the end, Benjamin argues that "The past carries with it a temporal index by which it is referred to redemption. . . . To be sure, only a redeemed mankind receives the fullness of its past – which is to say, only for a redeemed mankind has its past become citable in all its moments."[3] While not entirely repudiating the notion of redemption, Benjamin conceptualized history as "the subject of a structure whose site is not homogenous, empty time, but time filled by the presence of the now [Jetztzeit]."[4] His notion of now-time refers to the site of the actuality of the past, to the moment in which we experience an event of continuity and rupture and of something spiritual. In all three dimensions, now-time never aims to return to the beginning, nor does it aim at a completion (the completion invoked by Hegel's universal end).[5] Now-time, or the present, is the unfolding of a continuity and, as such, is subject to change. Within this continuous transition, the present is a site for action and transformation as much as for destruction.[6] As Benjamin puts it, the present moment can be blown apart at any moment.

In political terms, Benjamin's conception of now-time was meant to resist Hitler's fascism, German social democracy, and Zionism, all of which articulated the idea of redemption through political projects and called for specific interpolations of "return." Zionism saw the Jewish people as the redeemers of the future; of fascists, the German people, social democrats, and the working class. In this context, Benjamin argued that there could never be an original founding moment in history to which a return could be made. Yet his own notion of now-time remained politically ambivalent. This ambivalence was due to the political upheaval and the predominant melancholic intellectual setting of the inter-war years. In addition, Benjamin remained agnostic. He concluded his "Theses on the Philosophy of History" by noting how the Jews have been prohibited from investigating the future. In Benjamin's words, "This does not imply, however, that for the Jews the future turned into homogenous, empty time. For every second of time

3 Walter Benjamin, "Theses on the Philosophy of History," in Illuminations, 254.

4 Ibid., 261.   5 Andrew Benjamin, "Time and Task," in Walter Benjamin's Philosophy, ed. Andrew Benjamin and Peter Osborne (London: Routledge, 1994), 235.

6 "For Benjamin 'destruction' always meant the destruction of some false or deceptive form of experience as the productive condition of the construction of a new relation to the object." A. Benjamin and P. Osborne, "Introduction: Destruction and Experience," in Walter Benjamin's Philosophy, xi.

was the strait gate through which the Messiah might enter."[7] Elsewhere he used this notion of Messianic time in critically reflecting on the "condition of the world" in 1935:

> Naturally, one must wish for the planet that one day it will experience a civilization that has abandoned blood and horror. . . . But it is terribly doubtful whether *we* can bring such a present to its hundred or four hundred-millionth birthday party. And if we don't, the planet will finally punish us, its unthoughtful well-wishers, by presenting us with the Last Judgment.[8]

If there were a beginning, this Ankara Chronicle would have investigated time in the triad of time/space/being. Let us begin with a simple statement: Here I am, before the one-hundredth birthday party of a civilization that has abandoned blood and terror. Here also is the water depository of my childhood, where I am addressing an audience through interpreters. Regardless of my and others' national origins, I remember that we are imprisoned in language and translation, both of which are irreducible to meaning, knowing, and understanding. My own speech limits my being just as much as time limits my being. I accept the limitations imposed on me by the mortality and fallibility of time, language, and translation.[9] Under the guise of a hospitable welcome to the audience, I, in fact, welcome myself to limitations, restraints, constraints, misunderstandings, misinterpretations, and muteness.

Here I am, felicitous: everything that needs to be known about time has been written. Everything unknown about time has long been relegated to messiahs, 12th-century Imams, and Western and Eastern philosophers. I confess: I have given up my will to know, to predict, to measure, to make sense of world politics, and to live up to the requirements and expectations of our times. Hence the concept of time and all related assumptions, conceptions, perceptions of epochs, beginnings, and ends become empty constructs, which I am reluctant to reproduce in this talk. By the same token I am reluctant to float with the tide of nostalgia. In personal and political terms I find it dangerous and destructive. To be more blunt, this felicity which comes with giving up the claim to know is at the same time a submission to a list of powers that continue to shape the world we live in. By willfully giving up the claim to know, I give up the task of choosing between the devil and the deep blue sea. Whoever or whatever they may be, their voices always oblige me either to repent or to curse, to ask for redemption or to redeem someone. As Galileo once remarked, "Time. I know nothing very specific about time, but if I let a heavy enough eyelid fall back on an event, any event whatsoever. . . ."; Derrida adds, "The first Frenchmen bombarding Algiers in 1830, if you like, bombarded themselves from Algiers about 1800. . . . I haven't the time to go into the matter at greater length."[10]

The present is my focus in theory as well as in practice. In the present one continues to live in the past but one cannot bring the past to the present. In elaborating on the relationship between the past and the present, it is useful to recall that since the discovery of time, mankind has acquired a particular consciousness of his own by constricting time zones. Ptolemy, whose views on the universe were predominant in both Arab and Western thinking throughout the Middle Ages, summarized this particularly masculine conception of time: "Mortal as I am . . . I know that I am born for a day, but when I follow the

7 W. Benjamin, "Theses on the Philosophy of History," 264.

9 These limitations arise from the fact that like time, language and translation do not have an original founding kernel in the ways in which they are conceived, perceived, remembered, and experienced. For an elaboration of this statement see W. Benjamin, "The Task of the Translator," in Illuminations; On the impossibility of translating proper names, see Jacques Derrida, "From 'Des Tours de Babel,'" in A Derrida Reader: Between the Blinds, ed. Peggy Kamuf (Hertfordshire: Harvester, 1991) and Jacques Derrida, Of Grammatology, trans. Gayatri Spivak (Baltimore: Johns Hopkins University Press, 1976), Part II.

8 W. Benjamin, quoted by Hannah Arendt in Illuminations, 38.

10 Jacques Derrida, Glas, trans. John P. Leavey Jr. and Richard Rand (Lincoln: University of Nebraska Press, 1986), 106.

serried multitude of the stars in their circular course, my feet no longer touch the earth; I ascend to Zeus himself to feast me on ambrosia, the food of the gods."[11] Benjamin's generation had received its fair share of this universal historical consciousness, which was articulated in psychoanalysis, philosophy, and literature, along with its implementation in politics during the inter-war years.[12] The common element in this generation's conception of time, space, and being is a realization that Zeus does not feed his sons ambrosia, that history is in ruins, and that the future of civilization brings the wrath of gods. In this setting haunted by the prospect of an inevitable end, man's personal and historical consciousness yearns for redemption in his own death. This realization makes man nervous and anxious in his relationship with the present. If Ptolemy was the "prophet" of universal historical consciousness up until the 1930s, for future generations Marcel Proust set the pace for an uneasy relationship between the past and present, a relationship characterized by a nervous state of being in relation to time, to space, and to oneself.

According to Proust, the past deforms men as much as it is deformed by them. In this uneasy relation with the past, characters in *In Search of Lost Time* experience time as the double-headed monster of damnation and salvation. Proust's notion of redemption resembles Benjamin's: damned salvation is a condition of resurrection to the extent that it becomes an instrument of death. Man's consciousness, in this relationship with the double-headed monster, tells him that "an experienced event is finite, confined to one sphere of experience," whereas a remembered event is infinite because it entails everything that happened before and after the event. In Proust's estimation, involuntary memory is explosive and immediate. What makes this explosive, immediate remembering so delightful is an acute consciousness of being, living, and experience, which I call the will to death.

Remembering, voluntarily or otherwise, establishes man's ties with both the past and present by means of an inevitable end: death, resurrection, and/or resolution. In Proust's narrative, man's relationship with space is ruled by the same dictum. It is as if when Marcel walks through rooms and gardens, he is always accompanied by a longing for an inevitable separation. What makes separation inevitable is Marcel's own uneasy relationship with the present in and of itself. To the extent that the present is part of the past, it too is damned by both the longing for an end and by remembering the dead mother, grandmother, or lover who, in Marcel's imagination, is destined to depart for good.[13]

If actual or imagined loss, absence, or parting underlies the consciousness of historic man, Henri Bergson's conception of time, space, and being offers a different dimension of this phallocentric will to end. In a gesture that resonates with Benjamin and Proust, Bergson projects the notion of time into space. In his words, "Time, conceived under the form of an unbounded and homogenous medium, is nothing but the ghost of space haunting the reflective consciousness."[14] In Bergson's framework one experiences time as a flux, as an immediate and continuous process of becoming.

11 Quoted in Daniel J. Boorstin, *The Discoverers: A History of Man's Search to Know his World and Himself*, (New York: Random House, 1983), 21.

12 Some of the most prominent works produced in this period include Freud's *Civilization and its Discontents* (1929); Edmund Husserl's essay "Crisis of European Humanity" (1935); and José Ortega Y. Gasset's *The Revolt of the Masses*, (1930–31).

13 For an elaboration on these themes see Samuel Beckett, "Memory, Habit, Time"; Walter Benjamin, "The Image of Proust"; Richard Macksey, "The Architecture of Time: Dialectics and Structure," all in *Marcel Proust's Remembrance of Things Past*, ed. Harold Bloom (New York: Chelsea House, 1987); Julia Kristeva, *Proust and the Sense of Time*, (New York: Columbia University Press, 1993); Marcel Proust, *In Search of Lost Time*, vol. 1., trans. C.K. Scott Moncrieff and Terence Kilmartin; revised D.J. Enwright (New York: Modern Library, 1993).

14 Henri Bergson, *Time and Free Will*, trans. Frank Pogson (London: George Allen & Unwin, 1910), 99.

What is different in this conception of becoming is the construction of consciousness. In *Matter and Memory*, Bergson explains the relationship among time, space, and being according to five dimensions: the mind, body, emotions, senses, and the soul. In his formulation, human consciousness is "possessed" by spirits: "We understand then why a remembrance cannot be the result of a state of the brain. . . . Pure memory is a spiritual manifestation. With memory we are, in truth, in the domain of spirit."[15] This implies that between memory and action there are "thousands of different planes of consciousness."

According to Bergson, in order to "act freely" one has to recover possession of oneself out of this plenitude and return to "pure duration," a quality that has no magnitude. Pure duration is the realm of existence that leads men to grasp their inner state as a living thing, constantly becoming, which is not amenable to measurement.[16] If I may momentarily tickle the masculinist conception of consciousness, what Bergson's spirits offer us is a possibility to return to the realm of the living by means of remembering that "Although we are free, whenever we are willing to get back to ourselves, it seldom happens that we are willing."[17]

I hasten to add in a more somber tone that a willingness to come to one's senses, possession of oneself, the free will to act, and the will to live are all part of the same phallocentric logic of beginning. Each of these affirmations assumes an original, founding kernel to which one returns. In Bergson's conception, we return to the will to live and the will to experience time by means of intuition and sympathetic insight. It is as if the founding kernel of being is presented in reverse. Instead of postponing spirits to the end, Bergson reinstates them at the beginning: in matter, in reality, in time, and in space. Thus, in being, there is assumed the presence of spirits.

According to this phallocentric logic, when we come to the present, "to our times," we need an update on the return of spirits, ghosts, and the notion of Messianic time. In the 1980s Fredric Jameson, among others, contemplated the difficulty, if not the impossibility, of retaining the past and the conception of a unique self as trademarks of postmodern culture. From this perspective, the commodification of everyday life, the space-time compression of urbanization, coupled with the rise of information and communication technologies, paved the way for pastiche, schizophrenia, and amnesia, through which we experience time and space. While these so-called postmodern trends continue to influence our perceptions and conceptions of time, Jameson, in one of his recent works, notes the re-emergence of *hauntology* as a sign of our times being "still out of joint." He argues that in Hong Kong, the search for a building to haunt is becoming more difficult due to land speculation. At the same time, there are ghost stories about haunted multistory apartment structures.[18]

What is notable in the global circulation of finance capital is not so much the "spectres" it produces as the effect of dizziness it leaves in historic man's universal consciousness. As Jameson accurately notes, in a setting where time is out of joint, there remains a longing for the process of abstraction from the concrete object, together with a desire to "return

15 Henri Bergson, *Matter and Memory*, trans. N.M. Paul and W.S. Palmer (New York: Zone Books, 1988), 240.

16 Bergson, *Time and Free Will*, 231–32.

17 Ibid., 240.

18 Fredric Jameson, "The Brick and the Balloon: Architecture, Idealism and Land Speculation," in *Anyhow*, ed. Cynthia Davidson (Cambridge, Massachusetts: MIT Press, 1998), 106–21.

to realism [in] plots, agreeable buildings, decoration, melodies and so on." Perhaps as a side effect of having lived with ghost stories since my childhood, I hear Proust's voice in this longing for realism and abstraction: "We are imprisoned in time." Here "we" are those "unique selves" who have always had the privilege of having a historical consciousness of humanity. We who wished for Zeus to feed us. We who longed for our dead mother. We who waited for the Messiah to enter through the strait gate. We who? Who are we, who have forgotten that Zeus killed his own son? Who are we, men of letters and sounds, who killed our mother, lusted for a lover? Who are we, who have done all this with the same passion and lust for a demon? Whose involuntary amnesia is this, indeed?

Here thousands of ghosts speak to me through Proust, who admitted to being a victim of his own time. But who has control over time? What remains a part of concrete reality in these times of ours is that the compression of space-time makes us more conscious of time as a loss. In concrete terms, each of us has limited time to speak here. We have other tasks to perform, deadlines to fulfill, the dull compulsion of work, taxes to pay. Each of these tasks binds us to time as a quantity. On a more abstract level, we tend to forget that capital in the now-time is a ghost that haunts our everyday life. In spite of the different, local, and vernacular temporalities each of us lives in, there still remains a repetitive, circular motion brought about by the ghosts of capital. Everyday life gets faster beyond our individual control. Speed makes it easier to forget the ontology of the present.

As if there were a big conspiracy brought to bear by speed, the themes of efficiency, productivity, and precision are repeated within academic circles, in Hollywood movies, commercials, sports, air traffic, and high-tech military destruction. We are compelled to reduce the time spent on any given task by hours, minutes, and seconds. As Paul Virilio notes, with the question of "time saved," "we return to the origins of social 'metamorphosis'. We are here at the level of the 'revolution of three eights' so dear to the men of 1848 – eight hours of work, eight hours of sleep, eight of leisure time."[19] He notes the theme of return elsewhere: "Speed is Time saved in the most absolute sense of the word, since it becomes human Time directly torn from Death – whence those macabre emblems of decimation worn down through history by the Assault troops, in other words the *rapid troops* (black uniforms and flags, death heads, by the uhlan, the SS, etc.)."[20]

In the present moment, we are also imprisoned in time because what has come to be known as nationalism – the politics of ethnicity, race, and religion – forces us into localized interpretations of a paradisiacal site: the beginning, the birth of a nation, a prophet, or a race. Custom-made, specialized niches of memories, now politicized in ethnic, religious, and racial feuds, somehow bring to mind what Ernst Bloch wrote in the late 1920s with regard to nonsynchronous contradictions that are experienced in pent-up anger and result from an unsettled past.[21]

Enter the ontology of the present through the historical consciousness of modern man, who lives the split between reason, emotions, senses, and sympathetic insight. Can someone explain why Yugoslavia has been blown apart? Why must new nations be

19 Paul Virilio, *Speed and Politics, An Essay on Dromology*, trans. Mark Polizzotti (New York: Semiotexte, 1986), 28. 20 Ibid., 22.

21 Ernest Bloch, "Nonsynchronism and the Obligation to its Dialectics," *New German Critique*, 11 (1977).

blown apart by civil strife and civil wars and then reassembled in the name of some new nation-state with such and such ethnic origin and religion in order to become a member of the United Nations? Now is the time to remember Benjamin's longing for a messiah to enter the "strait gate" and tell us that the planet Earth is preparing for the one-hundredth birthday of a civilization that has abandoned blood and terror. Yet after a century, we, the loyal supplements of the universal consciousness of historical man, have received in return the themes of Final Judgment, liberation, and demons speaking in tongues through the dead masks of history.

Imprisonment in time is accompanied by a submission, by a will to die as quickly as possible. Together with this will to death, hauntology resurfaces in the ontology of the present in different disguises. We are now conscious of the earth; we are made to experience the spirit of nature while we have a hard time breathing in cities. Campaigns to save the planet, whales, and rain forests, New Age spirituality, and Oxfam campaigns to feed hungry children are all cries for salvation of one form or another. Back to the beginning, in 1998 there is the same messianic cry for help. "Zeus where are you? Come and uplift my feet. Come and provide for 'hungry third world children' and for those who yearn for a planet free from horror."

Enter the present of future, in the now-time. At the beginning there were the Father, the Son, and the Holy Ghost; God, Adam, and Eve; time, space, and being; past, present, and future. All beginnings are conceptualized and experienced based on the founding premises of damnation and salvation. The law of the universe has always been made to silence its own libidinal economy of lack. Scarce resources, limited time, as well as the desire for eternity all stem from an invention of finite and infinite experiences. Yet, "At the close of our century, *the time of the finite world is coming to an end*; we live in the beginnings of a paradoxical *miniaturization of action*, which others prefer to baptize *automation*."[22]

Enter the present as present moment, filled with infinite possibilities of transformation, innovation, and change. "To gain the present," writes Cixous, "one can think that we never lose anything, that we are in a continuity, in a succession of full times that add up." This thirst for the instant requires a different relationship with death. Rather than expecting one's death in the future and adding up years as negativity, aging, losing (whatever one loses in aging, whatever one compensates for death), there is the possibility of entering into *now*, the moment as big as a particle. "Admittedly, being able to live in the instant all the time is nearly impossible. But one can live very often in the instant; it is a practice, a necessity."[23] It is a necessity for all concerned, for we who are imprisoned in time, civilization after civilization, imprisoned in involuntary amnesia, burned in gas chambers, driven to commit suicide at borders, and dead from longing for our dead mothers.

Between now and eternity there is here-now, which lasts for as long as one allows. If I were wealthy enough I would commission an architect to design a building of the incredible moment, as big as a neutron, if there were an architect wealthy enough and willing to entertain the possibility of building here-now for living non-being.

22 Virilio, *Speed and Politics*, 140.

23 Hélène Cixous, *Rootprints* (London: Routledge, 1997) 96, 90, 54.

BANU HELVACIOĞLU HAS TAUGHT AT QUEEN'S AND RYERSON POLYTECHNIC UNIVERSITIES IN CANADA. SHE IS ALSO A VISITING PROFESSOR AT BILKENT UNIVERSITY IN ANKARA. HER RECENT RESEARCH HAS FOCUSED ON ETHICAL FEMINISM.

D1

JEAN-LOUIS COHEN This panel is revealing all sorts of patterns in which time and duration, that is, lived time, are involved. I like the image of the Ise Shrine being frozen in time by the repetition of rebuilding the very same building with ever-changing materials. I liked also Arata Isozaki's high-tech references to the history of a lightweight structure as it was transferred to a much heavier, more solid structure. Damisch also clearly triggered our imagination with May Ray's film that pushes architecture upside down. The challenge is not only to register movement but to do so with a continuously moving perspective. The dynamics involved in Zaha's forms are also an example of how architecture is capable of integrating the dimension of change. And finally, Banu Helvacioglu showed how the encapsulation of time, that is, of personal memories, can take place in a particular building. So if we return to the idea of architecture as frozen time or frozen duration, we clearly see that architecture is a freezer of the past, as well as a freezer of its own history. Zaha's ability to transform and absorb a Malevich or an idea of Kandinsky's is important here, for it raises architecture as a frame for change. At the same time, that frame can imprison or incorporate, sometimes even strangle, what I would call the horizon of expectation. I think that architecture finds its limits in this imprisonment of expectation and finds its major contradictions somewhere between overplanning the future, and therefore freezing it, and underplanning it, which sometimes negates its own goal.

PHYLLIS LAMBERT I'm not sure that I agree with that last part. Does somebody have a comment to make?

CENGIZ BETKAS I cannot help thinking about the differences between my "now time" and Isozaki's. Like Banu's water tank example, my "now time" includes the five thousand bombs that exploded yesterday within an hour of who knows where. This definitely does not matter to you at all. It would be a miracle if my "now" and yours would converge. This could be a great delight. However, when you push too far, what kind of insistence is this? Isozaki breaks an office building at the middle with a sundial. As far as I can see, those who can see the sundial are outside, not inside the building. Perhaps those inside can only see it when going in and out of the building. They may not even experience it when going out. What a formalistic phenomenon this is. How could I claim to be ethically right in doing something like that? Because in our culture we see time in a different way. For example, I know a Seljukid caravansary with a holy place inside where both Muslims and Christians can pray. With different roof openings, holes, and lines, it continually speaks of the flow of time to its inhabitants. I wonder whether sharing "time," sharing "now," would be more appropriate for the architect than a situation confined to self-expression and that fails to be anything more than formalistic.

ARATA ISOZAKI I'm sorry. My earphone didn't work, so I couldn't hear. Maybe Asada can reply.

AKIRA ASADA Well, Isozaki is a Japanese architect. As far as I know he misread Dogen, but his tea ceremony house seems very Japanese and, at the same time, very modern. With his commission for Disney, the ultimate American entertainment industry, he is clever enough to insert his own metaphysical thinking in the guise of this colorful structure whose entrance recalls the shape of Mickey Mouse. Actually, the whole shape somehow resembles an atomic plant and its related nuclear/ military complex, which is not so far from the structure of Disney. It is full of irony, and within this kind of deliberate simulation of American entertainment, he somehow inserted a certain segment of metaphysics. The problem is not that of sharing a common time. He was talking about certain differences. Everybody has his or her own watch, which tells the time. But the sundial shows a different time, one that is always different from the watch. Those small differences are more important to Isozaki than communal experience.

ISOZAKI Perfect.

BANU HELVACIOGLU When I talk about the "now time" in the context of the ontology of the present and the miracle of the moment in that context, I'm being very careful. I'm not talking about the relativity of time. On the contrary, in the context of the ontology of the present, I was trying to explain by giving different examples how that temporality, even though experienced in different cultural, religious, political terms, is a homogeneous time, and what gives that homogeneity is the presence of ghosts, so to speak. It can be explained and formulated and represented in different shapes, sounds, and representations. I didn't make it very clear, but I'm not talking about relativity; I'm talking about something constant, something unbound, but unchanging at the same time. Now as to how that miraculous moment can be represented in architectural form, I don't know.

HUBERT DAMISCH Isozaki's sundial may seem to be an entertainment, but in the cathedral of Bologna there is a sundial that crosses the old building. It means that the building itself is functioning in some way as a sundial. So what is the purpose of that sundial? Is it part of a code? Is it part of the time of the church or the time of the religion? What is it? I have no answer, and I don't think that you have an answer either.

BETKAS Banu, I do not think that my ideas are contradictory to yours. Time goes as fast as my speed of perception, but this is not relativity. Isozaki spoke about something totally different, therefore the convergence of those speeds is very important. In his building, someone else, say a sculptor, could have placed that sundial. For me, it is not in perfect harmony with the whole of the building.

ISOZAKI In Japan we have only one word for space and time, ma. Ma means a space between two points as well as the silence between two sounds. The silence occurs in time, and the vacuum or vacancy in the space between two objects. These are the same concept for us, there is no differentiation. Our language is always the way to understand this. As an architect, this is what I always think about. Time itself is a very important subject in designing space, but there are many definitions for understanding time. The main thing I want to point out is how we should feel in the space. When we feel or understand space, it already includes time; when we see time, space is also present.

Now, you made many comments on my Disney building. Yes, this is an entertainment building, and there is an ideology for making entertainment architecture. This company always tries to build entertainment, so this was one of the very rigid frames I had to follow at that time. But inside this difficult frame, we have to find something different, something more general, with universal meaning, so I proposed the sundial. It was a way to create a dialogue with the entertainment business people.

CHARLES JENCKS I want to talk a little about the physics of time and then introduce some ideas on physics and architecture. Einstein said, of course, that time was probably a dimension of space. We have the illusion that because we're all in the same room, we're occupying the same time. But as Einstein showed, there is no such thing as the absolute present, there is no such thing as simultaneity. In the same way that I can't occupy your body, Phyllis, I cannot be in your space-time. None of us can occupy each other's space-time. The relativity of everybody's monadic space-time structure differs, even when we are in the same room.

But from that basic insight, Einstein went on to make a great blunder when in the 1920s he wrote to a woman whose husband had died. He wrote, "Don't worry, darling. Your husband's dead; it doesn't really matter – time is really an illusion." Others have cited this letter for its appalling misconception of a dimension of time. As mortals, we are all irreversibly involved in time. Architecture, which is the most potent of the seemingly lasting elements that we build in civilization, actualizes these contradictions. Perhaps time is such an incredibly potent subject for us today because architecture really crystallizes the contradictions in all its different guises. The Romans said that you build architecture to immortalize memory, to give a physical presence to something that outlives our own pathetic transience, and yet we are terrifically aware of how architecture rusts and crumbles. So cutting across all these time spans, from the moment of today's weather and fashions to the proton, which will last 48 billion years, we can see that architecture is located somewhere between a few seconds and a few thousand years, and therefore internalizes the dilemma. Interestingly, capitalism also internalizes these and speeds up the cycles. As Banu said, we don't know where it's going, which makes us even more conscious of it. As architects, we have traditionally tried to slow time down. I am very interested in the way the Japanese apparently slow it down with tea ceremonies and by trying to make a transient moment into something eternal, or a symbol for something eternal, like rebuilding the Ise Shrine every 20 years.

GREG LYNN I have a question for Asada and Damisch. The panel suddenly seems to sound a little bit conventional in its notion of memory, and I'm wondering if it's just the preconceptions about architecture as monuments that store memory, which is later thawed through experience. There is a kind of freeze-thaw cycle which the panel seems to have fallen into, that sounds more like gestalt psychology than Bergsonian duration. Is this a privileging of experience as the model for duration, rather than, say, the construction cycle, demographics, or economics? A lot of things other than experience can come into play. I wonder whether the building, which is thought in motion but never actually seen moving after it's built, might somehow open up other pathways in architecture than the merely monumental or memorializing kind.

ASADA I would rather refer to what Banu said about now-time, or **Jetztzeit**. Now Jetztzeit is a kind of cut of the continuous flow of time. It's a critical moment that somehow reveals a multilayered structure of time. It is not necessarily a Hegelian synthesis of memory. Rather, it is a fairly violent operation that somehow makes visible this multilayered time structure with its gaps and contradictions. I talked about the cut or the severance of the continuous time in the sense of eons, Deleuzian eons, and Banu, as far as I could understand her, talked about the Jetztzeit, the now-time of Walter Benjamin. So it's rather the opposite of the Hegelian synthesis of flows in music, which somehow synthesizes within itself all the layers of memory of mankind.

DAMISCH It's true that I referred to time coming to architecture in terms of experience itself, expressed most of all in terms of the experience of movement, but I also emphasized that I was dealing with only one way of time coming to architecture. I didn't use the word "memory," for instance, because I think that we are aware of how time becomes part of the experience of architecture. But there is another, more important side of the issue, which is how architecture comes to time, how architecture becomes part of the fabric of time or the fabric of history. Partly it has to do with memory, of course. Architecture has to do with the past, but it has to do with the future as well. At the Anyhow conference last year, I asked, how are we to deal with history in terms of architecture? We cannot deal only with history in the past tense, for architecture also has to do with the future. You do not build for the past.

LAMBERT There is also the issue of paintings, music, and literature. Each generation looks at these things differently, but this hasn't come into the discussion at all.

LYNN In **Matter and Memory**, Bergson doesn't really talk about time being something you can experience. He says it may be open to what he calls a sensible intuition, but I think the move from sensible intuition to the experience of time through motion, again, sounds more like gestalt psychology than Bergsonian philosophy. Is there a critical difference between those two modes of thought or are they compatible?

ISOZAKI At the very beginning of our work in the 1960s we raised the problem of severance in the design process in architecture and in city planning. The image of severance came to me because when we design a building, it is not a fixed image. It's moving, like a computer graphic or like organic bodies. To transform this moving image into a real building, at some point you have to find the moment to cut the movement and to freeze the whole. When we freeze the image, we can transform it into real production, with drawings and so forth, on the construction site. But there is always a moment in this process when we must intervene in this movement, to make a cut. When and how do we decide to do that? Which moment do you choose? We struggle with this. From the beginning, we used any; any is exactly the undecidability it refers to. If we accept any situation, we cannot find the exact point; the exact finds a moment within many possibilities. Probably after we are very tired, after lots of work, almost unconscious, maybe even drunk, we decide it's time — let's do it. I don't know how we can legitimate a kind of action that finds the exact moment.

DAMISCH Greg raised the issue of psychological experience. Man Ray is by no means a psychological experience. The meeting of two systems, film and architecture, is nothing psychological. I only showed one part of the film — the whole thing runs 35 or 40 minutes. The film shows the old program of the villa, which was, for modernistic life, sports, the swimming pool, dancing, and so forth. It was by no means restricted to a psychological experience. It's a discovery; it asks, where are we? And when Man Ray gets outside, he turns the building upside down. The only way to deal with such a building is to turn it upside down. It's not an experience; I would say it's an experiment.

ZAHA HADID There is another thing. Man Ray's camera was often moving backward. The film was not shot moving forward. It deliberately moved away from light, and in one instance I think it moves clockwise.

HELVACIOGLU I'm glad Greg brought up Bergson's **Matter and Memory.** I was going to bring it up in relation to Jencks's comments about the physics of time. One thing that needs to be clarified in Bergson is that unlike other philosophers, like Hegel, who wrote about the metaphysics of time, Bergson has a different metaphysical understanding: the whole concept of matter is explained in four different dimensions. Each has subsets, so to speak: mind, emotions, soul and senses, and body. He talks about the experience of matter, which is both spiritual and real, in these four dimensions, and there is nothing psychological about it. When he talks about the experience of mind and memory, he makes a distinction between the mental state and cerebral state, and so in terms of the experience of time, space, and being, it's important to keep in mind that he proposes a different sort of metaphysics.

SASKIA SASSEN In the economy we speak of a collapse of time. It's really a bad description. What we are talking about is a change in duration, really a change in customary or established duration. My question is, how does this work out in architecture? Does the change in duration that we experience in so many realms of life today get inscribed in architecture? Do architects deal with this question of the change of duration?

DAMISCH In the Villa Noailles there were something like 30 clocks, one in each room, because so many things were taking place during the day that everyone had to conform to a strict schedule. This was a very strange scene in terms of the collapse of time; all of these clocks functioned according to a central system, but they stopped at different times. How could they stop at different times if they worked according to a central system? One says twenty-past-four, the next one ten-to-six, and so forth. There is absolutely no reason for the time of the day.

SASSEN When I see the slides that Zaha showed, I see a multiplication of fragments that signals something about duration, perhaps an acceleration of the length of duration, or a shortening of duration. Perhaps the language I'm using isn't quite clear, but as I said, when we deal with economic activities, we really are experiencing, because of telecommunications, the dematerialization of products, etc. — this change in duration. The question is, do you experience this in architecture and do you feel the need to incorporate this fact in the design of spatial structures?

HADID I think the effect of time has made us much more critical. Technology, or a translation of it, and materiality have led to processes that have shrunken so much that eventually the process is collapsed. I'm not sure that this leads to something more fluid or more simple. I do think that it eliminates all smaller particles, because when time shrinks, you have to make very strategic decisions. It could illuminate the presence of error, which is sometimes interesting. I'm not saying that it's more accurate; it just eliminates many emotional aspects that are sometimes interesting. But something I've noticed recently is that in the corporate ranks, buildings are beginning increasingly to look like models. In real life a model looks very strange. It could lead to many diagrammatic buildings, which I think would affect process a great deal.

MARK GOULTHORPE It's very difficult for us to represent **process** in architecture; we generally represent **things**. In Zaha's work, there is an extraordinary sort of cyclical creative process going on that overlaps itself, and it seems very different from the kind of linear modeling of much architecture. Greg seemed to suggest that we can think of buildings in processural terms much broader than simply experiential. I think Zaha's process is largely experiential – how can one experience this space, how do the spaces come into being, how is material squeezed or stretched or morphed, etc. Could we actually incorporate all of the economic and political aspects into our models in a way similar to what Zaha does to get an extremely rich processural model that is constantly subject to change and not subject to this sort of moment of cut that a physical model seems to suggest? The engineer Peter Rice used to suspend the final moment of an engineering project to the absolute last possible minute – he kept it floating. In a lot of the industrial processes used today, a computer model can feed in all sorts of different criteria, which develop in ways that represent process but at any moment can adapt to changing circumstances. You end up with nonfixed images and a more processural representation. But perhaps this doesn't enter into Zaha's work.

HADID There is a kind of emerging interest in terms of management and in terms of politics that coincides with an interest in architecture. That kind of project is only possible when the state empowers you to do a work for public use. If you are only dealing with rather small commercial work, it's very difficult to integrate that kind of civic aspect. All these ideas have to do with degrees of flexibility, transience, and accessibility. Civic spaces rely on these flexes. I hope this will eventually happen, but in my 20 years of professional experience I haven't seen it.

PETER EISENMAN We have seen three radically different views of space-time presented by three different architects today, Winy Maas, Zaha Hadid, and Arata Isozaki, yet this multicultural audience seems only to be able to digest these three things as if they went together like pickles and ice cream. Last year after the first day of Anyhow, the different "hows" brought about an incredible anxiety among generations and different architectural philosophies. I find it curious that no anxiety has been provoked by these three radically different space-time conceptions. I hope that the lethargy that seems to surround this issue will soon be disturbed.

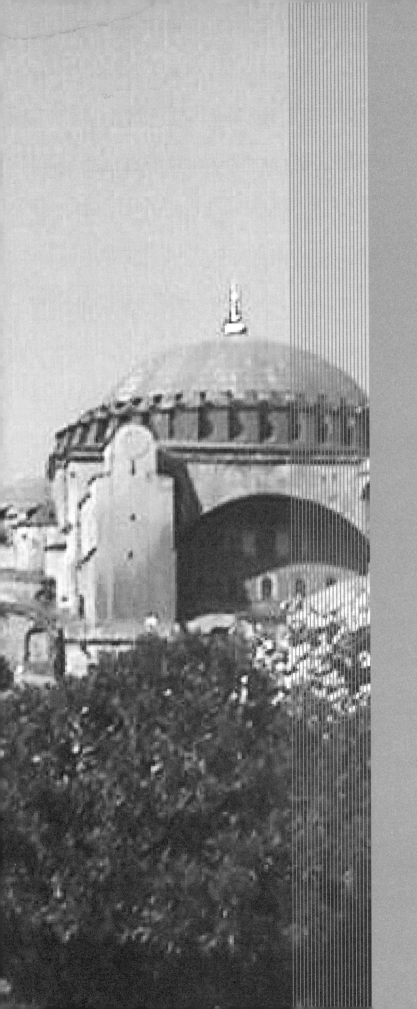

The Collapse of Time In systems which refuse transgression and defy the intervention of an outside, systems which seek thermodynamic, political, or social equilibrium, there is the inevitability of collapse, of "heat death." Does the intervention of an outside, whether the outside posed by cultural, social, sexual, or political otherness, or the otherness posed by the latencies of the system itself, hasten or delay collapse? Does the collapse of a singular time — the time of the system — produce or hinder the advent of multiple times? Is time implosive or explosive? Are cultural otherness, migration, nomadism ways in which one time collapses into many?

Juxtaposed Temporalities: Producing a New Zone

Saskia Sassen

1 Of course if we are simply deploying the word time rather than the category and its long lineage, then we can use it any way we want. Using the category allows me to juxtapose time and temporality. Similarly, we can use various words to represent instances of nontime, and deploy nontime as we like. But in my analysis nontime has a temporality; indeed, different nontimes have distinct temporalities. Nontime can be represented as escaping the strictures of time but not of temporality.

I would like to address two questions whose connection is not necessarily self-evident, but my past experience at Any conferences suggests that rather than being a problem, this may well be a source of exciting debate. The first question is whether matters of duration and temporality in today's economy, a period of enormous transition, do or do not engage the practice of architecture. The second question concerns a dynamic I have named "de-nationalization" in an attempt to capture two distinct temporalities. One of these is the collapsing temporality of the national state as a historic institution, a master temporality often thought of as historic time. The other is the new temporality of economic globalization. In the intersection of these two coexisting temporalities we see the formation of new economic dynamics and opportunities. New strategic economic projects have emerged in the play between these two master/monster temporalities within which we exist and transact (and enact all kinds of *microtemporalities*). These new economic projects materialize partly in new types of built environments (that is, in physical structures) and partly in digital space. (The hyperspace of international business is emblematic – a cross-border grid of brand-name airports, state-of-the-art office buildings, and luxury hotels whose construction is a response to new business practices.) What kinds of questions are raised for architecture by the formation of these new economic projects?

First, then, the question of duration and temporality in the economy, and its possible resonance for architecture. I find the concept of time – time as category – problematic. Akira Asada's presentation in Ankara is excellent in this regard; it touches on some of the same aspects I find problematic. I do not speak of time; I don't know what "collapsed time" means.[1] I do know what collapsed temporality and duration might mean. As a category, time functions as a sort of benchmark against which we measure and situate – a condition with an objectivity all its own. This is perhaps similar to the representation of space as container, as given, rather than space as produced spatiality of various dynamics. I find categorical representations of time and space problematic. Temporality and spatiality suit me better.

When it comes to the economy, we are all familiar with how technology has altered the duration of a whole variety of economic practices. This of course has a very long history. It has been an accelerating history over the last few decades because of the features of these technologies. Telecommunications is the typical referent here. But it is not only the capacity to neutralize distance that matters in telecommunications.

It is, I would argue, also an organizational capacity. Today's globally integrated markets are not a necessary outcome of these technologies. The latter are necessary, but the fact of market integration in commodities, and especially in finance and specialized services, required a separate and distinct effort, dynamic, and will – in short, agency. The agency that leads to the integration of markets is to be distinguished from whatever agency is de facto incorporated in the technology. Technology by itself would not have created these integrated markets. This is very important for understanding economic globalization today because it introduces questions of power – the will to new forms of power.

The dematerializing of a growing number of economic activities is one concrete outcome of the interaction of new technological capacities and the will to new forms of power. The project is to dematerialize entities, goods, and processes we have hitherto thought of as being material, for example, real estate. The strive to dematerialize cannot simply be attributed to the technology; there is plenty of agency in all of the economic processes involved.

Of course, these transformations have taken place with every new technology. Again, it is the acceleration of the impact that marks our contemporary experience, partly because of globalization and partly because of some of the features of the new technologies (e.g., connectivity and simultaneity), which makes this perhaps a particularly dramatic instance of how technology affects the economy.

It is not acceleration per se that is crucial. It is the sharply different rates of acceleration in different economic activities that is decisive. This is not a homogenizing process. The differences engender the possibility of differing temporalities. This is what matters. The changes in duration for certain economic transactions have today reached a scale that allows one, or at least allows me, to think of the production of new temporalities. The whole notion of a temporality or temporalities is transformed. This is one window through which one can look at the economy. It is not the theorists of the economy who would look at it in terms of the juxtaposition of different temporalities embedded in different sectors of capital. It is, rather, the practitioners, who, unwittingly or not, engage in practices and develop business opportunities that negotiate the different temporalities and extract new types of profits from their coexistence and their sharpened difference. This, however, is not the language they would use to describe what they do.

The ascendance of finance and the dematerialization of many economic activities assume their full meaning in this juxtaposition of different temporalities. They are an enactment in the economy of this sharpened differentiation – between their temporality as dematerialized/digitalized activities and the slower sectors of the economy, which still deal with the material.

Let me illustrate this with a particular case. A few years ago I had a chance to speak at length with the head of engineering at Volkswagen. One particular item in our conversation is of interest here: "Yes, we produce cars, but 45 percent of our profits come from auto-parts manufacturing, half come from our financial services operations, and only about 4 percent come from making cars." One might well ask, "Why, then, bother to manufacture cars?" I don't know how many readers can guess the answer. In my terms it revolves around the different temporalities of each of these three types of investment. The strategic difference is between the temporalities of manufacturing a car and providing financial services: the first takes about nine months, while the second, could take a day or less.[2] In the exchange, in the trade-off between these two, lies a world of business opportunities. The sharper the differentiation between these two temporalities grows (with dematerialization/digitalization), the more intense this world of new business opportunities will be. Wall Street is emblematic.

2 The other element in the explanation is the fact that through the manufacturing of products such as cars or airplanes, an enormous amount of capital is concentrated under one management, so to speak. Market economies always face the challenge of securing a concentration of sufficiently large piles of money that can function as investment capital. For the financial services division of Volkswagen, the manufacturing of cars secured vast amounts of capital that were not continuously used at a similar level of intensity over a cycle of nine months, and hence allowed financial uses at various points for shorter term operations.

3 By the notion of "analytic borderlands." I seek to open up a line that is represented or experienced as dividing two mutually exclusive zones into a border zone that demands its own theorization and empirical specification, and that can accommodate its own distinct practices. My notion of the global city is one instance, clearly at the macro level. My current work on the state is another such borderland, particularly the notion of incipiently denationalized (highly specialized) institutional orders that negotiate between a) the world of the exclusive sovereign authority of national states over their national territories and b) the implantation of global operations in those same territories. Both this work on global cities and on the state resists the duality global/national.

Does the emergence of this whole new world of business activities at the interface of the distinct temporalities of different sectors in advanced economies bring with it questions and agendas for architecture? It does for urban economies, particularly insofar as many of these new activities tend to locate in cities and create new sources of growth *and* new hierarchies of profitability. It also does for theory, in my view; analytically these new business activities constitute a sort of border zone that belongs to neither of the two or more sectors among which it negotiates its own existence and sources for profit.[3]

A specific kind of materiality underlies this world of new business activities, even if they take place partly in electronic space. Even the most digitalized, globalized, and dematerialized sector, notably global finance, hits the ground at some point in its operations. And when it does, it does so in vast concentrations of very material structures. (I have written about this in my work on global cities and will not dwell on it here.) These activities inhabit physical spaces, and they inhabit digital spaces. There are material and digital structures to be built, with very specific requirements: the need to incorporate the facts that a firm's activities are simultaneously partly deterritorialized and partly deeply territorialized, that they both span the globe and are highly concentrated in very specific places. This produces a strategic geography that cuts across borders and across spaces yet also installs itself in specific cities. It is a geography that explodes the boundaries of contextuality.

One question I would ask is whether the specific kind of materiality underlying this interface economy carries implications for architecture, as distinct from simply "building." There are three issues here. The first is the particular type of sub-economy this is: internally networked, partly digital, mostly oriented to global markets, and, to a large extent, operating out of multiple sites around the world. The second is a more elusive, and perhaps purely theoretical, issue – though I do not think so; it involves the point of intersection between the physical and the digital spaces within which a firm or, more generally, this sub-economy, operates. The third is the matter of contextuality in architectural practice. The particular characteristics of this networked sub-economy would seem to unbundle established concepts of context, the local setting for building, and so forth.

A NETWORKED SUB-ECONOMY.

To a large extent, this sector is constituted through a large number of relatively small, highly specialized firms. Even if some of the financial services firms, especially given recent mergers, can mobilize enormous amounts of capital and control enormous assets, they are small firms in terms of employment and the actual physical space they occupy when compared, for example, with the large manufacturing firms. The latter are far more labor intensive, no matter how automated their production process might be, and require vastly larger amounts of physical space. In addition, specialized service firms need and benefit from proximity to kindred firms – financial services, legal services, accounting, economic forecasting, credit rating and other advisory services, computer specialists, public relations, and several other types of expertise in a broad range of fields all use each other. The production of a financial instrument requires a multiplicity of highly specialized inputs from this broad range of firms.

Physical proximity is clearly an advantage insofar as time is of the essence and direct transactions are often more efficient and cheaper than through telecommunications (it would take enormous bandwidth to do some of this digitally and there would still not be the full array of acts of communications). Face to face is the shorthand way in which enormous amounts of information can be exchanged. At the same time, however, this networked sector has global span and definitely operates partly in digital space, so it is also networked in a deterritorialized way that does not pivot on physical proximity.[4]

THE INTERSECTION BETWEEN ACTUAL AND DIGITAL SPACE.

A new topography of economic activity is sharply evident in this sub-economy, a topography that weaves in and out of actual and digital space. Today there is no fully virtualized firm or economic sector. Even finance, the most digitalized, dematerialized, and globalized of all activities, has a topography that weaves between actual and digital space.[5] To different extents in different types of sectors and different types of firms, a firm's tasks now are distributed across these two kinds of spaces; further, the actual configurations are subject to considerable transformation as tasks are computerized or standardized, markets are further globalized, etc. More generally, telematics and globalization have emerged as fundamental forces reshaping the organization of economic space. This reshaping ranges from the spatial virtualization of a growing number of economic activities to the reconfiguration of the geography of the built environment for economic activity. In both electronic space and the geography of the built environment, this reshaping involves organizational and structural changes.

My question for architects is whether the point of intersection between these two kinds of spaces in a firm's or a dynamic's topography of activity is one worth thinking about, theorizing, and exploring. This intersection is, unwittingly perhaps, thought of as a line dividing two mutually exclusive zones. I would propose, again, to open up this line as an "analytic borderland" that demands its own empirical specification and theorization and contains its own possibilities for architecture. The space of the computer screen, which one might posit is one version of the intersection, will not do; at most it is a partial enactment of this intersection.[6]

Admittedly, I have been somewhat obsessed with the question of this intersection and have not gotten very far with it. It is for me part of a broader condition pervasive in the social sciences, namely, the use of the dividing line as an unproblematized way of relating and separating two different zones (whether those zones are conceptual, theoretical, analytic, empirical, or related to meaning or practice). What operations are brought in and what operations are evicted by putting a line there?[7] Quite possibly these are analytic operations linked to the type of work I do and have little meaning in architecture. They are certainly not an issue in conventional social science.

4 I examine some of these issues, particularly the future of financial centers given electronic trading and the new strategic alliances between the major financial centers, in a nonspecialist version in "Global Financial Centers," *Foreign Affairs* (January/February 1999).

5 Another angle into these issues came out of the Aspen Roundtable on Electronic Commerce (Aspen, Colorado, August 21–23, 1997). The annual event brings together the CEOs of the main software and hardware firms as well as the key venture capitalists in the sector. The overall sense of these insiders was one of considerable limits to the medium. In their opinion it will not replace other types of markets. See *The Global Advance of Electronic Commerce. Reinventing Markets, Management and National Sovereignty* (Washington, D.C.: The Aspen Institute, Communications and Society Program, 1998)

6 The work by John Seely Brown (Xerox Parc) on the space of the screen is among the most sophisticated and promising

7 Here I find Gayatri Spivak's thinking on the hyphen compelling.

8 I also see this in the political realm, particularly the kind of "global" politics attributed to the Internet. I think of it rather as a multiplicity of localized operations, but with a difference; they are part of the global network that is the Internet. This produces a "knowing" that re-marks the local. See "Electronic Space and Power," in my *Globalization and its Discontents* (New York: New Press, 1998).

WHAT DOES CONTEXTUALITY MEAN IN THIS SETTING?

A networked sub-economy that operates partly in actual space and partly in global digital space cannot easily be contextualized in terms of its surroundings. Nor can the individual firms. Its orientation is simultaneously toward itself and toward the global. The intensity of its internal transactions is such that it overrides all considerations of the broader locality or region within which it exists. On another, larger scale, in my research on global cities I made clear that these cities develop a stronger orientation toward the global markets than toward their hinterlands. They thereby override a key proposition in the urban systems literature, to wit, that cities integrate and articulate regional/metropolitan territory and urban systems do this at the national level. Such may have been the case during the period when mass manufacturing and mass consumption were the dominant growth machines in developed economies and thrived on the possibility of vast metropolitan and national scales, but it is not the case today.

In digitalized, globalized, dematerialized sectors such as finance the connections with other zones and sectors in its "context" are of a special sort – one that connects worlds that we think of as radically distinct. For instance, the informal economy in several immigrant communities in New York City provides some of the low-wage workers for the "other" jobs on Wall Street, the capital of global finance. The same is true of Paris, London, Frankfurt, and Zurich. Yet these other zones and other workers are not typically considered part of the context, the locality, of the networked sub-economy I have been speaking of – even if, in my reading, they are.

What then is the "context," the local, here? The new networked sub-economy occupies a strategic geography, partly deterritorialized, that cuts across borders and connects a variety of points on the globe. It occupies only a fraction of its "local" setting; its boundaries are not those of the city in which it is partly located or those of the "neighborhood." The sub-economy interfaces the intensity of the vast concentration of very material resources it needs when it hits the ground and the fact of its global span or cross-border geography. Its interlocutor is not the surrounding, the context, but the fact of the global.

I am not sure what this tearing away of the context and its replacement by the global could mean for architecture. The strategic operation is not the search for a connection with the "surroundings," the context. It is, rather, installation in a strategic cross-border geography constituted through multiple "locals." The local becomes one mode in a complex global interaction. I see a re-scaling: the old spatial hierarchy local-regional-national-international no longer holds. Integration is no longer achieved by going to the next scale in terms of *size*. The local now transacts directly with the global – the global installs itself in locals, and the global is itself constituted through a multiplicity of locals.[8]

This last point brings me to the second subject I want to discuss here:

DE-NATIONALIZATION.

Embedding the global in the local happens under specific conditions. Implementing today's global economic system in the context of national territorial sovereignty requires multiple policy, analytic, and narrative negotiations. These negotiations have typically been summarized or coded as "deregulation."

There is much more going on in these negotiations than the concept "deregulation" captures. The encounter of a global actor – a firm or a market – with one or another national state can be thought of as a new frontier. It is not merely a dividing line between the national economy and the global economy. It is a zone of politico-economic interactions that produces new institutional forms and alters some of the old ones.

Nor is it just a matter of reducing regulations. For instance, in many countries, the necessity for autonomous central banks in the current global economic system has required a thickening of regulations in order to disengage central banks from the influence of the executive branch of government. The case of the central banks also illustrates another key aspect in the process whereby national economies accommodate a global economic system; "national" institutions become home to some of the operational rules of the global economic system.

New legalities had to be produced in order to encase the new global operations that cut across borders. I use the term "legalities" to distinguish them from higher orders of the legal (jurisprudence, law), to bring them down, so to speak. These new legalities encase the cross-border topography of economic activities I mentioned earlier. Along with the operations of the new global actors, such new legalities constitute this topography as a strategic geography for globalization.

The strategic spaces in which many global processes are embedded are often national. The mechanisms through which new legal forms, necessary for globalization, are implemented are often part of state institutions. The infrastructure that makes possible the hypermobility of financial capital at the global scale is embedded in various national territories. Each country, or more precisely, each particular institutional order within a country, has had or is having its own specific trajectory of implementation of the new global rules of the game.

It is this specific set of processes that entails de-nationalization – of a highly specialized, partial, and incipient kind.[9] The process of de-nationalization of national territories cannot be reduced to a geographic conception; this was the perception of the generals who fought wars to nationalize territories in earlier centuries. Further, trajectories of de-nationalization will vary from country to country, they will vary for different institutional orders, and they will have different temporalities.[10] To emphasize these trajectories toward globalization is, heuristically and methodologically, rather different from emphasizing globalization, in that the latter signals the condition to be attained.[11] There are conditions and new institutional orders that

9 I examine these issues in *Losing Control? Sovereignty in an Age of Globalization* (New York: Columbia University Press, 1996). An extraordinary account of some of these issues in historical perspective is Peter Taylor, "World cities and territorial states: the rise and fall of their mutuality," in *World Cities in a World-System* ed. Paul L. Knox and Peter J. Taylor (Cambridge: Cambridge University Press, 1995), 48–62.

10 A key issue in this regard, which I cannot touch on here, is the relation between digital space and national jurisdiction. See, for example, *The Internet and National Sovereignty*. Special issue of *Indiana Journal of Global Legal Studies*, vol. 5 (1998).

11 To study, name, and conceptualize these conditions is not easy, whether I am dealing with globalization or de-nationalization. The categories for analysis, data sets, and methods all presuppose the nation-state as container, as unitary condition, as providing meaning. This embedded statism is a significant obstacle insofar as the new developments we are confronting signal a transformation in the particular form of the articulation of nation-state sovereignty and territory that has marked the history of the modern state and inter-state system until quite recently.

12 See the chapter "Whose City is It?" in *Globalization and its Discontents*.

are best described in terms of globalization. I am using "de-national-ization" to see, detect, and represent processes and temporalities that are lost when I use "globalization."

Does all of this carry any implications for architecture today? I am not sure. The issues are partly related to the ones I raised earlier. So the question would be whether focusing on the specific trajectories and temporalities of different institutional orders as they accommodate the global, rather than simply the fact of the global, make a difference to a discussion about architecture. Given a de-nationalized strategic geography, the meanings of representation and articulation with the surroundings need to be reinvented. This is true especially when the local is seen as situated in a hierarchical scaling that is subsumed under some larger entity, whether a region or a country. Further, what is the edge, the border, the surrounding, in this configuration?

A second issue concerns vocabulary. There is doubtless a new set of international standards in some of the most globalized economic sectors, notably in financial, legal, accounting, and telecommunications services. These standards operate across borders and are part of the new legalities I have mentioned. This has in turn meant certain "stan-dardized" built environments for those circulating professional and executive elites who reconstitute themselves as transnational – even if architectural "authorship" is a key input. Is there more to it than the hyperspace of international business? Is this becoming a conditioning fact in architectural – as distinct from simply building – practice (and theorization)? In the case of the economic sectors I research, there is much more than the general description in terms of "deregulation" would suggest. Is there more to it in architecture?

Possibly another issue connects to the question I ask regarding cities: "Whose city is it?" This question arises in certain settings – global cities, key nodes in the new cross-border geography of the global economy.[12] This geography, after all, emerges from the juxta-position of two different trajectories and temporalities – those of the national state and those of globalization. When it comes to architecture in this new topography, does it make sense to ask, "Whose architecture is it?" I am not sure such a question ever made sense on some general level, but it certainly did in the case of very specific architectures: for instance, in various periods what I think of as the architecture of power. That architecture belonged to power. A "contextual" building "belongs" to its context in some sense. But what is the context in this new cross-border strategic geography for global capital?

SASKIA SASSEN TEACHES AT THE UNIVERSITY OF CHICAGO AND THE LONDON SCHOOL OF ECONOMICS. HER MOST RECENT BOOKS ARE GLOBALIZATION AND ITS DISCONTENTS AND LOSING CONTROL? SOVEREIGNTY IN AN AGE OF GLOBALIZATION. HER BOOKS HAVE BEEN TRANSLATED INTO NINE LANGUAGES.

The Temple of the Vedic Planetarium in Mayapur, India. Completion anticipated 2015.

Abstract and Ancient Futures Romi Khosla

Following the triple collapse of empire, socialism, and time, a view of the world today shows that modernism, now "too late," is being isolated as the "ancients," or traditional societies, inherit the right to predict a future. This is a wide-angle, almost fish-eye view of contemporary activities in modern and ancient worlds. It is necessarily historical and has to do with periods. No matter what Bernard Tschumi says, history is just not going to go away simply because late capitalism filled the void left by the collapse of the socialist project with globalization and simultaneity. Modernism does have a narrative and its development and movement through time continue. The central character of the story simply cannot step outside of the story without losing his identity. Because of globalization, in fact, polarities are increasing. For example, the bipolarity of the Cold War has been transformed into the bipolarity of futures. It is possible to discern patterns in this new polarity that react against plurality and view the relationship between contemporary time and future times as part of a bipolar view.

Futures are being projected, on the one hand, in the debates of the transatlantic nations, and, on the other, in debates in much of the rest of the world.

The transatlantic debate explores issues concerning the dynamism of the present, the potential for invention in an uncertain future, and the accumulation of wealth. Meanwhile, large parts of Asia, Africa, and the entire Islamic world have begun to reinvent ancient times, hoping for stability and constantly fighting the contemporary period's arbitrary notion of time. While advanced capitalist cultures explore the joys of choice and simultaneity in a new global environment, the less developed world embraces its cherished spiritual assets and resurrects them for revelations of the future. As the Anglo-Saxon capitalist engine extracts the surpluses from the lands and people of ancient civilizations, these countries defend themselves with cultural and religious assets contained in sacred books and practices. For these degraded civilizations, modernism is the claw of blasphemy and exploitation.

We have lived through the most violent and destructive century in human history. In it some 187 million deaths have been brought about through human decisions and actions. There is still one more year to complete the 20th century and the toll shows no signs of letting up. Of course, it has also been arguably the most exciting century. Entirely new systems

of production and capitalism arose, were destroyed, and rose again. A new socialist project, a pure philosophical invention, was conceived, born, and died. It was a century of enormous innovation, a period in which man's perception of time was reformulated. World War I and the end of feudalism and ecclesiastical power helped to ground the modernist belief that mankind's future lay beyond the world of driving stability and uninterrupted time, and that the passage of time and the natural environment were both within human control. Wars and revolutions proved that divine stability and celestial time were unreliable guides for human destiny. It was in this century that the enormous destruction of life, property, and human ideas enabled a new agenda to be adopted for the future. Since much of the destruction took place in Europe, it was natural that the new agenda – the modern agenda – should rise from its ashes.

Even before the Great War, the theoretical, philosophical, and empirical bases for defining the terms of the modern agenda had been laid. The ideas for this foundation were contained in the disciplines of biology (Darwin), sociology (Marx and Engels), clinical anatomy, astronomy (Einstein), economics (Adam Smith, Malthus), and the arts. The boundaries of the natural phenomena that could be used to advance scientific knowledge expanded enormously. The clinical dissection of the human body and the mapping of human organs opened up enormous potential for intervening in the human body and its "natural" life span. In 1922, the first 100-inch telescope put an end to the idea that there were no distant galaxies. Not only were there distant galaxies, there was also a large universe that, as Einstein argued in 1917, was expanding and in constant motion, a theory confirmed by Hubble in 1929. In all these ideas, the central issue was one of dynamism and movement versus classical stability. Modernism proposed that the universe, the world, and all human affairs were dynamic and hence capable of being influenced by human intervention.

In the non-Judeo-Christian world, exactly the opposite notions began to take root. As colonial rule was withdrawn and as the lands that had once been the territories of ancient civilizations (Arabic, Persian, and Indian) regained independence, whole societies searched for their identities in ancient texts. (China, an exception, will not be discussed here.) As Judeo-Christian societies began

to redefine time as a brittle unit of measure, the rest of the world began redefining perpetual, cosmic time.

As the European modern agenda developed it split into two currents. One was taken up by the capitalists and the imperialists and, through trading offices, it spread the new concept of clock time throughout the Near, Middle, and Far East. This is the current that is taking us into the next century. Modernism's other current was the socialist project, which was intent on recasting society and creating a man-made future paradise. In order to realize that utopia, the present had to be destroyed.

In fact, the destruction of the present for the sake of the modernist future was inherent in both schools of thought. The socialist project, of course, ended up in a dead end. The capitalist empire powered by the entrepreneurs of Western Europe and the United States laid a crust of modernity over the ruled territories, a superficial layer that began to peel off after the 1950s. Europe had paid a great price to modernize itself. The collective memories of at least two generations were gutted in the trenches, prisons, and urban rubble of two world wars, one civil war, and one revolution. Within three decades, two generations of the best educated

and skilled minds were wiped out. The surviving generations turned to the modern agenda to redefine their futures.

The postwar period created new systems of education and new institutions that introduced a hitherto isolated America into the affairs of the world. The most powerful modernizing influence, coupled with advanced capitalism, began to transform the globe. These changes had profound effects on the lands and people who had just been liberated from colonial rule. Imperialism's demise also ended the colonialists' sustained efforts to "modernize" the colonies through the prosperity of private enterprise. The independent, national leaders who emerged – Kwame Nkrumah of Ghana, Gamal Abdel Nasser of Egypt, and Jawaharlal Nehru of India – faced a choice between two modernizing systems: the postwar American one or the Soviet one. Their choice was between the two currents into which modernism had originally divided itself. The original split in the modern movement had defined one current with an ideological content that strove to redefine man, to create a new paradise and harmonious equality, while the other current simply improved technology to increase the accumulation of wealth, letting the market

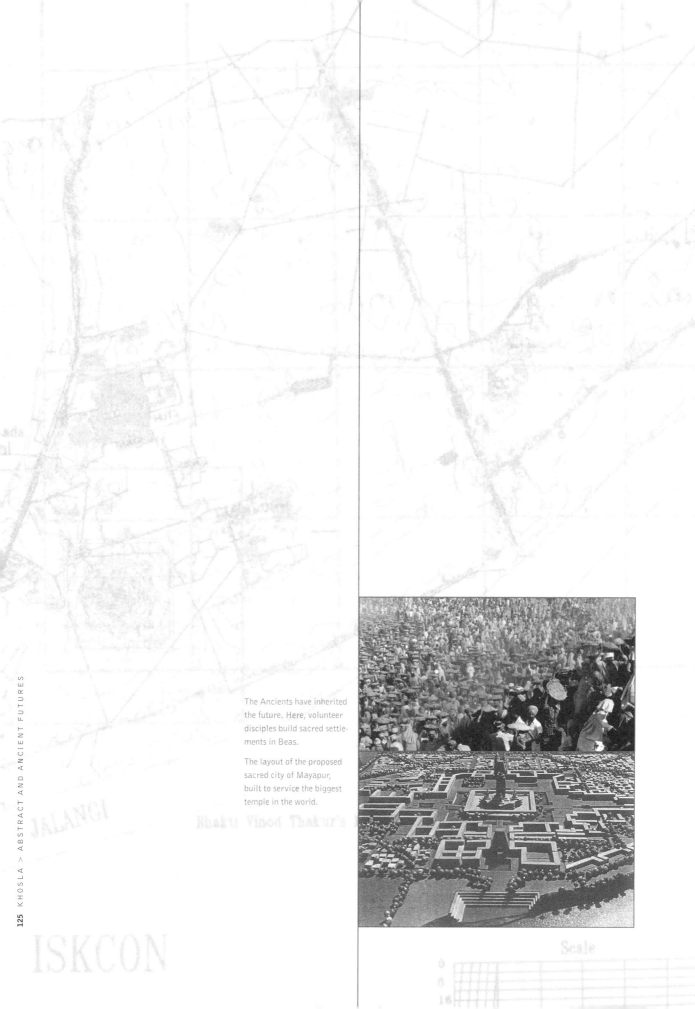

The Ancients have inherited the future. Here, volunteer disciples build sacred settlements in Beas.

The layout of the proposed sacred city of Mayapur, built to service the biggest temple in the world.

Frank O. Gehry and Associates, Guggenheim Museum Bilbao, detail. The abstraction of future modernism

Temple of the Vedic Planetarium, detail. "The construction of the temple was predicted in the 16th century by Lord Prabhu. He said that an extraordinary temple will be built for Lord Caitanya in Mayapur and that an unparalleled exhibition of daily glorification of the Lord . . . will take place which will have an effect all over the world" (Shri Mayapur Dham, v. 41).

ROMI KHOSLA IS AN
ARCHITECT IN NEW DELHI
AND AN INTERNATIONAL
ADVISOR TO BULGARIA IN
THE U.N. DEVELOPMENT
PROGRAMME. HE IS THE
AUTHOR OF BUDDHIST
MONASTERIES IN THE
WESTERN HIMALAYAS AND
URBAN REVITALIZATION
PROPOSALS FOR UNESCO.

forces sort out individual paradises. All three leaders chose the socialist project. Large parts of Africa and Asia saw in it the opportunity to define a new future – new in comparison to what their own theological systems of thought offered. It was also, with or without the political rhetoric, one way to adopt the modern agenda. Nobody in Africa, Asia, or the Middle East wanted the corporate form of modernism; nobody wanted to adopt a modern agenda that had only a materialistic content and no ideology.

Today, the collapse of the socialist project has exposed the situation and dried up one of the modern currents. In the non-Judeo-Christian world, the institutions established by both the colonial rulers and the half-baked socialist rulers have begun to fall apart. As the crust of modernism flakes away, it reveals societies that cling to ancient wisdom to guide their destinies.

As we move toward the next millennium and as societies of the non-Judeo-Christian world search for their identities, a belief in the divine determinants of time and futures is emerging. Ancient futures are being reformulated and reinterpreted according to traditional wisdoms, which themselves form important sources of information and control. Because these

societies have not seen holocausts and because the old social systems are, by and large, intact, collective memory is relatively undisturbed. The deep roots of tradition have ensured that the modern agenda will no longer be adapted and grow.

Today there are two basic versions of the perception of time and the projection of futures in global societies. The first, prevalent in Western cultures, is formulated from the abstraction of the modern agenda and is disconnected from any divine supra-system. The other, prevalent in the rest of the world (save, perhaps, China), is part of the ancient divine system resurrected in contemporary times. These societies are rejecting the modern agenda as a symbol of Western exploitation and culture and are increasingly advocating ancient futures. A duality persists between societies who believe in the modern agenda and those who are shielding themselves from the modern. It is possible to interpret this as part of a growing plurality, but I suspect more and more that this is going to be part of a narrative of irreconcilable differences.

The way that futures are defined is closely linked to the way resources are invested: every investor places his bets on the future. Architectural

projects are therefore quite unique because they symbolize the commitment of investors to a future resource. Two projects, the Guggenheim Museum Bilbao in Spain and the Temple of the Vedic Planetarium in India, provide examples of the positions I have outlined in this paper. Of the two projects, one is complete and the other is about to be built. Both are extremely important symbols of the future. One, the Guggenheim, is about abstract futures, and the other, the Temple, about ancient futures. Both have been funded in unconventional ways. The one set in Europe is abstract in the extreme, its titanium forms generated by aircraft design software. It houses contemporary art from a museum system in New York and is set in the middle of Basque country, where an armed struggle is underway for regional independence from Spanish domination. The other, set among ancient temples, is a project of visions, built according to ancient geometric principles to last one thousand years. It is symmetrical, regular, and promises salvation – an act of devotion placed in the cycle of cosmic time and immersed in local culture. It is a new city in which all the inhabitants devote themselves to worship and self-improvement.

Homecoming after the Time-Collapse
Hasan Ünal Nalbantoğlu

1 Stephen Kern, *The Culture of Time and Space: 1880–1918* (Cambridge, Massachusets: Harvard University Press, 1983), 314. In spite of the close relationship between changing the conception of time and the rise of new conceptions and myths regarding polity and government, especially regarding nationalism and nationstate, this issue will be bypassed here. Suffice it to say that the importance of this historical phenomenon has been highlighted by Benedict Anderson in his *Imagined Communities: Reflections on the Origin and Spread of Nationalism* (London: Verso, 1983), 28–40.

2 This point is vividly raised both in Roland Barthes, "Research: The Young," in *The Rustle of Language*, trans. R. Howard (Oxford: Basil Blackwell, 1986), 69–75, and Louis Althusser, *Philosophie et philosophie spontanée des savants* (Paris: F. Maspero, 1974). For the English translation of the thesis and discussion on the slogan of "interdisciplinarity," see Louis Althusser, *Philosophy and the Spontaneous Philosophy of the Scientists & Other Essays*, ed. G. Elliott (London: Verso, 1990), 79.

3 For an illuminating article on the (hi)story of the Western "concept" of time, see, Hans-Georg Gadamer's "The Western View of the Inner Experience of Time and the Limits of Thought," in *Time and the Philosophies* (Paris: UNESCO, 1977), 33–48.

4 The confusions to which this particular statement paves the way when divorced from the historically determinate material social conditions is persuasively argued in David Harvey, *Justice, Nature and the Geography of Difference* (Oxford: Blackwell, 1996), 207–326; 207–47 in particular.

5 "History is an irreversible process," says Lukács, "and it therefore seems natural to start the ontological investigation of history with the irreversibility of time. It is evident that we have here a genuine ontological relationship [ontologischer Zusammenhang]. If this characteristic [Wesensart] of time were not the insuperable foundation of any existent [unaufhebbare Fundament eines jeden Seins], then the problem of the necessary historicity of being [notwendigen Geschichtlichkeit des Seins] could not even arise." Georg Lukács, *Ontology: Marx (Marx's Basic Ontological Principles)*, trans. D. Fernbach (London: Merlin Press, 1978), 70./*Prolegomena zur Ontologie des gesellschaftlichen Seins* (Darmstadt und Neuwied: Luchterhand, 1984, 1986; [hereafter *Prolegomena zur Ontologie*]), 1. Halbband: 612–13.

6 For Georg Simmel, see, for example, "The Sociology of Space," in *Simmel on Culture*, eds. D. Frisby and M. Featherstone (London: Sage, 1997), 137.

7 The current nostalgic literature on the fragments of everyday life in, say, Istanbul is just one concrete example of such historiographic/historiological [*historisch*] writing. Even in such a "completely unquestioning age (Weltalter der gänzlichen Fraglosigkeit)" as ours, "[a] historical (geschichtlich) confrontation, however, is essentially different from a historiographical reckoning (als die historisch verrechnende Kenntnisnahme) of and acquaintance with the past, as Heidegger attempts in his 1937/38 lecture. See Martin Heidegger, *Basic Concepts of Philosophy* (Bloomington and Indianapolis: Indiana University Press, 1994), 12, 13. *Grundfragen der Philosophie* (Frankfurt am Main: Vittorio Klostermann, 1984), 11–12, 13. It seems to me that the underlying problem here is the refusal to recognize that every tradition can also be seen as a simulation, and it is futile to search for any authentic tradition in the ongoing flux of things. Needless to add, such nostalgia, when deployed with concern toward present and past "quotidian" as an alternative to the metanarratives of a supposedly defunct modernity, has little in common with the solidity of certain exemplary narratives of the *quotidienne* even when following in the footsteps of such works of historiography as those of the *Annales* school (e.g., Marc Bloch's *Les caractères originaux de l'histoire rurale française* or Emmanuel Le Roy Ladurie's *Montaillou*), which were, in turn, partly inspired by the Durkheimian sociology.

8 Luc Ferry, *Homo Aestheticus:The Invention of Taste in the Democratic Age*, trans. Robert de Loaiza (Chicago: The University of Chicago Press, 1993), 11.

This essay is a thought-experiment, so to speak, a personal stroll along an alternative path, taken earlier by others, though not too frequently as far as I can see.

The present state of inquiry has something to do with the collapse of belief in and the consequent assault on what Stephen Kern once aptly called "a universal, unchanging, and irreversible public time," a collapse into the private time(s) fashioned by the now "radically interiorized" experiences of bourgeois "individuality" as the ideological mainstay of modernity. Unlike other earlier modes of time, namely, the sense of the past and of the future, this gives rise to a new mode, to a sense of present that, Kern contends, "expand[s] spatially to create the vast, shared experience of simultaneity" increasingly abandoned to the mediation of technology.[1]

The question of time and space is also on the agenda of certain theoretical interventions. These have the express aim of opening up the social sciences by transgressing their jealously kept traditional boundaries, of radically transforming the very *object* of "interdisciplinarity," without seeking refuge in the old and stale protocols of interdisciplinary research. All the better; any specialized language that advocates interdisciplinarity from behind the jealously guarded walls of its particular discipline or profession is the mortal enemy of the newly posited interdisciplinarity.

The spirit of this essay has, in its own way, something to share with such attempts to cultivate an alternative interdisciplinarity and its proper "theoretical object,"[2] which has yet to appear on the horizon of thought.

The homogeneous empty time of historicism that has thoroughly domesticated the so-called "West"[3] can no longer be called on for help and we must recognize that there is no solace to be found in chestnuts such as "time and space are social constructs."[4] Given the ontological irreversibility of the process of history,[5] any dialogue with contemporary architecture as part of a historically determinate space-time beyond self-serving nomenclatures and "languages of specialty" is likely to take issue with two things: first, the concrete times and *topoi* of architectural practices of all sorts;

and second, the still-hegemonic Cartesian (shall we say, *simulated?*) approach to the "time/space" couplet of modern science – an abstract and empty husk so often filled by anytime and anyplace at will[6]– at times with an almost capricious, trendy recklessness.

Our all-too-familiar and ever-fashionable escape into nostalgia provides a conspicuous example of these failures, especially amidst the debris of a time-collapse. Moreover, it does so without fundamentally challenging a basic trait of the modern mentality, namely, the instrumental-calculative thinking so pervasive in our everyday and disciplinary lives. Within the various practices, including architecture, that are largely conditioned by market conditions, such nostalgia often aims at reviving bygone ages via various means. Coffee-table books glorify everyday life of some past society or the architectural wonders of a certain region of the world; old structures and even streets are rebuilt or restored to fuel a romantic yearning for lost times while simultaneously catering to a variety of industries, particularly those associated with tourism. We are swimming in an ocean of symbols uprooted from their original contexts in order to form a simulated reality. This does nothing to develop an "authentic" memory that embodies a true sense of time and history. On the contrary, such nostalgia, harnessed to serve today's pragmatic ends, is the most seductive enemy of any authentic building that is involved in the memory and consciousness of times and places. Nostalgia of this kind is not merely one symptom of our incapacity to cope with the existential problems of the present; it is, in fact, an escape from time as it actually unfolds.[7]

Still, such hasty manufacturing practices serve a utilitarian function by creating fictitious pasts. Besides being an item within the *Regelkreis* (reach of the law) of information demanded by both the modern nation-state and various industries such as tourism, they tend to turn any "work" into a producer-artist's *carte de visite* under pressure from a culture industry that increasingly promotes and packages the producer's public persona.[8] Seen in this light, the persistence of the producer's signature even in works intended to break the yoke of time ("timeless" architecture is perhaps an example[9]), ultimately joins hands with the idea of the timeless work of art à la the Romantic spirit of the 18th century.

This sits well with the idea of the modern architect-cum-master-builder for modern times. Yet questions arise as to what happens to such abstracted subjectivity in the wake of emergent technologies such as softgels, nanotechnologies, or even the prepackaged architectural software that is widely used today. Considering the qualitative difference of Cartesian "manufacture" from the ancients' *tekhné*, does not this new rhythm of things truly threaten such jealously guarded crafts as the architect's vocation? Might it even undermine the long-cherished creative powers of the subject-architect, already jeopardized by the very corporate world of architecture?

"Architecture is the most spatial of arts," declares one platitude among others. This, one suspects, provides ground for any theoretical "intervention" on the part of various architectural discourses, including those aiming at "timeless" architecture. As is obvious in so-called Western, logocentric architecture and its derivatives elsewhere (as in what one is tempted to call, *das neuzeitliche Morgenland* [the new modern East]), self-reflection on the part of any architectural discourse does not appear to take us far; for such discourse aims at providing the very foundation of all historically shaped knowledge while simplifying and universalizing the meaning of dwelling and shelter. More important are the historically determined human relations taking place within those merely physical shells promising "dwelling," be they the ancient (or modern) *oikos-domos* or the temples of modern consumption. In this context, we must examine how such determinate relations are affected in the emergent spaces under the tutelage of "form" in modern times, given the conditions imposed by a historical spectacle so persuasively portrayed by Theodor Adorno in the early 1950s.[10]

In fact, one can go further, joining Heidegger in rethinking this "homelessness" as the essential trait of human existence, despite continuous attempts at "building" and "dwelling."

9 This somehow reminds one of the fixed Platonic form and its pseudo-Hegelian corollary, the so-called "end of history" forcefully criticized by J. Stallabrass in view of cyberspace as the quote below exemplifies, and has to be rethought over the silent premises of a timeless architecture: "...data, which must be handled in the visual arena of cyberspace, like numbers on the stock market, has already been abstracted from the real world and made fungible. Its particularity has already been stripped away in its reduction to number. In cyberspace, where it is given an apprehensible form, this data must be constantly animated, as if in a movie. Given that the function of virtual representation is tied to movement, a fixed perfection like that of architecture will certainly elude these forms. Yet even these clean, mobile cyberspace forms can never show the material suffering behind a row of financial figures, for this has been stripped away long ago in the very collection of data. When a form is restored to this data, the 'reality' it adopts is utterly cleansed of anything that cannot be exchanged." "Empowering Technology: The Exploration of Cyberspace," NLR, 211 (May–June 1995), 3–32.

10 See Theodor W. Adorno, *Minima Moralia: Reflections from Damaged Life*, trans. F. N. Jephcott (London: Verso, 1978), 38–39.

11 Not for the weak-hearted, of course. Still, we cannot rest content, in support of our argument here, by merely pointing to Heidegger's somewhat enigmatic statement in brackets within the published text of his Freiburg seminar in the first trimester of 1940, that *"The world is shifting out of joint – if indeed it ever was in joint – and the question arises whether modern man's planning, even if it be world-wide, can ever create a world order. / ...der Erdkreis geht aus den Fugen, gesetzt daß er je in solchen war; und die Frage erhebt sich, ob die Planung des neuzeitlichen Menschen – und sei sie planetarisch – je ein Weltgefüge zu schaffen vermag."* ("On the Being and Conception of FUSIS...": 224. / "Vom Wesen und Begriff der Fúsij...": 242 [Heidegger's emphasis]). One also needs to pay attention to his further comments in a 1942 seminar *Hölderlin's Hymne, "Der Ister."* If the two keywords of the seminar in question, namely, *Wanderschaft* and *Ortschaft* are thought in the light of Heidegger's earlier understanding of Aristotelian *ergon* and *Kunstwerk*, then the homecoming via "otherness" in a world permanently out of joint makes perfect sense, given the concerns and priorities of our present-day conjunctures in particular. In fact, this is expressly put by Heidegger as follows: "Homecoming into one's own implies that, for a long time and perhaps always, man [human existence] is not at home; and this, in turn, implies that man ignores, rejects, and denies – perhaps must deny – the site of home. Homecoming for this reason is a transit through otherness"; quote from Fred Dallmayr, "Homecoming through Otherness," *The Other Heidegger* (Ithaca: Cornell University Press, 1993): 161. / *"Dieses Heimischwerden im Eigenen schließt in sich, daß der Mensch zunächst und langehin und zuweilen für immer nicht heimisch ist. Und dies wiederum schließt ein, das der Mensch das Heimische verkennt und verleugnet und flieht, vielleicht sogar verleugnen muß. Das Heimischwerden ist so ein Durchgang durch das Fremde."* M. Heidegger, *Hölderlin's Hymne "Der Ister,"* (Frankfurt am Main: V. Klostermann, 1984), 60. In spite of a recent excellent translation of the German original [cf. *Hölderlin's Hymn "The Ister,"* trans. W. McNeill and J. Davis (Bloomington and Indianapolis: Indiana University Press, 1996), 48.], I have here preferred to use Dallmayr's translation/interpretation of the immediately relevant text for my purpose [emphasis added].

12 I can't see here any reason not to agree with the thesis Max Horkheimer once posited: that is, doing science in the spirit of Cartesian rationalism ahistorically takes knowledge as something stored-up and invested, put into circulation, consumed, etc., without asking what theory means for human existence; cf. "Traditionelle und kritische Theorie," (*Zeitschrift für Sozialforschung*, vi/2, 1937: 245–92); trans. in *Critical Theory: Selected Essays* (New York: The Seabury Press, 1972), 188–252. Secondly, like any other tradition, Cartesianism is just one simulation among others before and since, albeit a very powerful one for *more geometrico* is still the dominant *paradeigma* with its "legislative" power of abstraction (for which it is indebted to the language of the courts and the commercial law) in all social practices, including various levels and spheres of architectural practice. Thirdly, such historically determinate "enframing" for which the Cartesian view provided an early abstract model and within which the simulated reality of manufactured products effectively made their presence, represented an early modern anthropocentric rupture. I have in mind, specifically, the separation between *res cogitans* and *res extensa* which did not only

anticipate "possessive individualism," "transcendental ego," and the myth of "creative genius" (which is so indispensable for the "spontaneous ideologies" of art and architecture), but further prepared the ground for an essentially Subject-centered, "sanctioned-ratified history" in Bachelardian parlance (l'histoire sanctionnée, as opposed to its actual generation and flux of knowledge with all its attendant irruptions and waywardness, in short, its l'histoire périmée). Such l'histoire sanctionnée had its parallel in examples of official historiography within the architectural discourse of modern times. One salient feature of such histories is that they tend to retrofit the abstracted profile of modern Subject-cum-architect into the mental spaces of distant times and peoples, and especially the ancient Greeks in the case of the geneaology of the historical construct, "The West."

13 Louis Althusser, *Essays in Self-Criticism*, trans. G. Lock (London: NLB, 1975), 112, note 8; *Eléments d'Autocritique* (Paris: Librairie Hachette, 1974), 27, note 1.

14 Although the origins of the word are well known, what is often overlooked is that the language and the *psuché* dwelling in the bodies of, e.g., ancient Greeks were not yet conducive to employ the word *àrkhitektón* in a restricted way to mean precisely and solely the builder of material structures, as it came to mean only in later times.

15 The possible advantage of architecture perhaps can be found here, despite all reductivisms, for it produces a surplus which cannot be contained by any language of or about architecture. For further discussion, see Peter R. Gleichmann, "Architecture and Civilization," *Theory, Culture & Society*, IX/4 (November 1992), 29, 33, 35.

16 Cf. an oft-quoted, passage in Descartes's *Discourse on Method [of Rightly Conducting the Reason and Seeking Truth in the Field of Science]*, Part Six : "It is possible to reach knowledge that will be of much utility in this life; and that instead of the speculative philosophy now taught in the schools we can now find a practical one, by which, knowing the nature and behavior of fire, water, air, stars, the heavens, and all the other bodies which surround us, as well as we now understand the different skills of our workers, we can employ these entities for all the purposes for which they are suited, and so make ourselves masters and possessors of nature. This would not only be desirable in bringing about the invention of an infinity of devices to enable us to enjoy the fruits of agriculture and all the wealth of the earth without labor [sic!], but even more so in conserving health, the principal good and the basis of all other goods in this life." René Descartes, *Philosophical Essays*, trans. L. J. Lafleur (Indianapolis: Bobbs-Merrill, 1977), 45–46. [emphasis added]. Again, one recalls the radical difference between the world of Greeks and that of the Cartesian tradition which is easily overlooked; for a detailed discussion of the difference between being "object as Object for a subject and object as an 'over against one' [Gegenstand als Objekt für ein Subjekt und Gegenstand als 'gegen einem über']" see Martin Heidegger, *The Principle Reason*, trans. R. Lilly (Bloomington and Indianapolis: Indiana University Press, 1991), 81–2./*Der Satz vom Grund, Siebte Auflage* (Pfüllingen: Verlag Günther Neske, 1992 [1957]), 139–40.

We might, at the same time, find in "labor" the *Lichtung* – a potential "opening" (to which I will return) – and seize a real possibility of "homecoming" without any need to escape into nostalgia.[11]

All these have a bearing on recycled discourses on the "end of history," the "collapse of time," and the like, the original and better versions of which have in fact long been dwelling in the ecology of the mind.

With such considerations in mind, I am tempted to think that just as there is no "theory-in-general," there is no such thing as "architecture-in-general," for both point to a "no-good-to-no-one" timelessness of one kind or the other.[12] At best, each can be deployed "as the minimum of generality necessary to be able to grasp a concrete object."[13] This also holds true in the case of using the word *architecture*.[14] Without it, thinking cannot produce the "concrete-within-thought" with respect to the specific times and places of architectural practice, even in the *Neuzeit* (new-time), in terms of their essential tension with the notoriously abstract entities of Time and Space.

Even so, I must admit that I experience a certain degree of frustration as an individual agent/vehicle of thinking from another, equally modern but relatively recent disciplinary practice: sociology. I find this to be especially the case in its attempts to deal with the question of time in relation to the practice of architecture and its discursive space in particular. There is a twofold reason for my anxiety:

First, the agent has to convey its thinking in propositional statements,[15] no matter how much he or she has to be on guard against speaking the pervasive and often covert language of "Law" (the power of which rests on a "subject-object" distinction involving an inevitable property relation, which turns the realm of *Dinge/Gegenstände* [thing] into that of *Objekte* [object].[16] The prison house of language is no mere metaphor. What should be feared in an exposition of this sort, therefore, is that it will result in just another set of propositional statements, or worse still, another discursive edifice or system pretending to contribute to a likely *poíesis* by its own presencing (*Anwesenheit*), while in fact being nothing more than another product of intellectual manufacture circulating in the sphere of cultural artifices/commodities. If the latter is the case, then it means that this little exercise of "will-not-to-will" could never succeed in producing its own "authentic-time" and is simply a prisoner of a commodified "now," if not another potential stockholder in the Heidegger industry.

Second, the thinking/writing process that led to the intervention taking place here/now cannot fully escape the common representation of time in terms of the holy trinity of past/present/future, which collapses into each actual present as a succession of *nows*. The question is: How can one let architecture and its discourses *be*, while simultaneously allowing for its presencing and letting it produce its own limits in "authentic" (*eigentlich*) time? How can one thereby think architecture rather than think *about*, *on*, or, worst of all, *above* architecture? To what extent is it possible to break the spell of the current dangerously familiar representation of space-time that is understood as the distance measured both quantitatively and qualitatively between two points in time? This calculation casts its shadow even if one struggles for a heteronomous stand against objectifying architecture, its inner motions, rhythms, and tensions.

This problem looms large for architects. It is even compounded by the dominant language that speaks through the statistical average of the modern architectural profession; its increasingly monopolistic corporate structures; the power hierarchies within the profession, on its margins, and beyond, its power-holding and power-exercising clientele, the very institutional contexts of architectural education that adapt themselves to the *Regelkreis* (reach or extent of the law) of a techno-scientific, information era; architectural competitions (including alternative ones) and their sponsors; and, last but not least, the constant danger of infiltration by the culture industry, even where countertendencies stand a chance to prevail.

With all this in mind, one is further tempted to ask: What about now, for example? What of Any's particular "now" considered as a "futural project" (to which I will return) that

forces the framework of sequential "now-times" (*Jetztfolge*) or rather, hopefully, its *Jetztzeits* (Walter Benjamin) onto its past gatherings?

To the extent that it is a time-filled project, pregnant with a baby named futurity, any such project (or Any, for that matter) is a challenge. It goes through its successive happenings via the presencing of various discourses on each occasion and as a series of now-times spread over our habitual chronological time. It appears to offer, existentially, the emergence of a heteronomous, open-ended space-time without providing a rain check for posterity. My self-assigned task within this now-time is to pursue, as rigorously as possible, a reasoning that incorporates a significant pointer toward what has not been addressed earlier in Any's ongoing activity and which should be carefully thought out. This is the case in the very nature of every *Dasein*, despite the fact that it has to accommodate itself to the time with which we are blindly familiar: namely, a series of perpetual presents, a sequence of nows. Whether or not the "measuring-calculation" intrinsic to such now-times is quantitatively employed is of no consequence here.[17]

Once we accept Heidegger's assertion (*lógos*) that time is not nothingness and, moreover, precedes space[18] while further agreeing with Benjamin concerning the very nature of "now" (*Jetztzeit*),[19] then it should not be difficult to conceive of Any as a possible alternative to "the now" of dominant rationality as manifest in the economics and politics of existing "culture": to conceive of it, for instance, in Jean-Luc Nancy's terms as the "spacing of time itself [which] is nothing else than otherness, heterogeneity emerging in time."[20] Any has the potential to produce its "authentic" space-time in Heidegger's sense of an "openness which opens up in the mutual self-extending of futural approach, past, and present." Heidegger's next assertion also fits here: "This openness exclusively and primarily provides the space in which space as we usually know it can unfold. The self-extending, the opening up, of future, past and present is itself prespatial; opening up of openness only thus can it make room, that is, provide space."[21] Unlike Nancy, however, I would stop short of characterizing this yet-to-be-seen spacing (*espacement*) of time which is "full of openness and heterogeneity" as "the space of community in its existence." That remains to be seen and is contingent upon the trajectory of the development of *lógos/legein* in this "gathering" which stands a chance to allow the "third" thing of every authentic conversation to emerge (Gadamer à la Aristotle).

Likewise, our presencing here with respect to the *Holzweg* (if you will) of Any, produces, I hope, its alternative "now," its "true-time," and not the other way around: namely, the manufacture of "things (already) said." This is also a position of resistance vis-à-vis the lure of our current understanding of time, simultaneously a point of transgression and accommodation (if we recall the discussion at the Anywise conference in Seoul).[22] Such "alternative" time that generates itself by presencing out of Any's futurity via minimal exercises of the "will-not-to-will" is also a mover for other possible modes of *poiésis* and not *creatio*. This involves the production of a peculiar space, an opening for the emergence of what Henry Cobb described as the "sense of poetry that transcends mere artfulness."[23] This is precisely the product of "labor" as understood by both Aristotle and Lukács, that is, the *poiésis* of thinking as *tékhne* and therefore as *phúsis* (*elementary substance* and *outward form*) wherein thinking submits itself only to its own necessity, and the *Da-sein* of any project such as this one opens up as a temporary "clearing" (*Lichtung*) for the "presence" of a certain enigmatic *à-létheia* imposing its own temporality during the split-second stay prior to its immediate withdrawal.

If the space-time of "true-time" is three-dimensional, we are told that there is still a fourth dimension at the very heart of this three-dimensionality as the very ground for the calculated one-dimensionality of space-time (as the distance between two time-points, and mostly, but not exclusively, measured in quantitative terms). We are told that this fourth dimension is both independent of and antecedent to all calculations of time (and to calculation as such), as well as to any spatiality. Our familiar time and space are nullities in and of themselves. This in fact had

17 *"Time familiar to us as the succession in the sequence of nows is what we mean when measuring and calculating time."* / *"Die als Nacheinander in der Jetztfolge bekannte Zeit meint man, wenn man die Zeit mißt und berechnet."* Martin Heidegger, "Time and Being," *On Time and Being*, trans. Joan Stambaugh (New York: Harper & Row, 1972), 10. / "Zeit und Sein," *Zur Sache des Denkens* (Tübingen: Niemeyer, 1968), 11 [emphasis added].

18 Following a lead on the basis of an intervention by one of the participants in M. Heidegger and E. Fink, *The Heraclitus Seminar: 1966/67*, trans. C. H. Seibert (University, Alabama: The University of Alabama Press, 1979): Sixth Lecture, 60, 62–3, which directs one on Heidegger's earlier lecture concerning Time and Being, *Zur Sache des Denkens* (1959). Further, one has to point out that, for Heidegger *"space"* [is] *something for which the Greeks had neither a word nor a concept. For us today space is not determined through place, but rather all places, as constellation of points, are determined by infinite space that is everywhere homogeneous and nowhere distinctive."* Martin Heidegger, / "On the Being and Conception of FUSIS...": 229. / "Vom Wesen und Begriff der Fúsij...": 248–9. Earlier, Heidegger states that *"...in a certain sense what Aristotle means by 'change of place' is something different from the modern conception of the change of location of some mass in space. Tòpoi is the pou, the place where a determined body belongs."*

19 Walter Benjamin, *"History is the subject of a structure whose site is not homogeneous, empty time, but time filled by the presence of the now [Jetztzeit]."* "Theses on the Philosophy of History, XIV," *Illuminations*, trans. H. Zohn (New York: Schocken Books, 1969): 261 and the note concerning *Jetztzeit's* radical difference from *Gegenwart*, the "present." Cf. Jean-Luc Nancy's modified translation and the treatment of "now" in "Finite History," *States of 'Theory': History, Art, and Critical Discourse*, ed. Davis Carroll (New York: Columbia University Press, 1990): 170.

20 Nancy, 167.

21 Martin Heidegger, "Time and Being": 14. / "Zeit und Sein": 14–15. Heidegger's later remark that his earlier *"attempt in Being and Time, section 70, to derive human spatiality [die Räumlichkeit des Daseins] from temporality [auf die Zeitlichkeit]"* can no longer be defended (M. Heidegger, Op.cit.: 23/24) in this vein as well; see also, Maria Villela-Petit, "Heidegger's Conception of Space," *Martin Heidegger: Commemorations*, ed. by C. Macann, *Vol. I: Philosophy* (London and New York: 1992): 117–140. The pertinent question concerning the trinity, future/past/present, pursued within the flux of rigorous thinking/writing at any 'now' is whether it lets them freely self-extend prespatially in the present case (*Anytime*) as well, consequently contributing to the emergence of an 'authentic,' 'true' time-space through the succession of pregiven spaces and their impositions due to all kinds of *"properties peculiar to site [Eigentümlichen des Ortes]."*

22 See *Anywise*, ed. Cynthia C. Davidson (Cambridge, Massachusetts: MIT Press, 1996).

23 Henry N. Cobb in Discussion 5, in *Anywise*, 235.

Philosophical Hermeneutics, trans. by D. E. Linge (Berkeley: The University of California Press, 1976), 9.

27 "What results is that we happen if to happen is to take place, as other, in time, as otherness (and what is time, if not the radical otherness of each moment of time?). We are not a 'being' but a 'happening' (or rather, being is in us exposed to the beginning). This happening as the 'essential' otherness of existence is given to us as we, which is nothing but the otherness of existence (more than the existence of otherness). The 'we' is nothing but finitude as a subject, if subjectivity could ever be finite (rather, it is, as such, infinite). And this is the reason that the 'we' is a strange subject: who is speaking when I say 'we'? We are not – the 'we' is not – but we happen, and the 'we' happens, and each individual happening happens only through this community of happening, which is our community. Community is finite community, that is, the community of otherness, of happening. And this is history. As Heidegger writes: 'History [Geschichte] has its essential importance neither in what is past, nor in the 'today' and its 'connection' with what is past, but with the proper happening [Geschehen] of existence.' [from Being and Time, para. 74]" Jean-Luc Nancy, Op.cit.: 161 [emphasis added].

28 Martin Heidegger, "Overcoming Metaphysics," The End of Philosophy, trans. J. Stambaugh (New York: Harper & Row, 1973), 94. / "überwindung Metaphysik," Vorträge und Aufsätze (Stuttgart: Verlag Günther Neske, 1994), 77.

29 What I have here in mind is the brief and highly exceptional diagnosis by Barthes: "…no longer the (narrow) sphere of French society but far beyond that, historically and geographically, the whole of Western civilization (Graeco-Judaeo-Islamo-Christian), unified under the one Theology (Essence, monotheism) and identified by the regime of meaning it practices from Plato to France-Dimanche." Roland Barthes, Image – Music – Text, trans. by S. Heath (London: Fontana, 1977): 167. Barthes' remark can be read as a step outside the Western metaphysics over the three-hundred years since Descartes has collapsed into a state whereby not only are "an "unworthy attitude of mind in which fear would jostle its counterpart, possessiveness" prevails more than ever, but its char-

24 Dasein: "…that entity in its Being which we know as human life; this entity in the specificity of its Being, the entity that we each ourselves are, which each of us finds in the fundamental assertion: I am. The assertion 'I am' is the authentic assertion of Being pertaining to the Dasein of man. In its specificity, this entity is as mine. / …das seiende in seinem Sein das wir als menschliches Leben kennen; dieses Seiende in der Jeweligkeit seines Seins, das Seiende, das wir jeder selbst sind, das jeder von uns in der Grundaussage trifft: Ich bin. Die Aussage 'Ich bin' ist die eigentliche Aussage vom Sein vom Charakter des Daseins des Menschen. Dieses Seiende ist in der Jeweligkeit als meiniges." Martin Heidegger, The Concept of Time / Der Begriff der Zeit, trans. William McNeill (Oxford: Blackwell, 1992): 3/3E; 6/6E (hereafter CT/BZ). This is further attested by Heidegger's talk at the Greek Academy of Sciences and Arts in April 1967, where he says: "No space could grant things their place and ordering and no time could become and pass [as] hour and year, that is, temporal extension and duration, had not Space and Time been given the opening governing their belonging-together." / "Kein Raum könnte den Dingen ihren Ort und ihre Zuordnung einräumen, keine Zeit könnte dem Werden und Vergehen Stunde und Jahr, d.h. Erstreckung und Dauer zeitigen, wäre nicht dem Raum und der Zeit, wäre nicht ihrem Zusammengehören schon die sie durchwaltende Offenheit verliehen." M. Heidegger, "Die Herkunft der Kunst…": 148 [emphasis added; translation mine, with a little help from friends].

25 CT/BZ: 15/15E.

26 CT/BZ: 14/14E. The very "futurality" underlined by Heidegger also finds an echo in Gadamer's hermeneutic understanding: "[h]istory is only present to us in light of our futurity." Hans-Georg Gadamer, "The Universality of the Hermeneutical Problem,"

been boldly asserted, in the wake of Einsteinian theory of relativity, by Heidegger himself, who wrote in 1924:

> The space is nothing in itself; there is no absolute space. It exists merely by way of the bodies and energies contained in it (an old proposition of Aristotle's:) Time too is nothing. It persists merely as a consequence of the events taking place in it. There is no absolute time, and no absolute simultaneity [Gleichzeitigkeit] either.[24]

In Heideggerian parlance, this fourth dimension at the heart of any three-dimensionality is both a pre-temporal and a pre-spatial "opening," and must be thought as a "giving" (hence, Es gibt) with respect to Sein. What determines time and Being (the latter understood "now" as "presencing") is their belonging-together, the Event of Appropriation – in short, Ereignis.

Now, all this is old hat, as subject to become dangerously familiar as any kitsch, and hence uncanny to any probing mind in today's academic market, especially when deployed as just another standing-reserve for the manufacturing process(es) of a contemporary Heideggerbetrieb, a globally oriented Heidegger & Co., with its flexible techniques and technologies of investment and accumulation in "cultural capital."

So, what is new to say here? In spite of the dangers mentioned above, Heidegger can still provide an initial impulse. If Dasein, in its everydayness, "is supposed to be time, as reckoning [rechnend] with time, indeed measuring it with the clock and is therefore never alongside time in its authenticity [Eigentlichkeit],"[25] one alternative point of departure may be the following:

"Maintaining myself (think Any for a moment) alongside my past in running ahead, I have time. All idle talk [Alles Gerede], that in which such idle talk maintains itself, all restlessness, all busyness [alle Geschäftigkeit], all noise and all racing breaks down. To have no time means to cast time into the bad present of everyday [Alltag]. Being futural gives time [Zukünftigsein gibt Zeit], cultivates the present [bildet die Gegenwart aus] and allows the past to be repeated in how it is lived [läst die Vergangenheit im Wie ihres Gelebtseins wiederholen].

With regard to time, this means that the fundamental phenomenon of time is the future [das Grundphänomen der Zeit ist die Zukunft]."[26]

acteristic "cerebral mode of consciousness;" culminates into a final stage of paranoia; see Joseph Needham, "Poverties and Triumphs of the Chinese Scientific Tradition," Scientific Change, ed. A. C. Crombie (New York: Basic Books, 1963), 149.

30 An oeuvre at the center of which stands the volumes of the Science and Civilisation in China, an 'event' once described by Arnold Toynbee as "a Western act of 'recognition' on a plane higher than the diplomatic." For the immediate purposes of this occasion, however, I have in mind Joseph Needham, Time and Eastern Man: The Henry Myers Lecture 1964 (London: Royal Anthropological Institute of Great Britain & Ireland, 1965); see also thought-expanding articles in Time, Science, and Society in China and the West [The Study of Time, V], ed. J. T. Fraser, N. Lawrence, and F. C. Faber (Amherst: The University of Massachusetts Press, 1986). For a recent rethinking and recasting of the world of Greeks in this light, see, G. E. R. Lloyd, Adversaries and Authorities: Investigations into Ancient Greek and Chinese Science (New York: Cambridge University Press, 1996).

31 Harvey, Op.cit.: 210–12 and passim.

32 Besides Heidegger's work cited earlier, one can point to the following sources in support of such argument: Jacques Taminiaux, "The Origin of 'The Origin of the Work of Art'", in Reading Heidegger: Commemorations, ed. John Sallis (Bloomington & Indianapolis: Indiana University Press, 1993), 392–404; Dennis J. Schmidt, "Economies of Production: Heidegger and Aristotle on Physis and Techné," in Crises in Continental Philosophy, ed. A. B. Dallery & C. E. Scott with P. H. Roberts (Albany: State University of New York Press, 1990), 147–159.

Schmidt, who starts with Heidegger's 1931 dictum, *"WoWelt-daWerk, und Umgekehrt"* (*Where world, there work, and vice versa*), also adds the following, which I think further lends support to my first suggestion: "*the sites and frames (the topoi) for thinking – the call to displace those seemingly irreducible oppositions must be heard as a call for a topological shift. It is equally well described as an economic shift – that is, as a shift not only of sites and frames, but of the mediating laws and measures of transfer and translation between those places. This is the meaning of the epochal shift, the 'step back,' the return to the Greeks that Heidegger wants to effect. It is a return to the Greeks that throws them out of 'the' so-called Western tradition they are said to found, a return that gives them what Hölderlin characterized as their 'Oriental vitality,' a return that belongs to the project of blasting the borders of the Western world that takes itself to be heir to 'the Greeks'."* (148) [emphasis added]. Further evidence in this direction can be found in M. L. West, *Early Greek Philosophy and the Orient* (Oxford: Clarendon Press, 1971); on time, in particular, 35 ff. and on Heraclitus's *aion*, 158–9.

33 See Fredric Jameson, *Signatures of theVisible* (New York: Routledge, 1992), 1; and G. Lukács, *Ontology: Marx*: 49./ *Prolegomena zur Ontologie*, 1. Halbband, 596.

34 Bob Dylan during the *Jeweiligkeit* of putting down his lyrics for the song, "Up To Me," for instance. See Dylan's recollection in the liner notes to his album, *Biograph*. The verse, "*Someone had to reach for the risin' star*" calls to mind Octavio Paz's "*star of the present*" in "Poetry and Modernity," *The Tanner Lectures on HumanValues*, XII, ed. Grethe B. Peterson (Salt Lake City: University of Utah Press, 1991), 75.

What if we were to approach any human project(ion) that produces a *Jeweilige*, such as the Anytime "happening," not considering it just another ritualistic occurrence within a time-series comfortably couched within the empty husks of traditionally understood time and space but, alternatively, as a possible opening allowed (yet by no means guaranteed) by the "futurality" of Any's *Da-sein*?[27]

This, of course, does not have enough power to disturb in any major way the uncanny stability of what Heidegger called representative-calculative (empowering) [*vorstellend-planende (machtende)*] thinking,[28] the promises of which we are accustomed to await yet cannot really be delivered, except often in dissimulation these days. Still, the futurality of Any, if pursued rigorously, stands a real chance to let the freedom of a *Jeweiligkeit* (a particular while [*özgean; özgesüre*], a specificity in the temporal sense, radically distinct from a "static specificity," *die Eigenart*) prevail, and, in turn, we may all turn it into an enriching *Jemeinigkeit* (mineness), architects and nonarchitects alike.

In this vein, I can end my intervention on a conservative yet cautiously optimistic note. I suggest rethinking, in a *Wanderschaft* such as Any's, two interlocking moments that would help ground my discussion and might further contribute, beyond Heideggeriana, to the spacing in the future of similar projects, a "future" with the difference each occasion/ locality (*Ortschaft*) may bring forth.

One possible *Wanderschaft* is to address the consciousness of time and space outside the overall animus of Greco-Judaeo-Christian-Islamic civilizational complexes.[29] This is not to seek refuge in the stale variants of East/West distinction. Nor in the very New Age attempts to demolish that distinction, which simply turn the so-called wisdom of the East into just another marketable commodity. Rather, it should be possible to turn our gaze toward a distant point beyond such variants in this endeavor (here I have in mind possible knowledge-effects of the monumental *oeuvre* first spurred by Joseph Needham).[30] Yet such endeavor is hardly sufficient to complete the suggested detour unless it is grounded somewhere.

Still more fundamental, therefore, is the renewed attempt at an *ontological grounding* of the consciousness of time through a rigorous thinking similar or at least parallel to Georg Lukács's largely unappreciated, sisyphean effort to weave around a largely Aristotelian understanding of "labor" (*êrgon*) a *nonanthropomorphic* theoretical intervention concerning *gesellschaftliche Seins* (the very historical process understood nonhistoriologically, which, in fact, dismisses our uncannily familiar time-conception).This would provide an opening for the proper spacing and dwelling of my discussion of time, space, and place.This, I think, not only helps us to turn them into clearer heuristic devices along the lines of discussion elaborated, for instance, by David Harvey.[31] It is also very close, if not identical, to the clearing/opening (*Lichtung*) that *Dasein* turns out to be in Heidegger's later work (already anticipated in his early entanglement with the Greek *tékhne* and the "work" of art).[32]

Moreover, such grounding could very well prove to be a yet uncultivated dwelling place in pursuit of Fredric Jameson's somewhat hesitant point concerning the need to develop a new ontology.[33]

Who knows, we may even convince those who have in mind Rimbaud's "*Je est un autre* [I is another]"[34] that reaching for the risin' star is solely "up to me," nor is time necessarily an enemy once it is taken as the refreshing river of an alternative *Wanderschaft*.We may even find ourselves casually thinking of some past saying concerning time at an occasional *Ortschaft* while backstroking downstream. And that particular while does not turn into *anymineness*, there is no need to worry; "the rivers pay court to the sea" anyway, as the old Chinese adage goes.

HASAN ÜNAL NALBANTOĞLU IS A PROFESSOR OF SOCIOLOGY AT MIDDLE EAST TECHNICAL UNIVERSITY IN ANKARA AND HAS ALSO TAUGHT AT DURHAM UNIVERSITY IN ENGLAND AND THE UNIVERSITY OF CALIFORNIA, BERKELEY. HE IS THE AUTHOR OF SEVERAL ARTICLES AND MOST RECENTLY AN ESSAY FOR A COLLECTION ON HEIDEGGER AND THE MODERN AGE.

Netherlands Embassy Rem Koolhaas

The Dutch Embassy in Berlin, located on the Rolandufer in what was the earliest settlement of Berlin, has been an exciting project in the sense that it was a double rediscovery: of Berlin, a city from which I had been banned, and of the Dutch civilization from which I had been more or less exiled. Berlin has become a kind of seamless city as a result of a relentless effort to erase the signs of the traumatic realities that characterized it for decades. This effort has been pursued via an incredible insistence on the orderly reconstruction of the city according to a predetermined model. I find the results both paradoxically exciting and slightly tragic in that Berlin has been effectively transformed into a kind of Chinese city. Through massive building projects, tightly controlled by legislation, Berlin has become the construction site for a new German identity, a synthetic whole not based on the original ingredients of the city as context but from the official definition and annexation of what is missing from recent German history: unity and uniformity.

In the midst of this citywide project, we expected the worst. The Berlin dogma would dictate that the embassy simply needed to complete the block, but to our surprise we found a formerly East German and therefore formerly communist bureaucracy that had in fact been insulted by the dogma imposed on it by the West at the moment of its liberation. They encouraged us, within certain limits, to be fairly independent.

From the other side, the Dutch Ministry of Foreign Affairs wanted a solitary building, clearly distinguishable from its urban environment, that was an expression of "Dutch openness."

In order to deal with both the wishes of the Dutch government and the local zoning laws, the building was conceived as a glass cube on a socle. The conflict between perimeter block and free-standing building was resolved by combining the two. The embassy creates its own context: against the firewall surrounding the site, apartments for embassy staff form a theatrical backdrop to the cube. It is suggested that the entire entity was once a solid, and that the smaller building has been excavated from the solid. The building is separated from its surroundings by an access road along the rear edge, a drop-off area on a socle that can be read as both an internal court and a park.

In order to activate the entire volume of the embassy, one continuous promenade, the trajectory meanders through the building. It is a singular spatial element excavated out of a cube of generic office floors and workspaces. From the street-level entry to the roof, the trajectory links the collective, public spaces of the embassy by means of ramps and stairs. The direction and organization of the trajectory is based on visual relationships with the building's surroundings: the Spree River, the omnipresent TV Tower, the park, the apartments. All elements of context, each part of a different natural and political past of the city, are treated with the same seriousness.

Where the trajectory reaches the facade, it interrupts the regular rhythm of mullions. At those points, the facade uses nonreflective glass, and load-bearing glass mullions support the facade itself as well as the apparently floating vice ambassador's apartment above. It is even possible to see diagonally through the building from a park on the south by means of the sliding trajectory.

The embassy is a ductless building; all services are integrated into the architecture. Pressurized, the trajectory acts as an enormous duct. Fresh air migrates into the offices through openings in the structural walls and into the negatively pressured facade plenum.

Although the building looks somewhat bland from the outside, it has a very agitated and complex interior. It was fascinating to find a building project that so needed to incorporate a demonstration of freedom or architectural shamelessness in the context of a relatively generic cube. This is in part addressed by the structural solution; every point where walls or other parts of the building are superimposed is mobilized to structure the building. It is a cumulative rather than a systematic structural stability which is generated by enlisting and exploiting every moment of coincidence.

REM KOOLHAAS IS PRINCIPAL OF THE OFFICE FOR METROPOLITAN ARCHITECTURE (OMA) IN ROTTERDAM. HE IS THE AUTHOR OF **DELIRIOUS NEW YORK** AND **S,M,L,XL**, IN COLLABORATION WITH DESIGNER BRUCE MAU.

D2

FATIH UGURLA Today Saskia Sassen is posing the kinds of questions that I have been expecting from the Anytime meeting. She did not reply to them "architecturally," but her approach encourages me, as an architect, to ask my own questions of sociologists. Is it possible to make predictions about the future on the basis of the current trend of global change or on the basis of the transformations expected in the family structure, the structure of national economies, or factors like individualization and socialization? Can we make future projections? If so, architecture will definitely be affected by them. Will we be able at the end of this meeting to open a window and look 20, 30, 40 years into the future?

SASKIA SASSEN There are several issues in my mind vis-à-vis the practice of building, which may be more general than architecture. One relates to the technological issue that has to do with relocating activities. When I saw Rem's presentation of the Bordeaux House, I realized that I always think in terms of the economy, but of course it is the same thing in household spaces and in many institutional spaces. Technology makes it possible to relocate activities between digital spaces and actual space. The second issue, which comes more from this notion of denationalization, is probably more connected to matters of cultural vocabularies. I object to the notion of an opposition between culture and techné, but let me just use that language to invoke some of the comments made by our Turkish colleague here. I think, for instance, that the world of finance has a culture of practices, a culture of beliefs. Many of the incredible innovations that were launched in the 1980s traveled worldwide in this very strategic geography because there was a subculture in finance – the financiers in Tokyo and in Hong Kong, etc. There is a cultural vocabulary attached to all realms of activity. Anthropologists have criticized me for saying this, but I am at a loss for finding another term to name what I am trying to name. If we take the notion of this denationalized, strategic frontier-zone that I talk about, which cuts across the old north-south divide, there is the issue of a different cultural vocabulary. This has been partly captured in notions of the hybrid space of international business. That trope is now familiar to everybody, but there are far more subtle forms in the making. A third issue that I am very concerned with is the transparency of power. There was a time when power made a point of its own representation. Banks and stock markets were built with Greek columns; there was a whole architecture of power. There are two aspects to what has happened today in terms of this: one is a technological issue that necessitates rethinking how power materializes in something that you can capture in actual space, and the second is an issue of perhaps a diminished transparency of power, compared to how we knew it. I was on a panel with the CEO of what was NYNEX, the major telecom firm in the New York region, which had a headquarters in the suburbs – beautifully landscaped, everything perfect. A year and a half ago this CEO moved back to Manhattan and into a very modest office. He was asked, "Why did you move to a modest office?" and he said, "I didn't move to Manhattan to be in my office. I moved to Manhattan to be in the loop," that is, the information loop. There is something about the less-accessible and the more intermediated representations of power that is happening – it's built into the new constraints and the new possibilities of economic systems, and thus is an issue. Somewhere in that model of new conditions and new possibilities lies a question for building practice, which at times may become architecture.

BERNARD TSCHUMI Saskia, you were actually turning that question toward us architects and talking about the liquefying of buildings as investment. You said, "Will it change aspects of architectural practice? Does it make a difference in terms of architectural practice?" Occasionally we architects talk to developers — they talk a very different language, which is certainly not the language spoken by the architects invited to the Any conferences. They talk a language of investment, of interchangeability, of moving money from one place to another — in other words, of a certain type of indeterminacy of space, but one that is extremely qualified as an investment. What we do — the other type of architecture, in this room — is exactly the opposite. They are highly specific things — to use Rem's term, very nongeneric — while the large investment powers are looking for a generic quality that can be bought and sold over time. It has been this way throughout the 20th century, but it is now excessively developed. The two projects that Rem showed today are highly specific and very different from the liquid, interchangeable space of those large investment companies. So we find ourselves in a situation where either we are architects who make highly specific works commenting on a highly specialized, highly personalized view of architecture as culture, or so-called corporate architects who respond to the large financial investment and movement of capital.

When Romi opposed Gehry's Bilbao museum to the temple by the so-called graphic designer from Australia, it struck me that the lingo, the ideological wording for that temple, was not so far removed from the ideological wording used by those large financial powers. Although it is interchangeable and neutral and generic, the temple tries to have a so-called ideological view — that architecture is contextual, that it's a response to the neighborhood, etc. It's not an issue of style, it's not an issue of what it looks like, but of specificity. The temple is not specific. For me it's ultimately a generic piece of architecture. So on the one hand we have very generic views that are highly consumable by financial logic and, on the other, those which are highly specific, like Rem's house in Bordeaux or the embassy in Berlin. Are we condemned to that opposition?

REM KOOLHAAS I think that's the danger of generalization. We are actually in a very exciting position in the sense that the generic has formally become an issue now. I think that it allows us a wider repertoire. We are not necessarily condemned to a life of endless specification, but we are now able to read perhaps with more precision what in every single client, or in every single mission, is the pertinent issue. I could have shown a very generic building; Greg Lynn's church also has a kind of certain generic quality. I think that our repertoire is widening through a greater awareness of these different domains.

TSCHUMI I still have this question for Saskia. Why don't those clients, those financial powers, go to Peter Eisenman, for example, for the design of a building? What is the situation?

SASSEN When I heard your first statement, Bernard, I thought in a sense that it signaled the possibility of a critical architecture. I'm thinking of Renato Rizzi's comment yesterday, "How do we develop a critical architecture within the dominant discourse?" This is one way of interpreting what Rem just said; that you practice within, say, the generic domain but with a self-consciousness about what you're doing. In my research, what is generic or nongeneric is itself subject to transformation. What I think of as denationalizing, like these central banks — whether in Iran or Germany, etc. — is that they're part of a shared epistemic community. The generic itself has been transformed.

HANS VAN DIJK I was very intrigued by Saskia's remark that there is a correlation between the completely digitalized world of the financial markets and the, may I say, "bigness" of the impact when it solidifies in real space. On the other hand, when Romi showed this temple, I thought there is no correlation between bigness and duration anymore. Although the temple was predicted to be built four centuries ago, and it took two years to pour the foundation, it is now being built in a very short time. The same conditions that allow it to be built in a very short time could also mean it will be demolished very fast. The pleasure of megalomania will be short-lived because a big building that can be built fast can also be demolished very fast and replaced by another one while this condition remains.

ROMI KHOSLA As I understand it, the generic in architecture is the activity that helps you to accumulate more surplus, whether you liquidate it quickly or not. The process of building generic architecture and liquidating real estate is getting very rapid now because capital is accumulating in fewer hands. But this whirlwind activity throws out surplus parts that help to generate new ideas. The whirlwind process itself throws out individual, nongeneric substances that help guide it where to go. I think both activities are important. The difference in the temple itself is this; the founders of that temple went into the whirlwind and reaped the surplus to take out a new generic item. This money, which has gone into the city, has been made on the stock market – in Russia, the United States, and Asia – so we have a slightly different kind of activity here. We are talking about a group of people who are doing a generic activity, but actually moving away from multiplying surplus in an effort to multiply ancient beliefs. The implication is different because this kind of activity is going on at a microlevel in many parts of the world.

CENGIZ BEKTAS Saskia crystallized a topic that I have been trying to work out for quite a while. It seems that the essential word underlying the concepts of globalization, corporation, and internationalism, or rather the one word we should be thinking more about, is **denationalization**. However, sincerity is even more important in this denationalization, for a kind of Trojan Horse part has been acted out in several previous intellectual activities by the mention of the supra-national. Which one would carry us to a better end, denationalizing to become citizens of the world or struggling for an international identity?

I would also like to ask Ünal Nalbantoglu what he thinks about the situation of the architect who wants to achieve philosophy without passing through a sociological substructure.

SASSEN When I say denationalization, I am trying to get at a specific process that is different, say, from the formation of supranational organizations, which has been going on for a long time. I'm trying to identify specific trajectories of how countries get engaged, at what point do they deregulate, etc. Second, to answer your question about citizenry and what is a better world: I am not one who thinks that the national state was the best thing that ever happened. I do not believe in nationalism, and I'm very disturbed by the renationalizing of politics that goes along with the denationalizing of strategic economic spaces. But one concern I do have is where do we locate the project of social democracy if we don't have national states? Your question is really deeply involved in my new research project, which is a five-year project and hence very big, but I want to mention two things. We need to recover our national states. That doesn't mean nationalism. I want to strip it of the symbolism. I want to look at it as a capable administrative structure within which we can locate projects of social democracy. At the same time, I believe in these new transnational geographies for activity. If you look at international migration, at feminist groups, at environmental groups, you see a lot of transnationalism going on. Those geographies, which are now geographies of activity, could also become political geographies. I believe that what lies ahead is a new kind of politics; it's a new concept of citizenship. I do not believe for a minute in a world state, nor do I believe in the world citizen. I do believe that the Internet is potentially a very interesting political space for the politics of localities. I have also been part of the political initiatives against a multilateral agreement on investment, against all kinds of things that have simultaneous operations in many countries around the world, north and south, all connected via the Internet, which means that they are operating within the temporality of two days, given the transformation in the time zones. But there is a new politics afoot with some notion – which comes with this denationalization – of rethinking what constitutes membership. The whole project of our identity and of membership has been dominated, in the West especially, by the sovereign national state. The sovereign has marked our project of identity formation – that is the modern project, and that is not going to go away because of structures of power. However, there are other political projects of membership that escape that, and that operate in other transnational geographies.

CHARLES JENCKS Something that hasn't been addressed specifically is the collapse of space-time, an idea that's been in the air for thirty or forty years. In his book **The Postmodern Condition**, David Harvey talks about how the globalized network of the economy actually produces a condition in which all points on the globe become the same point. In other words, wherever you are in the global net, work and trade happens 24 hours a day. You're keyed into the same system, so it doesn't matter where you are because all spaces and places are of equal potential. Secondly, all times are now, so space-time has imploded or collapsed in this model. That's a very specific point, which makes everywhere and every-when the same. It sort of cuts our experience into blankness — it's called amnesia. It's connected to Karl Marx's famous line, "All that is solid melts into air." I think the fluid liquid has two meanings; one is the liquid architecture; another is literally the way capitalism has melted and continues to do at an ever greater rate, a point made by Joseph Schumpeter, an economist in the 1940s, who said basically that monopoly capitalism and welfare capitalism are destructive creative events. These are two ways in which traditional time has been threatened. These forces are much bigger than architecture and much bigger than personality. What is I think clear from these discussions so far is that there isn't one response to this but a spectrum of responses, and they're completely different. In fact, they're contradictory, because the biggest response is retribalization or renationalization, not denationalization. It doesn't make sense to talk about one paradigm or one spatial time response.

ÜNAL NALBANTOGLU When I go to that place called philosophy, that space is occupé. Every single hill and summit there is held. There is no tabula rasa. There is nothing that I can tell the architects — I may hold a place on those hills as much as they do. I believe that what we call philosophy is something that has exhausted itself. We should pass to something beyond philosophy, to a mode of thinking that would surpass philosophy. Not a mode of thinking but heterogeneous, multiple, and definitely with challenges; where we will try to find our ways. This is what I understand from Holzwege. A brand new world is opening up before us; a new world of artifices. There will be no more sociology in the coming century, perhaps no more philosophy. But there will still be thinking.

Charles Jencks's mention of everywhere and every-when dangerously reminds me of commodity exchange. For example, Carl Schmitt, in his book **Political Romanticism**, said that in 18th-century bourgeois romanticism, everything could be exchanged with everything else, for a hierarchy of values no longer existed. All things, including everything within this mushroom house called culture, can be bought and sold. We have to think about that, too.

GREG LYNN There seems to be a kind of emerging urban pattern of architectural objects as pilgrimage destinations. I actually thought Romi was comparing a kind of pilgrimage museum and a temple. Megashopping as pilgrimage destination is also very common. Given Saskia's comments about denationalization, the pilgrimage seems to cut across all of the panelists' presentations, and architecture always plays a destination role in it.

KHOSLA Undoubtedly, there is an underlying message; both places are pilgrimage sites. At the back of my mind is the idea of architecture as oracle, because these things are addressed to the future, and in both cases they are playing the role of oracles — the temple more literally than the museum, which is more ephemeral. This idea of the oracle hasn't left us. I see what Saskia is saying about the nation-states dissolving civil governments and reforming themselves, with the multinationals becoming the new oracles and being responsible for new oracle architecture. I think there is certainly a kind of effort to link up with the future. It's just that the future is getting much shorter, so the act of pilgrimage itself is becoming more complex. It is possible that the icons of architecture, in both divine and abstract terms, are going to be the new destinations for pilgrimages. Let me add something to help you understand the scale of the pilgrimage. We have a deity in India that one hundred thousand people go to see every day, 365 days of the year. Ten years ago, it was only two thousand a day.

PETER EISENMAN Rem always likes to chide me, so I would like to just chide him at the beginning of this comment. Fortunately, Rem's house proves to me that his first statement is a dissimulation, because for me his house is a triumph of architecture. It does not show any ambiguity about the role of architecture at all. The issue, though, that all three of the latter speakers presented in one way or another is the relationship of the generic to the specific. What we seem to be dealing with are the specific styles of the generic or specific. In order for the temple that Romi showed to exist, it must maintain its generic condition. In other words, it must oblige a certain typology in order to maintain what it is supposed to be. In maintaining that typology, it sustains a kind of dominant and normalized condition that can never be critical. On the other hand, those things that are specific — like Rem's project or, I would argue, Greg's church — can always have the possibility of being critical. That does not mean that all specific forms of architecture are specific; most of them are the generic masquerading as specific and therefore not critical. In a sense, only when the specific contains generic possibilities does it allow itself to be critical. I would argue that in one sense Rem is striving for the generic in the specific, which no longer represents a dominant condition of typology but rather a critical generic condition.

KOOLHAAS For me, the generic really represents an infinitely intriguing category. I find the most amazing shift in architecture in the prewar period and, to an even larger extent, the postwar period. The most important architects were those who were most concerned with the generic. Take Mies; I think that his later work is an endless reflection on the virtues of the generic, both in terms of the type of architecture it produces but also how it can generate not an emotion-free but a demand-free environment, a new environment where the architect is not permanently in your face. What I think you are rightly signaling, in a way, is that we consider ourselves — and I still don't know whether it is really true or not — we consider ourselves condemned to the specific. But I think it's not impossible to consider a project for the reconstruction of the generic, which is caving in to the commercial world.

TSCHUMI I wonder, where is the chicken and where is the egg? We think we architects are at the center of things, but in reality who comes to us to ask for such services? The large corporations may have found Mies to be a useful model – just look at Park Avenue – but they do not look at the architects that we represent for the development of their financial strategies. Those financial strategies go along with very sophisticated, very precise ways to build a building – how to make square feet valuable, etc. We do not function according to those parameters, however hard we try, because we always think we have the miracle solution; we work differently, our logic is different. So if I follow your argument, you seem to be saying that maybe we are the vanguard, like Mies was in a sense, giving capitalism an image to develop in a certain direction. I wonder whether we are not actually quite naive and idealistic in thinking that our processes – our cultural processes, because they are intensely cultural – will be absorbed and consumed and made allies of capitalist development.

JALE ERZEN I think that we have to consider that there are time habits that certain political habits take advantage of. For example, this dematerialization that Saskia raises has been resisted by the Turkish central banks. One is in the big building right across the way. It has accumulated more land and made more materialistic evidence of itself all over Turkey, including the appropriation of all kinds of cultural activities. The second example is the Turkish Building Bank, which continued to build so-called public housing when there was no demand. This is one thing we should look into. These powers take advantage of a time lapse. I would ask Romi Khosla whether or not the two systems he talked about, the modern agenda and the divine, in the end do not really even out? They come to the same thing by their different processes of activity. For example, the modern agenda fears this inevitable end, which is like some kind of divinity in itself – the inevitable outcome of human intervention. On the other hand, the divine activity, this temple, is made possible by human intervention, which is so earthly and so materialistic.

SASSEN Charles Jencks referred to — and I agree of course — multiple times. Again, I think that we are talking about temporalities, durations, rather than time, because time is a construction of a certain kind. My concern is a step further from that: the act of establishing that there are multiple times (I'm going to use his language). My concern is whether the existence of these multiple times contains a hierarchy that reorganizes the power of certain elements. For example, he mentioned the neutralizing of time and space. Well, that's a prerogative of certain kinds of sectors and certain kinds of activities. As I said, it can also go down to a certain grassroots politics. But my main point is that those sectors of finance that have the option of neutralizing time and space therewith gain enormous power. Let me refer again to Volkswagen, an example I left unexplicated. Given the temporality of finance, Volkswagen can use the temporality of manufacturing as a condition for access to capital. This is always an issue in capitalist economies — how do you effectively concentrate capital in orders of magnitude? Manufacturing serves that purpose. For Volkswagen, the manufacturing of the car is a mechanism for concentrating capital with a temporality of nine months. It uses its financial services — its subversion of the flow, right? — to utilize its capital in whatever different temporalities finance makes possible. This inverts the hierarchy that we had in the economy under Fordism, where mass-manufacturing of a certain kind — it was state-of-the-art — was the dominant sector that imposed its rhythms — political, social, legal, etc. — on other sectors of the economy. So it's not enough to say that there are multiple temporalities, though in itself it is a very important observation. Time is problematic because it's been constructed as a chronology of repetition. Temporality is a different kind of construction, where there is a subjection today of certain kinds of conditions to other conditions. Finance has managed to subject other economic sectors to its rhythms, including those sectors like building that we thought could not be made into financial instruments.

Now, Jale's example is very important because it comes back to this notion of the encounter between the global project — which can be carried out by national agents, by the way — and the national project. This really is a frontier zone where a lot of battling is going on. I don't know enough about the central bank in Turkey, but clearly we're talking about an elite that is doing the work of elites in a certain way, and it's resisting certain aspects of globalization. This is part of the point of this notion of denationalizing. It captures the process and the many struggles that are happening, and the sites of these struggles. In my fieldwork now, I'm looking at central banks, at ministries of finance, at courts, at legislatures, etc., in order to understand the battle. It's a frontier zone, but it is inside national territory, which creates its own engagements with existing legal systems.

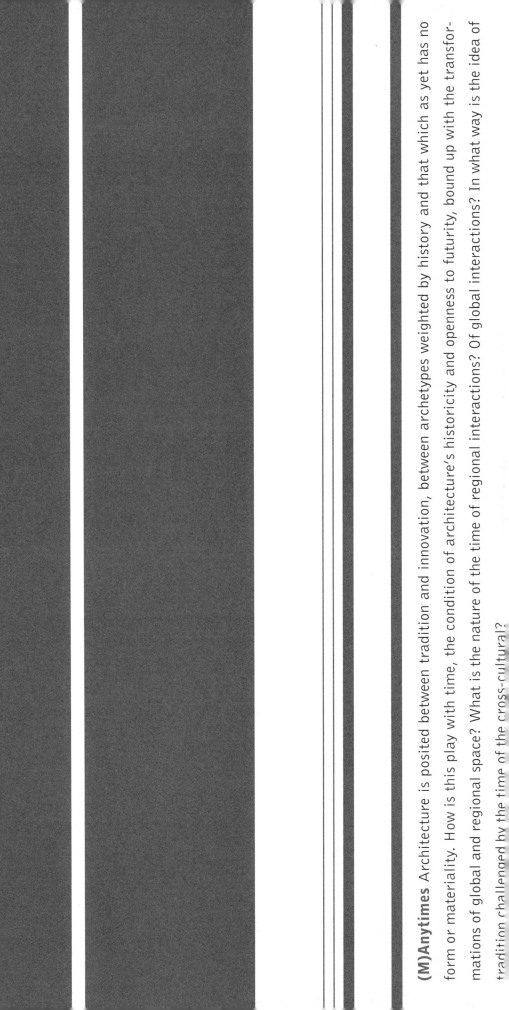

(M)Anytimes Architecture is posited between tradition and innovation, between archetypes weighted by history and that which as yet has no form or materiality. How is this play with time, the condition of architecture's historicity and openness to futurity, bound up with the transformations of global and regional space? What is the nature of the time of regional interactions? Of global interactions? In what way is the idea of tradition challenged by the time of the cross-cultural?

Time Out John Rajchman

1 On the relation between reductive modernism and pastiche, see Rosalind Krauss, *The Picasso Papers* (New York: Farrar, Straus and Giroux, 1998).

2 Le Corbusier's *promenade architecturale* might be seen as an instance of what Deleuze calls a "movement-image" or as matching with the invention of such images in cinema. Beatriz Colomina has opened up the question of the promenade in relation to image and "media culture." (Beatriz Colomina, *Privacy and Publicity*). But it is not sure that the idea of image or medium itself remains constant since the 19th century; and in distinguishing the arrival of time – rather than movement-images in cinema after the war, Deleuze remarks that ours is a civilization not so much of the image as of the cliché, the whole problem being precisely to create a genuine image– *pas un image juste, juste une image*, Godard would say. The relation of photography, video, and cinema to architecture might then be understood in relation to this search for "just an image" in banalized environments. Thus, already with the "disconnected spaces" and "achronological" times of neorealism we already find a whole new relation of the cinematic image to urban spaces (especially in Rome): while with Ozu we find an exploration of the various "times" that make up the traditional Japanese house; or later with Andy Warhol, a kind of "slow down" of the image, together with rituals of waiting. Deleuze associates the turn to such "time-images" with a new "architecture of vision," which would be no longer "gravic" and centered but would approach the light Earth of *trajets et parcours*. With the French New Wave, Deleuze thinks such an "architecture of seeing" frees itself from enclosure in a "veridical narration" of the sort one still finds in neorealism.

3 Mark Wigley "Lost in Space" in *The Critical Landscape*, ed. Michael Speaks, Rotterdam: 010 Publishers, 1996. Wigley returns to Kevin Lynch in an attempt to show how much Fredric Jameson's mapping of "postmodern" space owes to earlier modern assumptions, which

How does one introduce the question of time into architecture, which is traditionally thought to be an art of space? There have been many different views of time itself. I will try to identify some tendencies in architecture or architectural discourse and then ask in what ways they might usefully fit together with a particular philosophical notion of time. My question might be put in this way: what is an architecture that *presents* rather than *represents* time? And what is time when freed from enclosure in any prior movement – when freed from any image of, any story told by, God or Nature?

Francis Yates' study *The Art of Memory* contains a suggestive historical account of how "memory" was inscribed in architecture at a time (Antiquity, The Middle Ages) when it was thought that there existed a sort of hermetic prose of the world, spelled out in the signatures of things. Later, Walter Benjamin would complain that glass boxes, ignoring all traces of time, contribute to a new barbarism of an amnesiac modernity; and perhaps one can see the historicist pastiche of postmodernism as the guilty conscience of that.[1] Today we might discern yet another logic, another formation – perhaps also another view of time. One way to see it is in a departure from classical composition and monumentality in favor of what might be called a noniconic diagrammaticity.

Take, for example, what Rem Koolhaas calls "bigness." Here scale is not colossal or sublime but labyrinthine, without overarching plan. This is what allows him, even in a quite neutral or minimal container, to break up the classical relations of permanence, succession, and simultaneity and introduce diagrams that allow for odd simultaneities, hybridities, and unexpected encounters. In this way Koolhaas arrives at something other architects find along different paths: the Corbusian promenade is interrupted, its narrative broken, multiplied, its exits and entrances displaced, its plan made more informal and complex.[2] We are no longer in the nice postwar world of the "grammar" or orienting "map" dreamt of by Kevin Lynch; in its place, we have a freer space in which many unexpected things can happen at once, without overarching story or program, involving rather different relationships between image and city. It is as if the "time" of habitation had been set free from the "movement-image" and the kind of narrative and memory it makes possible.[3]

Architectures that "present" time in this way are basically not monumental or monumentalizing – or at least they pose the question of the monumental in a new way. There is a strange kind of "secularization"; it is almost as if we no longer feel ourselves capable of iconic or symbolic monumentality in any form other than nostalgia or kitsch. Even traditionally monumental typologies like mosques or museums are no longer linked alienation and disorientation in the 19th-century metropolis. But in making disorientation the supposition of his deconstructive critique, Wigley opens the possibility of another, more diagrammatic kind of orientation in space and time no longer given by window or frame (by perspective or projective geometry). Such an orientation would have the same feature that Deleuze finds in time-images, which allows for a deployment of life no longer subordinated to any veridical narration but forming part of a kind of "new vitalism" of trajectories and passages.

4 Gilles Deleuze, *Essays Critical and Clinical*, trans. Daniel W. Smith and Michael A. Greco (Minneapolis: University of Minnesota Press, 1997); see especially the chapter "What Children Say."

5 Deleuze takes up this Leibnizian theme in *Cinema 2*, trans. Hugh Tomlinson and Robert Galeta (London: Athlone, 1989). After establishing that the presention of time requires a departure from "hodological space" and "Euclidean geometry," he finds that the larger question of "incompossibility" shows how it departs, at the same time, from veridical narration.

6 It is such features that make Francis Bacon "Egyptian" for Deleuze. His figures break with relations of "gazes" in classical narrative painting, and so with "faciality" – the potential "facelessness" of the figures goes with another nonnarrative "spatialization." We might then see them as supposing another and diagrammatic relation to urban space.

7 One of the most sustained discussions of the idea of the missing people comes in chapter 8 of *Cinema 2*, in which Deleuze examines the political implications of time-images in third world and minority film. The idea is also to be found earlier, in Paul Klee's writing about the Bauhaus's lack of popular appeal as well as in Kafka's turn toward a minor literature.

easily understood architecturally in terms of the grand stories they preserve or the grand symbols they embody. Other considerations closer to contemporary demographics are starting to be expressed in their diagrams. Along with a departure from the classical language of geometric composition we thus find the notion of a kind of "nonmonumentalizable" time given diagrammatically through passages and intersections rather than iconically through symbols of the myths of holistic communities or already-given peoples. But what then, philosophically speaking, does such an architectural presentation of time involve? What, for example, does it have to do with the philosophical attempts to imagine a *nomos* or an ethos in which our modes of being would be composed of many times, many trajectories, hence many hybridities and simultaneities? In the 20th century's great philosophical attempts to work out a new concept and image of time in its relation to our very "constructions" of ourselves, we see a move away from mechanical or clock or segmented spatializations. Despite his reservations about the problem of time (too close to "project" or "program"), even Michel Foucault may be said to have rediscovered it in his idea of "histories of the present," the kinds of diagrams they suppose, and the kinds of questions they thereby ask. But among philosophers who have taken on the problem more directly, Gilles Deleuze is perhaps the most free of any Heideggerian mysticism of being and the "unrepresentable" and poses the problem of time rather as a matter of Life – of modes of being and the "plans" of their intersection and composition. He does not need a mysticism of absence and Law to imagine a time outside any "extensive spatialization," any "movement-image."

In his late "clinical" essays concerned with Life, Deleuze talks of an architecture of *trajets et parcours* – of ways of "going through" space and time that cannot be predetermined by any prior plan or fixed subjective position.[4] One might say that this architectural figure of a "diagrammatic" space-time plays a role in his thought (and his view of what it is to think) rather like that of the pyramid in Leibniz or in Hegel. As in those cases, it is a figure of time and possibility. In his *Theodicy*, Leibniz imagined a great pyramid of descending possible worlds. Each level contains another apartment in which something happens to Sextus that leads him to acquire new sorts of predicates or express new "worlds." Deleuze takes this pyramid as the architecture for the Leibnizean concept of "compossibility"; it helps show why the concept is an original one, irreducible to logical consistency or causal regularity. Deleuze uses it to imagine the logic of a situation in which many possible worlds might coexist in a single dynamic space. In such a space at each point in a given history there might arise another history that would redistribute or reorient it. (This is what

Deleuze calls an "event" or a "becoming").[5] It is rather as if the Leibnizian pyramid had been laid out horizontally and turned into a Borgesian garden of ever bifurcating paths – as if a principle of dissonance in disparate multiplicity had taken over from the more baroque music of Leibniz's "preestablished harmony." Instead of Leibniz's principle of the greatest variety for the simplest laws, we would have the idea of the greatest variability among disparate elements along a single plane; and the problem of selecting the "best world" would be replaced by construction of planes without predetermining organization or prior narrative, allowing instead for the chance of new histories, new "possibilities of life" – as Deleuze puts it at one point, many cities at once, and always another city in the city. This is a Fellini-esque encounter, it is precisely the "image" of such a "time of the city" that Deleuze sees cinema as having invented after World War II, starting with the "disconnected spaces" of neorealism. But such a time (and time-image) then involves a notion of potential or "power" (*puissance* rather than *pouvoir*) different from that of the mummified Spirit in the Egyptian pyramid, which Hegel tried to introduce into a grand "veridical narration" of Western philosophy. Deleuze looks to Alois Reigl for another kind of Egyptianism, one given through haptic rather than optic space, where movement is no longer laid out for a single transcendent or external eye of the sort developed by classical perspective but, rather, allows for singular vital points of view to emerge unexpectedly and at once within the same space.[6] As we move away from veridical narration, the problem of East and West shifts; there arise new spaces that allow for becomings belonging to neither. These are just the spaces that Deleuze adduces when, in his discussion of minority and Third World cinema, he advances the principle: the people are missing, the people are yet to come. It is precisely through time-images that cinema appears to such a people yet to be invented, not given in any kind of movement and, in particular, in the mass movements intellectuals have undertaken to represent. For while a majority has a history, only a minority has a becoming. Minority cinema explores this through the superposition of different times and places.[7]

What then does it mean philosophically to imagine time as freed from subordination to prior movement, unfolding instead through the play of disparate elements in unformed or indeterminate spaces? And how then does one "present" rather than "represent" it? Here is one way Deleuze puts the problem: rather than thinking of ourselves, our actions and our inter-relations, as being "in time," we should think of time as being "in us" or "in them" in a way that may divide us from our given selves (public and private). This exposes us to other worlds, other possibilities, other paths and trajectories.

Deleuze finds that Hamlet is the hero of such a time, captured when he declares that "the time is out of joint." Hamlet is not the hero who doubts or is skeptical; rather, he is the one brought to move in this other time that divides him from himself and exposes him to other possible worlds. It is as if with the discovery of this time Shakespeare were departing from what Benjamin thought of as the melancholy of baroque drama. This is what makes Hamlet different from Oedipus, whose destiny is still predetermined by the Law of the City, *his* problem being that he does not know it yet still *wants* to know. Deleuze thus says that this informal time of other possibilities into which Hamlet is plunged is not predetermined by any law and becomes "the time of the city and nothing else" – a time freed from cycles and seasons, no longer dependent on a Nature or a God that would precede it.[8] For the distinction between eternity and temporality tends to match the distinction between the City of God and the City of Man – the second being, of course, an imperfect copy of the first or the law of the first; and what Deleuze finds interesting in Nietzsche's concept of the "untimely" is that this whole eternity-time, God-Man scheme collapses, giving rise to a gay science of what is yet to come. Charles Baudelaire would have a sense of this time associating with the artifices of "modernity" in the 19th-century metropolis. Deleuze finds it as well in the literary theme of being "without qualities," "too smooth" for any quality to stick, as with Herman Melville and "those on the road" in American fiction.

But what happens to this sense of time, this sense of modernity and artifice, in our time or within our contemporary urban conditions? What happens, for example, in the megalopolis or global city where the old practices of flânerie and dérive no longer apply? *Can* we still devise new ways to present this time that is no longer subordinated to prior movement, prior story, or prior image, that allows instead for the odd juxtapositions or simultaneities, disparities, hybridities in the possible worlds of our relations with one another? Or has our problem changed altogether? And assuming it is still possible or desirable today to invent new ways to "present time" outside of movement, what kinds of architecture or architectural discourse would best be suited for it?

Deleuze sees Spinoza, the excommunicated Marrano in the "globalizing" Amsterdam of the 17th century, as formulating a "new vitalism" later developed by Heinrich Kleist and Nietzsche (in contrast to the "organicism" of Goethe and Hegel). Spinoza goes beyond the lingering salvationism in Leibniz's baroque theology to imagine a "plane of immanence" (rather than of "organization") in which singular modes of being are composed; thus he offered a picture of Life prior to the distinction between artifice and nature. In political terms this led him to a view of the city or polis (hence of politics) that might at last free itself from the assumptions of the theological-political tradition; thus Leibniz's sense of "modernity" was rather different from those of theorists of sovereignty like Hobbes, just as (unlike Descartes) he turned "eternity" into an uneliminative potential in life for the emergence of the new. But what might such modernity mean today for our global or globalizing cities and the stories about "modernization" that economists and sociologists are now inclined to tell about them? What – and *how* – would a contemporary Spinoza think? I think he could no longer rely on concepts of "place" or "ground" or "world" (hence of "regionalism" or "abstract space") developed through phenomenology. To imagine spaces that include the times of disparity or hybridity, freeing our modes of being and their composition from prior narrative and allowing new histories to arise in our histories, requires that one depart from the phenomenological "grounding" of space. And yet the philosophers who have departed from such phenomenological views of orientation and grounding in place have often done so in the name of a new transcendence, a sort of mysticism of the incalculable and unrepresentable; only through a kind of "negative theology" have they been able to imagine extracting time from its subordination to the "joints" of a prior movement. This is where a new Spinoza might come in – perhaps there is another more vitalist way for time to go "out of joint," a way that is less religious and more directly concerned with the worldly question of how to compose a life.

Today, of course, phenomenological views are often revived as an antidote to the electronic idealism of placeless interaction; but Spinoza's notion of Life prior to the artifice-nature distinction might point in another direction. Indeed, that is the kind of question Deleuze opens up in the last pages of his book on Foucault, where he talks of the form of such a vital "time out," such a "nowhere" within our contemporary biotechnotopian imagination. In the 1960s Foucault tried to work out in terms of an archaeology of discourse on language what would be supposed by the "madness" of the "absence of oeuvre" in modern literature and painting. Deleuze goes on to remark that today we might pose the same question in terms of the spaces of work and life – in relation to the biotechnological break-up and reformation of life and the digital break-up and reformation of work. The kind of heterotopia that Foucault found in literature and painting might thus be applied to the new biotechnotopia and so allow us to discern "a new form, neither God nor Man, of which one can hope that it will not be worse than the preceding two."[9]

8 Deleuze, "Four Poetic Formulas That Might Resume Kant" in *Essays Clinical and Critical*.

9 Deleuze, *Foucault*, trans. Sean Hand (Minneapolis: University of Minnesota Press, 1988).

JOHN RAJCHMAN TEACHES AT THE COLLÈGE INTERNATIONAL DE PHILOSOPHIE, PARIS. HIS BOOKS INCLUDE **TRUTH AND EROS: FOUCAULT, LACAN, AND THE QUESTION OF ETHICS** AND A COLLECTION OF ESSAYS ON ARCHITECTURE PUBLISHED IN **CONSTRUCTIONS**, PART OF ANYONE CORPORATION'S WRITING ARCHITECTURE SERIES.

16.06.98 MACAU: PORTUGAL WILL SEND POLICE REINFORCEMENTS TO MACAU TO HELP TACKLE SPIRALING CRIME IN THE PORTUGUESE ENCLAVE, WHERE GANGS ARE FIGHTING FOR A PIECE OF THE LUCRATIVE GAMBLING INDUSTRY.

The Emergence of Modern Time-Consciousness in the Islamic World and the Problematics of Spatial Perception

Uğur Tanyeli

Mihrimah Mosque sundial, 18th century.

1 Gerhard Dohrn-van Rossum, *History of the Hour: Clocks and Modern Temporal Orders*, trans. Thomas Dunlap (Chicago: University of Chicago Press, 1996), 13.

2 Lewis Mumford, *Technics and Civilization* (New York: Brace and Company, 1934), 12–18.

According to Werner Sombart, the measurement of time stands as a symbol for a whole cluster of processes of modernization and rationalization.[1] In *Technics and Civilization*, Lewis Mumford claims that the key machine of the industrial age was not the steam engine but the clock and that the first seven centuries of the machine age were characterized by profound changes in the categories of time and space.[2] However, these hypotheses, which were almost immediately accepted and tactfully proven, seem valid only for the Western world and cannot be directly applied to the Islamic realm. Though it was known and used in the Muslim cultural area beginning in the early-16th century, the mechanical clock could not deeply affect, let alone revolutionize, the social and intellectual life in this part of the world at the same pace that it had in Europe. The problematics of modern time-consciousness in the Islamic world seem more confusing, because the conception of modern abstract time and, in a broader sense, the process of alienation from nature are related not only to the mechanical construction of the clock but also to the social construction of time, which is indirectly connected with the former. This means that in the Muslim world, the mechanical clock alone was insufficient to dissolve the space-time unity which characterized all premodern societies. I will analyze the Islamic – and in some respects, all non-Western – resistance toward the construction of modern time-consciousness and its relationship with the problematics of spatial perception.

Before attempting this, an explanation is necessary; as far as the clock and modern time-consciousness are concerned, there is no sufficient information on its role in Islamic societies beyond those of the Ottoman world. The lacuna of references can be attributed to the relatively indifferent attitude of non-Ottoman cultures to the clock. They were not in such close contact with the West as were the Ottomans, who had a geographic proximity to Europe. This means that everything that can be said about Islamic societies regarding timepieces is based on the data obtained from Ottoman Turkey.

In Europe the manufacture of mechanical clocks first began in the 14th century. Turkey was the first Islamic country to encounter clocks, as early as the second half of the 15th century. There is nothing to indicate that mechanical clocks were made, imported to, or even known within the Islamic realm before that time. The first evidence of a Muslim wanting a clock comes from an early-16th-century Italian source, which states that after 1477, the Ottoman Sultan, Mehmed II the Conqueror, asked the Venetian government to send him a clock maker, a painter, and a maker of "cristallini" (probably lenses).[3] The reliability of this source is doubtful, however. Within the extremely broad historical literature of the Turco-Italian relations in the age of Mehmed II (1452–81), there is no information verifying a request for a clock maker at all. Nevertheless, the mechanical clock became widely known in the 16th-century Ottoman world. Clocks were imported and, after the late-16th century, produced in Turkey both by Muslims and by Europeans who settled in the Pera district of Istanbul.[4]

The history of the mechanical clock and watch in the Ottoman world is a unique case study that warrants broader discussion because of the cultural problems that emerged as Muslim society imported another society's technological novelty. The time-measuring machine quickly became a sign bearing new meanings in Ottoman Turkey, from the beginnings of its history until its collapse in the early-20th century. Put another way, the region underwent a "crisis of the clock." The

3 Francesco Suriano, *Il trattato di Terra Santa e dell'Oriente*, ed. Girolamo Golubovich (Milan: Editrice Artigianelli, 1900), 94. Quoted in Otto Kurz, *European Clocks and Watches in the Near East* (London: Warburg Institute, 1975), 20–21.

4 For Turkish clock- and watchmaking see P. Ülkümen, "Saatçiligimiz" in *Türk Etnografya Dergisi* (Istanbul, 1961) 4: 14–19. For European clock makers in Istanbul see Kurz's book, and A. Babel, "L'horlogerie genevoise a Constantinople et dans le Levant du XVI au XVIIIe siecle" in *Etrennes Genevoises* (Geneve, 1927), 61–74.

5 Dohrn-van Rossum, History of the Hour; David S. Landes, Revolution of Time: Clocks and the Making of the Modern World (Cambridge: Belknap Press, 1983).

clock also obtained new meanings in Europe, the site of its invention, but the semiotics of the clock in the Ottoman world were quite different from those in Europe. In every society, in fact, every technological "novelty" tends to be revalued semiotically within a new context that may gradually diminish its relation with the functional reality on which it is originally based. Because of this semiotical revaluation process, it can be said that each society has its own techno-cultural history. On the other hand, it can also be claimed that the techno-cultural history of a society is almost autonomous of the technological contents of its material culture. Theoretically, the equality of the technical/technological accumulations of any two societies never means that these two must have identical techno-cultural histories. For obvious reasons, this hypothesis has to be especially true of premodern societies. Different techno-cultural traditions operate differently in the context of the emergence of modern time-consciousness and the modern space-time conception.

The clock's history and complications in Europe were entirely different from its story in Turkey and elsewhere in the Islamic world.[5] In Europe the techno-cultural history of the clock did not lead to a denial of its functional or technical reality. One of its techno-cultural meanings was as a sign of prestige, not dissimilar to any rare and expensive item. For example, the clock quickly became a source of pride for an urban community, not unlike a large public building. First cities and then individuals regarded clock ownership as a sign of privilege. For several centuries, owning a clock or watch indicated social rank. The more expensive it was, the more strongly it indicated that its owner was a member of a tiny minority.

The second techno-cultural meaning of the clock in Europe was even more important in the *longue durée*. For the first time in history, the clock imposed on society and the individual a new rhythm and order of everyday life, totally free of the natural tempo of the day. All scholarly studies of the clock present it as the instigator of the emergence of modern time-consciousness. Social practices were organized according to a new rhythm. For example, one historical account shows that the people of Lyon wanted to have a new public clock for two basic reasons: first, they thought Lyon needed a decoration and a sign of prosperity, second, they needed a more orderly life.[6] Surprisingly, in a completely pre-industrial urban community, the precise determination, or measurement, of time and "a more orderly life" were quite useless, given the rhythm of life within the functional basis of this social system. It seems that the people of Lyon expressed not a "genuine" necessity but an "artificial" or "fictive" one that was mentally imposed on them by the clock itself. The abstract order of time of the mechanical clock was shaping the order of everyday life, even though it was almost unnecessary, given the organizational level of the productive forces in late medieval European society.

Nevertheless, it is widely accepted that all techniques and technologies condition lifestyles and mentalities in all ages. The clock, however, was quite different from the devices known at the time; it was the first "absolute" substitute for a natural reality in all of history. Before the clock, the order of everyday life was defined by the sun. As far as its temporal function is concerned, the clock gradually put the sun "out of order" and substituted for it, thus becoming the first "ersatz" object in history. Prior to the invention of the clock all technical devices, tools, and machines were merely auxiliary or supplementary to the means provided by nature. The clock, in contrast, is not a mechanism functioning to cooperate with nature. It cannot contribute to the preexisting means of

6 E. Vial and C. Cote, Les horloges lyonnais de 1550 à 1650 (Lyon, 1927), 4. Quoted in Carlo M. Cipolla, Clocks and Culture 1300–1700 (New York: Norton, 1978), 42.

7 Anthony Giddens, The Consequences of Modernity (Cambridge: Polity Press, 1991). 16.

8 Ibid., 17.

9 Ibid., 20.

nature. It is completely autonomous and forces men to live not according to the rhythm of nature but to a new order that it itself determines. This transformation formed the main axis within the process of the emergence of modern time-consciousness and modern space-time conception in Europe. For this reason, the techno-cultural history of the Western world should be divided in half, with the invention of the clock as a fulcrum, a historiographical division between the modern and premodern eras.

As concisely defined by Anthony Giddens, the separation of time and space is directly related with modernity so as to be one of the sources of its dynamical nature.[7] According to Giddens, until the uniformity of the techniques of measurement achieved by the mechanical clock found its expression in social organizations, time had always been thought in relation to a definite space. In other words, in premodern societies time could only be defined in terms of space. In such a society "no one could tell the time of day without reference to other socio-spatial markers: 'when' was almost universally either connected with 'where' or identified by regular natural occurrences."[8] But along with the diffusion of the use of the mechanical clock, this system began to evolve into the modern socio-temporal order, which depends on the dissolution of time-space unity. "The separating of time and space and their formation into standardised, 'empty' dimensions cut through the connections between social activity and its 'embedding' in the particularities of contexts of presence."[9]

What does Giddens mean by the formation of time and space into empty dimensions? In a premodern society, time and space could only be described – not defined – by what they contained. This means that time was described by the sequence of successive events or the chronological order of occurrences in a definite

place. On the other hand, space was an area spontaneously or intentionally organized to be the scene of some kind of activity – personal, communal, urban, and so forth. In this respect, space and time were only perceived socially and only within the culture of the society that created them. For this reason, no foreigner could understand and convert the spatio-temporal reality of another premodern culture into his or her own, even if he or she lived contemporaneously with it. Modernity, in contrast, defines time and space as separate categories with their own units of measurement. They are categories of reality that are measurable, calculable, and rational. In other words, time and space owe their autonomy in the modern world to the technical means that measure them; or, what make modern concepts of time and space are the specific measuring techniques employed to "represent" them. Time is represented not by the regular occurrence of a natural event but by the universally valid hour and its subdivisions. Space, on the other hand, is represented in its three-dimensionality by geometrical-mathematical techniques like surveying, descriptive geometry, and artificial perspective.

It is noteworthy that dissimilar historical processes occurred in the Islamic world. Contrary to its achievements in the West, the clock was unable to dissolve the space-time unity in the Islamic world for almost four centuries. We must, therefore, reconsider not only the history of modernization in the Muslim cultural area, but also the same process as it occurred in Europe. The scholars of the historical process of Western modernization generally tend to exalt the clock as the main factor of modern time-consciousness. But the process of the emergence of modern time-consciousness in the Islamic world cannot be explained in such a mechanically deterministic way. One has to think that the construction of the modern

10 For the sun quadrant and its use as a timepiece in the Islamic world see Muammer Dizer, *Rubu Tahtası* (Istanbul: Boğaziçi Üniversitesi, 1987).

space-time concept in Europe was a more complex problem. And paradoxically, as far as time-consciousness is concerned, the historical transformation toward modernity in the Muslim world may also provide the clues for reconsidering the same process in Europe.

The techno-cultural adventure of the clock in the Islamic, or Ottoman, world was almost completely different in its uses and meanings. In the West the clock substituted for the sun, but in Ottoman Turkey and the Islamic world in general, it "supplemented" it. The clock did not punctuate and determine the rhythm or order of everyday life. Rather, its function was restricted in an already differently determined socio-temporal life. The socio-temporal life of a Muslim continued to be shaped by the five prayer times (*salat*), which were, and still are, calculated daily according to the sun's position in the sky. Besides daily prayer times, fasting times in the month of Ramadan also necessitate the use of temporal hours – the unequal hours of the preclock era. In this system, sundials, astrolabes, and, later, sun quadrants were unavoidable devices that made the temporal order work in the predesignated manner of religious dogma.[10]

Thus, even before its penetration into Ottoman Turkey, the mechanical clock would not determine and condition the tempo of social life, for the essential punctuation of everyday life in a traditional Islamic society was by definition not secular but strictly religious. Since the clock could not radically challenge this reality alone, Ottomans who confronted these two unavoidable realities had to construct a consensus between the traditional religious socio-temporal order and the clock's equal, abstract hours. The result was the setting system called *alla turca*, in which hours were equal – contrary to the first Japanese experiments with the mechanical clock – but determined according to Muslim socio-temporal needs. In this

setting system, sunset was determined as 12 o'clock, and all clocks had to be reset daily – or every two days – according to the continuously changing time of the sunset. It can be said that the alla turca clock, which took sunset as its reference point, did not measure time but counted hours from sunset to sunset. Thus the socio-temporal life of the Ottoman world was still dependent on the natural rhythm of the sun, not on the mathematical or digital order imposed by mechanical clocks. Because of this not modern but perhaps proto-modern time-consciousness, even in the late-19th century, the sun quadrant remained practically the sole instrument utilized by the *muvakkits* (experts who determined the prayer hours). Sundials, too, were still in use. Even at the beginning of the 20th century, the *muvakkithane* (office of the *muvakkits*) of Yeni Cami in Istanbul, while not an observatory in the modern European manner, functioned as an Ottoman "Greenwich," determining prayer hours for the metropolis.

In the alla turca system, the mechanical clock and the sun were functionally collaborative elements. The practical uses of this collaboration are worth investigating. Apparently, there was no practical use for this time measurement system until the 19th century. In spite of the large number of clocks imported into the Ottoman world from the 16th century onward, almost no Ottoman text refers to the use of the clock for a precise determination of time for ordinary purposes. The alla turca hours only became useful in the second half of the 19th century, when Western-style schools were founded, theaters opened, and public transportation systems began to operate. Before the heyday of modernization in the Ottoman world, though clocks were widely known, imported, produced, and bought, the sun continued to be the primary source that punctuated the rhythm of daily life, even for the upper classes. These facts disprove the historian Otto Kurz's assumption that "the increasing use of mechanical clocks and watches led to the same results in the Christian and Muhammedan worlds: the temporal hours died out in ordinary life and equal hours took their place."[11] Rather, the situation in the Islamic world did not change for several centuries. Temporal hours were abolished here only after they had become a huge obstacle to modernity, and even then, the modern socio-temporal order could hardly efface the temporal hours in the personal and social life of the Muslim. Turkey, the first Islamic country to abolish the traditional temporal order only did so in 1925. Until the 1960s, Saudi Arabians, the most conservative of all Muslims, continued to set their clocks and watches alla turca, which they called the "Arabic way."

What, then, made clocks and watches such widely appreciated objects in a society that insisted on ignoring their utilitarian dimension?

In spite of its discarded principal function, what made the clock useful in Ottoman Turkey was a process of revaluation that made it "functional" within the existing cultural system. The clock functioned in the classical Ottoman world (16th and 17th centuries) as an object of tribute or as a gift. Among the Ottoman upper classes, official, reciprocal tribute-paying and gift-giving, which was sometimes misinterpreted as bribery by the Europeans, was a sociopolitical practice. The social system expected members of the upper class and foreigners to pay tribute as a way to denote hierarchical status. Gift-giving practices brought European clocks to the Ottomans, since almost every European envoy who arrived in Istanbul preferred to present the sultan and high officials with mechanical clocks – the most valuable and sophisticated of European gifts and therefore an unsurpassed novelty in the East. This Western preference led the Ottoman upper classes to regard the clock

primarily as a tribute object or a gift. Surprisingly, the Ottoman bureaucratic elite began to value and even request this instrument. For example, the tribute money paid to the Ottoman state in the 16th century by the Austrian government was accompanied by clocks because of the overwhelming demand expressed by the Ottomans.[12]

The situation was not dissimilar in China, where the upper classes also became increasingly fond of clocks through European envoys. Yet the Chinese passion for the clock was distinct from that of the Ottomans, for the Chinese appreciated the clock as a sort of mechanical toy or automaton, regardless of its use value.[13] In Ottoman Turkey, however, the clock was not considered a toy but something to be stockpiled as indicative of material wealth, high social status, and political influence. For example, the prominent Syrian-Ottoman scholar Taqi ed-din learned the mechanics of the clock by studying the Western instruments in Ali Pasha's house.[14] Traditional Ottoman society regarded the clock as something precious that had to be presented to a member of the upper class as a sign of reverence by a subordinate. What is important in an act of reverence is not the object that accompanies it but the act itself, thus we can conclude that in Ottoman Turkey the utilitarian function of the clock yielded to the social meaning it obtained in upper-class culture. For example, Salomon Schweigger, a German who was in Turkey from 1581 to 1591, wrote that the sultan's clocks were piled up in a room in the palace and not much attention was paid to their maintenance.[15] Nearly a century later, the Frenchman Tavernier similarly wrote that he was told by an Ottoman official that many clocks were in the treasury of Topkapi Palace.[16]

Among the members of the Ottoman upper classes, the clock seems to have been the sine qua non of hierarchical status. Clock-owner-

11 Kurz, European Clocks and Watches, 83.

12 Ibid., 30–42.

13 For the Chinese attitude toward clocks see Cipolla, Clocks and Culture, 30–42, and the sources mentioned therein.

14 S. Tekeli, 16. Yüzyılda Osmanlılarda Saat ve Takiyüddin'in "Mekanik Saat Konstrüksiyonuna Dair en Parlak Yıldızlar" Adlı Eseri (Ankara, 1966).

15 Salomon Schweigger, Ein newe Reyssbeschreibung aus Teutschland nach Constantinopel und Jerusalem (1604; reprint Graz: Akademische Druck, 1964 reprint of the 1604 edition), 61.

16 Jean-Baptiste Tavernier, Nouvelle relation de l'interieur du serrail du Grand Seigneur (Paris: Olivier de Varennes, 1675), 128–29.

ship, moreover, became almost a privilege granted to them, or at least the Ottoman system was not very tolerant of a broader ownership. The clock was a luxury, and like all luxuries in the Ottoman world, its use was limited to the bureaucratic upper class. The prevailing opinion was expressed by one of the most prominent and prolific of its early-17th-century representatives, Gelibolulu Ali, who writes in his book *Kava'idü'l-Mecalis* (Rules of the Communities):

> Especially Persian and Egyptian rugs and carpets, gold-embroidered sofa spreads, precious cushions and table mats, silver basins and candlesticks, gilded platters and silver incense-burners, likewise golden and silver pen-cases, and gilded chiming clocks . . . without doubt, have to be the privilege of those famed ones at the highest peak, the viziers and generals of eminence. Men of lower status, who ventured to have them, have to be lashed and punished severely by sharp-tongued critics because of this abuse.[17]

This cultural attitude made the members of the Ottoman upper classes keen "collectors" of clocks. Among them was Kapuağasi Yakub Ağa, whose property came to the Imperial Treasury after he died during the reign of Mehmed IV (1648–87). According to the inventory of his belongings, which is now in the archives of Topkapi Palace, he had numerous clocks.[18] Some high-ranking officials were not content merely to purchase these devices and employed personal clock makers in their households.[19] Without a doubt, this was the rarest privilege, and it was restricted to a distinguished few, such as Sokollu Mehmed Pasha, the grand vizier of Suleyman the Magnificent (1520–66).

Additional evidence that clocks had nothing to do with the socio-temporal life of traditional Islamic society was the rarity of clock towers or public clocks. There were some clock towers in 16th-century Ottoman Rumelia, but they were exceptional structures whose existence can be explained by some curious historical accidents. For example, the clock tower of Üsküp (modern Skopje in Macedonia) was built in 1566, and the clock that was reinstalled on it had been seized in the Hungarian city of Szeged when it fell to the Ottomans.[20] It can be seen as a sort of war memorial. It is certain that, contrary to Kurz's supposition, clock towers in the European part of the Ottoman Empire were not the remnants of the pre-Ottoman past of the Balkans.[21] Even though such structures were built in the Ottoman period, conventionally, the minaret from which muezzin announced daily prayer times – the temporal hours – continued to be more useful in fulfilling the needs of a Muslim society than the clock tower. The historian O.G. de Busbecq, who first tried to explain why there were no clock towers in Ottoman Turkey, assumed that the reason was the fear of undermining the muezzins' authority, but we know that muezzins themselves had, and have, no authority.[22] It is true, however, that in the Islamic world the mechanical clock was made almost useless by religious dogma, which maintained basic temporal order in society by decreeing five prayer times a day. In other words, what limited the number of clock towers in the Ottoman world was not the muezzins' authority but the semiological priority of the minaret itself. Perhaps the clock tower was regarded as an architectural and symbolic rival of the minaret, the very "concretization" of the socio-temporal order. The clock tower, however, was the concretization of a different, more secular, socio-temporal order, and for this reason, Ottomans built clock towers in the second half of the 19th century, when they intended to "secularize" the routine of daily life along with the newly emerging consciousness moving toward complete social modernization.

Doubtless clocks had, and have, some functions other than their social role. For example,

17 Gelibolulu Ali, *Kava'idü'l-Mecalis*, ms., Süleymaniye Library, Istanbul, Resid Ef., n.1146, fol. 139. For status symbols in Ali's works in general see Andreas Tietze, "Mustafa Ali on Luxury and the Status Symbols of Ottoman Gentlemen", in *Studia Turcologica Memoriae Alexii Bombaci Dicata*, ed. Aldo Gallotta and Ugo Marazzi (Naples, 1982), 577–90.

18 W. Meyer, *Topkapi Sarayi Müzesindeki Saatlerin Katalogu* (Istanbul, n.d., booklet in Turkish, English, German, and French), unpaged.

19 On clock makers employed in the houses of some high-ranking Ottoman officials see Kurz, *European Clocks and Watches*, 48–49.

20 S. Tihich, "Islamska Umjetnost na tlu Jugoslavije", in *Svijet Islama:Vjera, Mandi, Kultura*, ed. B. Lewis (Belgrade, 1979), 320.

21 Kurz, *European Clocks and Watches*, 99–100. All clock towers in the European part of the Ottoman Empire, except those in Hungary, must have been built in the Ottoman era, because the Ottoman conquest of the Balkans was so early (first half of the 14th to the early–15th centuries) that the installation of public clocks before that period was chronologically impossible.

22 O.G. de Busbecq, *The Life and Letters of O.G. de Busbecq*, ed. C.T. Forster and F.H.B. Daniell (London, 1881), 255.

23 Tekeli, 16. Yüzyılda Osmanlılarda Saat ve Takiyüddin'in.

24 Ömer Barkan, "Edirne Askeri Kassamı'na Ait Tereke Defterleri (1545–1659)" in Belgeler.Türk Tarih Belgeleri Dergisi, III/5–6, 1968, 224f., 414–16, inventories no. 35 and 87.

25 Meyer, Topkapı Sarayı.

astronomical observations required the use of mechanical clocks. Taqi ed-din, among the first astronomers to use the clock, founded an observatory in Istanbul and wrote the first handbook on clock making.[23] But his early attempt did not survive, and astronomical activities soon ceased in Turkey and in the whole Islamic world. The clock's astronomical life was extremely short in Muslim countries.

The least documented part of the history of the clock in the Ottoman Empire is its domestic use from the 16th to the 18th centuries. Several reasons lead us to believe that domestic clocks were extremely rare. For example, 16th- and early-17th-century *tereke defteris* (legal inheritance inventories) of the city of Edirne reveal that only the *bostancıbaşis* (high-ranking palace officials) had clocks.[24] This means that most clocks were in the hands of the upper classes. Curiously enough, clocks also appeared in mosques, where they might be used as a sort of confirmation for the time measured by other instruments according to the position of the sun. When the sun could not be observed because of the weather – Turkey is less sunny than the other Islamic countries – the prayer times could not be easily determined. Perhaps for this reason, the first documentary evidence of clocks in the Ottoman world belongs to the age of Bayezit II (1481–1512), who bought three European clocks, two of which were purchased for mosques. One was placed in the "New Mosque" (today Bayezit Mosque in Istanbul) and the second in Hagia Sofia Mosque.[25]

Nevertheless, the use of clocks in mosques cannot be seen as a mere fulfillment of a functional necessity to tell time. There were symbolic concerns behind this use. A precious object like a clock was thought to be appropriate to a mosque. Perhaps it was seen as a very expensive embellishment that could only be used in a sultan's mosque. In this sense,

clocks employed in mosques were also status symbols that indicated the importance of the institutions in which they were placed.

This brief historical analysis should not mislead us into thinking that medieval Islamic societies – whose techniques of time measurement were more advanced than those of the West – did not invent the mechanical clock before Europe because their religious attitude restricted them to the use of unequal natural hours. Nor should we assume that what made imported clocks practically useless in the Muslim world was religion's domination over social life. Such an analysis is only half correct. Though we cannot ignore the role of religious dogma in traditional Islamic society, we have to admit that similar dogmas existed elsewhere with the same vitality. If one considers the conflict between the abstract, equal, "secular" hours and the religious socio-temporal system in medieval Europe, it can easily be seen that religious obstacles were effective not only in the Islamic world. Dohrn-van Rossum's scholarship has revealed the complications of "church hours" in Europe.[26] Nor was religion the only opponent of modern time-consciousness. The scholar who wants to understand the problematics of space-time in Islamic societies has to further penetrate their inner intellectual and organizational structures.

Such an investigation cannot be done here, but we must at least realize that the clock did not dissolve space-time unity in the Muslim countries with the same ease that it did in the West. At least the mechanical clock was insufficient by itself. Contrary to common belief, the mechanical clock is not a magical instrument of modernity. It did not alter the socio-temporal life of Islamic societies during the first four centuries of its existence. To have made a radical transformation, the active part of the daily life of the Muslim needed to change structurally in order to add an important part of the

26 Dohrn-van Rossum, History of the Hour, 231.

16.06.98 ISTANBUL: A BOMB EXPLODES IN THE KARAKÖY DISTRICT, LEAVING 12 PEOPLE INJURED. AN ANONYMOUS CALLER CLAIMS RESPONSIBILITY ON BEHALF OF THE FUNDAMENTALIST, TERRORIST ORGANIZATION IBDA-C.

night to the daytime. In the modern socio-temporal system, night is an extension of day. In a traditional socio-temporal system, however, people wake up with the dawn and go to sleep at sunset. Such a society does not need sophisticated lighting equipment because they do not extend the day into the night. This can only be done by the abstract temporal order defined by mechanisms unrelated to the position of the sun in the sky.

Modern time-consciousness not only dissolves space-time unity but also ignores the human biorhythm. The Ottoman clocks, however, thanks to the setting system described above, chimed in accordance with the human biorhythm, which was defined astronomically. Ottomans lived their daily lives according to the path of the sun in the sky. Modern man lives according to the abstract rhythm of a clock that does not correspond to the astronomical cycles. Ottomans did not need to have much light in their interiors other than that provided by the sun. If one studies *tereke defteris* stretching from the 15th to the early 20th centuries, one seldom finds references to domestic lighting equipment. These extremely detailed inventories contain very few references to artificial lighting other than simple artifacts like candles, which satisfied the most primary needs in a direct way. For example, no one observed or was informed about the existence of a domestic chandelier in the Ottoman world before the second half of the 19th century. Ottoman architecture before modernization was an architecture of daylight. Not only domestic buildings but even the most technically advanced masonry structures verify this fact. The issue awaits detailed analysis.

The history of the clock in the Ottoman world reveals that technological transfers alone are not necessarily consequences of, or impulses for, a society's modernization. In other words,

modernity is not inherent in "modern" objects, whatever their significance may be. A traditional society can easily accept and adapt a technology and/or its products without being so influenced as to change structurally. Therefore, it can be said that what makes a society "open" and modern is not merely its ability to transfer foreign techniques. Throughout its long history, Ottoman culture was always eager to adopt, use, and even perfect not only clock making but many other techniques and technologies.[27] This eagerness, however, did not lead the Ottoman society to modernity, industrialization, and "openness" along the same lines as Western Europe. What needs to be investigated in this and similar cases is not only the know-how transfer itself but the process of revaluation of the transferred technology within its new social environment. It seems that every techno-cultural encounter initiates a mechanism of revaluation in order to work. The society that confronts the necessity of borrowing some cultural and/or technological phenomena also reevaluates borrowed materials in a new context that can be completely alien to their original uses and meanings. Within this process of revaluation, borrowed materials and technologies begin to be remolded into more acceptable forms in order to be internalized by this society. A technique or know-how can become a component of a techno-cultural system only after this internalization process. The Ottomans internalized the clock that they imported from the West in an existing premodern context of their own; thus they could not employ it to destroy traditional space-time unity.

Why is the separation of time and space and its perception by non-Western societies crucially important for architecture? What are the architectural consequences of the delay of the dissolution of time-space unity in the Islamic world?

27 This is a long-neglected part of Ottoman history. For a study which ignores the revaluation processes, see R. Murphey, "The Ottoman Attitude Towards the Adoption of Western Technology: the Role of Efrenci Technicians in Civil and Military Applications," in *Contributions à l'histoire économique et sociale de l'Empire Ottoman*, ed. Jean-Louis Bacque-Grammont and Paul Dumont (Paris, 1983), 287–98.

The dissolution of time-space unity had to be the raison d'être for modern architectural discourse and utopian thinking. What obligated architecture to be considered from outside the context of actual "built reality" was this disconnection, which created "empty" categories of time and space on which to speculate. In order to construct an epistemologically autonomous architectural theory, the first step should be to isolate architectural practice from its spatio-temporal reality. The premodern Islamic world, however, could discuss architecture in three hybrid textual frames, none of which could threaten the time-space unity; on the contrary, they indirectly stiffened it. Consequently, the three frames in which architecture was discussed can hardly be described as an architectural discourse. They were merely extensions of other, long-established traditional discourses into the realm of architecture. The first frame was legal discourse, in which architectural issues took place only as a part of legal practice. The second was bureaucratic discourse, in which architecture was discussed when it became an issue concerning the state. Ottoman archives contain numerous examples of this, showing that architectural matters took place within the interstices of bureaucratic activity and actual building practice. The third hybrid frame was the historical discourse, which only considered architecture in the context of the history of a city or a political entity.

Until the late-19th century, the Islamic world did not produce a theoretical essay on architecture because of these attitudes, which perceived building activities merely as independent cases. In this cultural geography architecture could not be conceived within a conceptual frame regarded as valid for all future structures and all cases. Architecture, however, can only be conceptualized if one isolates it from the actual problematics of building practice. Islamic societies did not go beyond the discussion of the actual building practice and related issues, which are inherently space-time bound.

On the other hand, utopia – a main distinguishing feature of which is defined by Françoise Choay as a model society "located outside of our system of spatio-temporal coordinates" – could also only be realized within the modern "empty" categories of time and space.[28] If one wants to imagine an ideal society, one has to mentally reconstruct it by dissociating the society in which he or she lives from the actual spatio-temporal reality.

I will not discuss utopia and architectural discourse epistemologically here. I intend only to define the complexities of the problematics of separating time and space. In order to dissolve the space-time unity and to create these two "empty" dimensions in the Islamic world, all of the structures and patterns of perception that prevented Muslims from conceiving of the spatial and temporal realities mathematically, or rationally, had to be demolished. This has begun in the last two centuries, and this gigantic social transformation has involved an entire reformatting of all intellectual, visual, and spatial culture. This has been a complex and difficult process, one which is far from completion today. The premodern systems were much more sound than can be recognized at first sight. Neither the clocks of the past nor the computers of today could painlessly destroy it. Modernity was, and still is, not inherent in its artifacts.

UĞUR TANYELI IS A PROFESSOR OF ARCHITECTURAL HISTORY AT THE YILDIZ TECHNICAL UNIVERSITY IN ISTANBUL. HE IS THE AUTHOR OF TWO BOOKS AND NUMEROUS ARTICLES ON MODERNIZATION AND ARCHITECTURE IN THE NON-WESTERN WORLD.

28 Françoise Choay, The Rule and the Model: On the Theory of Architecture and Urbanism, ed. Denise Bratton (Cambridge and London: The MIT Press, 1997), 34.

Diasync Bernard Tschumi

1.0   POLEMICS

1.1   It is less what a building looks like that counts than what it does.

1.2   It is less where a building sits in history that counts than what events and simultaneities it triggers.

1.3   It is less the diachronic than the synchronic that counts – less memory and its obverse, projection, than unexpected simultaneities.

1.3.1   Flashback: To revive an old structuralist diagram (as if there were two specific "times" in architecture):

Synchronic Time (simultaneities)

Diachronic Time

Bernard Tschumi Architects, Proposal for the Museum of Modern Art Expansion, 1997.

2.0   ABOUT SIMULTANEITIES

2.1   Simultaneities of movement / form / experience: architecture's multiple temporalities.

2.1.1   Simultaneity of movements = architecture as dynamics.

Simultaneity of forms = architecture as heterogeneity.

Simultaneity of experiences = architecture as (see 3.6).

2.2   Is there a simultaneity that collapses the movement of history into a single set of images, which at no moment tells a story? Is there an anti-narrative?

2.2.1   I have never been terribly interested in diachronic time, in the idea of moving from past to present to future. (Today everyone seems to be writing or rewriting history; every building seems to "have" a story or to "be" a story.)

3.1 Fragments of narrative are narrative, too.

3.2 Jean-Luc Godard, in **Breathless** and **Alphaville**, and Raymond Chandler, in **The Big Sleep**, do not tell a story; they establish a sequence of simultaneities. Pauline Réage in **The Story of O** does not tell a story; she sets up simultaneities (much like Sade does in **Justine**). In **Ulysses**, James Joyce is not so much telling a story as he is dealing with simultaneities.

3.3 A good film or story is non-narrative (i.e., a-narrative in the sense of a moral). It is even better when you miss the beginning and do not see the end.

3.3.1 For example, good pornographic movies or texts have no real beginning or end; they are made up of simultaneities.

3.4 In Godard's latest film, **Histoire(s) du Cinéma**, the narrative is not linear; it jumps back and forth. Montage relativizes the narrative using jumpcuts, fade-in/ fade-out, juxtaposition, and superimposition. Is there one "true" history, or are there several true histories? As Godard says, "There are only relative truths." There are also only relative narratives.

3.5 Does pornography require a story or script (a narrative) to achieve its aims? In their crudest and most precise description, are not images sufficient? To eliminate all narrative and, consequently, all meaning in order to achieve immediate effect – this is one aim of making images collide in the service of an exacerbated sensuality. A porno film without a story, a cinema without a story – this is not only possible but, as everybody knows, not unpleasant.

3.6 We also know, however, that eroticism is not to be neglected. It is the source of another type of pleasure, which is more diffuse. Eroticism is narrative; it is temporal; it tends to heterogeneity and intertextuality. In contrast, pornography is spatial; it tends to autonomy, to homogeneity; it is abstract.

3.7 How to combine refined desire and brute pleasure, representation and abstraction?

many questions

4.0 DISTINGUISHING PROGRAM AND EVENT

4.1 Program is about time as duration, in which a previous state cannot be separated precisely from a future state.

4.1.1 Program is about fixity and repetition. It fixes states.

4.2 "Event" is about simultaneities, irreversible moments, and discontinuities. (You cannot predict events.)

4.3 To cite Fernand Braudel: Program suggests a homogeneous and unified space / time. "Event" is about unpredictable rupture and dislocation.

4.4 Intelligence understands repetition (program but not "event"). Intelligence is only practical; it fixes states.

4.5 Braudel again: Against a view of history as made only of a succession of events, for events inevitably reveal longer cycles and durations.

Continuity = homogeneous and unified, without layers or series: a slow evolution of history.

Discontinuity = phenomenon of dislocation, rupture within the social throughout history.

Social discontinuity = structural break.

No more singular or unitary history but many histories, partial histories, multiple histories.

4.6 If architecture throughout history has been about duration and continuity, can it now be rethought to be also about simultaneities – so that the simultaneity of time, form, space, politics, and events would reveal a truly heterogeneous history of architecture?

5.1 John Rajchman, citing Deleuze, has said: "Time becomes a form." I could not agree more.

5.1.1 Time, however, has always been an **abstract** form (an a priori of knowledge, as Kant said).

5.2 To paraphrase Henri Bergson: Time is not a thing of the past but is appropriated as an **act**, with its creative or unpredictable dimension.

5.3 Time cannot be solidified. Architecture as frozen music, as frozen time, is exactly what these points are **not** about.

5.4 Any representation of time in space (for example, a line divided into homogeneous intervals) misses **duration**. It fixes states instead of understanding the fluidity or mobility, the movement itself. To use such a spatial diagram shows how intelligence tends not to understand duration.

5.4.1 Real time, experienced time = duration. It is a qualitative time, continuous and unexpected, where a previous state **cannot** be separated from a future state.

5.5 A dynamic architecture as opposed to a static one?

Our design for the spatial organization of the new MoMA reflects our view that architectural considerations are never independent of urban circumstances, and that the internal logic of a building must respond to its external conditions. In order to reflect its own "historicity," the unique texture of time and culture that distinguishes its period and needs from others, the new MoMA could introduce a new form of museum by reversing conventional a priori. We therefore proposed three reversals which, together, constitute an operative concept rather than an arrangement of arbitrary forms.

1ST REVERSAL The museum is not conceived as a sculptural object but as an interior city or route. Its exterior form must be derived from and expressive of its interior dimensions. Moreover, the route is not a linear sequence with a fixed beginning, middle, and end but a multiple sequence that can be accessed at many points.

2ND REVERSAL The new MoMA is not a unitary totality but a heterotopia. It combines three distinct types on its site: a received type – the museum's historical 25-square-foot column grid and double bay – for its departments; a borrowed type – the columnless factory – for its temporary exhibitions; and a new type – our proposal for fixed spaces, variable spaces, and interspaces – for the permanent collection.

3RD REVERSAL The third reversal is strategic rather than constructed. It is about architecture as form. The constraints of the site, program, and zoning regulations are such that imposing a simple external model onto it would be a losing proposition. A different strategy is necessary, as in Judo, in which the forces of the opponent are used to one's advantage. The site conditions, the historical and artistic heterogeneity of the Museum, and the demands of new art are productive forces that require a reversal of architectural conventions.

Double Screen
for Signs or Art

Sculpture
Terrace

Four Floors of
Continuous Staff Offices

Trustees Suite

MUSEUM
PERMANENT
COLLECTION
GALLERIES

Loading
Docks

Restaurant, Cafe,
and Theater Entrance
in 53rd Street

DEPARTMENTAL
GALLERIES

53rd/54th Street
ENTRANCE
(FIFTH AND A HALF)

SCULPTURE
GARDEN

NORTH
COURT

EAST GARDEN
GALLERIES:
TEMPORARY
EXHIBITIONS

UPPER
GARDEN

TOWER COURT

Street Gate

LOWER
SCULPTURE
COURT

THE DYNAMIC
INTERLOCKING
OF GALLERIES
AND COURTS
AROUND THE
GARDEN

UPPER
SCULPTURE
COURT

1964 COURT

COURT 54

THE COURTS: A SEQUENCE
OF ART AND SOCIAL SPACES

BERNARD TSCHUMI IS AN
ARCHITECT AND DEAN OF
COLUMBIA UNIVERSITY'S
GRADUATE SCHOOL OF
ARCHITECTURE, PLANNING,
AND PRESERVATION. HE IS
THE AUTHOR OF SEVERAL
BOOKS, INCLUDING **MANHAT-
TAN TRANSCRIPTS**, **EVENT
CITIES**, AND **ARCHITECTURE
AND DISJUNCTION**.

Architectural Time – Between Melancholy and Narrative

Charles Jencks

ARCHITECTURE AND BONES

Time and architecture are intimately connected, like Romeo and Juliet locked in an embrace of erotic death. We mortals all grow, mature, and die in time; our structures, our teeth and bones, like buildings, are the only things that survive us. They are the fossils of time that tell the trained eye of the archaeologist how we have lived and evolved.

Architecture, as Adolf Loos pointed out, resides in the monument and the grave; it preserves memory against the ravages of time or, like a medieval memory theater, allows information to be stored. Architecture is a form of inactive DNA, a type of frozen time that elicits thoughts of the past. If you have lost someone you have loved deeply, you cannot enter a room or drive through parts of a city you have shared without the architecture evoking those experiences. We believe architecture will outlive us and pass on something less mortal.

The Neanderthals, who, some sixty thousand years ago, were the first to bury and memorialize their dead, understood this truth. The grave site of a man of forty, a cripple, was recently discovered. Apparently he was cared for and loved even after he had been hurt in an accident. That he was tended to by a nomadic tribe and given a ceremonial burial shows that even primitive species can memorialize time's negative arrow – that is, entropy and death. Was this the first act of architecture – bones, teeth, and burial pit?

ARCHITECTURE OSCILLATES BETWEEN THE DIFFERENT CYCLES OF TIME

Architecture also perishes, has its own form of mortality. While it cuts across a larger spectrum of time than the human, this greater range makes us all the more aware of its limitations. Compare it to our eyesight. Although we see a great many colors of different wave lengths, we see only a small part of the total electromagnetic spectrum. Some animals can see ultraviolet light, which is invisible to us. Donald E. Carr has drawn a depressing implication from the fact that single-cell animals do not edit sense impressions the way our brains do: "This is philosophically interesting in a rather mournful way, since it means that only the simplest animals perceive the universe as it is." Likewise, architecture, extending across cycles of time greater than those of our lives, makes us conscious of the fact that it does not work well at the very small or the very large time scale. Its relative superiority makes us aware of its shortcomings.

There are at least six different kinds of architectural time: ephemeral, personal, urban, cultural, evolutionary, and cosmic. Each of these types involves a way of looking at architecture, and is thus a paradigm for considering architecture. The conflicts between them generate an extreme consciousness of time. Architecture thus embodies *hyper-time*. Without stopping to define the six types, let me suggest what they mean. Ephemeral architectural time is that of the Eskimo and Bororo, peoples who are constantly on the move and yet eternally rebuild their structures in cyclical periods. A more contemporary avatar of ephemeral time is the architecture of capitalism which, in Marxist terms, "melts all that is solid into air." This includes tents, inflatable buildings, or even vast and quick urban renewals where neighborhoods and skyscrapers come and go in ten-year cycles.

All these institutions and practices of quick obsolescence constitute a paradigm first celebrated by the Futurists in the 1910s and, as if to underscore the irony of time's strange contradictions, was revived by the Metabolists in the 1960s, Archigram and Cedric Price in the 1970s, and the lightweight avant-garde in the 1990s. A *revival* of quick obsolescence – what a telling irony of our time!

Another theory of architectural time, the personal paradigm, comes from looking at the individual's life as the unit: Martin Pawley's Time House, which records the existential moments of birth, maturation, decay, and the attendant transitional moments, generates another set of assumptions in which the unit of, say, a seventy-year life span is the measure for architecture. Buildings may last far longer, or they may be renewed on a shorter cycle, say every fifteen years or at each change of generations, so there are inherent conflicts between these three physical systems. One might consider the quick change of fashion, which is ephemeral like a light and sound show (the archetype of 24-hour architecture). Or one might look to the individual's lifeline, based on 20-year cycles that reflect momentous change in a person's life, such as the birth of children, or a change of profession or spouse. Then there is the building's lifeline to consider; if it is subject to capitalist development it may be three years, if it involves bricks and mortar, one thousand. Changes at the larger urban or cultural scale only add to the conflict and tension. There is thus an inevitable clash of paradigms, and these not only heighten consciousness of time's arrow but lead to a fundamental psychological truth about architecture.

Architecture, necessarily suspended among all these models of time, makes one conscious of differences and lays bare the inability of any time cycle to be perfectly accommodated. This leads to the argument for architecture's immortality. As the Romans and many other cultures knew, architecture should memorialize significant acts and great events. Its role is to freeze significant moments preserving history for future generations. The Renaissance discovery of the ruins of Rome was also the discovery that architecture is the melancholic art. *Sic Transit Gloria Mundi* was the theme of countless paintings. The ruins of Rome and the bittersweet pleasure of the past *as destroyed but still present* became a stock-in-trade of thinkers and creators. These culminated in Piranesi's grand but morbid celebration of melancholy, which in turn was followed by an entire Romantic meditation on the loss of past triumphs. Egypt's colossal statues sit desolate in the desert, all of the surrounding architecture removed, pillaged for another site. They speak to the hubris of immortality through architecture: to paraphrase King Ozymandias, Look on me all ye architects and despair. But Egyptian ruins did not discourage the Romans, who, like most cultures since, continued to look to architecture to bestow immortality on human events, important values, statesmen, and poets. Hitler's Thousand Year Reich, which he imagined as a ruin in stone one thousand years on, is one version of this tradition. Lloyd's of London is another.

The Christians, even though they built cathedrals of stone to last forever, were the first to lampoon the vain hopes of the Romans. Immortality, they pointed out, was a paltry notion to pit against eternity, the universe, and the kingdom of heaven. The notion of eternity has since then been broadened. After the 18th century and the discovery of geological ages, we have had to deal with the shock of what is called Deep Time. The fact that the earth has lasted for billions of years completely dwarfs the concept of individual, personal time, the Christian's cultural time, and even a species' evolutionary time. Deep Time is unthinkable, beyond our experience, beyond the way we usually measure things, that is, by generations or by cultural periods. Even Deep Time, we have discovered, is not long enough, because the most long-lasting thing in it, the proton, may decay after 48 billion years; the universe itself might even disappear. Or perhaps it will implode into a supermassive black hole and reemerge as another baby universe, in another space-time forever cut off from our own. The fact that these things are quite possible changes our relationship to time.

Some of these unhappy thoughts were conceived in the 19th century. The discovery of Deep Time and an indifferent cosmos led Nietzsche, as it did so many Romantics, to all sorts of escape routes: the hope for a reversible time of eternal recurrence; the view that historical destiny must be taken into our hands by the creation of the Superman, a new species of evolved hero. Other avenues opened up – the celebration of the eternal present, as Sigfried Giedion, the modern architectural historian, phrased the concept. All of history could be conceived as a *frozen now*, all comparable, all alive, all worth celebrating. The modern art historian Herbert Read wrote a book about *40,000 Years of Modern Art*, and artists such as Picasso navigated across vast stretches, from Lascaux to Velasquez. We are close here to the Post-Modern appropriation of everything; close to pulling diachronic time into a wide synchronic present; close to time warp. Cultural time has been restretched into cultural space, as if Einsteinian space-time operated in the art world and mental landscape. So we navigate today between two dangers: the Heritage Industry, where there is too much pastiche of the past, and the minimalists, who give too little acknowledgment that we have come from it. Their whitewashed surfaces and empty concrete do not have the spiritual overtones of the Cistercians, but rather signify the depthless present, or "presentism."

But, leaving these problems aside, I want to return to architecture as the Peculiar Melancholic Art, the art located between all periods, between past, present, and future and therefore adequate to none. Not only does the ruin of a Palladian southern mansion make us con-

scious of the entropy of time, it embodies this melancholy directly. Even a well-restored mansion, such as Palladio's Villa Malcontenta, carries another evidence of this condition. Presented with Le Corbusier's Villa Savoie outside Paris contaminated by an adjacent school building, one has the unmistakable feeling that the party is over, the guests have left, real culture is happening elsewhere or else is simply dead. Great architecture from the past calls up the pastness of history, great cathedrals such as Chartres remind us of the death of high Western culture; it is not only ruins which evoke time's melancholic arrow. The curious truth is that great architecture, more than sculpture or art, provokes such sad feelings because it presents a dead way of life at the same time that it transmits more purely architectural messages.

Of course, the better Post-Modernists have shown that this property of architecture can be reversed. Since architecture necessarily binds different kinds of time – past, present, and future – the combination can work in a synergetic way to heighten the density of meaning. Jim Stirling demonstrated at Stuttgart that architecture's peculiar melancholy is also its potential potency.

James Stirling and Michael Wilford, Neue Staatsgalerie, Stuttgart, 1977–84. The juxtaposition of different typologies, styles, and epochs – past, present, and future – reverse the melancholic sign of architecture.

Noyon Cathedral,
elevation of the nave

Laon Cathedral,
elevation of the nave

Paris, Notre Dame,
original elevation of the nave

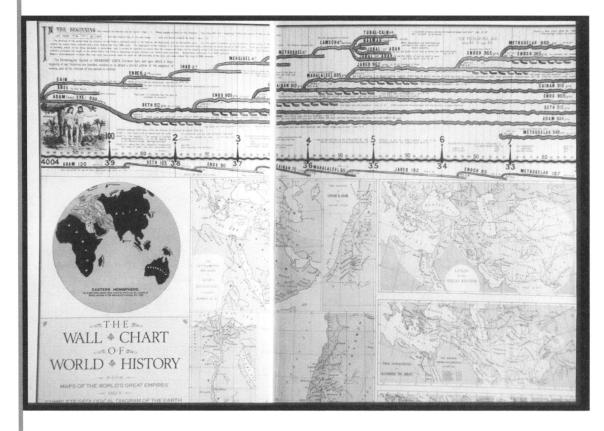

Linear-sequence, progressive development, the evolutionary timeline can be found in short periods of architecture: the development of the Greek temple in the 5th century, the Gothic nave elevation of the 12th century, and the curtain wall, 1950–60. Such progress within a problem situation is the archetype for linear time and the usual way architectural history is recounted. After Nikolaus Pevsner, Outline of European Architecture (1945).

Timeline of Judeo-Christianity ("The Wall Chart of World History," 1900) leading from Adam and Eve, 4004 BC, to cultural evolution and then the triumph of the West.

IMPERIAL VERSUS PLURALIST TIME

The idea that time could be pregnant with meaning was formulated by the Jews, in the *Genesis* account of creation, the story of the Fall, Noah and Moses, the foundation of the nation of Israel; these are all projections of narrative onto abstract time. Narrative triumphs over the pathos of empty time, gives it meaning, direction, and drama. As I will attempt to show, it is the only instrument that can put us in scale with the Deep Time of the cosmos. Other explanations or devices that attempt to put billions of years into human scale only make the time of the universe seem more absurdly big.

Furthermore, these stories which give shape to time also condition the Western psyche to accept the linear unfolding of events. The Judeo-Christian tradition projected mankind into cosmic time, giving it a beginning, middle, and end. Jews and Christians had a linear path to follow to salvation. So ingrained was this way of thinking that it became possible for modern scientists – Copernicus, Galileo, Descartes, and Newton – to believe both in a benevolent God and a mechanical, linear history. It was this conjunction of meanings – God as a rational law-giver and laws that inexorably drive history – that led Christian thinkers to decode the simple, deterministic laws of the universe. It was the Judeo-Christian religious tradition that created modern science. Hinduism and Buddhism, by comparison, emphasized the unfathomable nature of reality. The Chinese, who in 1450 were technically and scientifically more advanced than the West, were not motivated to discover the abstract laws of the universe because their worldview did not emphasize so rational a law-giver.

If modern science and linear time grow directly out of the Judeo-Christian worldview, then the collision of Darwinism with the Biblical account of humankind was an accident

waiting to happen. Here were two different interpretations of evolutionary time, both progressive in some sense, both leading from simplicity to complexity, both ruled by laws: those of God or natural selection. Since the publication of *The Origin of Species* in 1859 there have been continuous attempts to combine and resolve these two accounts of the story of the universe; as the Pope would now have it, God created the Big Bang. Versions of this story at the turn of the century outline an amusing, if politically incorrect, theory that Adam and Eve's descendants evolved into the tribe of Israel and from there, undergoing several more speciations, to the triumph of the white man and the West. In this picture of 1900, a Darwinian family tree of evolving humanity culminates, implicitly, in the six-foot Englishman. One is reminded of Le Corbusier's Modulor Man based on such a character.

The point is that *all* Western thinking becomes evolutionary after 1859, however much it may be a misunderstanding of evolution. The linear-sequential paradigm dominates all historical accounts, whether they are those of nations or architecture or species. The linear sequence has become *the* model for thinking about changing technology, be it Gothic architecture or a new building: mentally we put them in a time line, or evolutionary tree, or space of possible sequences, a series. These mental maps give time its shape, to use George Kubler's phrase, and explain the meaning of an invention in the context of a constellation of possible inventions: in the mainstream or in a backwater. Urban thinker Kevin Lynch's famous question, "What time is this place?" is partly answered by the linear sequence.

There are basically two versions of this view, what I call the *imperial* and *pluralist* pictures. According to the first, history is made up of winners and losers, nations or architects who compete in a Darwinian landscape for limited territory. Imperial history is written by the winners, which in architecture means the accounts of modernism by Nikolaus Pevsner, Sigfried Giedion, Reyner Banham, and William Curtis. Architectural Darwinism accentuates the struggle for the job, the fights between Bernini and Borromini, the competition for jobs between Lord Richard Rogers and Sir Norman Foster, SOM and KPF, Richard Meier and Frank Gehry – with Philip Johnson usually ending up with the lion's share. The imperial sense of time and history values staying on top, keeping ahead of trends, occasionally stealing jobs, and making one's peace with corporate culture.

During the Modern Movement's creative phase in the 1920s, no one predicted that it would align itself almost completely with the assumptions of late-capitalism. But architectural Darwinism proved to be a unifying connection between the worlds of business and architecture, and by the 1960s, late-modernism became the dominant expression of late-capitalism around the globe, even more so than Post-Modernism. It still is, with the neo-neo-International Style and minimalism, boutique Cistercianism, and other modes that have been assimilated by Armani and NEXT.

In depicting the evolution of architectural species since the late 1960s, I have brought out the point that there are two basic types of time, reversible and irreversible, which can be shown together as pulsating blobs. Species – that is, architectural trends – wax and wane along pulsating lines, fibrous bundles that show roughly the strength, or visibility, of an emergent tradition. I have assumed, following Claude Levi-Strauss and other structuralists, that there is some logic to these basic traditions. Their coherence is caused both by psychological and epistemological pressures: architects follow each other because they share habits of mind, training, and techniques, and these things lead to coherent species. When a tradition pulsates through the years, time appears reversible or cyclical: for instance, versions of abstract classicism and the International Style both tend to be revived every twenty years or so. These recurrent patterns give one a feeling of déjà vu, the strong sense that most architecture today is a revival of a revival, and they support the paradoxical notion that Modernism has now become old-fashioned and conservative.

The recurrent revivals *and survivals* suggest that there are different wavelengths of linear time. Following economists, and putting together the two types of time in the same diagram, one can talk about short, medium, and long waves. If we look at the economy for a moment we can see that capitalism has a five hundred-year trajectory with many short-term restructurings, or waves, that change its character. Different kinds of events and institutions have to be considered simultaneously – business cycles, the stock market, revolutions, and evolutions. Five basic stages of capitalism can be distinguished. The mercantile capitalism of 1500, overseen by monarchies, partly gives way to industrial capitalism after 1750. By 1875 this mutates and slides, at least in Europe and America, into monopoly capitalism, which reaches a crisis with the crash of the 1930s. Welfare capitalism (and Keynesian economics) restructures the scene around big Fordist companies until the next crisis, in the 1970s, forces another stage of development – post-Fordism, and an economics based largely on fast-changing, smaller companies networked by computer into the global market. The long wave is capitalism and the five smaller waves are types which cope with different social, technical, and economic changes. While each stage is classified by its leading type of institution, there are obviously continuities and *medium* waves that are obscured in my diagram.

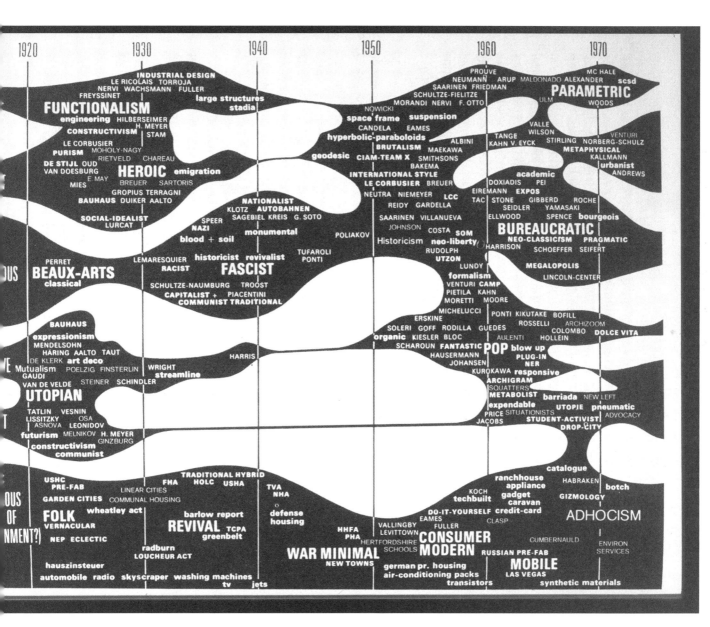

Charles Jencks, Evolutionary Tree of Architecture 1920–70 (1971) incorporates three aspects of time: linear-sequential time (the lines), reversible time (the recurrent blobs), and discontinuous events (noted incidents).

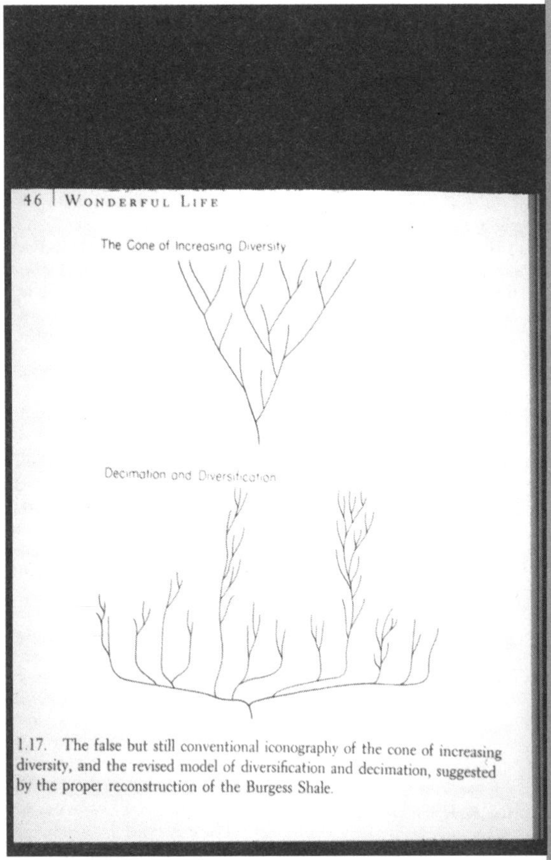

46 | WONDERFUL LIFE

The Cone of Increasing Diversity

Decimation and Diversification

1.17. The false but still conventional iconography of the cone of increasing diversity, and the revised model of diversification and decimation, suggested by the proper reconstruction of the Burgess Shale.

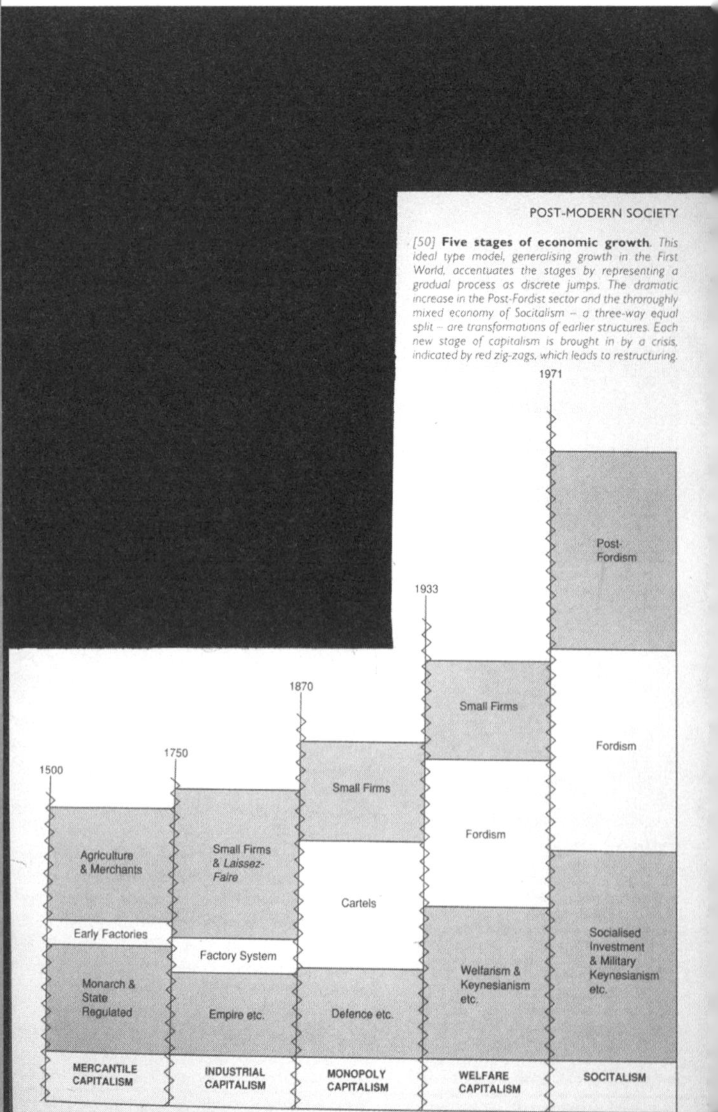

POST-MODERN SOCIETY

[50] **Five stages of economic growth**. *This ideal type model, generalising growth in the First World, accentuates the stages by representing a gradual process as discrete jumps. The dramatic increase in the Post-Fordist sector and the thoroughly mixed economy of Socitalism – a three-way equal split – are transformations of earlier structures. Each new stage of capitalism is brought in by a crisis, indicated by red zig-zags, which leads to restructuring.*

| MERCANTILE CAPITALISM | INDUSTRIAL CAPITALISM | MONOPOLY CAPITALISM | WELFARE CAPITALISM | SOCITALISM |

What do these different kinds of waves imply for architectural history? Should we consider the revivals and survival of classicism over the last two hundred years as one long wave? Even more than classicism, the International Style, and versions of it in the 1960s and 1980s, make it seem like this century's longest wave. Why should it be so? Architects take up formal problems, drop them, and take them up again, so considered from the point of view of the formal, this tradition has a long duration. Economic history and the fact that most corporations commission architecture in versions of the International Style suggest that it is the leading mode of imperial history.

While the imperial view of history tells us some basic truths about who wins, it tends to overlook a greater truth of evolution. The story of architecture is not a single, linear progression of a great tradition but a narrative made up of many minor trends and countless failures, thousands of species which make up the background environment, and, importantly, many inventive buildings which contribute architectural ideas that are picked up by others. Similarly, the evolution of life is not the story of increasing diversity — as depicted in evolutionary trees and biology textbooks — but the account of mass extinctions in which 99.99 percent of all species disappear while individual genes continue. The new metaphor for life is not that of a tree that has more branches at the top but of a mangy bush having few live twigs. The pluralism of life and architecture shows great fecundity and death, a thousand failed experiments, incoherence of overall pattern, and yet incredible creativity at the level of genetic combination. By analogy, most architects are forgotten, most buildings disappear; but if there is not a single pattern to world evolution there are, nevertheless, new types which are constantly incorporated into surviving traditions.

An analogy with natural selection: all species are competing for limited space, time, reproductive success, and resources. They are always changing in relation to other species, or co-evolving, and their ecology is the other species. In this world, represented as a fitness landscape, there is constant movement and transformation as each species reacts to changes in its competitors. They adopt behaviors from each other and at the same time specialize away from each other. In architectural evolution, because the medium is ideas, values, and forms carried in the mind — and not the genes — change occurs much faster and can result in complete transformation. One architect can quickly incorporate another's best solutions. In this way, countless ideas are propagated into the future even if they are not part of mainstream, or imperial, history.

Furthermore, pluralism feeds on itself, and this has consequences for the experience of time. Many architects are emboldened to stress their idiosyncrasies, to fashion a difference, and this bends our sense of time in extraordinary ways because history seems to have no direction. With Post-Modernism it leads to the illusion that anything is possible, that any style or solution will do. Today one is encouraged to live in an eco-house, underground, perhaps as Neanderthals lived, or in an electronic cottage — the 14th century with smart thatch. Inasmuch as space is shrunk by the electronic village, then time is warped by the incessant recycling of all architectures.

THE PLEASURE OF THE NEXT STEP

Thus pluralist time competes with imperial time. Any city is a palimpsest of both: some citizens of New York live in an Italian district that has affinities with 18th-century Naples, but they consume products that are constantly progressing. For instance, audio equipment has developed linearly in this century: first there were 78 rpm records, then 33, then audio tapes, then CDs. If one draws an envelope-curve over each successive technology, one can see the cultural escalator, always going up: in terms of speed, greater miniaturization, lower cost, more precision and control. In industrial society, this norm of progress is just assumed. In the early part of the century it constituted the futurist dream, and by the middle it created the Fuller elevator ("Doing more with less"). Modernity, the spirit of surfing the envelope-curve, developed equally within the business world and the worlds of fashion, the arts, and developing technology. That is why "the pleasure of the next step" is so rooted in city culture. Negatively, it multiplies its fashion victims, its amnesiacs whose sense of history is ten years deep; it is likely to create its corporate outlets – the Emporio Armani, NEXT, and MoMA. Its byproducts are schizophrenia, anxiety, and pretentious nonsense.

But it also has its real pleasures, innovations that change a paradigm and redirect history. There are the conceptual breakthroughs, the Barcelona Pavilion of Mies van der Rohe, the Vanna Venturi House of Robert Venturi, and the Moebius strip, to name inventions which are not comparable. I want to focus on two reasons why there is so much pleasure in extending a tradition of architecture and why leaders of architecture invariably seek to make the next step. One reason is quite obvious, although rarely understood: there is an implicit drive to be part of history, to make a difference in a historical sequence, and usually the easiest way to do this is to be out in front (although not in periods of reaction). In any case, leading from the front, or the rear, amounts to the same thing if one considers the deeper motive: to be part of the narrative of time, to project oneself onto the future and into Deep Time.

The pleasure of the next step is the cosmic supposition that, like a turning point in history, one changed the future for the better – one's life and work mattered. According to this psychological explanation, the experience of changing time in architecture becomes a major drive for architects, especially those with a historical imagination.

Second, there is the rare positive synergy that can result from innovating at the same time in widely disparate areas of discourse, especially that of cognitive development and sensual expression. When we experience a sensual work of architecture that extends a tradition, Gehry's Guggenheim Museum Bilbao or Peter Eisenman's Aronoff Center, for instance, there is a double charge to perception that can be mutually reinforcing, that creates the real pleasure of innovation.

Such buildings may also have force today because of the premium put on fast change and quick learning. The shrinking of space-time, as David Harvey points out in *The Postmodern Condition*, is rooted in the global economy. Twenty-four-hour electronic trading and the information world pull every point in the globe to any point and make every time an instant now. Space-time implosion means, at the psychic level, that time has sped up dramatically, that generations of ideas evolve in the belly of a computer just as generations of software evolve every year. The collapse of space-time was pointed out more than twenty years ago by Andy Warhol ("In the future everyone will be world famous for 15 minutes.") and, since the '60s, many critics have pointed out that the art world is becoming as fast-changing as fashion (an art generation is now about two years).

However, there is a paradox. With Time's Winged Chariot going ballistic, those involved in quick evolution wish even more to slow things down and distinguish between real change (significant invention within a tradition) and novelty. Furthermore, as Levi-Strauss pointed out, humanity's deep desire is to slow time down to a repetitive pattern, to achieve a crystalline structure to life. Such contradictory desires, to stay ahead of the wave *and* slow down, lead to the well-known contradictions

Peter Eisenman, **Aronoff Center**, Cincinnati, 1989–96. Two codes extended at once, the sensuous and cognitive – cogniroticism – have more power than either alone. Innovations in methods of design and fabrication imply that matter itself has a dynamic organizational property. The metaphor of large tectonic plates pushing against each other while still attracted to formal organizing principles is heightened by the fractal geometry.

among avant-garde artists: they may advance taste in one area and have reactionary opinions in several others. Tastes for fast *and* slow change tend to develop together, for the obvious reason that a trade-off in cognitive development is inevitable: one cannot be an expert in all of the fields that are racing ahead.

WHICH PHASE TO FREEZE?

The implications of such contradictions for architecture are profound. The public, most clients included, does not want architecture to change every year, they do not want to live the futurist dream nor its Archigram transformation. They do not want architecture to be very flexible nor change with the responsiveness of fashion. The architecture of ephemerality may be desired for a few functions, such as pop concerts, but architecture remains the art of slow time, the twenty-five- to one hundred-year cycle. It remains "frozen music" that crystallizes values meant to last for more than one person's lifetime. But under the pressures of space-time implosion, more is also asked of it today – and here I invoke the *zeitgeist* in order to explain it.

The feelings of fast change, the facts of quick evolution, are now an essential part of our culture and, inevitably, people want architecture to reflect this. The taste for both time warps and time sequences has become a long-lasting convention. The question for architecture thus becomes somewhat paradoxical: how to represent evolutionary series, the change of time, and, contradictorily enough, to freeze it.

The computerized image of a growing thunderstorm has become something of an icon for this discussion. Simulations of a severe storm show clouds, rain, and pressure systems developing between Oklahoma and Texas over a period of two hours and 20 minutes. Edward Tufte, who has made information display an art, has redesigned this simulation to show how the graphics can be improved, especially at the cognitive level, so that one can see, feel, and understand the process of the storm in its various phases. Time travels from left to right, the storm gathers power in six distinct phases, and its dimensions are clearly marked. The fluid forms depicting this process

in phase space are enticing and suggest that, if the cloud were frozen architecture, one might design a composite building of these stages. Again, the question is: which stage to choose? It strikes me that Tufte has not picked out the really dramatic changes in his six freeze-frames – where does the lightening strike, the hail pour down? Perhaps neither occurred but, in any case, his tiny clouds at the bottom are too much like each other to dramatize the events, the perception of time.

At the Anytime conference, Bernard Tschumi and I disputed the role of narrative in architecture, but on one point we agreed: events should be captured in architecture. In fact, events structure our sense of time, and in Tufte's depiction of the severe storm, nothing very dramatic appears to have happened.

Several architects, such as Ben van Berkel and Greg Lynn, have started to generate a new architecture based on events that unfold over time, engaging the interesting question: which phases of time should one freeze? For instance, for his H2 House project in Austria, Lynn has frozen various stages of solar orientation into the shape of the building. He analyzes several sweeps of movement – that of the sun on one side and of cars on the other – and collages the results as a new whole. On one side, the sun generates a curving roof form; from the autostrada cars generate a series of six cuts. The result is a refreshing mixture of continuous and discontinuous change that reflects both nature and current social reality. But there is a problem. Like Tufte's story of the severe storm, it is not quite dramatic enough. There is no heightening of the narrative strategy, no directional or climatic movement seems to occur; there is only continuous and stepped change. Cars and sun come and go and their movement is captured in the architecture – but is this content significant enough, does it have a culmination?

In a way I have adopted a related strategy in designing a Black Hole Terrace that is also directly related to time. Here too the transitions have been smoothed out to give priority to the whole process. Phases of space and time are marked but the fluid form is continuous.

In other ways the intentions are quite different. The functions of the shape are simple: to provide a terrace for eating under a tree and viewing the landscape, and to provide seats and nonskid surfaces, as one falls into the Black Hole. But the main intention is to present and represent a dramatic cosmic process that changes the laws of the universe, one that warps space and time and creates rifts in nature or, in this case, the landscape. In other words, it is to take a fundamental and extraordinary discovery of our time and turn it into a dramatic narrative.

One first approaches a wide curve, the event horizon, beyond which matter and light cannot escape. Then, as one descends into the Black Hole Terrace, literally pulled at an oblique angle by the tilt of the earth, by gravity, one sees space being stretched. The stretch marks are V-shaped grooves cut in the aluminium, which also make it sticky, a necessity because the space-time warp literally pulls one down toward the culmination, the singularity. While the warped grid shows space stretched, it also shows time being compressed: as one heads for the zero point, the units of Astroturf and aluminium grow closer and closer together. Finally one reaches the singularity, the point of disappearance, and steps over this "nothing" into a white hole, which is seen as the rush of continuous creation in another baby universe. As one steps over this void onto the dining terrace one contemplates several of the amazing but standard speculations of scientists.

Black holes do exist, and physicists even uphold the uncanny idea that the universe as a whole constitutes one! Perhaps they are very

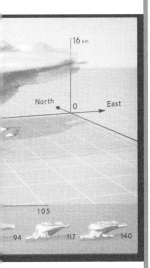

plentiful: the cosmologist Lee Smolin and others have calculated that there may be as many as 10 to the 18th power in our universe (100,000,000,000,000,000). A black hole rips apart our space-time; hence the cuts and slashes I have designed in the landscape, a tiny series of long black waves that radiate out from the event horizons. Furthermore, Smolin and other cosmologists believe that black holes may create white holes in another universe, one where the laws are *slightly* different. The small variations matter. A succession of universes evolving into other universes through the medium of black holes, Smolin contends, might lead to more successful universes, with the laws well-balanced, emerging through a process akin to Darwinian selection. This could explain why the laws of our universe are so *extraordinarily well-balanced*, a key discovery of our time.

For complex life to have evolved, a series of highly specific and unlikely conditions must be fulfilled, and it is this notion that is dramatized in the architecture: the idea is conveyed by the space-time warps on each terrace being similar to, but not the same as, each other. The warped squares slide into each other as self-similar, fractal shapes. Thus, while my design is similar to both Tufte's and Lynn's sequence in showing a smooth and stepped process, it has one culmination point — the singularity — and its story relates to a process that is extraordinary and cosmic. Narrative is dramatized.

TIME TURNS INTO NARRATIVE & NARRATIVE TURNS INTO THE UNIVERSE STORY

Behind every linear sequence, time series, and evolutionary tree is a story waiting to be told. Time is the great builder and destroyer and as such it is naturally meaningful. There is also the morphological similarity between the unfolding of a story and the lapse of time; both occur in a line. We all are born, grow up, and die, and this, the most important time sequence to us, creates the basic narrative structure behind all others. It explains why biography has such a hold on the mind, why we all have, as Frank Kermode has written, *The Sense of an Ending*. It is also said that the mind grasps things, and retains them best, through narrative, even if a story is a rather inefficient way of packaging information.

The Judeo-Christian narrative and the modernist, progressivist narrative (with its Darwinian implications) have been the two primary metanarratives of the West, and although each has been thrown into doubt, as Jean-François Lyotard has argued regarding all stories, they remain locally coherent and points of orientation. Following others, I have constructed a metanarrative of cosmic history because it is the measure of other histories. There is nothing more encompassing, and in the end more meaningful, although not many people may agree with this or understand it to be true. But as the universe story becomes more embedded through further discoveries and more convincing retelling, I believe it will become accepted as the grand metanarrative to which all others will relate. My argument in *The Architecture of the Jumping Universe* is that this story will shape other areas of culture, including architecture. It can be conceived as an instantaneous narrative and as a whole, but it also allows different interpretations and it *does* invite various metaphorical inventions. Because it is a collective construction, it continually invites better retellings. To bring out this restricted freedom in interpretation I have conceived it in three different ways: as a trumpet-shaped vortex, an expanding globe, and a four-stage warp.

Each visual metaphor captures *something* of the truth of cosmic history and collapses it

into a unified story: a single, creative, unfolding event that is depicted in jumps. The idea of the jumping universe comes from the notion of symmetry breaks, the fact that the universe story is not only a narrative of linear sequences but also of leaps in organization. Each stage of cosmic time emerges from the previous one.

At the beginning of time the universe is a pure energy event, misnamed the Big Bang; a better metaphor is that it is "the hot stretch of space-time," an expansion that suddenly jumps into matter. The next major jumps in organization are from matter into life and then from life into consciousness. Seen from the human perspective these are the four most dramatic symmetry breaks, but there are other possible interpretations and I have conceived the process in two other designs, in eight and 30 shifts.

Again, as with the thunderstorm or Lynn's H2 House, there is a selection of the major phases, a choice of metaphor, and the relative freedom to accentuate some dramatic moments rather than others. Moreover, the cosmos is shown as a whole, as if seen from the outside and from God's view of eternity because, presumably, the universe is unified and tells a story. Why? Because the four basic forces and its evolution make it a universe not a pluriverse. As far as we know the laws are everywhere the same in our space-time.

Although no one could actually experience the universe story, or live through the Deep Time of approximately fifteen billion years, and although this scale is unimaginable, impossible to grasp in terms of the usual human dimensions, it will become, I believe, the major assumption for all space-time coordinates. Other narratives, on this account, will have to accommodate themselves to this, the largest possible metanarrative, and in that sense it could become the model for architectural and cultural evolution. The argument here is too long and complex to be unraveled and, in any case, I have made it elsewhere. Suffice it to say that narrative is the human shape of time, something that gives its abstract duration a particular meaning and drama. Narrative also structures personal, local, and national identities. Narrative is one of the most potent ways to communicate ideas and relationships. Of course it cannot become the only idea behind architectural form, nor an excuse to avoid pressing concerns – as was mentioned at the Anytime conference. But it can, most importantly, articulate process and the passage of time and give them a direction and drama. Narrative, any locally important narrative (not just the universe story), might be mapped onto the abstract phases of the fluid architecture that Lynn and Eisenman so ably design and give it a greater dimension. This I believe, but at the conference it was subject to strong disagreement. In any case, it is true that narrative contains the semantic expression of time, gives abstract time a human scale and meaning, and it can embed us in a universe otherwise out of scale and hard to grasp. Because of the primacy of time in the cosmos, the scientist of dissipative structures, Ilya Prigogine, has recently claimed that narrative has replaced geometry as the leading explanation of the universe. Perhaps he is right. If so, this should change architecture.

The universe in four jumps. Reading from left to right across the terrace: 1) from energy (explosive straight lines) to matter (curved lines), then from matter, which curves space and time, to life (the bowl) and then to consciousness (the hedge).

The universe in eight jumps (Model and drawing). The expansion from a center produces the metaphor of a globe held together by the four forces (gravity, electro-magnetism, the strong and weak forces) – shown as spiraling structures which actually hold the circular hoops.

CHARLES JENCKS IS AN AMERICAN ARCHITECT AND ARCHITECTURAL HISTORIAN LIVING IN LONDON. HE IS THE AUTHOR OF THE LANGUAGE OF POST-MODERN ARCHITECTURE, WHAT IS POST-MODERNISM?, AND THE ARCHITECTURE OF THE JUMPING UNIVERSE.

AUDIENCE Yesterday somebody said the end is over in the sense that we no longer think with a teleological problematic or narrative. Here, both John Rajchman and Bernard Tschumi spoke of the notion of simultaneity and the Deleuzian notion of time, or duration, that came from his **Cinema** book. Do you mean that the grand narrative is over or do you think that being critical of the grand narrative and saying that it's over are different things?

JOHN RAJCHMAN The theme of the end of history, the end of grand narrative that was proposed in the 1980s by Jean-François Lyotard, is connected to what I was trying to say, but it's not the same as what I was trying to say. Essentially I was proposing a model of capitalism according to which there can be no end. Capitalism is fundamentally the endless deferment of judgment. I think that's slightly different from the idea of a narrative coming to an end. What is interesting now is to try to rethink the whole relationship of narratives, politics, and time, and to make some place for it. I see lots of different philosophers trying to talk about this, but I like the Deleuzian version because it presupposes no transcendence and no mysticism. I like its empiricism.

BERNARD TSCHUMI The limitation of John's and my responses is that we share common cultural presuppositions. The grand narrative, as analyzed in terms of the end by Lyotard, is interesting to connect with a Roland Barthes text, which was written at almost the same time, about the structural analysis of narrative. This was a very useful text for making certain architectural parallels insofar as you could literally map an architectural trajectory around the narrative structure. At the same time, one quickly arrived at the difficulty, which we all know through our conversation with Charles Jencks, that structural analysis of narrative is dependent on the idea of meaning. How about removing it altogether, but not by making mini or fragmentary narratives.

CHARLES JENCKS I find that Bernard uses a funny argument. Like Robert Venturi, he says, "I like simultaneity and I don't like history"; a series of personal judgments, which are then backed up by a bit of Bauhaus argument, a bit of modernism, and a bit of a historicist argument that is necessary or of our time – in effect, you only have one choice and it's my choice. Venturi does the same kind of historicizing of his anti-historical position, and of course it's absurd, there's no reason to do it. I think you are just holding onto your virginity like mad, so much so that you've even said that pornography has no narrative. Now, I don't know what kind of pornographic shots you just showed, but my point is that everything we do, human time, is shot through with beginnings, middles, and ends. Let me give you a pornographic narrative: it's boy meets, maybe, girl – let's be classical Western, okay? They look at each other; they find each other attractive. One is a non-Westerner, however. They are sexually attracted to each other; they start to fall in love, at least for the moment; they undress; they start making love, as in your pictures; and then he goes on having intercourse for a day and a half because he's a Tantrist; and she has 48 orgasms, at which point she dies; she didn't know she was making love with a Tantrist who has been trained to withhold orgasm. That's the end of an unhappy pornographic story. Now I tell this because it's got a very dramatic structure to it; it's what stories are about, expectation. The whole point of structure in music and literature in the cosmos is that we can relate to it, because the time has the same shape as a narrative. If you want to convince people of something, you tell them a story. It's the easiest way. Now, a story may be a very bad way of storing information, but it is the way that the human builds. I do not think that metanarratives have ended. I do think that the grandest metanarrative is the story of the universe, and it's going to sublate all other stories – all religious stories, all progressivist stories, all modernist stories will become an adjunct to this grand story. Our generation is the first to be able to tell the story, which has overwhelming implications. So I fundamentally disagree with the position of the panelists on my left.

TSCHUMI I'm struck by your reconstruction of the narrative. For your information, every one of those images comes from different reels and a different story.

RAJCHMAN I want to respond to Charles and his disagreements with the left side of the table. I am struck by something else that comes from a style of analysis that emerged in the culture that Bernard referred to, which is shown in the work of Michel Foucault. How are discourses, and particularly forms of knowledge, constituted and formed? Foucault thought there was an interesting answer to that question and an important point to analyzing it. In the '60s, the main science that he thought needed an explanation of this sort, a genealogy, as he called it, was the science of language, or linguistics, its relationship to formalism and so forth. So the hypothesis now – I form this in response to Charles – is that we have another formation, which could be called cognitive Darwinism, that combines selfish genes and computer brains. This discourse brings back the vocabulary of evolution and makes it seem inevitable. Perhaps I'm wrong and Charles is getting this from some completely other source, but I would say that is the discursive formation of Charles's analysis of architecture.

JENCKS No, no, that's wrong.

RAJCHMAN Oh, sorry.

JENCKS I'd be critical of Darwinism, and especially the selfish gene. In fact, my writings attack the progressivist nature of that, explicitly politically. My disagreement with work like Peter Eisenman's and Greg Lynn's — even though it's the most interesting — is that it doesn't yet address narrative content.

JALE ERZEN I'd like to come back to the practice of architecture. Since yesterday we've been seeing the cantilever as a recurring theme of dynamics and freedom. If we're really talking about simultaneity, of many times existing together, don't you think that the architect who takes the liberty of expanding into free space or acting in a very free manner looks like the guy with a racing car, rushing through the city at 200 miles per hour without considering the time of others, who may be much slower? This notion of dynamics and freedom cannot be considered on an individual level if we're talking about urban space, or the space of people who live together. I think this is a problem. To what extent does this create dynamics, other than visual, in the sense that we live in the city?

TSCHUMI If I remove your point about visual dynamics and the cantilever, I couldn't agree more with what you said. Clearly, whether you talk about one body in space or a multiplicity of bodies in space, we're talking about the same thing. Ultimately, ours is an urban society. Every one of the projects I showed is about urban society. So in this respect, the fact that you use a cantilever as opposed to a load-bearing wall becomes relatively secondary or, more importantly, circumstantial, contextual — not in the sense of a sort of analogy of forms, but simply reactive or provocative in terms of the context. But it is separate from the issue that you bring up. It's not about conditioning a design but about designing conditions, and conditions for exactly what you described, to appropriate pieces of the city. There are multiple strategies and tactics that can be used in how you design those conditions.

AYSE ERZAN I would like to thank Ugur Tanyeli for some very interesting remarks that have helped me pull together a number of questions that have been evolving over the last two days. I am a physicist and therefore, I should admit, out of my element. On the other hand, I am a little surprised at the willingness with which people are almost deliberately using the same words to mean very different things. So I was very happy to hear Ugur say that time in antiquity or before modernity could only be thought of as space. From his subsequent remarks, I understood this to mean the following: that when time could only be thought of as space, there was one overreaching motion, one canonical trajectory, that of the fictitious trajectory, in fact, of the sun across the sky, which could be used to parameterize time by identifying the different stations of the sun with different times. He went on to remark that in modernity, time could be disconnected from space only with the invention of the empty categories of abstract integrals of time and space. Now, it is surprising to me that many speakers are carrying on a discourse as if they were unaware or unwilling to acknowledge this separation. When they are willing to relinquish the existence of one canonical trajectory to which time can be referred, when they become aware that there are many different and quite unproblematically simultaneous trajectories, they prefer to talk about different times rather than just different trajectories, according to which time could eventually be parameterized. So I would very much like to support Saskia Sassen's proposal that one should talk about different temporalities; in doing so one underlines the fact that what is at issue here is a matter of representation, of different internal representations of abstract durations or intervals of time that can be associated with different motions, different processes, and different trajectories at different spaces or at different hypothetical spaces, even different cyberspaces. At the speeds at which we move in all the different processes that we've been talking about since yesterday, relativity in the sense of Einstein's special relativity is never an issue. None of these processes involve relativistic speeds, so simultaneity, or the definition of a diachronic time, is never problematic. The only problem we encounter is again an issue raised by Ugur Tanyeli, and that is a cultural rather than a technical one. It's a matter of willingness to synchronize your time with one overreaching historical trajectory – in this case, one overreaching historical narrative, or ahistorical, if you want to refer to the evolution of the universe. But this is a cultural wish to identify or map the different epics or historical moments of your own society with an overreaching historical or ahistorical trajectory.

RAJCHMAN We find in 20th-century philosophy lots of people who try to get away from the so-called mechanized view of time, or clock time. They say that our experience in some way has another logic, or is formed in another way, in order to get out of the spatialization of time. That's actually an expression of Henri Bergson. His model of memory was an attempt to give us another model of time that wouldn't be mechanized, and, of course, he gets into this argument with Einstein. Heidegger too very much opposed this idea of clock time. He wants to get back to the time of the life-world, and he has an even more complicated idea about epochs and history. I would say that one of the features of modern Western philosophy has been an attempt to give us some other kind of model, and it comes in different forms. One reason for liking Bergson rather than Heidegger here is that Heidegger seems to get back to some kind of mysticism or devotional relationship to being. The Bergsonian direction becomes interesting to think of in terms of narrative and in cinema and photography.

AUDIENCE In order to better frame my question, I would like to refer to the first two slides that Charles Jencks showed. The first was a picture ordering energy, matter, life, and consciousness in the form of a table. Right after that he projected a single image presenting two abstractions and configurations, one of energy, the other of traffic. His own interpretation as a critic, rather than as an architect, was concerned with only one form of this matter, the energy. He interpreted these two as related to only one part of energy: light. But wind is another possibility, and heat, and many other types could be thought about. We could also list many factors related to traffic: transportation, communication, noise, etc. How could we develop a logic of these or criticize them?

JENCKS If the relation of time to architecture, to us, and to the universe is a key question today, then I think it's important that we look to science to give us interpretations of what is a very long meditation on the universe. At the same time we need to criticize that and turn it into form, into architecture and landscape, which is what I'm doing in those slides. That's why it's not about traffic. I showed three different ways to interpret the same evidence, three different metaphors. One was the metaphor of a trumpet with jumps; another, an expanding universe like that globe; and the third, a twist with jumps in it. Each time you choose what is important, you are making an evaluative choice – you are interpreting the story of the universe. But you don't have what I thought John was implying at the end of his talk. It is not entirely a free choice.

GREG LYNN There seems to be something at stake about the role of architecture as a cultural practice. One role is that architecture would somehow express or narrativize or represent the cultural values of society. I think the other proposal is that architecture's role would be to experiment with those values and that society. It's very interesting that interest is growing about architects who would experiment on these values rather than architects who would express them. One of the most interesting proposals is that architecture could become an experimental discipline rather than a conservative and expressive one. Personally, that's why I want to postpone the narrative questions rather than begin with them. It's more interesting to see what narratives develop out of experiment.

TSCHUMI The alternative that you suggest is unbelievably clear and worth using as an instrument for a moment. But then we must also acknowledge the limitations of this alternative – any experiment occurs within a culture and therefore has its own cultural bias. I think that architecture will always be a cultural practice. However, when it constantly refers to its past cultural practices and endlessly quotes itself, that is a problem. If I had to fall into one trap or another, I would totally understand what you're saying. It's probably better to fall into the trap of experiment than the trap of repetition.

RAJCHMAN I like the word **experiment**, the idea of an experimental architecture, maybe even the division between an expressive and an experimental architecture. But I was trying to say that the notion of experimentation may be a little bit different than in physics, where it tends to be repeatable things that are interesting. This notion of experiment supposes a certain idea of time and . . .

AUDIENCE Physics is about laws.

RAJCHMAN Yes, well, that's the question.

RENATO RIZZI John, you started your talk by saying that our architecture should not represent time because we are presenting time. I need to know the differences between representation and presentation, because if we still discuss the notion of time within the paradigm of a nihilistic culture, then our architecture represents a nothingness of a nihilistic paradigm. I want to ask what you think about this paradigm. Do you want to be inside or outside this nihilistic paradigm, because our discussion is useless if we don't have a consciousness about this.

RAJCHMAN We might have a quarrel about exactly what is meant by nihilism – that's a philosophical question. I'm sympathetic with part of what you're saying, if I understand it correctly, which brings us back to this morning's very interesting problems about a critical architecture. Maybe the question of a critical architecture and what has now been called experimental architecture are in some ways connected. But as I understood the architects' debate, the problem of the generic and the specific is not the same as the problem of this kind of banality. There is something interesting in the generic that isn't the same as the banal. The vision of the urban and architectural conditions of this very banalized condition I associate with what you're calling nihilism. This might be an interesting way to give us sharper categories to think about.

HANS VAN DIJK I'm very happy that Charles mentioned "manytimes," which is the title of this session. But now we are also talking about the acceleration of time, of the need to experiment, etc., and hardly ever talking about the history of the long durée. How does the long durée play a role in the thought or work of Bernard Tschumi or even in the teaching at Columbia? How do we see the long durée vis-à-vis the present situation with all its acceleration and uncertainty? Is there still a role for that particular time?

JENCKS You can interpret Bernard's Le Fresnoy in a long durée, in allowing the past to be an accretion that challenges a building. You can also interpret it as a palimpsest, as a reminting, that has a way of relating to deep time. I'm sure that our identity is built out of being able to respond with forgetfulness, with no memory. We need amnesiacal time; we need the time of changing our mind, of forgetfulness. It's just as important to be able to forget as to remember. But if we are only into consumer-society time and the time of everything melting into air, then it's corrosive of our identities.

RAJCHMAN I have a slightly different response having to do with Rem Koolhaas. Of course it has different components. One is the urban investigations that he does and others are the details of his actual architectural projects. Now Fernand Braudel associates the long durée with climate, demography, things like that. People have disagreements about Rem's architecture and how he treats those subjects, but I think he is someone who has helped to make things like these big demographic patterns seem important to architecture. Saskia talks about this as well, a sort of redrawing of geographies and so forth. Some future historian who looks back might see that it is the long processes that Rem is somehow trying to tap into.

JEAN-LOUIS COHEN Braudel never viewed the long durée as the only patterns in historical interpretation, but as one of the ways of understanding change. Long durée was constructed against the dogmas of political and instantaneous history as another representation of continuity, not an absolute continuity but rather lines of continuity that did not eliminate issues. Apparently historians of history are now discussing figures of anticipation and belatedness – how the old remains encapsulated in the new, how the new can be encapsulated in the old or in the present. It is here that notions of experiment, rather than experience, are so important. I want to return to a different interpretation of history, an old one of the 1960s, and perhaps forgotten today, put forward by Louis Althusser in **Pour Marx**, in which he developed the notion of the conjuncture of time and space in which Marx's theories and hypotheses were appearing. I think this notion of conjuncture is extremely important for architecture today. In Le Fresnoy, Bernard responds to a specific conjuncture that is not simply a context and an ad hoc site but is also the creation of a particular experimental institution at a particular moment. I think the chronicle of current architecture could be read with the help of this concept. Another important concept is the chronotope, which was developed by Mikhail Bakhtin, the Russian literary historian and semiologist. In his work on the medieval novel or on the medieval mystery, Bakhtin identifies the notion of chronotope, that is, the convergence of space, time, and narrative – a particular narrative taking place at a certain moment in a particular place. For instance, a story or a narrative that is told on the Pont Neuf in Paris in front of a particular crowd and at a particular moment in a broader history. I think we look for projects that in a way are first built as a chronotope and then as a response to a series of hypotheses that are made to be looked at as chronotope. This question of discontinuities with the chronotope as opposed to the long durée is extremely important if architects are to respond to historical theories of the present and not of the past.

TSCHUMI The chronotope is constantly rewritten. It's another history. Therefore, the chronotope becomes another chronotope every time. You have three parts in the equation: the space, the time, and the narrative. If you change any one of the parts of the equation – if you remove the time but keep the space and the narrative constant, it is another thing; or if you alter the space and keep the narrative, keep the time, it's again a change. The chronotope itself is something that is in constant instability.

AKRAM ABU HAMDAN I'd just like to comment on a point made earlier that was never fully answered. It's to do with energy and light. I feel we have sidetracked light as a time-relative energy and as a maker of space and form – i.e., "And then there was light." I make reference also to John's association of light with God. This raises a couple of questions. I'm not looking for immediate answers but for something we can think about. First, are we subconsciously trying to reach God through ultimate abstraction, as light is not only an astral phenomenon but also an abstracted means of transporting power and telecommunications? Are time and abstraction related? Are the birth of time and the collapse of time processes or are they accidents? Do they have abrupt beginnings and ends? If so, they must have some form of pre- and post-resonance. Is that related to space and form? These are points that I feel we should also be thinking about.

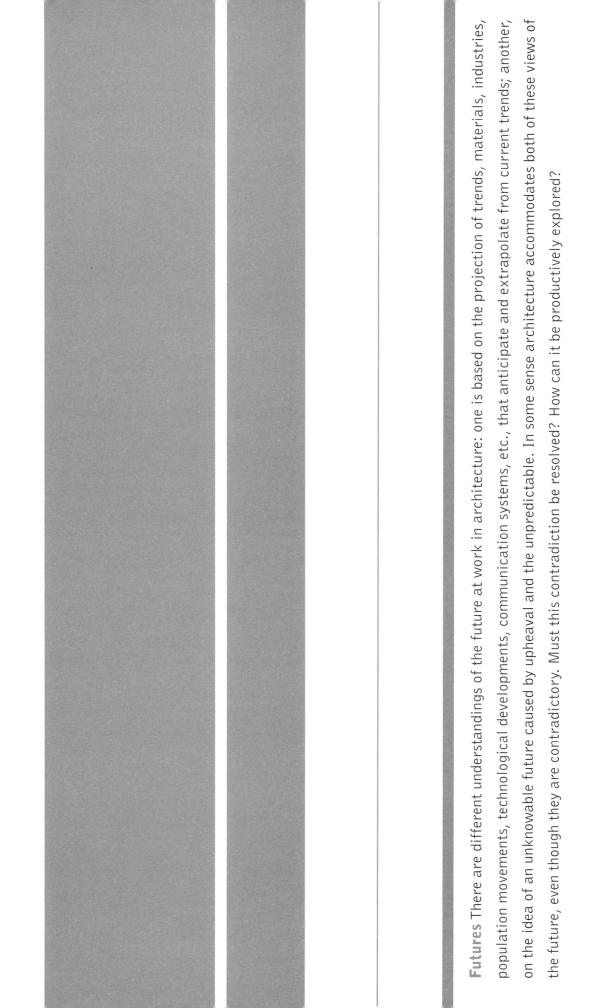

Futures There are different understandings of the future at work in architecture: one is based on the projection of trends, materials, industries, population movements, technological developments, communication systems, etc., that anticipate and extrapolate from current trends; another, on the idea of an unknowable future caused by upheaval and the unpredictable. In some sense architecture accommodates both of these views of the future, even though they are contradictory. Must this contradiction be resolved? How can it be productively explored?

Getting Engaged Bruce Mau

To call the 20th century an era of change is to understate the obvious. The last century has seen the world swept along by an extraordinary tide of change. We have been exposed to instances of invention, discovery, growth, and rupture that have transformed our lives in ways that we cannot yet fully comprehend. The effects of global modernization continue to shape and connect us. To fully appreciate the scope and impact of globalization on culture and identity, we need to place our thinking in the flow of the world.

To fully engage our moment in history, we need to develop speculative projects that illuminate the context in which we produce our work. Only a willingness to tackle the big questions, the tough assignments, the tasks we often consider boring or beneath us, will reinvigorate the practice of design. Only a full-fledged, exuberant engagement – neither *Wired*-style boosterism, nor mud-stuck nostalgic "resistance" – will fashion a practice of depth and meaning. This sort of engagement means calculating every move against the volatile milieu that envelops any new object, gesture, or configuration. Engagement means tenacity and entrepreneurship, along with creative, intellectual, and even physical stamina. It means postponing judgment while we search for an exit. It means not knowing the answers but fearlessly asking the questions.

To better understand the work we produce, and the work we ought to produce, I have attempted a preliminary inventory of the "background" conditions that increasingly constitute the substance of our work. Here I propose that there is little or no distance between foreground and background. On the contrary, our work and the objects we produce – whether they are books, cinema, systems, or language – are embedded in the thickness between the two. They are, in effect, formed of the world beyond them. That world has brought about the evolution of a new set of volatile forces, conditions, and practices.

The inventory touches on a range of phenomena currently shaping and constituting our global image context. It includes: inscribed surfaces, circulation, surveillance, infrastructure, camouflage, tourism, freeway condition,

Michael Friedel/Grazia Neri, Micronesia, 1996.

Robin Collyer, Yonge Street, Willowdale, 1995, retouched photography.

Robin Collyer, Yonge Street, Willowdale, 1995, retouched photography.

Kyochi Tsuzuki, Statue of Liberty.

Cape Concealment Specialities Sniper in Training, USA, from Colours (March 1996).

franchise, celebrity, the unstable image, e-media, violence, aura, and communication.

What becomes apparent in studying the inventory is that things are now more connected than ever. The attempt to find the boundary of any practice – where one ends and another begins – is increasingly artificial. We live in a 24-hour market world where there is less and less "unregulated" terrain. Events, cultural styles, technologies, memes, comments, rumors, scares, and insults pass through the global economy, distorting one another and reverberating.

INSCRIBED SURFACES
Image technology, global markets, and digital infrastructure all demand and support a predatory colonization of open space – whatever its physical, virtual, or temporal form. There is an endless need for inscribed and inscribable surfaces.

Openings of every sort – in schedules, in urban space, on clothes, in events, on objects, in sightlines, in democracy, in philanthropy, in cultures, on bodies – are all inscribed with the logic of the market. Regions once thought free from this logic find it ever more difficult to retain autonomy in the face of corporate cultural sponsorships, corporate educational initiatives, and so-called "civic" gestures. Nature (what remains of it) is perhaps all we have left that is free from the hostile takeover of the space of the logo, the regime of inscription.

CIRCULATION
What goes around, goes around. Circulation is the lingua franca of the new context. All objects, even apparently stable and singular ones like buildings and places, now exist in many places simultaneously. Statues of Liberty (the original was appropriately conceived as a love letter from its French creators) now proliferate all over the globe. So do signature architects: Frank Gehry is Frank at work in his Los Angeles studio, but he is also 400,000 Web site entries and an ad for Apple computers, Bilbao, and a line of bentwood furniture.

Within our reprographic culture, value is directly linked to circulation. Michael Jordan and Dennis Rodman function as currency. Their value is pegged to their performance on the court, but it also lies in their ability to circulate fluidly as brand images, in their capacity to be compressed and packaged to suit various communication formats.

SURVEILLANCE
Surveillance is the logical, even inevitable, outcome of a system with unlimited capacity to record. (Credit cards, magazine subscriptions, and mail-order catalogues are part of a vast network of data mining.) All information is ostensibly captured with the best of intentions – to improve service, to improve a product, to give us more of what we want – for our own good. As the recording systems become increasingly "responsive" to our "interests," as expressed by our purchasing patterns, we may only encounter things that interest us. Picture a world that rolls out in front of us like a red carpet of our own design, a projection of our own desires.

INFRASTRUCTURE
We all know about the "old" infrastructure. It involves large-scale, capital projects that are often visually prominent, politically sensitive, and typically the "pinnacle" of their "chief architect's" career – railway terminals, hydroelectric projects, and museums on hilltops (with railway terminals).

The "new" infrastructure, by contrast, is distributed, decentralized, and evolutionary. Built or grown by users, or in response to users, the new infrastructure consists of agreements, alliances, standards, and systems. It includes:

1. Mastercard, Visa, credit systems: In this vast e-commerce network, connection is more important to retail practice than physical real estate.
2. Currency exchange: Currency exchange is an ever-expanding system of shifting values. Once a currency is posted, everything within its domain enters the realm of infrastructure.
3. The global image business: Standards allow film purchase in Jakarta, processing in Toronto, and projection in Zurich.
4. The global media business: This system promotes the free circulation of "items" and "clips" measured in column inches and sound bites. (Paparazzi are the parasitic infrastructure.)

5. Containerization: The dispersed infrastructure of containerization liberated acres of the old-fashioned kind – ports and cargo terminals – triggering vast downtown real estate expansions in cities worldwide. The latest development (now in prototype), will use jet boats to guarantee on-time international cargo delivery in any weather, imposing just-in-time manufacturing from Houston to Kuala Lumpur. The problem overcome is not speed but inconsistency. The new system allows for further denationalization. Hold on to your minimum wage.

6. The software business: The software business is infrastructure produced line-by-line by millions of programmers. In a race to generate market share – and gain control of the infrastructure (what is called "an installed base") – they are giving it away.

Software produces a range of mini infrastructures: *the global typographic system* – digital fonts are accessible the world over; *the world car* – Ford is launching a world design studio connecting designers in Europe, Asia, and North America to produce a world car; and, of course, *the Internet* – the greatest distributed evolutionary infrastructure, still in its infancy. Conceived as a defensive posture to protect the old-fashioned kind of infrastructure, the Internet is still linked to an American system of command and control.

CAMOUFLAGE

The past half century has seen the creation of a vast industry that manufactures appearances that are subtly at odds with reality. In response to the collective stress of the changes we are undergoing, we have dedicated enormous resources to propping up and confirming our shared state of denial. We deny our newness, our ruthlessness, our violence, our modernity and focus instead on managing our image through public relations and spin-doctoring. The media, fully integrated into the camouflage industries, shift the debate from content to form, from "what she said" to "how she said it." The effect of all this is, paradoxically, that reality now seems at odds with appearances.

TOURISM

Every city is now in the business not only of making itself but also of marketing itself. Decisions that affect tourist "optics," like whether a city has a professional sports franchise or a crime problem or a police problem, take on added significance. Thanks to Milton Glaser, who brought us the I ♥ New York logo, cities around the globe compete for tourism dollars with their own logos and slogans. Celebrities – some long gone – are pressed into promotional service. The destinations themselves are increasingly design driven: nighttime golf courses carved from the Asian jungle, cinematically engineered theme parks, the latest massive-scale cruise liners. The latter, too big to actually dock anywhere, are no longer a form of transportation but are themselves a floating destination.

Abetted by transnational designers and architects, the forces of globalism are working their way into every pocket of the world. As a result, the places we arrive at are increasingly similar to the places we depart from. The most successful "attractions," like Jon Jerde's City Walk at Universal Studios, are franchised and reproduced around the world with subtle local inflection, increasing attendance and decreasing travel time.

The question becomes: Where to from here?

As the global middle class expands exponentially and global infrastructure transports vast hordes to increasingly distant and exotic destinations, every local "difference" becomes fodder for touristic exploitation. But as franchise operations continue to extend their global presence, wiping out uniqueness in food, culture, custom, and product, the practices that remain distinctive have become increasingly extreme and eccentric – bull fights, sex industries, violence, risk, fundamentalism, primitivism, isolation, disaster . . . architecture. In our age of global tourism, the natural environment represents the only significant and unmanufacturable difference, but even that is not holding on very well.

As thrill-seeking tourists look further and further afield to experience the ideal trip, one can imagine increasingly eccentric niche market offerings: South Central L.A. Survival Adventures; Ethiopian Famine Tours; Antarctic Isolation Tours (you may simply never come back); Disease Tours (complete with guaranteed cure).

Oasis, from Colours (May 1996).

Kyoichi Tsuzuki, EroDynamic Museum.

Kurita/Gamma, Private Ocean, from Colours (May 1996).

Freeway Condition.

Maria Aufmuth, Kentucky Fried Devil, 1997.

Reagan in Fur.

FREEWAY CONDITION

To drive the Pasadena 110 – the first freeway in America, famous for its treacherous 20-meter on-ramps – is to understand the cultural significance of the freeway condition. It is the profoundly modern idea that we can enter a flow, be carried along with it, and exit again effortlessly, unscathed.

As actual places decline in significance and particularity, the space between them increases in prominence and "quality." As Tracy Metz notes in the book *Snelweg – Highways in the Netherlands*, "Roads no longer merely lead to places: they are places."

The metaphor of the freeway condition, of constant movement and velocity, has become so ingrained in our collective psyche that it is now applied to politics, to (assembly-line, just-in-time) manufacturing, to the information industry. It is even applied to parenting. We are now a "streamlined" culture. We "go with the flow" and look for the best on-ramps. It is only when we try to decelerate that we realize there's a problem. In a freeway condition only robust entities survive. Only brand franchise signals can be apprehended. With culture set at cruise-control, clarity trumps complexity. The known quantity "Toys-R-Us" wins out every time over enterprising but ambiguous "mom and pop."

Uniqueness is a traffic hazard when you're traveling at breakneck speed. Difference, no matter how subtle, is an unnecessary detour. Both are impossible with life lived "on the fly."

FRANCHISE

Franchise is the application of reproduction technologies to intangibles. Franchise is founded on the idea that not only products can be designed, produced, circulated, and branded. Space and time can be branded too. Franchise is the packaging of sensibility – smiles, greetings, prompts, and employee "performance."

Franchise supersedes national boundaries. Franchise thrives on and sometimes generates a tabula rasa – a flat-nothing-on-the-edge-of-nowhere. For Franchise, no context is the best context.

Franchise is ruthlessly efficient, a form of centralized economy where development costs are endlessly amortized, where profits collected worldwide support the next phase of planned innovation at a head office.

Franchise is the logical outcome of the freeway condition. The "known" quantity, even of dubious quality, wins every time.

Franchise demands clarity. The capsule, the slogan, is the format of choice. For Franchise, "we bring good things to life" = "even finicky eaters love the meaty taste" = "we do it all for you."

The perceived limit of temporal, physical, and "attentional" real estate that one Franchise can occupy now prompts production of false variety: The Gap, Banana Republic, and Old Navy, apparent competitors, are all engineered by one design enterprise.

In a twist of irony, the ubiquity of Franchise has also provided an Esperanto of media formulas and clichés for culture jammers. Images now circulate beyond the control of central planners. The swoosh, the colonel, the arches, the bunny; all these have become fodder for culture jammers who threaten to blow apart the system of sign value.

THE UNSTABLE IMAGE, OR PHOTOSHOP TILL YOU DROP

We are faced with a fundamental paradox: as special effects become *more* real, that is, more convincing, the original image becomes *less* real – drained of its connection to an actual moment in time.

At its apparent apotheosis, the image arrives without its credibility intact. Even the straight shot seems suspect, easily accused of digital manipulation. Deadpan, amateur, snapshot chic is inflated with the potential of providing an "honest" alternative.

At the other extreme, the morphed image exposes us to deeply disturbing feelings of instability; call it ontological vertigo. As visual landmarks melt and reform before our eyes, many of us sense that the world will never be the same again.

CELEBRITY: BRANDED HUMANS

Celebrity is a clear human signal in a noisy corporate world.

Celebrity is a short form for personality, a way of "stuffing" complexity into a package that need never be opened.

Celebrity is efficiency applied to qualities.

Celebrity is a brand of DNA. It functions as a reductive index of personality and behavior.

Celebrity is the knife that cuts all of human history into 15-minute slices. It is the price you pay for being part of the future.

Celebrity is no longer based on accomplishment. It can be bestowed by virtue of mere proximity (Kato Kaelin), victimization (Nicole Brown-Simpson), mistaken identity (the Atlanta bomber), relation (Nicole's parents), evil intent (Mark Fuhrman), incompetence (Mark Fuhrman), or happenstance (Marsha Clark).

Celebrity occurs at every scale. Madonna = XXL celebrity, but every small town has a celebrity, typically seen hawking cars or carpets on late-night TV.

E-MEDIA

With 500 channels distributing events 24 hours a day, we have created a "need" for 12,000 hours of "drama" every day of the year. Since we can't possibly generate that volume "naturally," we have developed elaborate and sometimes bizarre strategies to produce it artificially.

> 1. Bottom Feeding: "My _____'s _____ is sleeping with my _____." This is a dismal format capable of infinite variation.
> 2. Depth: An imagined demand for "more" creates mind-numbing mountains of detail.
> 3. Television Verité: The MTV of police work, television verité has all the harshness of its cinematic cousin with none of the aesthetic ambitions.
> 4. Aerial Surveillance: The helicopter – a quintessentially American technology – can be seen scouring the landscape for a competitive edge. (A recent shotgun suicide on a Los Angeles freeway was broadcast live during children's cartoons, prompting bizarre apologies from the networks.)
> 5. Media Daisy Chain: We have reached a level of saturation where we regularly watch the coverage of the coverage of the coverage. A feeding frenzy on major stories has brought about increasingly abstract, minimalist programming. "Waiting" – for the jury, for a confrontation, for the standoff to end – is the content.
> 6. Amateur footage: There is a growing industry for amateur coverage of violence, disaster, and

pratfalls. The Rodney King video, one of the most broadcast clips in television history, had far-reaching consequences, not least among which were the Los Angeles Riots. These, in turn, provided ample opportunity for use of all of the above strategies.

A club with infinite membership, e-media represents a conduit between the production and consumption of events.

VIOLENCE

If the music business is about love, then perhaps the image business is about violence. Nowadays, the image business splits broadly into two camps: the utopian (advertising + Hollywood) and the dystopian (media + Hollywood).

Commerce produces utopia. Its line is: "There will be a future. It will be good. You will be there." Violent dystopia is the domain of today's newsmakers. Their line is: "There may not be a future given how violent today is. If there is, it will be violent and brutish, and you will be there."

AURA

Contrary to Walter Benjamin's assertion that mechanical reproduction drains the work of art of its aura, the inverse has come to pass. The circulated image does not steal the aura, it borrows and invests it. Today, the works of the greatest value – both in monetary and in auratic density – are precisely those images that are most reproduced.

It seems more and more apparent that virtual reality will never be a substitute for real space. On the contrary, the "virtual" now acts as an enormous advertisement for the real. Because the reproduction cannot ever hope to generate the dynamic range or bandwidth of the original; the better and closer it gets, the greater and more elusive the original becomes.

COMMUNICATION:
THE FIFTH DIMENSION

Communication is an infinitely flexible yardstick capable of measuring anything. Every gesture, every object, every event, has a communicative dimension that can be calculated and sometimes controlled. But that dimension

University of Illinois
at Chicago Biomedical
Visualization.

Body Builders.

Stock Market

Kirk McKoy/L.A.Times,
L.A. Uprising, 1992.

Misrach, **Target Practice.**

Thomas Struth, **Art Institute of Chicago 1, 1990.**

is not stable. It changes with perspective, with time, and with market conditions. Those capable of wielding the yardstick effectively have an uncanny ability to calibrate these factors. Some examples:

1. In a modern business context, the old-fashioned device says, "We care about our history," unless the service is bad, in which case it says, "We're poorly managed and haven't yet upgraded our equipment," unless the business is convincingly grassroots, in which case it says, "We care about the environment." No system of meaning is sacred. Every market sign is fundamentally unstable.

2. My stylish new haircut says, "I'm hip to the latest trends," unless I'm a White House intern, in which case it says, "I'm being handled by a book agent," unless I'm being attacked by the president's wife, in which case it says, "I'm not trailer park trash. I'm just a gullible, somewhat ambitious girl from the West Coast being handled by a book agent."

It is what it is, and it is what it says. Bhopal for Dupont. Valdez for Exxon. Nazi gold for Swiss banks. These are events with a considerable communicative dimension. Their meanings are enlarged or reduced by the way they are managed.

TIME AND ATTENTION

What I propose in response to these accelerated, frenzied, torrential conditions is an engaged design methodology. Engagement means enlisting to our advantage all of the restrictions, conditions, and limitations of the context in which we work. It means – like it or not – taking on the background of every foreground.

Unless we come to terms with our global image context and the way it permeates the things we make and see, we are doomed to spend our lives decorating and redecorating.

If freedom can be defined as the ability to apply one's energy to objects of one's own choosing, then our attention (our time and energy) is our most precious resource and ought to be guarded jealously. By understanding our working context we open avenues of liberty not yet established or explored.

BRUCE MAU IS HEAD
DESIGNER AT BRUCE
MAU DESIGN TORONTO,
DESIGN DIRECTOR OF
ZONE BOOKS, AND AN
EDITOR OF SWERVE
EDITIONS. HE IS THE
ASSOCIATE CULLINAN
PROFESSOR AT RICE
UNIVERSITY, AND A
RECIPIENT OF THE 1998
CHRYSLER AWARD FOR
DESIGN INNOVATION.

Time and the Concept of Modernity Fredric Jameson

1 Bioethics is clearly enough the new wrinkle in this old picture; it is a new problem that clearly breathes new life into an outmoded discipline. But the historical originality of this problem is that it is political rather than ethical in the older sense and meaning of the word.

2 See my *Cultural Turn* (New York: Verso, 1998), 93–103 in particular.

The title and topic of *Anytime* suggest two lines of inquiry, which I will pursue successively in what follows. First of all, the theme of time commits us to some reflection on history and periodization, both within architecture and outside of it; I want to register some peculiar and unexpected recent developments in this domain. Time is also a philosophical issue and an existential one, and demands a few thoughts on temporality as such. Those will follow briefly at the end.

In full postmodernity, or rather, as Ilhan Tekeli very nicely put it, in full *Anyfication*, there had until now always seemed to be a certain general agreement, a certain general consensus, on those features of the modern which were no longer desirable. The asceticism of the modern, for example, or its phallocentrism (whether it was ever altogether logocentric I am a little less sure); the authoritarianism and even the occasional repressiveness of the modern; the teleology of the modernist aesthetic as it proceeded on triumphalistically from the newer to the newest; the minimalism of much that was modernist as well; the cult of the genius or seer; the nonpleasurable demands made on the audience or public; all these things, which are of course interrelated and often simply aspects or different versions of each other, have been systematically and repeatedly named by the commentators.

Yet in the midst of all these healthy movements of disgust and revulsion, indeed, to the very sound of windows breaking and old furniture being thrown out, we have begun in the last few years to witness phenomena of a very different order, phenomena which suggest the return to and the reestablishment of all kinds of old things rather than their wholesale liquidation. Thus one of the great achievements of postmodernity – of "theory" or theoretical discourse on the one hand, and of Richard Rorty's *Philosophy and the Mirror of Nature* on the other (along with Pierre Bourdieu's critique of the disciplines) – was surely to have discredited "philosophy" in the traditional disciplinary sense and to have stimulated a proliferation of new kinds of thinking and new kinds of conceptual writing. Yet now we begin to witness the return of traditional philosophy all over the world, beginning with the hoariest subfields, such as ethics;[1] can metaphysics be far behind, one wonders (there are New Age speculations about physics that suggest it), if not theology itself (of which negative theology had promised an undermining)?

So it is that something like political philosophy reemerges as well, bringing back with it all those ancient questions about constitutions and citizenship, about "civil society" and parliamentary representation, as though nothing at all had been learned from the revolutionary century and from the experience of power, and as though all those problems were not in reality historical reflexes of the transition from feudalism to capitalism – an event now deeply lost in the world's past – rather than of some putative transition from communism to democracy.[2] Along with all this, an older political economy totters forth like a shade and offers us a prodigious new development, namely, the reinvention of the market, something about as exciting as the reinvention of the wheel. People can no doubt be left to their own tastes (another archaic concept, as I will imply in a moment), but no one is going to persuade me that there is anything glamorous about the thought of Milton Friedman, a Hayek, or a Popper in the present day and age.

And then there is the resuscitation of aesthetics, a discipline we thought modernism had both invented and deconstructed simultaneously, the various modernist forms of the sublime effacing aesthetic questions as swiftly as they began to emerge. Yet today, once again, people are beginning to raise the issue of beauty, the central subject of an aesthetics whose bourgeois motivation can be registered in its twin endpoints: the trivializations of the purely decorative and enjoyable on the one hand, and the sentimental idealism of the various ideologies of aesthetic justification on the other.

It must not be thought that these returns and revivals pose no problems for a history of ideas that is called on to justify them (as well as to discredit the modernist interests they wish to declare old-fashioned). Jean-François Lyotard's preemptive strike – that there are no longer any "grand narratives" and that therefore a historical and narrative justification was unnecessary, that "actuality" is not systematic and is nothing but a random coexistence of irreconcilable Nietzschean presents of time – is not very satisfying when it comes to dealing with these obviously regressive or reactionary phenomena. (It works much better for the experimental, which, naturally enough, frets and chafes under the alleged demise of modernist teleology.) Indeed, Lyotard himself, when it came to aesthetic matters, found himself obliged to reinvent one of the most archaic models of temporality, that of circular if not cyclical time, in order to justify his own proposition about the return of the aesthetic; namely, that the postmodern does not follow but rather precedes and prepares the return of modernism itself. Indeed, it was actually this dramatic and paradoxical formula which suggested that it was not so easy to get rid of historical narratives and historical storytelling by simple fiat; that narrative knows its own irrepressible return of the repressed. Lyotard's own proposition of some historical "end" of grand narratives was itself a new grand narrative (as must be all other versions of the now familiar "end of history"). It is an unexpected eventuality that leads us to some first thesis in the present context (the first of four to follow), namely, that whatever our philosophical or practical objections, we cannot not periodize. Beings condemned to think in terms of storytelling cannot but tell their own stories in periodizing terms – a negative formula I prefer to positive or affirmative concepts of periodization, which must all necessarily be ideological in their own distinctive ways.

This is the context in which I want us to consider one final return or reinvention of the outmoded in full postmodernity, and it is no doubt the most paradoxical of all: the return of the idea of modernity itself (my other three theses will bear more specifically on this peculiar matter). It must be a postmodern thing, one thinks, this seeming return of this or that concept of the modern. It is at any rate not a mere historical reconsideration of the type we would expect to find when some later historical stage reconsiders an earlier one and its self-justification. What could be more appropriate than a reconsideration of the very nature of modernity from the vantage point of the postmodern? Yet that was precisely what the critique of the modern constituted; this "new" and very different return is rather the reminting of the modern, its repackaging, its production in great quantities for renewed sales in the intellectual marketplace, from the biggest names in sociology to garden-variety discussions in all of the social sciences (and in some of the arts as well).

There are many reasons why this should be happening, although few enough of them justify it. Postmodernity came to seem a relatively disreputable idea in the established disciplines when some of its nastier consequences – a retheorization of late capitalism, a coming to terms with so-called "relativism" and the constructedness of social reality, an affirmation of social difference in the so-called multicultural – became more evident. Even if you distrust periodization as such, the concept of modernity, which traces its lineage back to the founding fathers of sociology – and with which indeed sociology itself is coterminous as a field of study – seems respectable and academic enough.

But there are deeper motivations, deeper advantages, and they lie mostly in the new global market, not least in the global marketplace of ideas. For one of the inescapable dimensions of the concept of modernity was that of modernization (itself a much later post–World War II coinage): modernity always had something to do with technology (at least in "modern times") and thus eventually with progress. But World War I dealt a very serious blow to ideologies of progress, particularly to those related to technology, and in any event bourgeois thinkers themselves had serious and self-critical doubts about progress from the late-19th century on. The invention of modernization theory after World War II allowed the bourgeois idea of progress a certain afterlife, while modernity and modernization knew a rather different version in the socialist countries based on the Stalinist promise of catching up with the West and its industry. However, the vociferous denunciation of Stalinist versions of modernization, which was strategically associated with the general proposition that Marxism and socialism were in their very nature bad "Promethean" ideologies, ought not to obscure the parallel discrediting of Western versions of modernization by the ecology movement, by certain types of feminism, and by a variety of left-wing critiques of progress and industrialization (the right-wing or conservative variants of these positions seem to have waned and ebbed since the onset of the market era, if not well before that). Yet, as Romi Khosla pointed out here,[3] if you have no program for future change to offer people – in other words, if you have no version at all of some vision of historical progress – you can scarcely compete politically. The revival of the concept of modernity is an attempt to solve that problem: in a situation in which modernization, socialism, industrialization (particularly the precomputerized kind of heavy industry), Prometheanism, and the "rape of nature" generally have been discredited, you can still suggest that the so-called underdeveloped countries might want to look forward to simple "modernity" itself. Never mind the fact that all of the viable nation states in the world today have long since been "modern" in every conceivable sense, technological and otherwise. What is encouraged is the illusion that the West has something no one else possesses, but which everyone ought to desire for themselves: that mysterious something can then be baptized "modernity" and described at great length by those who are called upon to sell the product in question. The lost object of desire. . .

Under these circumstances, a renewed investigation of modernity seems in order, one which is able to fulfill at least two positive requirements: to deal with the matter historically, and to provide operational rules for the use of a word that will surely not go away, however ideological its deployments may be.

The historical requirement ought not to tempt us back into the more questionable practices of a traditional history of ideas, which used to assume the existence of something like a stable concept that was modified over time and passed down with the kinds of alterations one finds in a building or a text. The philological method, which traces a material word down through its own changes, along with those of its vocabulary field, is surely the more satisfactory one here.[4] This process will in fact, in the present instance, persuade us of the validity and pertinence of my second thesis, namely, that modernity is not a concept, philosophical or otherwise, but rather a narrative category. It cannot be used without implying a before and an after, without generating what Jacques Derrida called the supplement of its opposite number and of the otherness of what it is not, namely, the unmodern, the premodern (and eventually the postmodern).[5]

So "modernity" always means setting a date and positing a beginning, and it is always amusing and instructive to make an inventory of the possibilities, which tend to move around in chronological time, the most recent – nominalism – being among the oldest. The Protestant Reformation obviously enjoys a certain priority for the German tradition in general (and for Hegel in particular). For the philosophers, however, Descartes's thoroughgoing break with the past is not only the inauguration of modernity but already of a self-conscious or reflexive theory of it; the cogito itself stages reflexivity as one of modernity's central features. In hindsight – the hindsight of the 20th century and decolonization – it now seems clear that the conquest of the Americas brought with it a significant new element of modernity,[6] even though traditionally the

3 Romi Khosla, "Abstract and Ancient Futures," presented at the Anytime conference on June 14, 1998, and published in this volume, 122–27.

4 The basic work has been done by Hans-Robert Jauss in his "Literarische Tradition und gegenwärtiges Bewusstsein der Modernität," in Literaturgeschichte als Provokation (Frankfurt: Suhrkamp, 1970), 11–57.

5 See Jacques Derrida, Of Grammatology, trans. Gayatri Spivak (Baltimore: Johns Hopkins University Press, 1976), 144–64 especially; the subject is of course Rousseau's own theory of history and concept of modernity.

6 See Enrique Dussel, "Beyond Eurocentrism: the World-system and the Limits of Modernity," in The Cultures of Globalization, eds. Masao Miyoshi and Fredric Jameson (Durham: Duke University Press, 1997), 3–31.

French Revolution, and the Enlightenment that prepared and accompanied it, has been credited with modernity's most momentous social and political break. Yet the reminder of science and technology suddenly sends us all the way back to Galileo if we are not content to affirm the existence of an alternate revolution in the Industrial one. Adam Smith and others make the emergence of capitalism an unavoidable narrative option, while the German tradition (and more recently the Michel Foucault of *The Order of Things*) affirms the significance of that special kind of reflexivity which is the historicist kind, or the sense of history itself. After that, modernities fly thick and fast: the Nietzschean death of God; Weberian rationalization in the second or bureaucratic/monopoly stage of industrial capitalism; aesthetic modernism itself, with its reification of language and the emergence of formal abstractions of all kinds; and last, but still not least, the Soviet revolution. In recent years, however, breaks that once would have been characterized as so many modernities have tended, rather, to be termed postmodern. Thus the 1960s brought momentous changes of all kinds, which it somehow seems superfluous to call a further modernity: modernity's own moment of modernity, perhaps, but the conceit would demand analysis in its own right.

That makes some thirteen proposals. One can be sure that many more are lurking in the wings, and also that the "correct" theory of modernity is not to be obtained by putting them all together in some hierarchical synthesis. Indeed, in my view, such a theory is not to be obtained at all, since what we have to work with here are narrative options and alternate storytelling possibilities, as which even the most scientific-looking and structural of purely sociological concepts can always be unmasked.[7] This does not necessarily mean that all options are equally viable, all stories equally interesting. Some have argued that the priority of a historical narrative derives from the amount of material it can encompass and absorb: perhaps, instead of grand narratives, it is simple narratives that we no longer particularly care for. I have a different proposal, and it will constitute my third thesis on modernity.

Descartes teaches us many things, but what I would like to retain from the lesson of the cogito – it is, to be sure, a perverse kind of edification – is the unrepresentability of subjectivity or consciousness itself. The cogito is not figurable; this is the consequence I draw from the most recent studies.[8] If the word stands for anything, it stands for the impossibility of formulating or representing, even conceptualizing the subject itself (which, it should be remembered, Kant numbered among the unrepresentable "things-in-themselves"). In our present context, this is an excellent lesson, for it allows us to discard a great number of narratives of modernity which are organized around this or that thematic of subjectivity, beginning with the narrative appropriation of Descartes himself. The cogito is not some primal form of self-consciousness, and it may come as a relief to realize that we may now abandon all those narratives which tell the story of modernity in terms of self-consciousness or reflexivity. It is clear enough, as Johannes Fabian, Bruno Latour, and others have warned us lately, that any definition of the modern in terms of self-consciousness produces its otherness in the form of the unmodern or premodern subject – the primitive! – who is thus by definition not self-conscious.[9] I think that this is not completely to be identified with Eurocentrism, although the two feelings certainly reinforce each other. The Eurocentrism that appears on the very first page of Max Weber's *Protestant Ethic*[10] has as much to do with the historical accident of capitalism's emergence in Europe as it does with fatuous ethnic or regional prejudice. Better to deal with this according to my thesis or formula: namely,

7 This is the argument of Arthur Danto's *Narration and Knowledge* (New York: Columbia University Press, 1985).

8 Jean-Luc Nancy, *Ego sum* (Paris: Flammarion, 1979); Claudia Brodsky-Latour, *Lines of Thought* (Durham: Duke University Press, 1996).

9 Johannes Fabian, *Time and the Other* (New York: Columbia University Press, 1983); Bruno Latour, *We Have Never Been Modern* (Cambridge: Harvard University Press, 1993).

10 "A product of modern European civilization, studying any problem of universal history, is bound to ask himself to what combination of circumstances the fact should be attributed that in Western civilization, and in Western civilization only, cultural phenomena have appeared which (as we like to think) lie in a line of development having universal significance and value." Max Weber, *The Protestant Ethic and the Spirit of Capitalism*, trans. Talcott Parsons (London: Harper Collins Academic, 1991), 1.

that the narrative of modernity cannot be told in terms of subjectivity, since the latter is unrepresentable in the first place. This then gets rid of the two other competing subjective options, namely, the telling of the story in terms of *freedom* and in terms of *individuality*, themes which no doubt invariably get mixed up with self-consciousness and with the privileges of the West.

But do we have anything left when we discard these long-cherished notions, which point to differences of inwardness, to unique qualities of subjectivity, to advantages of the soul? And however idealist such concepts are, has their historical role not been sufficiently preponderant for us to need to take them into account? In other words, the existence of new subjective virtues and qualities may not be a satisfactory explanation for modernity; on the other hand, any satisfactory account of modernity would certainly need to come to terms with the "modern" emergence of just such subjectivizing theories and arguments. Modernity is not some new form of subjectivity; but the new thematics of the subject are certainly modern in ways that remain to be accounted for (particularly since we have not yet offered any narrative alternative to these subjective ones).

What is minimally clear is that we have to make do here with our old friend, the subject/object split. It is around this event that the narrative of modernity is now being framed. It is with this event that modernity is said to begin. But is this yet another subjective narrative (consequences for the subject of the subject/object split), or has it now somehow miraculously become objective? In fact, the theory is objectively ambiguous, if I may put it that way, and can be read in either mode. I am unwilling to decide where this diagnosis of modernity comes from, however, except to observe that its theorists would necessarily be very modern ones indeed (and that the argument would probably begin as a test of strength between Hegelians and Nietzscheans). But it is undoubtedly Heidegger who has offered its most influential 20th-century version, and therefore Heidegger's theory of the subject/object dichotomy, in particular Heidegger's reading of Descartes and his interpretation of the cogito,[11] would have to be set in place here. I'll summarize it by suggesting that, for Heidegger, modernity resides neither in the subject nor in the object but rather in the situation.[12] In his narrative, the subject side of the dichotomy produces the now differentiated and separated object side by producing itself at one and the same time; subject and object "result" from this initial act of positing through separation, of separating through positing. This is at least the point I want to reach in this brief discussion and critique of theories of modernity: namely, that they need to be staged in terms of the situations of modernity rather than in terms of the latter's putative subjectivities.

And so on to the present day. For myself, the most interesting and productive "theories" of modernity are those which characterize it as a process of separation, something I would once again position in Descartes but in a rather different place, namely, the famous second precept of the *Discours* ("to divide up each of the difficulties into their simplest parts").[13] This process must be identified retroactively by way of its later stages – Weber's conception of rationalization, Georg Lukács's closely related formulation in terms of *reification*, and finally and most recently, Niklas Luhmann's theory of *differentiation*,[14] with which I will close this discussion of modernity.

The language of Luhmann's "differentiation" is clearly attractive to the present age and seems to offer concealed ethical perspectives and vistas of social and interpersonal difference. In addition, it is able to do an immense amount of work in correlating a variety

11 See in particular Martin Heidegger, "Der Europäische Nihilismus," in *Nietzsche* (Pfullingen: Neske, 1961), 2: 141–73.

12 The notion of the situation, popularized above all by Jean-Paul Sartre, seems to have originated (for contemporary philosophy) in Karl Jaspers.

13 René Descartes, *Oeuvres et Lettres* (Paris: Librarie Gallimard, 1953). 138. I will discuss the social determination of this procedure elsewhere; suffice it to say that without an indication of that social determination, Heidegger's model of the situation is incomplete and idealistic.

14 I have in particular consulted Niklas Luhmann, *The Differentiation of Society* (New York: Columbia University Press, 1982) and *Beobachtungen der Moderne* (Opladen: Westdeutscher Verlag, 1992).

of processes on all social levels. Finally, since it is a process rather than a static structure, it holds out a theory of history as a bonus: systems tend toward increasing internal differentiation (sometimes also called complexity), whether we are dealing with the state, with subjective feelings, with sociological theories, or with social groups. This is clearly a theory of modernity, yet it raises several narrative problems: that of a beginning, that of dialectical leaps, and that of the future. In fact, Luhmann's periodizations are the standard ones and identify the Renaissance as the general takeoff point for differentiation (anthropological notions of social order then serve to "differentiate" earlier kinds of societies and to identify forms of nonmodernity). The dialectic is certainly consistent with a general narrative of differentiation (even though Luhmann considers the dialectic to be less complex and thus less advanced than his own conception of differentiation, which can thus be seen to emerge from and to include it) and could add a welcome historical unevenness and unpredictability to what must otherwise be fantasized as an uninterrupted and relatively uniform process. But I am above all interested in the present, for which Luhmann offers no conception of postmodernity, but instead offers ever more complexity and differentiation, on an ever vaster and more minute scale.

His is thus, despite the relative novelty of the analysis, exactly that kind of regressive persistence of the older concept of modernity denounced in my opening pages. An ideologically motivated regression can here be detected by the reversion of description into prescription, the transformation of a historical analysis into a political program. Luhmann uses his own account of differentiation in order to warn against the dangers of a reduction in systemic complexity in current politics: "The obvious danger here is that we may replace the relatively large openness and variability of the classical, internal differentiation of the economic system by decision-making processes having too little selectivity and habitual and rigid premises. We would then let the economy sacrifice the maneuverability that became available after the external differentiation of the economy from the rest of the market." [15] This amounts not only to a warning against "socialism" but also rules out the maintenance of welfare-state type mechanisms or the return to even those milder forms of government regulation that have come to seem sensible after the worst excesses of the free market period. In such passages, then, Luhmann's ostensibly sociological theory of modernity unmasks itself as conventional free market rhetoric and the ideology of deregulation.

Such functional lapses are, however, mere symptoms of a deeper conceptual problem, namely, the insistence on maintaining older conceptions of modernity in the face of the situation of postmodernity, with its multiple transformations. I choose my terms carefully here, for the situation has changed and demands a modified theoretical response, without necessarily imposing any particular "concept" of postmodernity or even ruling out the argument that there has been no such transformation and that we are still in modernity itself, despite all indications to the contrary. That is why my fourth thesis must not decry the absence of a concept of the postmodern but only the omission of any attempt to come to terms with the situation of postmodernity (whatever the eventual diagnosis may turn out to be). Just such an omission certifies Luhmann's status as yet another ideologist of the modern as such.

15 Luhmann, Differentiation, 217, and see also 130, 162, 240, 287.

16 Jacques Derrida, "Ousia et Grammè," in Marges de la philosophie (Paris: Éditions de Minuit, 1972), 47.

17 See Henri Lefebvre, La Production de l'espace (Paris: Éditions Antropos, 1974), 475–77.

Now I must briefly comment on a theme frequently thought to be one of the principle constituents of modernism, if not modernity, which I have not yet mentioned. It is also the principal subject of this conference, and therefore the excuse for the lengthy preceding qualifications about modernity as a concept; I'm referring to time or temporality as such. I seem to have postponed the matter, perhaps too mindful of the remarkable warning Derrida hangs over it in an early discussion of concepts of time in Heidegger, Hegel, and Aristotle: "d'une certaine manière, il est toujours trop tard pour poser la question du temps"[16] (In a way, and from a certain standpoint, it is always too late to raise the question of time). He is speaking of the temporality of the very syntax (tenses, particles, the very order of words themselves in linear time) by means of which these philosophers set up the problem of temporality and then frame their "definitions" or even, as in his own case here, their refusals to define them. Temporality is always there ahead of them; their discussions, which ought ideally to have taken place in a space beyond or before the emergence of temporality, are always too late, presupposing what they were supposed to have discovered, reached, arrived at.

Perhaps this is not so true of the juxtaposition of time with architecture. For here, perhaps, it is precisely that buried temporal presupposition which it is a question of paradoxically bringing to light and revealing or unveiling: the deeper temporal structure of what seems absolutely spatial and at the antipodes of a temporal art like music or poetry. It would be useful to have not merely an inventory of the secret temporalities of the architectural but, above all, a chronicle of the moments in which architecture theorists have found themselves obliged to raise the subject in the first place.

I want to insert an intermediate step at this point. It is not enough to insist on time or temporality as an issue and a topic; or, rather, that is a modernist way of setting about it – the search for deep time within the spatial, as with nature in Frank Lloyd Wright, where the American landscape itself seems to offer a mediation with the archaic, sometimes by way of a preexisting culture, like the Maya, sometimes by way of the projection of the architect's own style as an ideal, imaginary, or utopian culture. Or indeed the very refusal of the archaic and of deep time, as with Le Corbusier, where the medical and industrial present mediates modernity, and hygiene offers a kind of *gestus* in which the past is removed like so much sedimented filth.

Today, however, I think we need a more explicit mediation because none of these immediacies is available to us any longer; we must therefore first interrogate the relationship between time and history. "History is time," affirmed Jules Michelet somewhere. But what is in question today is precisely this link between phenomenological time – existential temporality, the lived inner experience of the temporal – and of time that passes – history as such. Thus it is affirmed that our very sense of history, our very existential historicity, is today singularly enfeebled, as is our inner sense of time itself, compared to that of the modernists. Perhaps the implied question was itself poorly framed. The problem is not, as it seems to suggest, that of reviving older feelings of time but rather the other way round, whether a new sense of history is possible in the absence of an older existential time (or to put it in Henri Lefebvre's language, whether a spatial dialectic is imaginable.)[17]

Let me here set in place another remark, that of Gilles Deleuze, who in his film books raises an analogous problem and interrogates the political and historical possibilities of contemporary film: "Il y a quelque chose de paysan dans l'histoire"[18] (History has something peasant about it). History is a peasant rather than an urban experience: the cycle of the seasons, the immemorial, the rise and fall of dynasties, and again, that archaic sense of nature for which historical space is the landscape itself. The history of cities and modernities is too fast to be registered. The cities produce the aleatory rather than the historical. We may recall, in this context, the lessons of Louis Althusser: that temporalities and their accompanying historicities are not some eternal property of the human essence but are rather themselves produced by the modes of production. Each one – tribal or feudal society, the "Asiatic mode," the socialist, and the various stages of capitalism – generates the temporality appropriate to it, the unique mixture of desperation and empty waiting that it signs, the rhythms of the working time-unit, week or season, the form of generations, the visibility of change on material things. The quality of temporality is determined by the rate and rhythm of production itself.

Yet, at the same time there is no pure mode of production, and that very unevenness means a layering of temporalities, a surcharge and sedimentation of modes of the past and even modes of the future. The social units themselves have their own temporalities, their own technologies of memory and forgetfulness. So it is that history knew a particularly embodied existence in the period of the extended family or the class and about its mode of oral memory: storytelling in the peasant home or the manor house, the space in which several generations dwell together and the past of the grand- or great-grandparents is still present. You can reach out and touch it, even when their stories are tall tales or tissues of lies and rumors, for they are at least the lies and rumors of a time now gone by, they exist as testimony about the existence of the past, rather than about its events and contents. Such temporality lends its density to the duration of the buildings themselves; space itself is modified along with time when the older families yield to the nuclear and even the postnuclear kind, the isolated individuals, the anomie of the lone couple, the stacking up of dwelling units that can be added or subtracted at will. So perhaps existential time is itself a breakdown product of an older collective time, and perhaps it also generates its own space, the space it deserves. Perhaps the dilemma of the room as some inescapable final form of space is to be thought in this context, that ultimate existential room that was the stage of Beckett's plays but finds its most fitting representation, perhaps, in his one Film (1965).

That is to suggest that we cannot think beyond the room, and that the room marks some final arrested point of temporality. This is not necessarily such a terrible thing either, when one remembers Hegel's argument that when (as with Kant) you have reached the limit and mapped out the final boundary, beyond which the mind cannot pass, then in fact, by the very act of becoming conscious of that limit or boundary, you have already gone beyond it in a way, you have already drawn it inside thought and transcended it.

18 Gilles Deleuze, Cinéma 2. L'Image-temps (Paris: Éditions de Minuit, 1985), 332.

FREDRIC JAMESON IS DIRECTOR OF THE GRADUATE PROGRAM IN LITERATURE AT DUKE UNIVERSITY. HIS BOOKS INCLUDE LATE MARXISM; POSTMODERNISM; THE CULTURAL LOGIC OF LATE CAPITALISM; THE SEEDS OF TIME; AND BRECHT AND METHOD.

I prefer to get out of the time of the room in another way: by recalling its very construction. This is a unique species of time, which the very work itself seeks to conceal and to forget, to obliterate or, better still, to build over. For the time of the building site, of the excavation and the scaffolding, the cranes and the construction hats, of the paint cans and the wooden barricades, of dust and bulldozers, this time is the very temporality of praxis itself. Nothing better illustrates its internal contradiction than the haste of this time to abolish itself and to complete an object behind which this very temporality will disappear, its very memory become incongruous. The commodity, as has so often been said, is an object from which the traces of its production have been effaced. Production itself thus produces two temporalities, that of its coming into being and that of its persistence in being, its calm presence. These two temporalities are radically incompatible, even though so much of modern aesthetic attention and energy has been spent in the effort to create a form of the object in which its original praxis and production might still inhere. This is also the moment in which the relationship of the aesthetic to praxis and production is the most keenly visible. There remains a persistent strand in the Marxist tradition for which the very significance of the aesthetic itself lies in its projection of nonalienated labor or production. Art is then the space in which a uniquely Utopian vision of life and activity is accessible in a society in which work is alienated along with the objects it produces – and not only in its content but in its very form itself. So somehow this moment of production and of building is that figure of Utopia that ought to be present in all life and all activity, but which is at once forgotten and repressed when the project hardens over into a completed object. The forgetfulness inherent in that object is then a figure for the forgetfulness of the collective project itself, in that now global moment of a society for which praxis and activity have come to seem impossible and inconceivable, a society in which people, individuals as well as groups, have rarely seemed so paralyzed and helpless, so powerless and vulnerable, by virtue of the impossibility of imagining or remembering what real praxis or activity might be like in the first place.

Perhaps these losses, these diminutions and retreats of the temporal, mark a new situation in which it is vain to appeal to the past. Perhaps we were not wrong in feeling that the appeal to time was somehow anachronistic in a postmodernity that has so insistently been characterized by the transformation of time into space. Perhaps indeed our problems are no longer temporal ones, no longer those of deep time or of existential experience; perhaps our time is that of demographies and multiplicities, overcrowdings of people and buildings, an overpopulation of the urban, an overbuilding of the human and the social, the reign of the statistical, the externality of sheer number, which demands its own kind of monument. Perhaps then, in this sense as well, it really is too late to raise the problem of time; perhaps it is time once again to raise the problem of space.

Time and Self Incarnated Jale Nejdet Erzen

Moonflower.

Any, as a radical, forward impulse that feeds architecture with the most advanced science, technology, and philosophy, has come to Turkey — for whom history and tradition still have binding meanings — as a critical, subversive, challenging intellectual exercise, a provocation for self-examination. Any seems purified of all sentimentality; it is objective, sharp, futuristic. Anytime seeks to open up the realm of design and building to all potential inspirations, ideas, and means in order to free it from the control of a singular chronology, to energize it with many times, many futures, and multiple pasts.

Looking at the world of the powerless, one asks whether the forced and voluntary oblivion, ignorance, eradication of borders, wandering without direction, the search and exile have not already created a landscape of *any* in quite an unwanted way. Anatolian architecture, whose roots are thick, deep, and multiple, has a quality of *any-ness*. My question is can Any, as an avant-garde project, really come up with more unexpected and original solutions than those already proposed by the helpless, by anarchy.

Coming back to earth from the liberating world of abstractions, physical realities seem to subject all differences, all that wants to be independent of the earth, to the rules of nature and of the body. The Archimedean point of complete liberation and power has still not really been achieved. Any cannot truly exist.

Upon seeing the close resemblance among the traces of Eurythmie dance, the traces of water's movement, and the images of the Virtual House by Eisenman Architects, I became especially convinced that everything assumes a converging identity.[1] My text — no matter how aware I am that natural bonds often seem desperately romantic — frames the issue of Anytime from the vantage point of the earth and the body. Thus, I cannot proceed without paying respect to Octavio Paz who, in the 1960s, had already dealt with this issue in a most piercing way.

TIME/BODY/SELF

Time is a wanderer looking for a body. It acquires as many personalities and identities as the bodies it inhabits. Yet, if those bodies are in constant metamorphosis, time is forever without memory to link its many beings.

We humans believe we are more than flesh — anything but flesh — and, having not only physics but also ethics, we come to an idea of self. Where and when does the self emerge? It is coupled with time. Time is not only a catalyst for continuity but it is also the great divider, as implied in its Old English origin Di, to cut up, divide.[2]

What holds one together when the body and more than half of its cells are decomposing, decaying, and being reproduced? What constructs the self, which, in spite of all its many phases, has a common model or ethic around which it gathers? At the basic level of the cell, the memory of *identity* is passed from one dying cell to a new one as a pattern of movement. It is a trace in space. It is the body, or the embodiment of time.

1 Eisenman Architects, *Virtual House*, from the catalogue of the exhibition held at Borusan Gallery (Istanbul: Borusan Kültür ve Sanat, 1998)   2 John Ayto, *Dictionary of Word Origins* (New York: Arcade Publishing, 1991).

As such, even on a biological level, it is representation.

At the level of human consciousness, the link is constituted by representations: images, objects imbued with meaning, stories, language. In the most effective sense, continuity is rendered by cultural tools. When the body was the measure, infinitesimal variety and quality were not causes of fragmentation and disorientation. The body was the center of the universe and the great gatherer of truth. In such a world, art and culture adequately defined the self.

As the proliferation of images and symbols, as the diversity of associations have accumulated, the unity of the self has been threatened. Today, when culture is produced as an industry, it is no longer sufficiently related to the individual to serve as an *oikos*, the habitation of the self. This is now only possible with art, which functions outside the accepted consumer culture; within a true avant-garde there must be an experimental attitude where the past, present, and future find habitation. Such an art is only possible today if it is engaged. For this reason, I believe that we can appeal to architecture, which is always perforce concerned with the human.

Beginning in the 14th century, the gradual dislocation of the body from the mind, the gradual discovery of other worlds, and the realization of man's finality brought forth a stricter control of time, a more exact measure. As the notion of infinity appears against mortality, as the notion of many worlds, many universes, non-concentric orders, and many

different times appear with Giordano Bruno and Galileo, the mechanical clock develops, giving order to the uncontrollable. The clock can only measure earthly time; the clock is the "any," the appearance of the indefinite that has a meaning only if there are limits.

Man's decline from a central position as the measure of heaven and time, to a mortal fraction of an infinite and multiple world had to be compensated; exactitude would give him power over mortality. With the disjunction of the center, the eventual discrediting of the church, and the discovery of continents, planets, and galaxies, the clock gathered times and ordered them; art became the great faith.(Galileo, Giordano Bruno).[3] Art played a magical, unprecedented role at this curious time in defining the self of cultures and individuals. From the early 16th to the 18th centuries, state, church, and citizen, the sacred and the secular, found self-expression and self-revelation in art.

This happened again in the first half of the 20th century. Social and scientific disturbances and new theories and techniques gave a great impetus to art, both in unifying and defining the self and in moving toward the future. Art was both a psychic solution and a transgression. The power of art lies not only in its unifying capacity but also in the way it creates an increase in being, an increase in the time of living, especially in a society in which the regularity and routine of labor impoverishes everyday life.[4] The power of art is that it creates breathing space for

3 Giordano Bruno prepared the way for Galileo's theories, which were instrumental in the development of the mechanical clock.   4 Hans-Georg Gadamer, *The Relevance of the Beautiful* (Cambridge: Cambridge University Press, 1986), 45–46.

Jale N. Erzen, The Winds, detail.

5 In the Sistine chapel, Michelangelo's frescoes make use of varied viewpoints and spatial systems that reflect different understandings of time.   6 Navaho Indian night chant after Bitahatini from *Technicians of the Sacred*, ed. Jerome Rothenberg (New York: Doubleday, 1968), 79.

culture. In the visual arts, the endurance of the image carries us to the future. On the vault of the Sistine Chapel my gaze meets that of Michelangelo.[5] Architecture, the art that shapes and conditions our everyday life, becomes the domain of *aisthesis* in the most effective way; in architecture, this expansion of time is readily given to us.

ARCHITECTURE

Architecture, as the initial consciousness of form as spatial indicator, as territorial signification at its most nonphysical, unites immediately with time and composes it to form the shell of the individual, of the family, of the clan, of God, and of the people. Architecture also renders the identity of the days, the character of the seasons, and geographies. It becomes the definition of movement, of a life through time, of the individual through space. Architecture, as definition of movement and gathering of light, as founded in the earth and opening toward the sky, in its qualities of past, present, and future, is also the *oikos*, the habitation of time and of the self.

As in the Navaho Indian chant, after Bitahatini:[6]

> In the house made of the dawn
> In the house made of evening
>   twilight
> In the house made of dark cloud
> In the house made of rain
>   and mist, of pollen, of
>   grasshoppers
> Where the dark mist curtains
>   the doorway
> The path to which is on the
>   rainbow
> Where the zigzag lighting stands
>   high on top
> Where the he-rain stands high
>   on top

Time of darkness, of solitude, of growing, of growing old, of appearing and fading out. Time is like the moonflower, which lives only a night, perfumed and unseen, but maybe longer than you or I.

Architecture creates the spaces of history. Through and with and in architecture, the life of an epoch can survive in parallel to the actual. In art and architecture, many different times cohabit the world. Art is the simultaneous actualization of different modalities of time. In addition, there is art that actualizes one specific time and occasion, like jazz or most improvised or vernacular music. There is also architecture that is conceived not statically, but for a specific occasion or a specific experience and time. In this, it is almost like music; the narrative on the Sistine ceiling required the experience of *manytimes*; the painting moves us through different ways of being and different histories and time cycles; on the moon terrace the stones come alive and move to the rhythm of the waves when the moon is full; my painting unfolds in time as one begins to move with the brush strokes.

I am grateful for music; it is an ever-ready vessel that transports me from one temporality to another. It is like a ship in the harbor, immediate and ready, because I am surrounded by the music of the spheres, the rotation and agitation of heavenly bodies. Our first relation to time as well as to space is the body that we inhabit. But that body is itself within a body: that of the Earth, which has its movements, ups, downs, cycles, and moods. Our bodies are within the Earth, and are owned by it. Beyond are the celestial bodies, movements, cycles, and times of which have a direct bearing on the Earth.

Thus our frail bodies, consciously or not, live at the biological, metaphysical, and astronomical level, in various times. These manytimes are eternal in their own ways: the times of the cell, of the whole body, of the earth, and of the heavens and galaxies are the different music we are already tuned to.

In an architectural setting, walking from one space to another becomes something much more than going from one point to another. As in the Süleymaniye Mosque and complex, for example, we may be joining the movement of the celestial bodies in circumambulating, extending to infinite space and living eternity in a moment. Or, receiving the light of the day through an oculus may bring us close to the sun's power and orient us to the center of the universe, as at the Seljuk Medrese or the Pantheon. In Rome, standing on the hill above the Piazza del Popolo at sundown, you can feel the axis of the sun's movement through your body.

Time can be understood as the relation between successive happenings, as a flow that connects, like the harmony between two notes on a violin. Those two notes are only brief instances; what creates the music is the extension of one note into the other. In order to play the first note musically, the musician has to give his or her body and mind over to the flow of time and enter its rhythm. Understood as

such, time creates, conditions, and gives form to life's flow. The principle of Eurythmie, elaborated into a dance technique by Rudolf Steiner, considers life to be a rhythmic flow and gives priority to the notion of time over space; accordingly, the form of space is conditioned through the rhythm of the life force, Bergson's elan vital.[7] From this perspective, how similar are the traces of the bodies of Eurythmic dancers in space and the images of Eisenman's Virtual House?[8]

THE PRESENT, THE FUTURE, AND THE AVANT-GARDE

Music and art are the continued heritage of a perception and tuning of time that relates to the senses and to the body. They relate to genetic memories of many times, memories predating the invention of mechanical time and of mechanical measurements. Such perception, through synchronizing and *syn-aestheticizing* many ways of being, can also create a potential ground for sharing among peoples.

In contrast to the movements of time before the clock, mechanical time is supposed to be repetitious and lifeless. But I remember when the ticktock, like the heartbeats of an invisible visitor, used to echo and define the spaces where we lived. That ticktock has been silenced. The unarrestable quality of time has been substituted by the ever-fixed digit. Now, even the mechanical time of the clock may seem strangely animated, just as primitive machines once used to measure time now resemble Paleolithic fossils. The machine, after all,

7 Wolfgang Veit, *Eurythmie* (Stuttgart: Urachhaus, 1985). 8 Eisenman Architects.

had the body as its model. Representations and codes that refer to the body entail, through the universality of that reference, the possibility of bringing together varied minds, cultures, and times.

While progress claims equality through the standardization made possible by digital technology, and while a lot of discourse concerns the issues of equality and justice, the capacity to move, inhabit, and produce, and the capacity of speed, have become extremely uneven amongst the world's inhabitants. The elimination of qualitative difference has not created a just distribution of quantity. For power, it has made the demand for a difference in quantity even stronger.

One basic annihilation of qualitative difference occurs in the perpetuation of the present. The ticktock has been silenced; the to and fro between past and future has been reduced to the single beat of the now, a now that always anticipates the move onward; the ever-present rushing to an indefinite future. In the now, all times collide and are consummated in expectation of some future. In fact, the complicity between the avant-garde and mass culture consumes all plurality. What is presented as plurality or as avant-garde today is only the novelty to keep the appetite for consumption alive. The art biennials and world's fairs have become the sites for promoting a kind of intellectual, artistic Disneyland and exercising the greatest control over time.

From this point of view, the repetition of today's housing blocks, Disneyland-type hotels, shopping malls, recreation centers, and even museums offers little difference in the way it gives freedom and expression to time. Time, imposed as regularity, repetition, and order, becomes an instrument of control. Since humankind's only real investment in the world is time, it becomes the perfect tool for control when given over to the digital measure. The beat of much of today's popular music sounds more regulating, dictating, and repressive than the beat of the galley slave's oars.

I am deeply hurt by the impoverishment brought on by the importation of recent technologies to the poorer parts of the Earth. A technique that, in its original context, improved an already developed method or background, when insensitively transplanted, becomes a lifestyle, a model, a one-size-fits-all garment. Contemporary art, entertainment, commodity production, and the culture industry merge together, and the poor world joins this international mass culture with a rapidity that pushes all memory into oblivion.

CONCLUSION – KAIROS AND MANYTIMES

Every invention is power over nature; each one reduces human dependence on and experience of nature. Likewise, the reduction of time to a linear progression has taken control of nature's movements and robbed us of many temporalities. As Octavio Paz explained, the concept of linear time presupposes absolute, single time, with the human being as a protagonist whose action becomes the main

narrative. Linear time, furthermore, assumes hypotheses that legitimize progress, such as class struggle, better living standards, and longevity.[9]

As long as the blind faith in technological man's infinite superiority dominates value judgments, even the best intentioned efforts to make manifold time's possibilities will not be able to transgress the attitude that history is "a discourse that man had been delivering since the beginning."[10] The effort to create alternatives to the present conditions of impoverishment through concepts and abstractions can only end in blind circular motions.

Unlike the 20th century, which sought to deny the past and create a utopian future, the next millennium has to seek sanity and longevity in the pluralization of concepts of time and space. This must be done for the sake of the real and contingent present and the present of *all* of humanity, with its different times and lives.

According to Immanuel Wallerstein, the fragmentation toward which the capitalistic system has pushed us will inevitably bring about a transformation of our own systems.

According to him, we have to return to a qualitative notion of space-time which is *kairos*, as opposed to the quantitative notion of *chronos*: "Human beings... faced with kairos, faced with what I shall term transformational Time-Space, cannot avoid moral choice. It is thrust upon them, at the 'right' time and place, at a moment of qualitative time and space whose length and breadth are of uncertain measurement and

unpredictable locus. . . . We can be certain that there is a *kairos*, a Time-Space at which transformation occurs."[11] The end of the millennium is marked by unfulfilled promises of a better and more just world through pluralism and heterogeneity, at the same time that materialism has imposed on us its reductionism. The ensuing chaos is seen by some as the sign of a transition that will necessitate a revision of moral priorities and a revaluation of the concepts of time and space.

Moving forward is inevitably accompanied by remembering, without nostalgia and in a critical manner, who we are. Jacques Derrida, in *Mal d'Archive*, relates how Christopher Columbus discovered a new continent by studying old texts.[12] The new reality made possible by diverse approaches to time and space, which supply us with experiences of quality, will also be a liberating factor. This is the way to the real avant-garde which, as the only free domain within the industrialized world, is necessary as a means of cultural transgression.

Our basic alternatives are religion, nationalism, or a secularism that must relate to the objective, material world. The last option is my own choice and is possible only through education. Toward that end, we must start with Epicurus's philosophy of doing the most with the least. Art is the only means to help us in this. Let us start by looking beneath our feet at the patchworks of multiple times waiting to be rediscovered. These discoveries will help create the links and bonds with those of other times, spaces, and realities.

9 Octavio Paz, *Alternating Current* (New York: Arcade Publishing, 1990), 179. 10 Immanuel Wallerstein, *Unthinking Social Science* (Cambridge: Polity Press, 1991), 147–48. 11 Ibid. 12 Jacques Derrida, *Dem Archiv verschreiben* (Berlin: Verlag Brinkmann, 1997).

ERZEN > TIME AND SELF INCARNATED

Michelangelo, Doni Madonna.

13 It was Professor Leo Steinberg who noticed this upon a visit to the Anatolian Civilizations Museum in Ankara.

A radical conversion from quantitative to a qualitative values can only be initiated at the aesthetic level. Such a change requires both the participation of all of the sensory faculties and an appreciation of the Earth's and of life's physical and material qualities. Both contain the invisible fluidity of time. Against the misuse of time as a linear trajectory separating and alienating us from the present, we can cultivate a new sensitivity toward synchronizing, synthesizing, and harmonizing with the essence of time. This can be achieved through the arts and through architecture which, through allegory, embody different times as different lives, beings, and becomings. Each geography contains overlapping layers of time that can be redeemed through architecture to make us conscious of human bonds and responsibilities, of the possibility of sharing beyond the confines of time and location, of creating both universal and specific ties to time and space. Ankara's geography contains unlimited potential, which can inspire (its) art and architecture.

There is an image from around 6000 BC of an Anatolian woman holding a child. She sits the way Turkish women still sit today. She may be the mother goddess Cybele holding her lover-son Attis. This figure was only later remembered by Michelangelo in his *Doni Madonna* tondo. Great art never forgets. It always finds the link. [13]

Only a few miles from here, near a riding club, is a burial mound of a Phrygian lord who was cremated with his horses so that he could speed to a better world; an hour from there is the Gordion of King Midas, where Alexander later crossed; from a hill there, one can see the temple of Augustus, which offered the teachings of Rome in two languages; close to it, in turn, is the hill with the mosque of Haci Bayram, the Sufi sage. It was there that Timur the Lame exposed the defeated Sultan Beyazit the Thunderbolt in a cage. Perhaps even more important is the continued presence of the old fortress of Ankara and around it, on the road to the airport, of the felt manufacturers and Angora mohair storehouses, which bespeak a life on the steppes that goes on at its own rhythm, unmindful of the motorized traffic.

JALE ERZEN TEACHES AT MIDDLE EAST TECHNICAL UNIVERSITY IN ANKARA. SHE IS PRESIDENT OF SANART, AN ASSOCIATION FOR THE PROMOTION OF VISUAL ARTS IN TURKEY, AND THE EDITOR OF THE MONTHLY TURKISH FINE ARTS JOURNAL BOYUT.

Anytime as an Interpretation of Time and its Prospects for Reflections on the Future Ilhan Tekeli

The series of 11 conferences planned and organized by the Anyone Corporation has established an interdisciplinary platform for discussion in a period of profound global restructuring. Each conference is developed around a particular concept prefixed by the word ANY. As a result of the addition of this prefix, these concepts undergo a process that I like to call ANYFICATION, a term that refers to a transformation of those concepts into an INDETERMINATE state. In my opinion, this process of anyfication seems to be an intuitively developed research strategy, the goal of which is not clearly indicated but only roughly pinned down, a tactic that perhaps enables us to embrace many potentialities without restriction.

The topic of the eighth Any conference, Anytime, can be defined as an anthropomorphic interpretation of time. I would like to examine the prospects that such an interpretation holds for reflections on the future. In so doing, I will first focus on the changes anyfication can generate in thought and in society. I will then consider how the concept of time attains an anthropomorphic interpretation, and look at possible alternatives to this interpretation. Later, I will examine the emergence of the concept of the future in modernity and discuss the social repercussions of anyfication on the time of the future. Finally, I will tackle the possible implications of the anyfication of time for the practice of architecture.

Reinhart Koselleck, Futures Past, (Cambridge, Massachusetts: MIT Press, 1985).

Collapsing Space and Time, eds. Stanley D. Brunn and Thomas R. Leinbach (London: Harper Collins Academic, 1991).

Rafael Moneo, "The Indifference of Anyway," in Anyway, ed. Cynthia C. Davidson (New York: Rizzoli, 1994).

227   TEKELI > ANYTIME AS AN INTERPRETATION OF TIME

It is likely that the architects involved in the Anyone project enter into such a thought experiment in order to *transgress* the one determined by the existing order, that is, the order of consumer society, of society as spectacle, and even existing architectural practice. Assuming Any is a thought experiment, I will ask two critical questions: First, what kind of transgression are we talking about? Second, given one possibility of transgression, what kinds of limits should be considered for this kind of research strategy?

There are three dimensions to the possibility of transgression. The first is related to the context of the transgression: that is, do we aim to transgress the existing architectural practice or to transgress the existing social order in a comprehensive way? The second is related to the degree of radicality: in other words, do we intend a piecemeal (or incremental) transgression or a total (or radical) one? The third concerns intention: Do we aim to transgress at a conceptual level or to dislocate current practices?

There have been no specific attempts to answer these questions in previous Any conferences, and I will not attempt to answer them either. This is partly because searching for an answer is difficult, perhaps untraceable and unreachable and partly because putting possible answers in a framework of instrumental rationality is not very beneficial if there is no possibility to test it in practice. Nonetheless, posing these questions may still have practical benefits: First of all, this type of questioning will help us realize the differentiation of anyfication strategies if it is used for different aims. For example, if the aim is an incremental transformation, only some elements of a social system would face anyfication; that is, if some elements of a system are suspended by anyfication, suddenly new possibilities will exist for change in other elements of the system, and thus new hopes created for the emergence of new social orders.

The second question asks: What are the possible limits of transgression by anyfication? For every transgression has an implicit limitation. At the same time, each system remains open to new transgressions.

The overriding theme of all Any conferences is the indeterminate character of the term *any*. It is time is to examine this character. We can easily define *any* as referring to a being or thing that has no striking quality and is easily replaceable. At the same time, anyfication is a strategy that transforms being, with its apparently social importance and unchangeable existence, away from an ordinary, common, and dispensable one. This strategy brings about an opportunity for transgression and transformation. To carry out such a discussion, I will construct two groups of "any" through which anyfication can perhaps have different meanings: the first is comprised of things and persons, that is, to *Anyone* and *Anything*; the second, of processes and modes of doing, that is, *Anyhow* and *Anywise*.

In order to grasp the possible outcomes of anyfication we should first consider *anyone*. As everybody knows, the *self* has been one of the basic building blocks of the development of Western thought. Given this tradition, can a person who attempts self-actualization with particular attention to individuality and difference also consent to becoming anyone? Surely an anyfication process would take on different meanings in different societies. We cannot expect that an individual would be satisfied with being just "anyone" if he or she lives in a society that values individualism. However, a society composed of anyones might gain an entirely different meaning. A society of anyones could become a project aiming for equality, a free democratic society of free people. This shows that transgression realized by the concept of anyone would be effective if it were radical and comprehensive.

The Sufi tradition in Anatolia could represent another form of anyfication, in which the Ego is erased through *internal oriented training*. However, this alternative does not present an explicit or implicit social project. Others might argue that homogenization is another form of generating anyone in a society. However, reproduction of this kind of a unified society is only possible through the differentiation of some small fraction that achieves special recognition and thus establishes a hierarchical order. Consent is impossible in such a society.

What we are in fact looking for is a way to develop a social project without becoming trapped in a sharply hierarchical structure, a way in which society can reproduce itself with horizontal and anonymous relationships that enable individual human beings to thrive. This seems to be the only way for transgression, or anyfication, the only kind of social project in which individuals do not feel manipulated by others and can live their differences freely. If we can successfully envision such a social project, which internalizes a democratic and peaceful life, then we can also show the prospects of such a transgression.

In such a project, is a person in the process of "becoming anyone" merely the product of his or her own efforts and internal actualization? Is there a *monadization* or process by which individuals internalize everything everywhere and become echelons of every type of evaluation? When we consider "anyone" within this kind of project, should we accept that the meaning of an individual's existence depends on self-evaluation? If these questions are answered affirmatively, then such a project demands a great deal of individuals indeed; its success depends on their maturity and skill as well as their respect for each other as "anyone." But this should not be an inwardly oriented project. In it, anyone is basically an individual who has real external relations and responsibilities to interact anonymously in a social field.

When we dwell upon the strategy of anyfication as a basis for process and modes of action – rather than for individuals and objects – a variety of solutions should be considered. This in turn paves the way for a certain permissiveness, for an openness to innovation and a liberal way of thinking. This kind of anyfication could become an incremental strategy of transgression rather than a total one.

The meaning of time and space and the role each plays in constructing human knowledge are among the most complex epistemological questions. The primary difficulty is that one has to conceptualize time and space on the basis of their indirect relations with observable events, since they themselves are not directly observable. A child, for example, has no serious problem developing its own concept of time, which is then used throughout life. However, the more one ponders the concept of time, the more blurred and confusing it gets.

Today's common understanding of time is linear, unidirectional, irreversible, homogeneous, and measured. This concept of time comes from physics. Even relativism (which posits that time is generated with the sequence of events) and absolutism (which posits that time is independent from events) gather their support from physics. But such a time concept based on physics is not necessarily a satisfactory tool for the social sciences. In understanding social life, other kinds of time structures and time topologies can be used simultaneously and/or separately. Two different references seem to help to determine such time consciousness. First is the reference to the Earth, where life has developed. Second is the reference to lived experience, which sets the framework of human understanding, in other words, the anthropomorphic foundation of time consciousness.

Earth has important repercussions for time. First, practically all human activity is realized on the Earth's finite surface, which leaves little room for a discussion of absolute and relative *space*. Place, however, is the platform of all human activity; thus the absolutist and relativistic interpretations of the time and space of these activities overlap. Second, the Earth's diurnal and seasonal rhythms determine man's perception of the rhythms of life. This concept of time is found in the calendar, which has two coexisting vectors. On the one hand, calendar time produces a homogeneous and linear flow of time; on the other, periodical and rhythmical characteristics have been added to the time of physics, which have eventually made calendar time not anytime.

Manuel Castells, The Rise of the Network Society (Oxford: Blackwell Publisher Ltd., 1996).

Hans Reichenbach, The Rise of Scientific Philosophy (Berkeley: University of California Press, 1968).

J. R. Lucas, Space Time, And Causality (Oxford: The Clanderton Press, 1984).

W. H. Newton-Smith, The Structure of Time (London: Routledge & Kegan Paul, 1980).

Time's anthropomorphic characteristics are defined by human life experience. This has led to the development of various time concepts based on different topologies and measures of time in various periods of human and social development, for example, childhood, adolescence, etc. The most important anthropomorphic concept stemming from human consciousness is the tripartite yet continuously flowing time of past, present, and future, a division that without human consciousness would be meaningless. If we accept this linear, homogeneous, and continuously flowing concept of time, we can define the present as an instant that cannot be divided into smaller parts. Surrounding this instant, we face the past and future. In actual human experience, however, the present has been extended so that it is possible to define past, present, and future as the three instants of the present that overlap in the human mind. The past is actually the life experience that we remember now, and the future is the expectations of the present. The accelerating pace of contemporary society is determined by the continuous increase in the gap between the experience of the past and the expectations for the future.

Explaining anthropomorphic concepts of time should not be limited to this tripartite division of time. These three concepts refer to an image of time without beginning or end. However, the human life span is limited to birth, growth, and death. This limitation gives a beginning and end to the anthropomorphic concept of time. Religions have always tried to make a rapprochement between these two concepts of time, as both are shaped by life experience. Human life reaches its end with death, but religion introduces of the concept of resurrection and the concept of an afterlife in order to reconcile limited human life with the continuous flow of time. This is an important innovation in the control of human behavior.

Obviously, the anthropomorphic concept of time directly affects the organization of an individual's daily life, but its effects on society as a whole are less direct. They can perhaps be best observed in the writing of history. For example, the doomsday prophesy, whether posed by Christianity or Islam, suggests the existence of a predetermined endpoint that the world will eventually reach. Under these circumstances, future human experience exemplifies the already-known. There is no need to give meaning to the sequence of historical examples because the end is already determined. Another distinct time topology is found in *Mukaddime*, by Ibni Khaldun, who shows that states are born, develop, and die like human beings. Khaldun's concept of cyclical time allows history to escape from the problem mentioned above, but he makes this time *satiric*.

The Enlightenment's transition from divine to human rule brought about a change in the writing of history and time. This is perhaps best illustrated in the German language: *Historie* was replaced by *Geschichte*, which relates stories of progress in a narrative form, giving each event its own time and space, neither anytime nor anyplace. Instead, the sequence of these events produced its own unique continuity which, with its explanatory form, was called historicism. In this kind of history, anthropomorphic time was conceived in the form of the past, present, and future. Thus it appeared to be real life and thus very convincing, apparently ruling out the need for scientific explanation.

This kind of history writing seemed promising and optimistic; since the future was not determined by prophesy, it could actually be planned. This change appears to have transformed thinking about and forecasting the future into a central interest of society. But this in turn presented the historicist narrative with a crisis. The new analyses of causes behind events made forecasting the future a primary focus of the nomothetic social sciences. Futurology then flourished over these developments as a pseudo science.

Obviously, forecasting the future can serve as an early alarm system that benefits society. Equally, however, whenever forecasting becomes an aim, a serious danger immediately arises because the unpromising and unimaginative visions rarely go beyond the limits of existing systems and thus are hardly helpful in the quest for a more equal and free society. That is why ways of approaching the future are highly related to freeing society from the trap of existing systems. Thus now we can ask how Anyfication, as a transgression strategy, can function positively.

We know that modernity's strong inclination for controlling the future is in line with a broad view of progress. This concept of continual progress is not compatible with the concept of anytime. If modernity were not in crisis, we would not venture a thought experiment to combine anytime and the future in this meeting.

What do I mean by anyfication of the future? Anytime develops when, because it has collapsed, there is no possibility for time to move forward, meaning the formulation of projects for the future becomes impossible. This impossibility is strongly related to a social situation in which contingency has replaced causality. The concept of causality, which depends on repeatable, necessary, and contiguous cause-and-effect relations, was an important characteristic of modernity, and, in particular, modernity's guarantee of a predictable future. Its centrality was solidified by the adoption of the concept by the natural and social sciences. This laid the foundation for social engineering projects based on instrumental and rationalist logic, which seems to have encountered severe problems at the end of the 20th century.

The acknowledgment of contingency instead of causality becomes a strong tendency, especially after the development of critical realism. Critical realism expanded the range of changes possible in social systems by rejecting the theory of causality in the natural and social sciences. The anyfication of the future is strongly related to this with its understanding of the importance of contingency in social analysis. This approach would bring freedom and expand the possibilities of transformation in societies.

But such an increased flexibility of a system raises a new question. How can a society succeed in reproducing itself when everything starts to become contingent or context-dependent? The modern project answered this question implicitly in practice. Although every phenomenon in society is context-dependent, given institutional structures and norms, the hierarchy of these phenomena is not. The decrease in context-dependent areas leads to increased individual decisions and guarantees the reproduction of society. This independence does not depend on the laws of the natural sciences but on rules made by human beings. Hence, in a crisis in which society cannot reproduce itself, it is possible to see these seemingly unchangeable rules suddenly change. Crisis situations help us to grasp possible ranges of context dependency.

At this point I want to leave this discussion of anyfication as a thought experiment and look at real world situations. This may help us to recognize the clues that heralded the emergence of anytime in the globalized world. This emergence of anyfication can be analyzed here from two different perspectives.

The first is related to the development of cyberspace: an electronic universe made possible by computers and telecommunication networks. People enter this universe through an interface – in other words, a computer monitor. Because they can hide behind a screen, this interface can actually occur anyplace. Human experience in cyberspace does not have a narrative time. Its sequences can easily be changed; thus we can say that cyberspace is anytime and anyplace.

Equally, we can observe the development of anytime in society. In this globalizing world almost no political party in the central countries, including Turkey, can propose a program that has radical claims for changing the existing order. Interestingly, this disappointing situation has not been created by oppressing the promising alternatives but by making possible alternatives unfeasible and unpromising. What does this mean? That there is no hope for changing the world. This is where anytime replaces the future.

Manuel Castells calls this new temporality "timeless time," in part based on the concept of a network society in which a space of flows discards the sequence of events, making all events concurrent. If we do not want to identify the character of contemporary spaces with flows, that is, metaphorically, we can say that a network society exhibits the concurrent character of events and the importance of feedback relations between them, rather than of discrete events ordered in time. This network space is

Yhezkel Dror, "Future Studies–Quo Vadis?" and Bertrand de Jouvenel, "A Word to Futurists" in *Human Futures* (London: IPC Science and Technology Press Limited, 1974).

Peter Eisenman, "K Nowhere 2 Fold" in *Anywhere*, ed. Cynthia C. Davidson (New York: Rizzoli, 1992).

also in part dependent on the relative space-time interpretation of Leibniz: when there is no sequence of events, time also vanishes. As we accept all social events as taking place in the space and time of Earth, the concept of timeless time loses ground and the concept of anytime becomes more relevant.

Now, to what extent can time, which faces anyfication, provide for the continuation of society? This is not such a difficult question. I can make a single yet perhaps important point related to this: we can see the future of modernity as self-expanding, while the future of anytime is self-maintaining. So far we have only addressed the future, but this does not mean neglecting the present. If our present world has not become the world of anytime, we cannot state that the future can become anytime.

It is useful to make some connections between anytime (whether we regard it as an emerging reality or as simply a thought experiment) and architecture. Modernism's strong tendency toward progress attempted to resist entropy, which has shown its nature in different forms: for example, group identity centered hegemonic strategies in political life, social engineering research, developmentalist political-economic paradigms, the activities of the public realm, the use of territory as a means of social control, etc. Modern architecture as a *form-giver* can be thought in this way as well. In fact, this architecture, which developed an authoritative moral attitude in search of eternal solutions, will be valid in the future. It emerged as an architecture with an awareness of the past and the present, and it had high expectations for eternity and universality. On the other hand, in the architecture of anytime, the links of the present to the past and the future have been cut. Architecture here is thought to be the profession of the present: not the eternal but the ephemeral. It is a building which is rebuilt and a city which is restructured in every instance. If we can imagine a world with such a practice, then architecture would no longer be limited to the activities of architects; everybody would be an architect.

However, contemporary buildings are still constructed with a long life expectancy. For example, old Istanbul's wooden buildings, were reconstructed after they burned in precise accordance with their traditional forms, despite the risk of another fire; thus they cannot be seen as ephemeral. Now we can ask an important question: How can one decrease the tension between the seeming contrast of an emerging approach seeking ephemeral architecture and one seeking durability? There are various approaches which could decrease the tension. One is to construct buildings without symbols that tie them to a specific time, that would allow society to attribute some ephemeral symbols to them, without allowing their accumulation in the course of time. This is an attempt to avert the construction of time-bound places. A second way is to focus on changing interpretations (as in a text). The buildings themselves would not face substantial changes, but their textual interpretations could change continuously, bringing a kind of ephemerality to the built environment.

A third way is to search for ephemerality in the relationships between buildings instead of in a single building. Such continuously changing built environments would be free from any particular time sequence. When the environment is fragmented, that is, not under the hegemony of a single identity but anonymously able to reproduce itself, it becomes the ephemeral-eternal. This method does not result in chaos. Rather, it should be thought of as a reterritorilization of a subculture facilitated by what Deleuze calls a *rhizomatic development*.

The tendency of the modern to seek to control the future has also affected city planning, which modernism even used as a means of this control. The development and continuous transformation of a city is actually an open game. But as a child of modernism, planning changed this open game to one whose rules were determined in advance. What we are now witnessing is that anytime, as well as anyplace, is on the way to changing this game back to an open one. Thanks to this transition, the importance of individual and collective choice is likely to increase in the development of the built and natural environments.

It is not sufficient to think anytime only from the point of view of individual choice. It is necessary to simultaneously think anytime from the points of view of collective choice and social movements. These social movements are not based on meta-group identities seeking hegemonic control of the future. Rather, it is better to think the multiplicity of these movements, which attempt to actualize collective choice in specific issues in anytime. They will emerge in anytimes and actualize their choices in anyplaces.

Having considered the anyfication of time, we are now in a position to ask to what extent it has been useful: What kind of a transgression has been achieved? The modernist ambition to control the future with the idea of progress through a deterministic understanding of science based on causality is dissolved in the face of the anyfication of time. This dissolution gives rise to a great transgression in thinking about the future of societies. Thinking of society not as an arena of deterministic relations but as an arena of contingent relations offers abundant opportunities. It is too easy to build the social sciences on a deterministic understanding and to think about society on the basis of the development paradigm. But when we enter the realm of contingency, we must come to terms with much more complex and difficult thinking. Now there is no restriction for societies in terms of thinking opportunities. It is possible to suggest what these opportunities are, but only practice will show what kind of social life these opportunities will produce. It seems implausible to evaluate this life with the values of the present society.

We saw another example of transgression while discussing the ephemerality of structures in the society of anytime. A transgression emerged in the field of architecture that went beyond the form-giving character of architecture. At the same time, all of society became an architect, a dislocation in architectural practice. There are more examples related to these points, but I personally think these alone indicate that anyfication can indeed be an effective strategy of transgression.

ILHAN TEKELI IS AN URBAN AND REGIONAL PLANNER AND TEACHES AT THE MIDDLE EAST TECHNICAL UNIVERSITY IN ANKARA. HE IS A MEMBER OF THE TURKISH ACADEMY OF SCIENCE AND EXECUTIVE COMMITTEE PRESIDENT OF THE TURKISH ECONOMIC AND SOCIAL HISTORY FOUNDATION. HE IS THE AUTHOR OF SEVERAL BOOKS, INCLUDING THINKING ON HISTORIOGRAPHY.

Arturo Escobar, "Imagining a Post Development Era" in The Sociology of Development, Vol. 1, eds. Bryan R. Roberts, Roberts G. Cushing and Charles Wood (Aldershot: Elgar Reference Collection, 1995), 477–513.

Francesco Dal Co, "In Consideration of Time," Cynthia C. Davidson, "The Placeless Anyplace," Jeffrey Kipnis, "Three Questions of Any," and Rem Koolhaas, "Precarious Entity" in Anyone, ed. Cynthia C. Davidson (New York: Rizzoli, 1991).

Paul Roth, "The Anti-social Epistemology of Narrative Experiments" in Social Epistemology, vol. 5, 1991, No. 4, 301–10

Henry N. Cobb, "City of Any," Cynthia C. Davidson, "Introduction," Peter Eisenman, "Eleven Points on Knowledge and Wisdom," and David Harvey, "On Architects, Bees, and Possible Urban Words" in Anywise, ed. Cynthia C. Davidson (Cambridge, Massachusets: MIT Press,1996).

Akira Asada and Arata Isozaki, "Fabrication of Amyplace," Dara Birnbaum, "Finding Anyplace in Cyberspace," Peter Eisenman, "A Way From/To Architecture," and Fredric Jameson, "Demographics of the Anonymous" in Anyplace, ed. Cynthia C. Davidson (Cambridge, Massachusets: MIT Press, 1995).

Telling Time Michael Sorkin

How does a city dweller measure time?

A few months ago, New York City Mayor Rudolph Giuliani closed the 50th Street crosswalks at Fifth and at Madison avenues.[1] The nominal reason was to combat "congestion" in midtown Manhattan but, of course, what he really meant was automotive congestion. Forcing pedestrians to cross the street in order to cross the street enabled cars to turn right or left onto the opposing one-way avenues without having to worry about negotiating with pedestrians.

In the mayor's organization, walkers are inconvenienced in order to convenience cars. As a result, 50th Street has become a contested zone at the limits of the fight over the right to move. Crossing the street — at least on those midtown blocks — is now an act of civil disobedience. Reflecting this, a policeman has been installed on each corner to assure compliance. This is parcel with the mayor's (the ex-prosecutor, the urban disciplinarian) penal understanding of time. A prison, after all, is built on the abstraction of every dimension of time but length, producing its one-dimensional hierarchy of deprivation.

The basis for the mayor's strictures against street-crossing derives from a desire to enhance the "flow" of traffic, to save time. In the logic of flow, priority is always given to the faster moving means. Value here is derived from speed, from the idea that getting from A to B in an urban traffic system is always to be judged on the basis of the expenditure of time. This, in turn, requires a hierarchy of adjudication with which to vet what the traffic engineers call "conflict" between modes. Here, the slower invariably yields to the faster when territory is contested or shared, walkers yielding to cars, cars to trains, trains to planes, and so on.

1 In early 1998, police were stationed at the intersections to enforce the new crosswalk rules; later, fences were erected.

17.06.98 BUENOS AIRES: DINO SAKIC, FORMER COMMANDER OF CROATIA'S LARGEST CONCENTRATION CAMP IS EXTRADITED, BOUND FOR HIS HOMELAND TO FACE ACCUSATIONS OF WORLD WAR II ATTROCITIES.

The history of modern city planning is structured about an armature of conflict avoidance in transportation. Elevated highways, pedestrian skyways, subway systems, and the whole familiar apparatus of modernist planning are predicated on the desire to clarify relations between classes of movement. This idea of traffic segregation finds its mirror image in the idea of zoning by use, another strategy for schematizing social priorities under the guise of function, another set of rules for determining what goes with what.

The reproduction of this neat order of difference is powered by growth, which inevitably introduces a vector of distance and, consequently, time. Under the regime of growth, this relationship has escaped rational management. The typical American – and, increasingly, global – solution to the difficulty of this system has simply been sprawl, the urbanistic equivalent of the big bang. As stable relationships of adjacency and proximity are disrupted by the growth of the edge and the consequent transformation of the center, the system has produced the so-called edge city in which a variety of uses are continuously relocated to establish proximity and to save time otherwise expended on commuting.

In cosmology, the increasing disorder of the universe, entropy, gives a direction to time. Where to look, then, for the ethics of time? I would suggest that motion defines such an ethics. This extends beyond the simple Virilian calculus that an increase in speed implies a corresponding decrease in freedom. There is, I think, a teleology of speed that implies an ethical relation between speed and purpose. This gives rise to the need for a nuanced ethics of privilege in a complex system that must inevitably weigh the spatial rights of ambulances and flâneurs and assign them priority.

Just to get the last piece of the Einsteinian equation into this, energy, of course, is required to produce motion. The ethics of energy expenditure – which these days comes down largely on the side of conservation – could arguably be invoked in defense of either side of the pedestrian/automotive question. On behalf of cars, the argument would come from their greater momentum (derived from both greater mass and greater speed), in the idea that their efficiency derives from smooth and speedy operation, that the economy of stop and start is opposed to the conservation of automotive energy.

The counter-argument would run that cars are intrinsically wasteful of energy. This claim depends on a global paradigm of conservation and not just a local one. In such an argument, pedestrians become the alpha-means of energyless travel. Such a hierarchy puts walkers at the top, followed by human-powered transport – like bicycles – and so on down the line, the criterion being that the more energetic always yields to the least. Of course, at the moment that the rising curve of teleological privilege crosses the sinking curve of energy output, the whole is thrown into question.

But this position is further fraught with problems. To begin with, it defines walkers as energyless movers. Once the actual expenditure is introduced into the equation, another difficulty of difference arises. On the one hand, we know that the expenditure of aerobic energy by the organism increases (or at least conserves) the potential for further expenditure. This is called exercise. On the other hand, we know that this calculation is based on individual potential, on the difference between old and young, handicapped and fit, and so on.

However, identifying this individualist paradigm opens the way for a theory of exceptionalism. If such a theory were conceived in the same spirit as the ordinary traffic system, it would produce a hierarchy based on the ability to derive benefit from locomotion. This would be based on a blending of the physiognomic (whose ambulatory efficiency would be most increased by a given expenditure of energy) and the teleological (whose functioning arrogates the highest degree of necessity). Of course, we open up the road to absurdity through this calculation.

An exceptionalist solution would introduce other means such as an elaboration of the fundamental system and not as one of coequals, suspending the idea that a car, for example, can have rights. Such means would be judged based on their ability to abet or ameliorate the primary – pedestrian – system. Thus, energetic means of motion would be assigned first to those unable to produce sufficient energy on their own. The elderly, the handicapped, and the encumbered would, in order to enjoy temporal parity with other citizens, be the first candidates for the allotment of the energy that would become the means for a fair distribution of time.

I am trying to suggest that it is possible to frame an idea of temporal justice – still blind – in which the scales are replaced by an hourglass. Of course, in our system, money is a lubricant that permits the conservation of time, the enrichment of the experience of time, and, consequently, the prospects for speed. If time has a politics, then, it derives from the degree of access to the malleability of time, the ability to speed up and slow down at will. This is an entropic reading since the individuation of desires tends (at least in a condition of freedom) to an increase with variation, a chaos of happinesses.

Anti-entropic styles of order, on the other hand, are associated with the collapse of the universe and the possible reversal of time. The ultimate slowdown is the black hole, the ultimate celestial traffic jam. But one must be careful about the way in which this metaphor is imported into questions of traffic. Traffic systems in India and other developing countries feel very different to Western, "rationalist" desires. Traffic is completely mixed up, a slow-moving mass of cows and pedicabs, motor-rickshaws, trucks and busses, camels and pedestrians.

To me, there is something very democratic about this picture, not just in the sense that everyone is subject to a universal slowing down but in that this slowdown is the material basis for the tractability of the system. A student of mine who was studying traffic in Istanbul observed that its glacial pace was the guarantor of the absolute freedom to cross the street, that a by-product of slowness was both safety and convenience. This is a crucial – and practical – insight. Once we stop judging systems by the absolute speed of any given particle, a telling contradiction is collapsed; in many instances slow becomes fast.

17.06.98 RESTON, VIRGINIA: THE SAFETY OF OLESTRA, A FAKE FAT USED IN SOME CHIPS AND COOKIES, IS ENDORSED BY ALL BUT TWO MEMBERS OF A FOOD AND DRUG ADMINISTRATION ADVISORY COMMITTEE.

If privilege in the modern city is produced by those who speed through it, it is natural that the stroll should be the modern form of urban leisure. Time becomes the ultimate luxury; the image of the modern person of privilege is the business traveler on the Concorde who arrives in New York before the hour he left London. Delay is everywhere penalized. Taxi meters are set to charge for both distance and "waiting time," a kind of penalty that the traffic system imposes on slowness. To have time on your hands is, as always, to risk concert with the devil. Time is fully incorporated into the Protestant ethic; we "spend" it.

Of course, as I have suggested, there are cultural vectors, the system enjoys an elasticity of both privilege and meaning. I can remember reading some years ago that what was—at the time—the world's tallest reinforced concrete tower had been completed in Brazil. The article suggested that this was achieved via a reduction in the size of the building's elevator core. This reduction in the availability of vertical circulation was, in turn, held to be possible only in a culture in which the pattern of patience suggested that people were willing to wait longer for the elevator to come.

Contemporary sanctions on the expenditure of time require that it be spent wisely. Haste no longer makes waste, we are rather forbidden to use time uneconomically. This appeal to economy is another argument for slowness as a contemporary form of resistance. The stroll is the potlatch of time, a slowing down that foregrounds the scopic. Slowness is the precondition for seeing, be it the passing look of the window-shopper or the loving gaze of the urban physiognomist. While speed may or may not be the universal enemy of freedom, it is surely no friend to architecture.

Contradictions, of course, arise. Disneyland—the objective correlative for everything—is inter alia a bordello of time, a place to have the "time" of your life. At Disneyland, the walker is decidedly alpha and the stroll—often slowed to a tortoise creep in the form of lines—is the major means of circulation between attractions (which are themselves based on a kind of pure internal speed). All other means of motion offer absolutely no benefit in convenience or time saving. Rather, they exist for the purpose of pleasure, the ultimate expression of luxury, the conversion of necessity into superfluity. The time-wasting deceleration of the line as an antecedent to a brief burst of speed on a journey to nowhere both extends the pleasure of the potlatch of temporality and offers—via the associated annoyance and pleasure—a bit of moral instruction in how to value time.

If the pleasures of Disneyland are predicated on a slowing down of time, those of Las Vegas depend on its complete suspension. Famously, leisure is enforced by the absence of clocks, by the putative elimination of the anxiety bred in our culture by a life governed by "the clock." This suspension is reinforced by the windowlessness of the casinos, imposed, one presumes, to deny access to the sun, an alternative means of telling time. The ideal time in Vegas is nighttime, when solar cues are unavailable and hence when the Las Vegas daylight of artificial luminosity is most profoundly realized. Vegas is the Copernican model of late capitalism, linking the elimination of time to the practice of continuous expenditure. In Vegas, time is infinite as long as you have another quarter.

The casino effect – suspended time and perpetual night – is an increasingly widespread paradigm for urban life. This extends both to the related timeless interiority of megamalls, airports, and other impenetrable containers and to an urbanity that longs for night. It also involves the continuous expansion of the zones of continuous expenditure. A number of airlines have converted their cabins into miniature casinos, with video slot machines in the back of every seat. As Times Square remakes itself in the image of Las Vegas, it is interesting to note that the bulk of new construction – four huge towers – lies to the south of the narrow square, casting long shadows, assuring an illuminating shade for the neon that glares 24 hours a day. Likewise, the world financial system with its globalized markets creates a convergence of travel round the world and working round-the-clock by assuring a trade can be made somewhere anytime.

A key by-product of speed – embracing even relativistic effects – is a distortion of the useful routines of time. Whether in the form of the attenuation of life across the barrier of light speed or simply in the effect of jet lag, speed transforms time. Indeed, the casino effect produces the gateway to virtuality, our most successful – if fledgling – experiment in the defeat of time. It is also true that the space of casinos – with their endless, indistinguishable gambling stations – is the product of an artful impetus not to disorder but to confusion, to the end of hierarchical space produced by anything other than the arbitrary.

We have ceased to believe in our own mortality. We know, after all, that if we move fast enough, time slows down: our fantasies of speed (not to mention the endless vitamins, the attenuation of childhood, news of cancer cures, genetic secrets revealed, plastic surgery, and the imminent arrival of UFO salvation) are all linked to the idea of the defeat of death, as if we could hasten away from the reaper if we could only move fast enough. *Speed bears life* must surely be one of the mottoes of post-temporal cultural.

Disneyland is a playground of mobility, it entertains with pleasure-motion. For all its depredations, regimentation, surveillance, and control, part of what is experienced as enjoyable at Disneyland really is the passage through an environment of urban density in which both the physical texture and the means of circulation are not simply entertaining, but stand in invigorating contrast to the dysfunctional versions back home. One thus extracts from Disneyland a shred of hope, the persuasive example that pedestrianism coupled with short distance collective transport systems can be both efficient and fun, can thrive in the midst of a foreign and even hostile environment, and that the space of flow, sufficiently decelerated, can become the space of exchange. But only if we're not just passing through. The paranoid, privatized space of Disneyland could never make itself home to any but the most abstract – that is, monetary – exchange.

Democratic traffic deprivileges unim peded flow and favors concrete exchange. To promote the enabling deceleration, cities need to adopt supply-side transport management strategies. This will not necessarily be easy. Our culture – nursed on advertising round the clock – makes a fetish of demand: the whole system thrives on spurious need. But this is no signal of the autonomy of our desires; these, rather, are the sounds of their silencing and reveal how thoroughly trapped we have become in someone else's entrepreneurial dream.

To begin again will mean reconsidering the place of the body in democracy. For the most part, democracy does not traffic in bodies; it is theorized instead in terms of disincorporation, the beheading of the monarch, the emptying out of the central place of power, the establishment of body-blind tribunals of public justice, and so on. Yet, as I argued earlier, it is a mistake to take this disincorporation literally, as the mere excision of the physical body from space, for what democratic theory actually represents is a radical clearing of old notions of the body and an invitation to invent it anew.

The grid prefers a movement monoculture, and monoculture is tyranny. Uniform transit helps produce uniform neighborhoods. Conversely, it seems clear that the ability of neighborhoods to act autonomously is enhanced by their accessibility. Indeed, the solution to the traffic problem is not continuously to model its operations at larger and larger scales but radically to disconnect locality from larger systems which, on balance, ill serve it. For many places, the only way to come to terms with the hegemony of the automotive system is to secede from it. In inner city areas, starved for useful public space and clotted with traffic, the most logical and effective step is to reduce the

MICHAEL SORKIN IS PRINCIPAL ARCHITECT AT MICHAEL SORKIN STUDIO IN NEW YORK. HE CURRENTLY TEACHES AT THE INSTITUTE OF URBANISM AT THE ACADEMY OF FINE ARTS, VIENNA. HIS RECENT BOOKS INCLUDE VARIATIONS ON A THEME PARK, EXQUISITE CORPSE, AND LOCAL CODE.

17.06.98 PARIS: IRANIAN EXILE GROUPS THREATENS TO DISRUPT THE POLITICALLY CHARGED WORLD CUP MATCH BETWEEN IRAN AND THE UNITED STATES.

physical area actually available to the car. Roadways constitute the major portion of the commonly maintained public realm in cities. Cars have been given an enormous franchise on the use of this space – public property – for both circulation and storage.

Recently, working on a plan for East New York, a poor neighborhood in Brooklyn, I wondered what a minimum intervention might be that would begin to recapture the order of the neighborhood from motor traffic, promote greening, and reinforce new patterns of relative self-sufficiency and local autonomy. The answer, I decided, was to plant a tree in an intersection. Several consequences were anticipated. First, the space devoted to the automobile would be reduced by the instant creation of four dead-end streets: the tree would oblige traffic either to find collateral means of circulation or keep out. Second, the quieted zone would permit dramatic alteration to the ratio of green to built space with accompanying possibilities for new agricultural activities and architectural types. Finally, I hoped that street-life – its sparse commerce having been attenuated into useless, center-crushing linearity – would be densified in a series of locally scaled commercial and social centers that would restore legibility, convenience, and conviviality to a place ragged, over-large, and devoid of all character.

It is necessary to bear in mind, however, that the constraints, and even the scale, of the body are not what they were in the classical age when Aristotle famously called for a limitation of the agora to the space of a shout. We can hear and see much farther now than then, the result of myriad prosthetic devices of our own invention. It is easy to say – and so it often is said – that these prostheses have annulled, or alienated us from, our bodies. The truth, I believe, is more complex: the body itself is not what it once was. With the rise of capitalism it acquired the potential of a tool, something that could be used. The effect this redefinition of the body has on the notion of neighborhood has never been adequately dealt with by urban theorists or planners . If public space, the agora, was defined by Aristotle through imprinting of the capability of the body on it, this is because incorporation was the metaphor by which the alien – the foreign – difference could be accommodated without threatening their integrity and autonomy. Once the notion of body changed, once it was conceived as a tool, the notion of incorporation was replaced by that of assimilation and the foreign came under increasing pressure to surrender its difference in favor of some unqualified substrate.

No modern neighborhood – inasmuch as it is home to computers, televisions, phones, faxes, and so on – will ever be as small as the agora of antiquity; it is thus impossible to return to this scale in some real sense. Nor is it possible to return to the older metaphor of incorporation, since our bodies and our conditions are materially different. But it is possible – and indeed necessary – to think and construct our cities in a way that binds them to the body and what it can do. For the modern body has, it turns out, redoubled and contradictory functions: it serves not only as a tool but as that which incarnates the accident as such. That is, whereas in antiquity accidents had a place and thus a body could expect to meet with them, in modernity accidents are not given a place and thus only a body can be one. The body now bears the burden of being the only place where the accident resides. In other words, only the body – through work – can introduce difference into an otherwise uniform system.

Consumer research and focus groups, the media of planning not only for Disney's town of Celebration but for many of our global cities, are busy designing urban environments suited to the programmable body-as-tool. The question is what place the other modern body – the body-as-accident – might occupy in the global city. Against all the arguments about the dematerialization attendant on our "information age," it seems important to recognize that the modern body has the impossible role of giving a place to place. Neither nostalgic nor humanist, this recognition stresses the historical novelty of this role and the radical impossibility that conditions it. That is to say, what is at issue here is not an argument for an urbanism that would allow the body to develop its full potential. Cities must make room not for what is possible but for what is still impossible. This latter never wears a human face, which is the source of a great deal of difficulty, the major urban difficulty we now confront.

D4

AUDIENCE I want to congratulate Fred Jameson for being so self-critical. I think when you cited Derrida saying that it's too late to talk about time, that was a self-critical remark. I have a question. Do you know the concept of the ecological footprint? This is a calculation that ecologists make for a cities like London or L.A., for instance, about how much land an inhabitant of the city consumes in order to maintain his or her lifestyle. In a city like London, for instance, this footprint consumes an area 200 times larger than London's administrative area. Since architecture is an urban profession, I'm struck by the sort of blindness here about the boundaries of cities and the boundaries of buildings. I'm also struck by the absence of this kind of larger area in your cognitive mapping of contemporary post-modern capitalism. I find your kind of Marxism both totalizing and not sufficiently totalizing. It's a little bit like hegemony. Hegemony is always both totalizing and somehow exclusionary. Doesn't that kind of approach have a Stalinist implication?

FREDRIC JAMESON Well, I don't think I'll talk a whole lot about Stalin. This was not a statement about social conditions but about intellectual life in the postmodern period and the way in which it has stagnated and thrown back up all of these old things that really have nothing to say to us anymore. It was also a kind of warning that the current discussions of modernity really have nothing to offer anybody. If you want a vision of the future, that isn't it. That's a rewarmed nonconcept from the past; something else has to be invented.

Now, I would have liked to have had a little more time to pursue the urban because – and this is not my idea really; this is just what I've heard architects say – it seems to me that another end to the modern in architecture comes when too much has been built. Peter Eisenman remarked at a previous conference that today, given this tremendous occupation of space, you could design the most extraordinary building in the world, stick it in the middle of Tokyo, and nobody would notice it. I think that does something to the older notion of the building as a work of art. Meanwhile, of course, something's happening to the concept of the work of art in other fields as well. It seems to me that's the originality of postmodernity. It's that new situation of complete overbuilding, of the impossibility of any single edifice to make a real difference, to produce new space, and then the impossibility of urbanism. That's the situation we're in, and it accounts for the unsuitability of many of these older ideas. The way in which there is a kind of impossibility of thinking the urban and the architectural together (and yet they can't be separated out) is one of the contradictions that we're grappling with here without necessarily being able to solve it.

AKIRA ASADA First I have to apologize. Yesterday I was so tired I fell asleep on a magic carpet, and when I woke up I found myself in Capadoccia, where of course I found Michael Sorkin's eerie towers and an underground topological maze, which somehow is similar to Greg Lynn's crazy structures. Anyway, I was very much stimulated by Fred Jameson's lecture, especially when he put emphasis on the importance of the crisis of modernity, a kind of rupture between modernity and postmodernity. I would like to formulate it in terms of a somewhat aesthetic paradigm: It seems to me that there have been two basic paradigms — theatrical and cinematic. In philosophy, Hegel — and not only Hegel but also the critique of Hegel, which somehow insisted upon the importance of rapture or the suspension of the dialectic — somehow belongs to the theatrical paradigm, whereas a Bergsonian-Deleuzian philosophy of time somehow belongs to a cinematic paradigm. But as you mentioned, there seems to be a rupture now between the cinematic paradigm and what might be called an infographic paradigm, exemplified by computer graphics, etc. I think it is very important to take into account this new infographic paradigm. Of course we should not be talking simply about a linear transition from the theatrical to the cinematic, and then from the cinematic to the infographic. It is always a layered structure. The day before yesterday, I spoke about the importance of the truncation, the severance or the cut, which somehow exposes this multilayered structure with gaps and contradictions between layers.

Now, I'm a great fan of Octavio Paz, but I may differ a little bit from you, Jale, because it is very important not to talk about **kairos** as an eternal present filled with meaning, but **aeon**, which is again opposed to the **chronos**, the chronological timeline. This is not only an eternal present but also a kind of violent truncation that somehow exposes those multilayered structures.

JAMESON This business of continuity and discontinuity is very important. It seems to me that it would have been another way of describing the modern, that the modern teleology had some kind of dialectical continuity to it, whereas in our thinking and our paradigms, we want, for whatever reason, to insist on discontinuities and breaks.

CENGIZ BEKTAS I want to ask Ilhan Tekeli to elaborate his thoughts on **anyfication** — I liked the term very much — taking into consideration the possibility of "anonymity."

ILHAN TEKELI Let me try to develop this concept, because anonymous relations have quite an important place in my paper, but I couldn't elaborate all these issues. I emphasized that when we achieve anyfication as a total project, not a marginal or incremental project, we then have to guarantee the self-maintenance of society. In order to guarantee this self-maintenance, anonymous relations are a necessary condition, because in the society of anyones, each anyone will have the respect of other anyones because he or she is an anyone. An anonymous relation is a necessary condition for the reproduction of that system.

CHARLES JENCKS I was dazzled by a lot of the things said this morning, but I want to bring out some of the contradictions: Bruce Mau was rather like Marshall McLuhan and Oscar Wilde speaking on several levels at once with a soft tongue and dazzling us with the voice-over, which to me, in a really interesting way, analyzed how time has been completely blurred by the media. Anyway, Michael Sorkin's distemper with the present time and then his particular situation of having to give two lectures at once led to a contradiction between his going at double-time and yet speaking in favor of slowness.

MICHAEL SORKIN Slowness of time, not slowness of thought.

JENCKS Right. I know, but the two lectures do compete a little bit in one brain. But I want to focus on Fred's contradictions. I agree with Fred saying it's absolutely necessary to show the relationship between postmodernity and modernity and how they illuminate each other. I agree with a lot of things he said. But one thing that I will criticize — which I think he's always criticized for — is his totalizing the present at the moment that he is criticizing totalizing tactics. He said, "We can't talk about ethics," and he swam to one side and pushed away all those born-again modernisms. Then with the other hand he pushed down all those things that he had thought were dead. But of course a consequence of postmodern pluralism is that it has to include revivals of modernism. So my question about his totalizing narrative is derived from the way he was talking about what we can and cannot do now. I share most of your feelings, Fred, but you were saying that different production systems engender different senses of time, which can be talked about in some objective sense. Yesterday, I said that one-sixth of humanity is still in the Neolithic era. They may have a different sense of time, and who are you or I to say their sense of time isn't equal to your totalizing sense of the present?

JAMESON Look, our task as intellectuals, as critics of culture, is to make some sense out of the current situation, which no one may be able to do, which we may do poorly, but I wouldn't be embarrassed by that. I can't believe this figure about the Neolithic except as a poetic thought, because there really are no genuinely primitive tribes anymore that haven't been touched by so-called civilization, even deep in the rain forest. The rain forest itself is being attacked, so I can't believe that there are any areas on the globe that are untouched by this unevenly developing system.

Now we're not, as intellectuals, the ones who are doing the totalizing. It's capitalism that's doing the totalizing. It's happening in spite of us, and it's pulling the world together. Globalization is certainly totalizing; it is the very logic of the system. When people accuse me of archaic Hegelian tendencies, I always like to say that it's not my fault; it's the fault of the system. It's not that I want universal identity instead of difference, the system wants that.

Two more things. Modes of production: If temporalities and cultures are produced distinctly by modes of production, postmodernity is not a new mode of production. In my argument, it's only a third moment of capitalism. The modern was perhaps the second moment, and that's what creates this problem, because postmodernity is both distinct and a kind of break with the modern, but we're still in capitalism. It's just a much more advanced form. You could say that computers are something brand new, but when gas or electricity came in, that was a radical shift as well, yet the system was still capitalist, still pushed by the profit-motive. This is the problem with this particular narrative. You have to tell a little of the story of modernity and that stage of capital, but then you somehow have to add on this new one to it, which is both a break and a continuity at once. That's really a dialectic, I guess.

Now, why are these old things coming back? You make it sound like they're all sort of slowly rising back up to the surface again. Well yes, but they are also postmodern. That is to say, one of the things that postmodernism did, and one its logics, was pastiche and the revival of old things; so we have a baroque postmodern, we have a medieval postmodern, and all the rest of it. This is the pastiche of the modern. These concepts of modernity that contemporary sociologists and politicians are peddling are not the concepts of modernity when they were real and alive and forged by the great thinkers. These are imitations, Xeroxes of all those concepts. Current ethics – that's all a pastiche. Theories of civil society – a pastiche of the great moment of the Enlightenment. There is a postmodern reason for these resurfacings, but we have to understand them as being images of themselves and not the real thing.

JOHN RAJCHMAN I also was stimulated and intrigued by Fred's remarks, and I can understand why he's dissatisfied with a certain number of tendencies in thought and artistic architectural practice. But his way of dealing with them is different from mine, and perhaps that's the source of our disagreements, if indeed we have any. I think that the best way to think of these things is not to postulate a period concept and then put everything you don't like into the previous period so that if anything goes back to them, you can say it's not adapted to our present. That, I guess, is Charles's sense of the problem of totality. In a curious way, a lot of the aspects of modernism still appeal to young people, who are living in this "other moment," who do not want an amnesia of that very interesting modernist tradition. They want to do something new with it, to adapt it to new conditions. I liked Akira's remarks that perhaps those new conditions are no longer cinemagraphic but infographic, or something like that. That's an interesting intuition about where this modernism will be revived. I think that is also true of philosophical concepts; they can come back in an interesting way in a new situation. When Deleuze, for example, wrote about Bergson in the 1960s, no one was paying any attention to him at all. What was interesting in Deleuze's attempt to go back, not only to philosophical figures like Bergson but also to modernists like Kafka or Proust, was his attempt to give us a new way of thinking of those figures adapted to our emerging sensibilities. For example, Jean-Luc Godard is engaged in this interesting **histoire de cinema**, going back over the postwar history of cinema, with a sense that it will be used again. I wonder if you aren't too dramatically disallowing the recurrence of these things.

JAMESON We have to invent some way of feeling our way back into the modernist situation and the richness of modernist praxis without becoming modernists, because at that point it becomes historical. What Deleuze does with these things is more brutal and exciting. He doesn't just understand Leibniz and then show us how Leibniz can be. He seizes what he wants and fabulates a whole new fresh Leibniz in his own image; it's very exciting and a very contemporary practice. Maybe it's a different way that one should use the past – that is, not so much respect for telling-another-story-of-it in the sense that there are these multiple stories. If someone told me that Deleuze's Leibniz was historically incorrect this would not be terribly disheartening for me. On the other hand, it seems to me that it's the present that we're all concerned with. We don't have to be bored by these things that are being offered us – we can do something new. The real contradiction here is that we're still modernists in the sense that we want something new, even though we don't want that **modernist** sense of the new. It's a deep contradiction, which reflects this relationship of two moments of capitalism. Brecht said – this is the Brecht year, so one must quote Brecht – "Let's prefer the bad new things to the good old things." This is still, although modernist, an excellent slogan for us to follow.

AUDIENCE My question is also to Fredric Jameson. I was concerned when you said that we should not give accounts of modernity from the perspective of subjectivity. At the same time, you suggested that there's a deep Eurocentrism to the notion of modernity. If we want to recognize that deep Eurocentrism, if we want to make accounts of it, can we easily get away from subjectivity? In other words, regardless of whether we think that subjectivity is representable or not, the Eurocentric subject represents it anyway. It's a subject that always re-represents itself. Modernity not only suggests that there is a mode of production to it, which accounts for its temporality, but it also implies a constitution of subjectivity in very particular ways. I notice that you also make reference to this Cartesian notion of subjectivity. If you want to make accounts of that, aren't you too easily getting rid of this account of subjectivity?

JAMESON That's a very important question and I don't think I can take enough time to answer it, but I will try to clarify a little bit. Let's say that what I meant by descriptions of subjectivities was essentialism. That is, there's a modern subject. Well, then there has to be a nonmodern subject, so already things are being said about people and their selves and so on. On the other hand, I proposed – and I think this leads immediately to Eurocentrism; it's inevitable – that one should describe it in terms of the situation, but I didn't mean by that to be positivist or objective in some horrible and lifeless, mechanical way. I omitted the model that I was thinking of, Heidegger's reading of Descartes in his long book on Nietzsche. In essence he says: Look, there wasn't this modern subject that appeared and then did all these things (everybody talks about the subject-object split, which is modernity, that began with Descartes). Rather, he says that the subject, in order to make the object appear in front of it, had to construct itself in a certain way. So what you have is a mutual construction of subject and object. That's a genuinely historical event that's not an essentialism or attribution of some kind of subjective qualities to this new modern subject, but it does somehow take into account the situation. That's the model I would prefer. At that point, you're beyond Eurocentrism because you're simply describing the conditions of the appearance of this stuff, which has to do, for example, with the organization of military forces in Descartes's period in the Thirty Years War, and so on. You are no longer in the essentialisms of the modern soul or spirit.

Rethinking Space and Time How is space, the presumed object and ground of architecture, bound up with time? Space and time are continually reconsidered in the natural sciences (from cosmology to evolution) and in the humanities and social sciences, with time seen as duration, period, event, moment, episode, change, etc. How does the problem of space and time in architecture help us to rethink space and time in the larger, cosmic sphere? How has technology altered our perceptions of space and time? And of the space and time of architecture?

Time Warps: The Monument Peter Eisenman

In his book *Mason & Dixon* Thomas Pynchon writes, "Time is the space that is not seen." Should we take this to mean that time is a condition of space? Fred Jameson, for one, seemed to think so when he said here that the postmodern condition involved the transformation of time into space. I do not think that this is what Pynchon had in mind, however. Time has always been linked to space, at least since the Chinese circle, which was calibrated at 365.25 degrees to correspond to the number of days in a year. Jesuit missionaries broke apart the link between space and time when they changed the Chinese circle to 360 degrees.

While *Mason & Dixon* is ostensibly about space – the 18th-century survey to plot the Mason-Dixon line – much of Pynchon's discussion is about time and its disjunction from space. For example, he describes how difficult it is to use a watch on the high seas and how the Jesuit-driven move from the Julian to the Gregorian calendar cut 11 days from the year in 1752. Indeed, this is not so different from what is happening to time today, as our global economy has given rise to a global time that is both arbitrary and relative in terms of place.

Take, for example, the State of Alaska, the largest land mass in the United States. When Alaska was simply a territory, it had six time zones. To fly from Juneau in the southeast to Nome in the northwest took four hours. But because Alaska is in a circumpolar zone in which the time zones narrow with the curve of the earth, one landed before the hour one had left. When Alaska became part of the United States, however, it was not practical, economically or politically, to have six time zones. Alaska needed one time zone and it had to relate to California in the lower 48 states. As a result, all of Alaska was arbitrarily placed in a single time zone that is one hour removed from (behind) California. Due to this arbitrary determination, today there is no relationship between real time in Alaska, clock-time in Juneau and Nome, and the time that existed in Alaska 50 years ago.

Time today is not constrained by a location in space as it once was. In one sense this is because of the increased speed of travel, but in an entirely different sense it is also because political, economic, and social considerations have made time independent of space. However, time and space in architecture are quite another matter, for they raise another issue, one that involves the relationship between the subject and the stationary architectural object. Historically, the subject came to understand the object of architecture through an experience of it in time. The more the subject moved in and around architecture, the more the subject understood the object. This understanding was usually ordered by a series of referents: a grid, an axis, a *marche*, or a *promenade architecturale*; that is, a sequential ordering of a series of apperceptions in the experience of space. The time of the object and the time of its experience, and thus the subject's understanding, were inextricably linked.

With Einstein's development of the Theory of Relativity, the idea of space-time as a continuum outside of subjective experience became a conceptual reality, with time seen as a fourth dimension of space. In *Space, Time and Architecture*, Sigfried Giedion attempted to relate these developments in mathematics and physics to what was happening in modern architecture. Giedion introduced his idea of the interpenetration of space-time through the transparency of glass in order to allow the subject to conceptualize the interior and exterior of a building simultaneously. There was no longer a need for a classical axis or even the more recent idea of a promenade architecturale. Clearly, Le Corbusier's spiraling ramps at Poissy and for his Mundaneum project, as well as the encircling ramp at Strasbourg, were an attempt to displace the axis of bodily symmetry from the symmetrical axes of classical architecture. This displacement, however, still took place in narrative, classical time. Space and time were still understood as a simultaneous continuum. Giedion's reflection on the "so-called" fourth dimension of space, while seemingly canonical in 1940, today seems rather naive in light of the advancements in virtual space and time. Transparency has proved to be a literal one-liner and architecture has moved to even more refined ideas of space-time. In the poststructural moment of today, architecture has become critical of both classical and modernist conceptions of space-time. Indeed, there is a sense in which the idea of a space-time continuum has been pulled apart. Time is no longer necessarily delimited by space; in fact, time may inhabit space in ways that have never before been conceptualized in architecture. For example, while the virtual space-time of the Internet is not possible in architecture, it exists as a conceptual possibility.

In 1912, Henri Bergson introduced the possibility of a difference between the time of the object and the time of the experience of the subject in his book *Matter and Memory*. He suggested two kinds of time: chronological, or narrative, time and the time of duration. For Bergson, chronological time concerns what he called a difference in degree, while the time of duration proposes a difference in kind. While architecture is usually experienced in chronological time, Bergson's idea of time proposes a possible disjunction between the time of duration and the time of apperception. For example, in the dissolution of a sugar cube in water, the time of the cube's duration has little to do with the time of a subject's perception of the event.

Bergson's two conditions of time are attempted in two of our recent projects: one a stadium for the Arizona Cardinals and the other a memorial in Berlin for the murdered Jews of Europe. While they are quite different, both of these projects can be called poststructural monuments. The monument as stadium and the monument as Holocaust memorial are loci of hyperreality; that is, they are both constrained by program, one iconic and the other indexical, at the same time that they have been cut free from their former modes of representation. The indexical program of the stadium is a motivated one. That is, the sign and the signified are internalized; they cannot be separated from one another. For example, it is not possible to change the space of the playing field or the relationship of the spectators to the playing field, therefore these spaces are controlled by the delimiting functions of space. Equally, it is not possible to separate the internal time of the stadium from its condition in space. This is not the case with a Holocaust monument.

Adolf Loos said that architecture is about monuments and graves. This meant that an individual human life could be commemorated by a stone, a slab, a cross, or a star; in other words, by a conventional icon as opposed to a motivated one. This iconic function

Eisenman Architects, Memorial for the Murdered Jews of Europe. Competition model, 1997.

ended with the Holocaust and Hiroshima, that is, with the mechanisms of mass death. Architecture can no longer remember life as it formerly did because the markers, which were formerly icons of individual life and individual death, have been changed by those events. This change has had a profound effect on the idea of history, memory, monument, and, ultimately, on the relationship each has to time. If it is possible today to make disjunct the relationship in architecture between the time of the object and the time of the subject – that is, to separate the internal time of the memorial object from the time of its experience – then the Holocaust is a prime subject. Most architects take for granted the idea that time is constrained by space or by the movement of the subject in and around space. Today, the space of the iconic monument is an artificial constraint and the architect's only control is that of time, the time of experience as distinguished from the time of the object.

The enormous scale of the Holocaust, and Hiroshima after it, is such that any attempt to represent the horror by traditional architectural means is inevitably inadequate. When the memorial is the site of an actual prison camp, it becomes a locus of the memory of real time. It is a time and a memory that are necessarily time and place specific. But it is precisely the specificity that allows the memory of the Holocaust to be easily assimilated, because the camp acts as an icon of memory.

In *Remembrance of Things Past*, Marcel Proust suggests that there are two different kinds of memory: one is a nostalgia in touch with a sentimentality that remembers things in the past not as they were but as we want to remember them; the other memory is a living one, active in the present with no nostalgia for a remembered past. The Holocaust cannot be remembered in the form of an object or site from the past that enacts a nostalgia for the object itself because the Holocaust forever ruptured nostalgia from memory. The memory of the Holocaust today can only be a living condition in which the past remains active in the present. In this context our monument attempts to present a new idea of memory as distinct from nostalgia. In order to do this, the time of our monument, its duration, is made different from the time of human experience or any possible understanding. It is almost as if the iconic monument has imploded to become the indexical one. The context for our monument in Berlin is the enormity of the banal. It suggests that when a supposedly rational and ordered system grows out of scale and exceeds its intended purpose, it in fact loses touch with human reason. Our use of a dense, seemingly regular grid of pillars is no longer a guarantee of a coherence between space and time. Rather, this grid begins to reveal the innate disturbances and the potential for chaos in all systems of seeming order, to show that all systems of a closed order are bound to fail. This potential is manifest as a disjunction between the time of the project, that is, its internal time, and the subject's experience of the project.

This is achieved in the following manner. There is an initial order of some four thousand concrete pillars, each 92 centimeters wide, 2.3 meters long, and with heights ranging from zero to five meters. The pillars are spaced 92 centimeters apart so that only individual passage through the grid is allowed. The ground plane on which the pillars stand is inflected, falling from grade to some three meters below grade in places.

Equally, the top plane of pillars is also inflected, appearing as a rolling sea; it is inflected differently from the ground plane. This difference appears to be random and arbitrary, a matter of pure expression, however, this is not the case. The top plane of the pillars and the bottom plane of the ground are determined by a divergent set of topological grid lines that situate this particular volume of space within the larger site context of Berlin. These two topological surfaces describe a zone of instability between them. It is this zone that can never be understood in the experience of the object. This zone defines an internal time inscribed in the object field. The irregularities in the topography of the ground plane and the top plane of the field of concrete pillars cause each pillar to tilt slightly from one another. Each pillar tips three degrees to its orthogonal intersection with the slope of the ground. It is only possible to experience the undulation of the ground plane in the context of the individual pillar and the individual space around it. This causes an indeterminate space to develop in what would appear to be a rigid order, creating both a perceptual and conceptual divergence between the three entities: the topography of the ground plane, the field of the pillars itself, and the top plane of the pillars. Thus a time of the object is inscribed between the ground plane and the topmost plane of the pillars. This indeterminacy in the field shatters the axial directionality of the grid and makes it multidirectional. There is no one place to enter, no one place to exit; there is no center, no goal to be reached. It is neither mazelike nor does it have a hierarchy. Rather, the field destroys hierarchy and the intentionality of movement. In this it destroys the illusion of the security of the order of the regular internal grid as well as the frame of the Berlin street grid. This makes for a place of loss, contemplation, a memory void in the present.

The traditional monument is understood by it symbolic imagery, what it represents. Such monuments are not understood in time, as in traditional architecture, but rather as an instant in space. They are seen and understood simultaneously. In architecture that requires a time experience, such as labyrinths and mazes, there is a space-time continuity between experience and knowing. Our monument demands a time experience yet shatters the space-time continuum. The time of the experience of the individual will be the same today as it is 50 years from today. The monument grants no further understanding of the Holocaust because no understanding is possible. The time of this memorial, its own duration from top surface to ground, is apart from the time of our experience of it. In this context, there no nostalgia, no memory of the past, only the living memory of the individual experience in the monument. One has the sense of being lost in space where it is literally impossible to be lost. This feeling of being lost is a disjunction in time.

When the iconic function and the indexical function in architecture are detached, the result is the possibility that in each repetition there is the potential for an unpredictable result. This result is both a locus of the memory of real time as it was formerly known and a virtual time as it is known in the present. The monument is the loss of the possibility of icon or index. No beginning, no end, no meaning, no experience of time as space; it is memory as only the former possibility of memory.

PETER EISENMAN IS AN ARCHITECT IN NEW YORK AND THE IRWIN S. CHANIN PROFESSOR OF ARCHITECTURE AT THE COOPER UNION. HIS BOOKS DIAGRAM DIARIES AND GIUSEPPE TERRAGNI: TRANSFORMATIONS, DECOMPOSITIONS AND CRITIQUES ARE FORTHCOMING IN 1999.

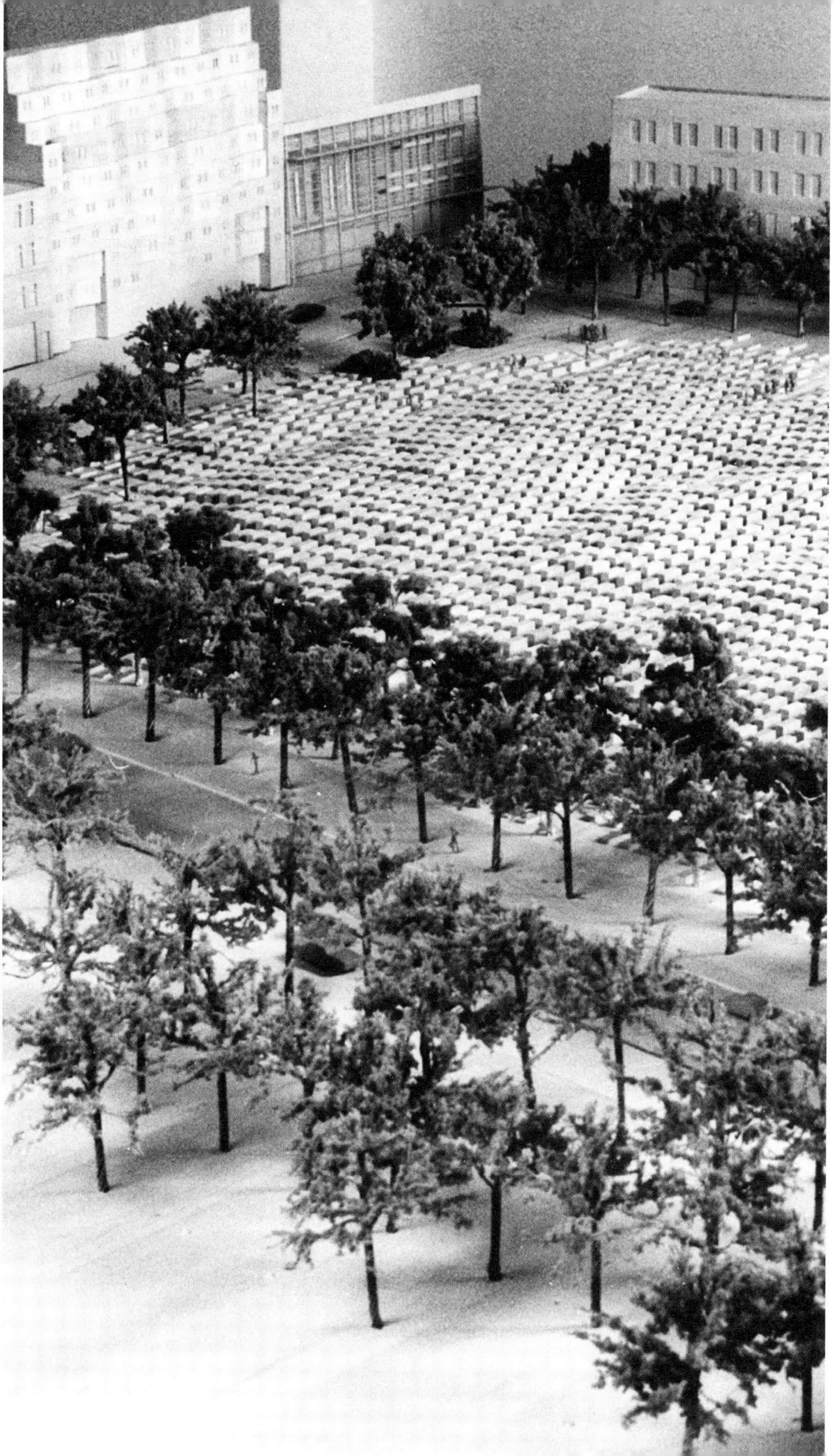

Abstract Machines and Calculable Grammars of Geometrical Shapes Ayşe Erzan

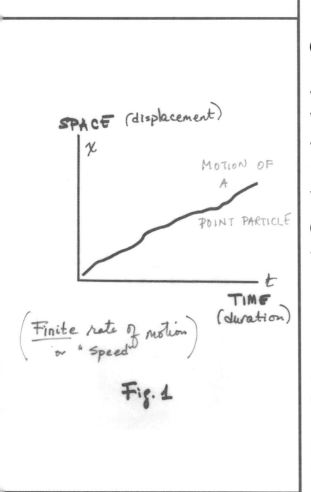

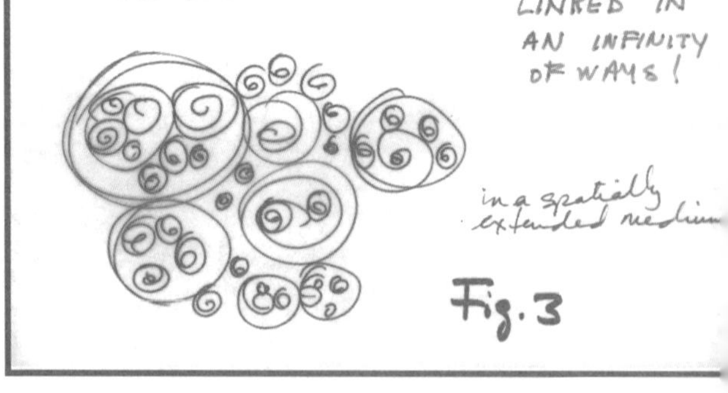

SPACE (displacement)

x

MOTION OF A POINT PARTICLE

t

TIME (duration)

(Finite rate of motion or "speed")

Fig. 1

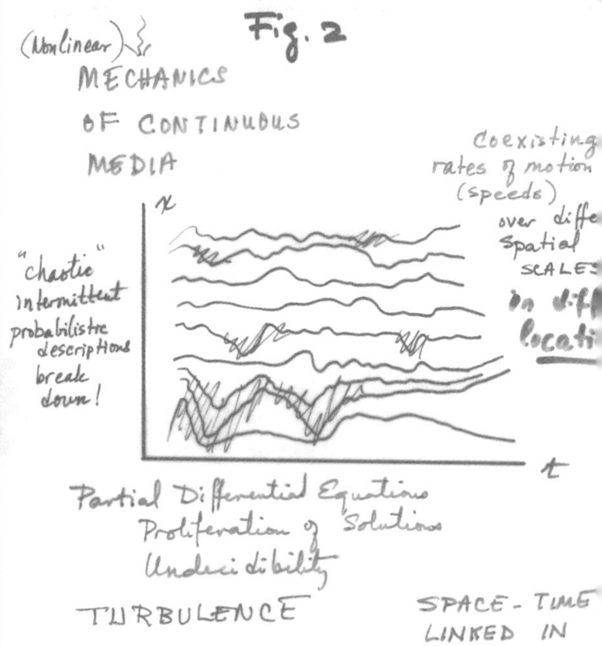

(Nonlinear) & MECHANICS OF CONTINUOUS MEDIA

Fig. 2

x

"chaotic" intermittent probabilistic descriptions break down!

Coexisting rates of motion (speeds) over diff spatial SCALES in diff locati

t

Partial Differential Equations
Proliferation of Solutions
Undecidibility
TURBULENCE

SPACE-TIME LINKED IN AN INFINITY OF WAYS!

in a spatially extended medium

Fig. 3

Fig. 1 The world-line of a point particle.
Fig. 2 Motion of a continuous medium: Trajectories of neighboring points, moving at different rates.
Fig. 3 Nested eddies in a turbulent flow.

Since architecture must at some point be based on assumptions regarding the spatio-temporal organization of human activity in order to shelter, facilitate, or shape that activity, it presumably has its own methods of modeling it. What are the minimal features that such models share? Which follow from the (necessary?) properties of space-time?

The tentative answers to these questions seem to hinge on the concepts of "orderedness" and "contiguity" in both space and time, the linkage of space and time via the concept of causality, and the existence of conserved quantities.

The necessary constraint or condition on the way in which we model space-time, however abstractly or noncontextually, is the quality of being ordered. Given any starting point and a notion of distance, one can order different locations as being more or less distant from that point of origin. Since the surface of the Earth is two-dimensional, we not only need distances but a whole map (distances and directions). What about time? Is it simply a one-way track on which all the events occurring in our universe are sequenced in a unique way? Or, does an event's position on that time track depend on where we are and at what speed we are moving?

Since antiquity it has been thought that space and time are linked together by motion. A displacement takes place over a

finite time interval, as long as the speed is finite (Fig. 1). If motion at infinite speed were possible, then displacement from any point to any other point could take place instantly and we could dispose with the notion of time. The mental picture this statement evokes in most of us is a trajectory traced out in space and time by a point-like particle – its "world line."[1]

All trajectories, processes, etc., initiated at some point in space are constrained within a region with a finite radius that increases with the velocity of propagation and the passage of time. This is a fundamental feature which must be incorporated into any model or simulacrum of space-time. We can think of this propagation into time as a cone – called the "causality bound" – with its point of origin as its apex. The cone delimits the region in space-time in which events can be causally connected via a particular process – the limit case being the propagation of information via electromagnetic waves. This provides a geometrical way of "seeing" the interplay between space and time.

The fact that all human activity is restricted to finite velocities immediately tells us that time and space are bound up inextricably in space-time. This real "causality bound" is often much more restrictive than the theoretically attainable bound given by the speed of light, and it leads to much more palpable consequences.

The idealized notion of Galilean "simultaneity" – the possibility of uniquely marking the occurrence of all events in the universe on a ticker tape issuing from a single clock –

actually needs to be modified for everyday use, not for relativistic reasons but for the very practical reason that human intercourse takes place at speeds much smaller than the speed of light. Apart from purely technical considerations, psychological and social factors also play a role in the perception of distances and the eventual reception of signals that place events on our Galilean ticker tape. It should be clear that in any particular medium of intercourse or communication, for the simultaneity of two events to be an issue, the observer should be placed in a region of overlap of the respective "causality cones" of the two events. In general it can be said that we function in a space-time of mutually overlapping "cones" with all the other "agents" that make up our world.

Rethinking space-time from scratch in the context of architecture is not at all a trivial question, for the following reason: the functions, processes, and so on defined by an architectural plan and eventually by the built object involve motions, circulation, and complex flows in space-time, which cannot be rendered in terms of the trajectory of a single particle. The moment we go from a single particle to a continuous, deformable medium, we have to face the problem of a multitude of – in fact, infinitely many – trajectories, one for every point of the medium (Fig. 2). The motions of these points are not independent from each other; each exerts force on the other, at least on neighboring points. Some of these interactions may be expressed in terms of constraints, or so-called "conservation laws": matter must be conserved, and most fluids and solids are not very compressible, so total volume has to be conserved. Just as distances can easily be associated with time intervals (the "time it takes to get there"), so can areas or volumes (the time it takes to paint a surface or to empty a pool or auditorium). This is how we customarily reparameterize time in terms of space, as in the hourglass, for example.

A particularly interesting problem is posed by the turbulent flow of a fluid. A turbulent flow is characterized by swirling, eddying motions, which take place over many different scales; the velocity of tiny volumes of the fluid differ wildly from one region in space to another. Such motion is termed "chaotic" (Fig. 3). If one observes turbulent flow from any particular point in space, one sees intermittent bursts of violent activity interrupted by stretches of relative but unstable calm. What is interesting for us here is that within such a medium, space and time are perforce linked together in an infinity of coexisting and overlapping ways.

In contrast to the motion of a single pointlike particle, described by so-called "ordinary differential equations" that admit a unique solution once the initial position and velocity are specified, continuous media extended over macroscopic regions of space have to be described by "partial differential equations," which present a greater degree of difficulty. Under certain conditions, the solutions cease to be unique and one faces a question of undecidability. The program

of building a statistical theory of turbulence still has huge obstacles to overcome.[2] It is particularly challenging because we are not simply interested in statistically describing all of the individual trajectories; we would also like this description to somehow incorporate the macroscopic structures, the swirls and eddies, in a natural, easily identifiable manner.

Spatially, extended complex systems far from equilibrium (maintained off-balance by forces like gravity) are capable of producing spontaneously evolving spatio-temporal patterns such as the swirls and eddies in a river. The astounding thing is that over long time periods and at large enough scales, the patterns produced by very disparate phenomena resemble each other, at least over large temporal and spatial scales. In fact, it is this feature that makes it worthwhile to study classes of partial-differential equations capable of describing, at least in some coarse-grained fashion, the spatio-temporal behavior of ecological systems, epidemics, the economy, urban development, or the weather.

Many spatially extended systems, however, are particulate, or discrete, to begin with. They are made up of identical – or approximately identical – units, or building blocks. An alternative way of studying pattern formation is via so-called discrete "cellular automata"[3] rather than with partial differential equations. These are very simple abstractions that represent an extended system using points on a grid, which may be either "on" or "off" (occupied or empty, black or white, "o" or or "1," and so on). They are

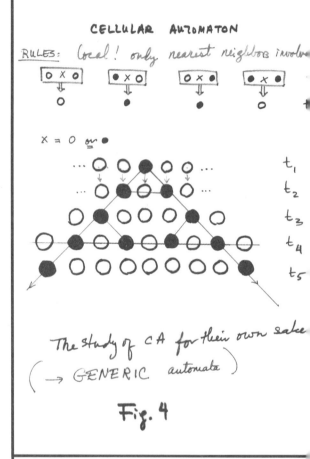

Fig. 4 A deterministic cellular automaton. We see that the system is capable of self-organization over increasingly large distances; at the fourth step, a whole set of alternating black and white sites suddenly turn themselves off, only to propagate at the outer edge into two other triangles identical to the first one, etc. This growth and catastrophic termination continue ad infinitum, and at all scales.

2 Although electronic communication ideally takes place at the speed of light, more realistically, it travels at the speed of many electronic relays that operate along its path. Nevertheless, compared to conventional means of communication, we tend to perceive it as "instantaneous." I understand the remark made at the end of this conference by Fred Jameson, that "time has been abolished" or "has ceased to exist" in this sense, namely, that since the exchange of information with any point on the globe is almost instantaneous, all points seem contiguous, or conversely, all processes simultaneous.

3 *Turbulence Modeling and Vortex Dynamics*, eds. Olus Boratav, Alp Eden, and Ayse Erzan (Berlin: Springer Verlag, 1997).

4 See, for example *Pattern Formation in the Physics and Biological Sciences*, eds. H.F. Nijhout et al. (Reading: Addison-Wesley, 1997), a publication of the Santa Fe Institute on Complex Systems, where there is a project underway on "Evolving Cellular Automata."

5 B.B. Mandelbrot, *The Fractal Geometry of Nature* (New York: Freeman, 1982).

thus particularly suited to digital computation. The temporal evolution of any given configuration is governed by elementary rules, which specify how each site must be updated with every step in time. In most cases, these rules involve only a given site and its nearest neighbors; interactions between units are very short range.

Two such cellular automata, one completely deterministic, and the other, stochastic, are illustrated here (Figs. 4 and 5). Remarkably, both spontaneously produce arbitrarily complex, scale invariant, fractal patterns.[4] The first gives rise to a hierarchy of nested triangles whose appearance does not change when we magnify the whole thing by a factor of two. The second is slightly more subtle, in that the rivuletlike patterns resemble each other under arbitrary scale changes, but only in a statistical sense.

It should be remarked that both of the cellular automata introduced above are completely "causal"; effects originating from a point source remain within a "causality bound" with its apex at that point. Effects cannot precede causes. How, then, do we model things that happen without any apparent cause (or due to a confluence of myriad causes)? With a random number generator![5] (When we call something random, we usually mean that it depends on too many things at the same time for us to be able to model it realistically using a dynamical system with a few variables. A random number generator is a computational device for generating a sequence of numbers that apparently comes from a system with a very large number of variables.)

It should also be noted that the rules of the game defining cellular automata are completely divorced from any particularities of the wide range of phenomena that they are able to mimic. The trajectory of a small, compact, rigid body acted on by gravity can be described by an ordinary differential equation, which does not depend in the least on whether that body is made of wood or stone. Similarly, the hydrodynamics equations depend on the particular fluid in question only with regard to its viscosity and cellular automata are able to generate patterns resembling those that might emerge from forest fires, epidemics, voter behavior, or the transport of fluids through porous media.

Such completely generic automata may be, and are, studied for their own sake. It is possible to show that seemingly different "rules of the game" may produce identical properties over large temporal and spatial scales and to show that it is possible to make the discussion about "universality classes" into which they fall quantitative.

II. *The cellular automaton as simulacrum. The problem of modeling and simulation. The nature of abstraction and explanation in today's natural sciences.* The cellular automaton approach to the world of complex systems is the exact opposite of a reductionist approach. I will call the former the "universalist" or "genericist" approach. The cellular automata claim to provide universal machines that are capable of modeling anything. Here, modeling something means mimicking the spatio-temporal patterns, motifs,

and rhythms exhibited by the system. The fidelity of the mimicry can be judged by more or less quantitative measures, some of which are very elegant and imaginative. But the classification of spatio-temporal patterns, and the classification of phenomena according to the spatio-temporal patterns by which they can be "recognized," has become the "aim" of a certain (very dominant) trend in scientific investigation. Mimesis has become a tool for scientific investigation.

In the reductionist approach, science sought the mechanisms that made that particular system work in the minutiae, in the nature and assembly of the most elementary building blocks to which that system could be reduced. With the universalist approach, the reverse is true. The claim is that diverse systems, over sufficiently long times and large distances, exhibit spatio-temporal behaviors that can be mimicked by generic "machines." The "explanation" is not sought in the building blocks and their interactions; *reproduction* of sufficiently coarse-grained spatio-temporal patterns by a generic machine is what constitutes an "explanation." The generic machine is the "explanation." The hypothesis is subject to the test of the quantitative measures that discriminate between different universality classes, which can be determined on the basis of how such features as, for example, the information content in a particular pattern changes with increasing or decreasing resolution. This quest for generic "explanations" and universal phenomena removes any specificity or contextuality and, in a sense, "denatures" the phenomena it aims to investigate. In terms of time and space, phenomena are to be identified solely by *the way in which they break the uniformity of space-time.* This denaturization is in fact part of the procedure of investigation and is eventually part of the "explanation."

Most interesting generic machines (cellular automata) are capable of exhibiting qualitatively different, and even seemingly incompatible, spatiotemporal patterns upon the tuning of a parameter. This extra dimension makes it possible to link behaviors heretofore thought to be singular or contextual. It is perhaps in this sense that the single, unifying generic machine most powerfully qualifies as an "explanation."

The study of cellular automata in and of themselves is one step removed from the numerical simulation or model-making that has supplemented, and in many cases has supplanted, the laboratory as a domain of scientific investigation. In fact, this phenomenon of "precession of simulacra" has been foreseen and discussed by Jean Baudrillard in an almost prophetic passage, which I quote here:

> Today abstraction is no longer that of a map, the double, mirror, or the concept. It is the generation by models of a real without origin or reality: a hyperreal. The territory no longer precedes the map, nor does it survive it. It is nevertheless the map that precedes the territory – precession of simulacra – the map that engenders territory. . . .
>
> But it is no longer a question of either maps or territories.

Something has disappeared. the sovereign difference, between one and the other, that constituted the charm of abstraction. . . .The real is produced from miniaturized cells, matrices and memory banks, models of control – and it can be reproduced an indefinite number of times from these. It no longer needs to be rational, because it no longer measures itself against either an ideal or negative instance. It is no longer anything but operational. In fact, it is no longer really the real, because no imaginary envelops it any more. It is a hyperreal, produced from radiating synthesis of combinatory models in a hyperspace without atmosphere. . . .

> The era of simulation is inaugurated by a liquidation of all referentials – worse: with their artificial resurrection in the system of signs, a material more malleable than meaning, in that it lends itself to all systems of equivalences, to all binary oppositions, to all combinatory algebra.[6]

As a physicist, the most eerie thing about this passage is that Baudrillard is not talking about cellular automata in particular. In the rest of the book, the problematic of the "precession of simulacra" is discussed in a much more applied manner, in the context of social and cultural practice. However, today, many scientists wonder in a very similar vein about the way in which the study of cellular automata, of their abstract, pristine structures, or "systems of signs," which pride themselves on their generality and genericity, in many ways preempts the more strenuous, arguably more serious efforts to model real physical, biological, or even sociological systems. Such maps of reality can

also engender new domains of scientific investigation, new territory.[7]

III. The cellular automaton as an abstract machine or Deleuzian diagram. I would like to turn now to the new and exciting prospect that has been touched upon by John Rajchman,[8] Greg Lynn,[9] and Sanford Kwinter.[10] This has to do with the possibility that instead of an archive of shapes (either as the signifier or as signified), one may use algorithms to generate sequences of geometrical shapes.

As opposed to a compendium of all possible shapes and sequences of shapes, cellular automata afford economically storable and classifiable sets of rules, i.e., diagrams or abstract machines.[11] Acting on an initial configuration, these are able to generate periodic or endlessly evolving sequences of shapes. The abstract machine can be used to model both finished buildings and the functions that will be discharged in and by them. These sequences can be completely deterministic or can incorporate stochasticity; they may be periodic, quasi-periodic, or chaotic; their use is completely up to the artist or architect. Whether or not they are pleasing, useful, etc., is a matter of experimenting with different parameters and configurations. But they suggest new ways to enlarge our vocabulary, not only of individual shapes and the relationships among them but also of self-propagating sequences.

Functions of more than one variable, or their discrete counterparts, namely, iterated maps of many variables, all generate

6 In practice, there may be situations where one might want to include the role of "chance," or the effects of causes exterior to the system at hand. This may be done by relaxing the "causality" condition, and allowing things to appear out of the blue, by picking a random site where an external intervention is allowed (for example, lightning is allowed to strike a tree).

7 Jean Baudrillard, *Simulacra and Simulation*, trans. Sheila Glaser (Ann Arbor: University of Michigan Press, 1994), 1–2.

8 John Rajchman, "A New Pragamatism," in *Anyhow*, ed. Cynthia Davidson (Cambridge, Massachusets: MIT Press, 1998), 212–17.

9 Greg Lynn, "Geometry in Time," in *Anyhow*, ed. Cynthia Davidson (Cambridge, Massachusetts: MIT Press, 1998), 164–74.

10 Sanford Kwinter, "Emergence: or the Artificial Life of Space," in *Anywhere*, ed. Cynthia Davidson (New York: Rizzoli, 1995), 162–71; "Leap in the Void: A New Organon?" in *Anyhow*, ed. Cynthia Davidson (Cambridge, Massachusetts: MIT Press, 1998), 22–27.

11 There is a huge amount of literature on "abstract machines," or cellular automata, beginning with, I believe, Alan Turing. See Alan Turing, *Pure Mathematics*, ed. J. L. Britton (New York: North-Holland, 1992). For a recent text book on automata, formal languages, and Turing machines, see, for example, Daniel I. A. Cohen, *Introduction to Computer Theory* (New York: John Wiley and Sons, Inc., 1991).

12 Umberto Eco, *The Search for a Perfect Language*, trans. James Fentress (Oxford: Blackwell, 1995).

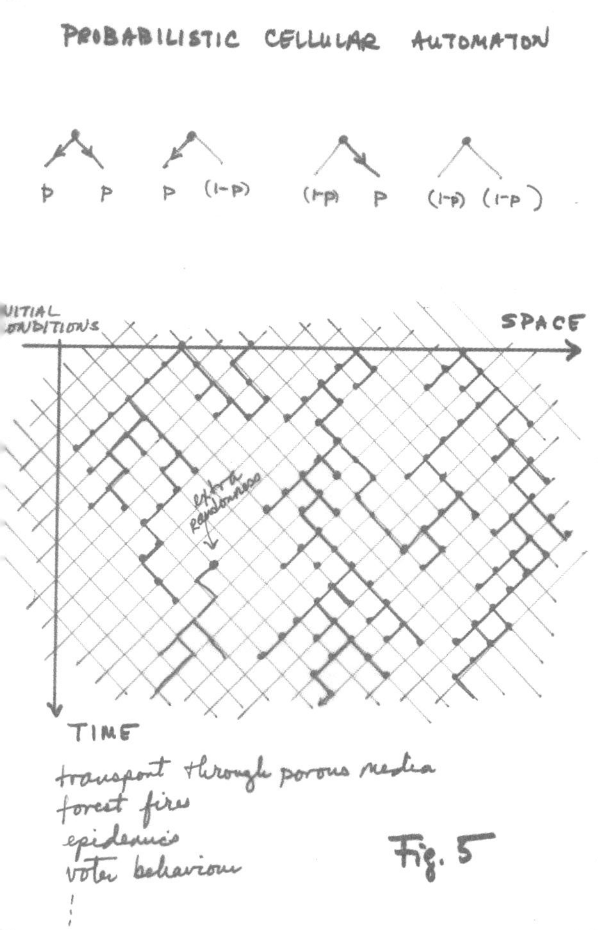

PROBABILISTIC CELLULAR AUTOMATON

Fig. 5 A stochastic cellular automaton mimicking the transport of fluid though a disordered porous medium, among other things. Each occupied site gives rise to either two channels issuing from it, or just one, or the flow may stop there altogether. A similar metaphor could be used to model the spreading of a forest fire; each burning tree has a different probability of igniting 0, 1, or 2 trees in the windward direction. In this case, it might be desirable to introduce an extra degree of randomness wherein a tree is ignited out of the blue (e.g., because lightning strikes it!).

curving, fluctuating, rippling surfaces or topographies that – as Greg Lynn and Peter Eisenman demonstrated at the Anytime conference – can be put to use to enlarge our repertory of shapes. Such functions, or iterated maps, provide compact devices, or abstract machines, and a computer can be programmed to "turn the crank" to produce three dimensional models that can be made to evolve over time. What makes cellular automata special, besides the Boolean (0 or 1) character of their components, the ease with which they can be manipulated, and the fact that they are particularly suited to digital computation, is the utter simplicity of the rules of evolution. These local rules are particularly transparent, making cellular automata highly accessible for modeling diverse phenomena. As such, they are unlike functions with many variables related to partial differential equations, which demand greater technical skill and intuition to connect them with real flows or processes. Perhaps the attraction of working with 0's and 1's, as opposed to arbitrary numbers, is the immediate way in which they can be translated into patterns (black and white pixels, for example). The rule can here be understood as moving directly from pattern to pattern, from one set of spatial relations to another, without the intermediacy of numbers.

I see this exercise is interesting in the context of a quest for algorithms that generate all possible propositions, going back at least to the Middle Ages.[12] Such was believed to be the power of language, that these algorithms were thought to correspond automatically to some reality. The algorithms were designed as ways of generating all connections between all possible signifiers. With the advent of the Enlightenment and nominalist thought, it became clear that not all possible propositions are true propositions, and in place of algorithms "to generate all propositions" (producing a one to one map of reality), the search was on for calculable grammars modeled after mathematics. These were, as in the case of Leibniz, often generated by mathematicians themselves. (By "calculable grammar," I mean one in which grammatically correct statements are also true. This can be checked by explicit computation whether a particular enunciation follows the rules of the grammar or not, and one may then independently verify that it corresponds to "reality.") This shifting of the emphasis from an archive of all objects, qualities, and conceivable relationships between them, to the admissible relationships between certain classes of objects and qualities is of course a great economy. But more importantly, the information content is now shifted from the objects and qualities themselves and concentrated, at much greater intensity, in the connections, in the grammar that governs connections.

The search for a grammar tight enough to allow only "true" statements (I really prefer the term "correct" or *juste* here) has led, eventually, to symbolic and functional logic. This is in fact a step back in the claims – or hopes – attached to such endeavors, in that it constitutes an admission that the connection between any language as a model of reality and "the world out there" is more tenuous than previously imagined. The difficulty seems to lie in attaching the nominative (the signifier) to enough of the attributes of the signified to be able to correctly orient new diagrams issuing from it in such a way that they may not only summarize already known data about the "real world" but eventually point to new, "undiscovered" connections or phenomena, the existence of which can then be independently verified.[13] Moreover, I agree with Gilles Deleuze and Félix Guattari when they assert that Bertrand Russell's logic or Noam Chomsky's grammar – both attempts at instituting a systems of signs that purport to mimic all of the functions of an underlying system of meaning – are both too abstract and not abstract enough:

> Regimes of signs are not based on language, and language alone does not constitute an abstract machine, whether structural or generative. The opposite is the case. It is language that is based on regimes of signs, and regimes of signs on abstract machines, diagrammatic functions and machine assemblages.[14]

Here the exciting possibility of computable grammars of geometrical shapes presents itself. I will try to suggest below that one may, using cellular automata, construct grammars that are both sufficiently abstract and also "verifiable" in that they correspond to some "reality" outside of language.

IV. *Cellular automata as generators of formal languages. Calculable grammars.* Certain aspects of cellular automata are interesting from a formal linguistic point of view. The elementary particles of this language are o's and 1's. Thus, a given sequence of o's and 1's corresponds to a statement. A map made up of local rules for updating a pattern is a one-to-one correspondence (a Deleuzian diagram) connecting one statement to the next in the sense that one implies the other. This relationship is transitive in that it generates a third statement that is also "implied" by the first, and so on. Each set of rules therefore corresponds to a different criterion of "correctness," a different logic. Given an initial statement (a premise), one may, using this map (or logic), deduce many other statements from it in a given sequence. Moreover, these statements do not arise in an arbitrary order but unfold in a particular order in time. (One may perceive a whole sequence of patterns as making up one pattern in space-time.) In this sense they resemble a narrative; the statements that constitute a narrative would not be valid if their order were scrambled. Propositions that do not follow from each other by implication may still correspond to some reality, if we have an independent criterion for establishing this. They may correspond to a different narrative, generated by a different rule or logic.

In this way we can keep inventing new diagrams (or implications) between narratives ad infinitum. This opens up the way to a calculus of narratives, rather than individual signifiers, a meta-language of

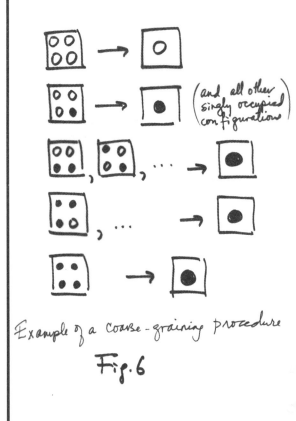

Example of a coarse-graining procedure
Fig. 6

Fig. 6 A possible rule for the definition of a coarse-graining procedure. An alternative would have been to take a majority rule by which one assigns a "1" to a box if the majority of the sites within it are "1," and a "0" if the majority of the sites contained have the value of "0." Tie votes could be assigned to either "0" or "1," with, for example, a 50 percent chance of each.

narratives, each representable in a geometrical fashion. One special case is transformations that map the narrative onto itself. An immediate example is afforded by the first cellular automaton mentioned in Section I. The sequence of shapes (or the narrative) generated by this device, at least for special initial patterns (premises), are congruent with themselves under the operation of rescaling by factors of two. When the sequence of patterns is not precisely reproduced under a simple rescaling, as in the case of the second example of a cellular automaton given in Section II, the rescaling operation needs to be defined with more care. I will call this "coarse graining." Coarse graining consists of making a calculable, irreversible map from one pattern or sequence of patterns to another. That, in this case, also turns out to map many different possible narratives that lead to the same configuration (see Fig. 6).

A further means of defining equivalence classes between narratives, where congruence does not hold, is via "measurements" that can be performed on them, i.e., with regard to their various properties, which may also be statistical in nature. (An important property in this respect is, for example, the rate at which information is lost in coarse graining.)

Clearly, maps from one narrative to another – equivalences between individual narratives – lead to diagrams between the rules that generate the narratives. Inasmuch as one may reduce different rules to a prototypical or "master" rule, we may claim in a very special

sense to "understand" all the different narratives generated by the rules within one particular equivalence or "universality" class. Alternatively, we may also build time dependence into our rules so that, over time scales large enough to allow for recognizable narratives to emerge, they will themselves evolve in time.

V. *Architecture, function, meaning.* Architecture, by its very nature, is the art of "the map which precedes territory," the narrative that precedes action. It is at the same time aware of the territory, the multiple narrative-generating trajectories, or the river-narrative, observed from a point poised above the flood, so to speak. I see every *theory* of architecture, on the other hand, as an attempt to construct a grammar of such narratives.

Simple human functions usually imply periodicity. We normally do not envisage functions that have no beginning or end – design that unfolds endlessly in time – except perhaps for divine beings or abstractions, such as "human society." This is all the more true of the functions that shape architectural designs. The hours, days, weeks, and seasons make up this periodic lattice on which human activity, made up of repeated actions, is hung. All architecture is based on this basic assumption. On the other hand, arbitrarily more complex functions could be identified with, or defined by, similarly complex spatio-temporal patterns. It has already been remarked that architectural design is one realization of a "machine" that once set in

motion, produces all of the complex behaviors identified by the functions discharged in this space of human activity. The fact that both periodic and complex spatio-temporal patterns can be generated by the same cellular automaton gives rise to the possibility that the complexity of architectural design can likewise be parameterized and the function to be generated coded in a universal machine.

This poses a new kind of challenge both to semiology in general and to architecture in particular. It is not an arbitrary (and for this reason meaningless) sequence of signs to which these motions can be reduced. Rather, it can be mapped to a coherent, in fact deterministic, sequence of arbitrary signs.

However, what Deleuze and Guattari call "the liquidation of all referentials" and the adoption of a "system of signs . . . that lend themselves to all equivalences"[15] in the end threatens the coherence of "function," as the latter cannot be completely divorced from "meaning." The designers and consumers of both computer games and architectural products are therefore either faced with the compulsive investing of such systems of signs with spurious meaning or the anxiety of unreceived intimations, which, in the absence of shared referentials, leads to perplexity, alienation, and isolation rather than ritual reaffirmation. I see this conference, with all its "productive misunderstandings," as an extremely interesting exercise in confronting this challenge.

13 On the other hand, quantitative sciences – physics, in particular – have been able to do precisely this. It is fascinating to consider to what extent the predictions of existence of the planet Pluto, the element Uranium, the W-meson, the effect of time-dilation, and the phenomenon of Bose condensation, to name a few, differ from that of the unicorn.

14 Gilles Deleuze and Félix Guattari, *A Thousand Plateaus*, trans. Brian Massumi (Minneapolis: University of Minnesota Press, 1987), 148.

15 Ibid., 136–47.

AYSE ERZAN TEACHES AT THE TURKISH ACADEMY OF SCIENCES AND IS A FOUNDING MEMBER OF THE GURSEY INSTITUTE, A RESEARCH INSTITUTE FOR THEORETICAL PHYSICS AND MATHEMATICS.

Bio Time Greg Lynn

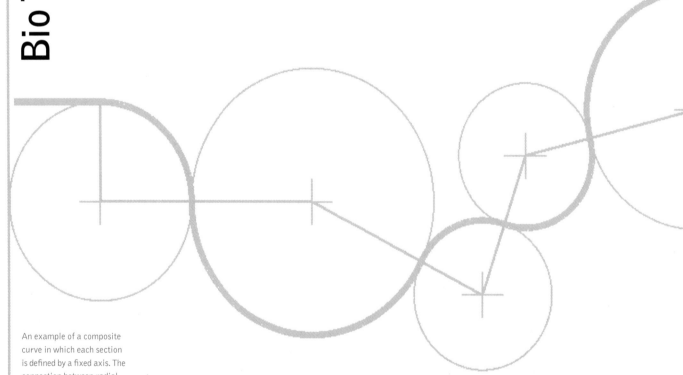

An example of a composite curve in which each section is defined by a fixed axis. The connection between radial curve segments occurs at points of tangency that are defined by a line connecting the radii. Perpendicular to these lines, straight segments can be inserted between the radial curves.

The Anyhow conference in Rotterdam ended with a discussion of the generic. And at the Anytime conference, Rem Koolhaas again raised the issue of the generic as one of the critical terms for the conference. I would like to continue to contribute to this discussion of the generic by defining it as different from the banal and related to development and growth. In addition, because I presented a paper on themes of animation and motion last year at the Anyhow conference, I will try today to extend some of those principles in order to talk about temporal morphologies. So far, architecture has been discussed primarily in terms of the experiential effects of time on form. I would like to discuss the effects of time on form, but I would like to arrive at this discussion through the issue of design-time, or the fact that form can be modeled, conceptualized, and generated as an evolving or growing process. The effects of understanding form as a dynamic condition rather than a static set of coordinates can support a discussion of a new generic, a concept of generic form that is defined from within a genetic field. The generic, in this case, is that which is yet to be differentiated and specified.

Let me first give a few examples of the cultural production processes that support these proposals. This new model of generic form is presently being deployed in manufacturing and fabrication industries. Rather than basing factory production on standardization, industry is moving toward generic envelopes of possibility. Take, for example, the trajectory of car manufacturing. Prewar mass production relied on one model of car that was fabricated and assembled in one factory. During the postwar period, many models of cars emerged, and in order to support the variation specialized factories were developed based on similar processes. Engine factories and body plants emerged to fabricate parts that were transported to assembly plants where the various models were assembled. Different models of cars were designed based on standardized components or kits of parts that could be differentially assembled. Now factories are being built in which the machines can be reprogrammed to fabricate a range of different parts and components. The engines and body panels of many models of cars can be fabricated with the same processes, even though the parts vary in specificity. Instead of designing a machine for a particular model of car, the machines are

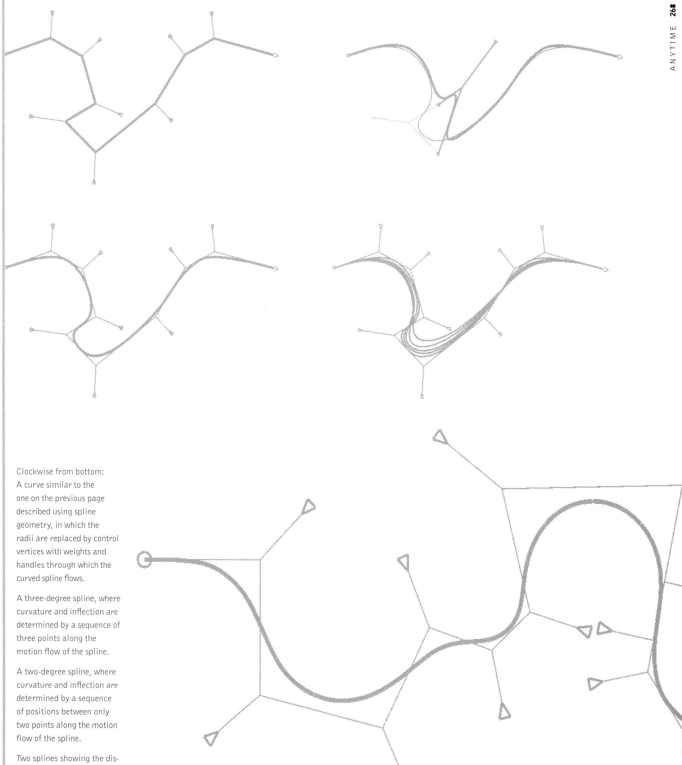

Clockwise from bottom:
A curve similar to the
one on the previous page
described using spline
geometry, in which the
radii are replaced by control
vertices with weights and
handles through which the
curved spline flows.

A three-degree spline, where
curvature and inflection are
determined by a sequence of
three points along the
motion flow of the spline.

A two-degree spline, where
curvature and inflection are
determined by a sequence
of positions between only
two points along the motion
flow of the spline.

Two splines showing the distributed effect of change in
one control vertex across
the length of the spline.

A superimposed series of
splines sharing the same
control vertices with different degrees of influence.

designed for generic processes that are limited by a performance envelope of parameters or constraints. The specific parts are variable, as is their assembly. In this way a single factory can produce various models of cars.

Historically, experiential time implies that architecture is frozen music that can be animated by the visitor or occupant. Form is static and the sequence or promenade of a visitor adds motion to form in order to render it dynamic. This processional model of motion and time is familiar and is based on an understanding of architecture as a collection of frozen frames through which time passes. There is another important model of time that many other disciplines have engaged that looks at temporal morphologies. Organization in biological systems that grow and reproduce over time must be understood in terms of developmental time. Evolution and epigenetic growth conceptualize form as a developing process rather than as a frozen or fixed condition. The principles of design within developmental time, along with the resulting architectural characteristics and effects, should not be evaluated based on the simplistic assumption that if architecture is to investigate time it must literally grow, move, or interact. Most complex organisms complete their growth process and achieve an adult form. The process of developing in time involves an internally constrained organism unfolding in complexity within a contextual field of influences. The effects of this process are the differences that emerge in the organism. These are in principle rhythmic.

At the Anyhow conference I discussed the introduction of calculus-based forms into architecture. Calculus is often described as the mathematics of motion pictures. The zero of steady state equilibrium equations is replaced with either a differential, as invented by Newton, or an integral, as invented by Leibniz. There are two kinds of variation, one discrete, or divisible, and the other continuous, or sequential. Calculus can represent time only as a continuous sequence, rather than as a series of exact points in space. In a Cartesian space organized around a zero point, time is subtracted from an equation only to be later added back. In the three-body problem invented by Lefler and popularized by Poincaré, the future or past positions of three interacting bodies in space cannot be calculated without sequentially calculating their interactions. Similarly, in calculus, as in any differential mathematics, position is always relative to a variable. Rhythm,

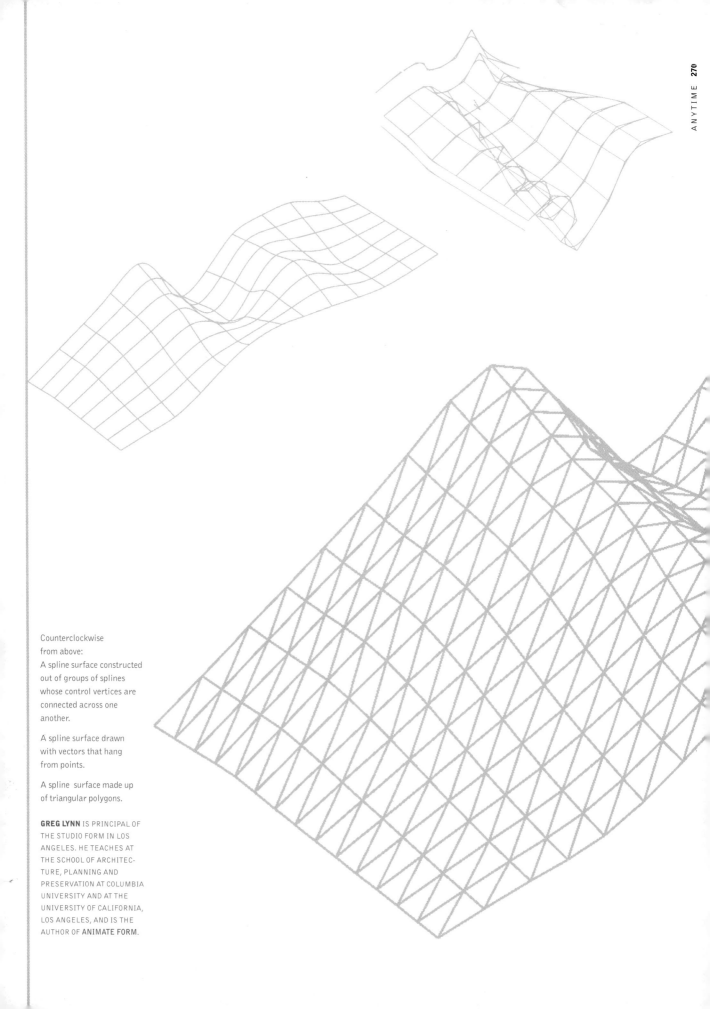

Counterclockwise
from above:
A spline surface constructed
out of groups of splines
whose control vertices are
connected across one
another.

A spline surface drawn
with vectors that hang
from points.

A spline surface made up
of triangular polygons.

GREG LYNN IS PRINCIPAL OF
THE STUDIO FORM IN LOS
ANGELES. HE TEACHES AT
THE SCHOOL OF ARCHITEC-
TURE, PLANNING AND
PRESERVATION AT COLUMBIA
UNIVERSITY AND AT THE
UNIVERSITY OF CALIFORNIA,
LOS ANGELES, AND IS THE
AUTHOR OF **ANIMATE FORM**.

then, is not related to some fixed point that is animated but rather occurs between elements. In calculus there are always differential rhythms and patterns. The primitive element of such a system is the spline. A spline is a curve that hangs from weighted points and creates a flow. Where in a radial curve any point can be defined exactly in relation to fixed radial points, a spline is a continuous multiplicity without points. In order to calculate position or shape on a spline, one must calculate in relation to many variable points as a trajectory in time. The constituent geometric elements of topology are themselves vectors or arrows that have a direction and weight.

Buildings can now be described not as single monolithic surfaces, as Winy Maas suggested (although I wonder whether his VPRO building is an example of a single-surface grotto typology), but rather as assemblies and distributions of nonmoving parts, the combination of which involves the management of connections and relations among elements. The question of time then should not only be posed in terms of the freezing and thawing of a form through a promenade but also in terms of the methods by which elements are rhythmically orchestrated and distributed relative to one another. Rather than freezes, most of our projects utilize sweeps. These sweeps have a beginning and an end, just as any growth process has a moment of fertilization and growth. There is no instancing of form but rather the distribution of elements in sequential patterns according to differing speeds, accelerations, decays, and trajectories.

This eliminates the problem of having to reverse-engineer a form generated in an unarticulated state. By engineering the relation between elements in design time, the architect guides the growth and mutation of a system that is internally articulated through it developmental process. Structure and tectonics are understood within a system of mutational rhythms rather than being imposed after a moment of instancing. Architecture, in this way, involves a process of unfolding complexity from within and an enfolding of complexity from a context. This implies a shift from chronological time based on positions in space to a model of biological time based on the differentiation of a generic organization that tends toward greater heterogeneity.

Fabula Tempus – An extempore speech on the need for extempore experience Ahmet Inam

I am the last speaker, so I hope my speech will not be tedious. My speech, as you see, will be *extempore*, which means improvised or impromptu, without any notes or previous preparation. Extempore is also an attitude toward the future. It means spontaneously, on the spur of the moment, improvised, without precalculation, without any planning. This is, in my opinion, very important because the much needed experience of spontaneity shows that precalculation or preconceived expectation is a hindrance to understanding time, to living through time, with time, and in time. The experience of time in this sense demands spontaneous change of attitude, especially in the midst of our technologically driven daily life.

I am not an architect but I may be, to coin a phrase, *tect* without *arche*. (*Tekton* in Greek means craftsman or builder.) As a *tect*, I have been studying the structure of the experience of time. I am a craftsman of meaning, of experience. In my work I have observed three different, yet complementary aspects of time: *Extempore*; *Ad huc*, *ad huc non* (till now, not yet); and *Kairos*.

First things first. Let us start with *extempore*. Like the French *experience vécu*, although you might not be prepared, you can be full of ideas, expectations, and hopes to such an extent that you live them spontaneously; you live open to the future and to the miracles of life. Although we live in the so-called Minkowski Cone, physical space-time, there is some hope and expectation, in the poetic sense, that one might leave Minkowski space-time, or causal space-time, through the interpretation of the experience of time.

The second aspect of time experience can be called *ad huc*. Ad huc means, in Latin, "hitherto" or "as yet." Ad huc experience requires the examination of the past. We turn to our past and study it and try to interpret it. This is, in a sense, an experience of extempore; we live spontaneously but at the same time we feel the necessity that this kind of experience should be complemented by the experience of ad huc. Ad huc refers to the experience of the our past, and ad huc non means not as yet, or not at this time. This is the experience of something missing, something negative. In English we might

say "so far so bad" rather than "so far so good." As we study and try to live through our past through ad huc non, we prepare ourselves for future extempore experiences.

Between extempore and ad huc or ad huc non, lies an experience of the Greeks: *kairos*. Kairos means the right time, or just time. In Latin one would say *intempore*, or seasonable time; fitting time; the time to move; the time to think; the time to rethink; the time to reconsider our lives.

In English there is the expression "the time of my life." The time of your life is your kairos. You have an important experience; you feel happy; you are very powerful and understand what happened in the past, what will be in the future, and what is happening "now."

Unfortunately, in contemporary life it is difficult to bring these three dimensions together. To overcome this problem we should move toward what I call the *polyphonic* or *polyrhythmic* experience of time. I call it polyphonic because time, in a sense, contains many sounds, many tones from our past. We experience the now and have expectations; we say, "I need more time." The ad huc leads us to the conclusion that we have lived life so far and have some objections; we are unhappy with some aspects of our life and we need time to correct them. We have to find a new starting place. We have to start afresh. We need a fresh life. This freshness, I think, requires a new understanding of time.

My Heideggerian inner voice tells me that the key is *tempus*. Aside from its usual meaning — time — tempus also refers to the right place, or vital spot. That is why we call the sides of our forehead temples. The meaning of space can be found in the word *tempus*. With it we can get from the right place or vital spot to *templum* or open space, space for observation, or sanctuary; sacred space or temple.

The concept of time in Western culture is striking when examined in a Heideggerian way, that is, *poetically*. Down that path we may find important hints about how to understand the relationship between space and time and its implications for modern, postmodern, and ultramodern architecture.

AHMET INAM IS A PROFESSOR OF PHILOSOPHY AND LOGIC AT MIDDLE EAST TECHNICAL UNIVERSITY IN ANKARA. HE IS THE AUTHOR OF SEVERAL BOOKS ON PHILOSOPHY AND LITERATURE, INCLUDING WHAT IS TECHNOLOGY TO ME? AND THE PLACE OF LOGIC IN HUSSERL'S PHILOSOPHY.

Give Time a Break Balkrishna Doshi

I was born into an extended Hindu family. Several generations lived together. Some members were 80 years old and some just a few days old. Birth, growth, and death were recurring and natural events. So were the celebrations of festivals, birth ceremonies, extended rituals after death, and trips together to temples or pilgrimage places. Everyone accepted and shared these inevitable events. Days, months, and seasons passed through good times and bad. Over time, changes in lifestyle – changes or breaks in the social, economic, and cultural structure of the household – became a living part of each of us.

With this evolution, the character, form, and style of the house in which we lived was also transformed. It grew organically, from just a few rooms to many and from one floor to several. Modified functions and revised movements appeared strange, and at times new, yet they were accepted and absorbed naturally. The expanding structure of the house and its evolving functions were like a big sponge, porous and absorbent, constantly providing us with spatial and aesthetic surprises. However, the kitchen, dining room, and prayer room remained focal points, dominating the overall ambiance and serving as the foundation for the shifting plan and functions. Such continuous evolution and transformation have become integral to my perceptions of life as well as my aesthetic experience.

I often went with others to nearby villages and temples to attend various ceremonies. The rituals appeared to be similar, but their purpose, manner of performance, scale, and location differed. They took place in diverse places: on a riverbank, in the open court of a house, or within the precinct of a shrine. These scattered events, held in both modest and profusely decorated settings, did not seem odd but rather gave one a chance to learn more about uncertainty and constant flux.

Ritual emphasized the sacredness of each event and deepened our understanding of our relationship to the cosmos. This comprehension of our tenuous connection to the unknown, the acquired sanctity of an everyday space, and the shift from local time to cosmic time established a deep rather than a superficial bond with the cosmos. Through our chanting, everything became part of the ritual, and soon the invisible but omnipresent gods would arrive. They participated, and, after the chanting of the final *aarti*, the devotees were blessed. The rituals lasted anywhere from 15 minutes to more than eight hours, but we did not notice the passage of time, the space, or our individuality. Psyche, emotion, and faith combined to make each event and experience mythical.

I now sense the how and the why of this continuing acceptance of life. It is the experience of constant sharing. Sharing multiplies the effects of joyous events and diminishes those of sad ones. It adds new dimensions to our understanding of life as a constantly turning wheel or a broken circle, whether the religious or social ceremonies we perform are planned or unexpected. Living together helps us to understand life's uncertainties, the successes and failures. This increases our tolerance and changes our values from material to spiritual. Even the conception of life after death and reincarnation brings about hope. The "present" is only a phase in a transition, part of an unending chain of construction and destruction. These experiences made me realize that life is full of surprise and paradox. Everything that occurred in the past can happen again in another time, place, and form. Once past, events become unrealities, memories, or visions. The endless fluctuation of experience between oneself and others, the immediate world and beyond, good and bad, and then and now, are simply God revealing and concealing his game, his *lila*.

Traditional Hindu architecture, which achieves expression through movement, is perceived not only as a part of this instant or of eternity but as an intimate experience. The broken wheel of time is expressed architecturally as a sequence of juxtaposed long and short corridors with a variety of pauses, scales, interspersed courtyards, and unexpected visual barriers. Such barriers include changes in structural expression and the quality of light.

Likewise, in traditional Indian architecture each space can be perceived independently to complete a unique experience. One can be transformed through a proactive dialogue with space and time. One can cross a threshold into another space, another time, and another phase of psychological and spiritual experience. Walls, columns, surfaces, rhythms, and light are among the instruments that activate these spaces. Such experiences can be had throughout India, in places both small and large, and in social, religious, and royal complexes. These complexes possess a natural pattern in which the normative activities connected to specific functions are transcended and surrounded by an immense number of peripheral links and areas with no apparent function. Even in the conventional temple complex, the zone of activity and the interaction with the participants are marginal. While the open, pillared *sabhamandap* invites assembly, the enclosed, dark *girbhagriha* admits few, thus establishing an inner awareness of silence, void, and timelessness. However, when a devotee undertakes the ritual circumambulation on the plinth around the exterior of the hidden deity's shrine, his perception of time and space is transformed, even though the physical space remains the same.

When I visit the Meenakshi Temple at Madurai, a vast complex built over seven centuries, the spatial experiences continually reveal life's dualities through the simultaneous coexistence of extremes. The spatial organization is characterized by the informal and the formal, the structured and the flowing, the finite and the infinite. The same spatial attributes are intrinsic to India's traditional towns and villages, where the built forms and open spaces enrich both the private and public realms. The temple's corridors of various scales are designed to instantly recall our ancient history. Columns and walls elaborately decorated with stories and myths immediately connect us to other worlds with different times, even as the clock continues to tick normally.

The varied sizes, scales, and types of the complex's open and semicovered courtyards extend my vision to the eternal passage of the sun and the moon, the changing patterns of the starlit sky, and the rhythms of the seasons. The saturated, diverse, and simultaneous experiences at the temple, as well as the deities in the wall niches surrounding the shrines, intercept my movements with their depiction of social contexts similar to those in towns. Nevertheless, these diverse experiences do not distract me from the goal but simultaneously connect me to the complex's main and multiple centers and peripheries. Strangely, this heterogeneous complex becomes condensed into a single experience. Its diversity appears simultaneously both close and far. For example, watching a statue of a deity hidden in the corner of a dark room near the corridor, I continually sense the presence of the main deity across a great distance and through layers of surrounding wall. A universal energy is generated by the dynamic relationships among solids and voids and between the built and unbuilt.

Another significant and completely different architectural example of the dialogue between space and time is the observatory at Jaipur, Rajasthan, known locally as *jantar mantra*, which implies magical contraptions. Here the visitor enters into a totally different time frame. All of the architectural manifestations are sculptural interpretations of scientific instruments that measure cosmic time through the movements of the planets and stars. The devices represent a condensation of all celestial movements in a permanent stage set of precisely located and oriented architectural forms. The casual observer may experience the geometry as enigmatic, but to an inquiring mind, the moving shadows somehow convey silent but certain connections with the sky, the cosmos, and the larger order of time.

In the Islamic complex at Sarkhej, Ahmedabad, built around 1466, a summer palace, a mosque, and several tombs are organized around a vast reservoir. Today it is the most frequented monument in the city. Some visit it simply to go to the mosque, others the tombs, while others simply sit in the shade under the pavilions. In the end, most visitors assemble on the steps that enclose the reservoir, performing the daily chores of washing clothes or bathing. The complex has designated focal points of tombs, mosque, and pavilions, but it is the unassigned, in-between spaces that have become unique, allowing for spontaneous

Stepwell at Adalaj.

activities ever-changing with the seasons, festivities, and intensity of visitors. Rather than physical architectural linkages, the visual, emotional, and psychological connections are what contribute to this complex's popularity and compelling force.

The traditional buildings of India have a strong relation to the sun, the moon, and water. The famous subterranean step wells, which connect changing levels of drinking water, are unique architectural monuments that celebrate the presence of and access to water. Narrow, long, and often more than five floors deep, the wells are located mostly in hot, dry climates where the water level changes drastically between the monsoon and summer seasons. They also transcend mere functionalism. The sequence and process of fetching water is elaborately designed to exalt the ceremonial and sacred aspects of water. Pauses in the spatial sequence and underground rooms for resting accommodate gatherings away from the hot sun. The passage of time is conveyed through the daily movements of the sun and shadows as they filter down through a lattice of beams and columns. Time is also evident in the seasonal changes of the water levels. In this inclined and horizontal space, planned and unplanned encounters with other community members encourage the discussion – and absorption and effacement – of experiences of daily family life. At the same time, in the shadows and the silhouettes against the sky, one discovers a period full of myths and realities.

On the Indian subcontinent, the shapes of towns and cities that grew over time narrate similar physical and metaphysical stories. The juxtaposition of linear and meandering streets with multifaceted, irregular open spaces in Delhi, Ahmedabad, and other cities; the high plinths of the houses with deep verandahs at Benares; the open-sky terraces and extra-large gargoyles in the desert of Jaisalmer; the finely carved *jharookhas* at Jaipur; all simultaneously express the needs of a very complex way of life and the aspirations of a particular people and place. Layers of forms, surfaces, and architectural styles vary in relation to climactic conditions, suggesting the continuity and

prolongation of time. The architecture expresses a lifestyle that has existed and will exist as long as the context does.

Recalling these experiences, I realize how much we have drifted from those so-called immeasurable activities and spaces that are essential to society's physical and social balance. We have to find ways to promote awareness of the changes in the seasons, the phases of the moon and their link to the rise and flow of tides, and the rising and setting of the sun. Only this will enable the inner self once again to perceive the unpredictable pauses that contain timeless energy.

Measuring the utility of a building by months or years does not reveal the quality of one's experience of it. This experience is really disconnected, personal, and time-bound. Imagine a design that has provided for a separation of zones of time, a layering of external and internal worlds, or alternate modes of movement with elements that slow down, break up, and change the course of the relationship of time and movement. Does not such a design provide choices and unexpected joys? Does not the absence of a sustained order lead to memorable experiences? This is always true of great architecture. Sadly, it is not true of our present buildings. New dimensions have entered our perceptions. Our measure of time is accelerating, and events are now coupled with rapid change and uncertainty. The relationship of man to built form has become transitory, and identity has become synonymous with quick, result-oriented action. Symbols are now dependent upon a constantly changing and increasingly uncertain worldview.

Against the well-structured, extremely regulated, mechanized architectural spaces engendered by this myopic worldview, only one constant can help us recover our sensibilities: the introduction of the pause, the "gap," the unexpected, ambiguous link. This gap or "open-ended ambiguity," through its momentary sense of repose in time and reorientation of space, counteracts stressful activity and replenishes lost energy and the spirit.

In architecture, this pause is the unassigned, loosely superimposed space, the accidentally

Vastu-Shilpa Foundation for Studies and Research in Environmental Design, Aranya Community Housing, Indore.

Stein, Doshi & Bhalla, Indian Institute of Management, Bangalore.

Vastu-Shilpa Foundation for Studies and Research in Environmental Design, Sangath, Ahmedabad.

Vastu-Shilpa Foundation for Studies and Research in Environmental Design, Gufa.

discovered corner or corridor or irregular courtyard. In these spaces, use is undefined and choice is unlimited. The spaces may not have tangible, measurable, or material value, but they have a permanent, immeasurable, and experiential value because they contain the possibility of spontaneity.

In the academic and cultural complexes and the townships that I have designed, I have included architectural elements whose only functions are to break the circle of time and to allow opportunities to pause, meander, or simply stray. Because time can stop. And when time is still, we discover the joys of getting lost in space, in time, or in a place. The traces of a linear, stressful life are effaced when we pause to register the changing nuances of shadows and rhythms in space, the quality of light, color, texture, the sound of falling rain, the smell of flowers. This, in turn, connects us to our primordial, timeless selves. This is the challenge I have taken up in my projects.

In our Aranya housing for the "have-nots" at Indore, a multidimensional use of time and resources was employed. To encourage unexpected but accepted participation, we integrated the form and pattern of flexible dwellings with the street patterns. We provided pauses in the form of open spaces that allow residents to choose time, contact, and activity before they reach a destination. Aranya offers residents a choice: they may live at either the pace of a village or at that of a neighborhood on the fringe of a metropolis.

Inspired by Fatehpur Sikri near Agra or the Meenakshi Temple at Madurai, the Indian Institute of Management in Bangalore makes use of unassigned open and semiopen architectural connections to mark the passage of time. The project was over twenty years in the making, during which time several directors modified the academic program, but this uncertainty helped to add new dimensions and flexibility to our design for the campus. The passage along the spine is modulated with changes in light, space, and scale in the covered and semicovered pergolas. This encourages the academics to pause and reconsider the existing and new interactive modes of communication.

Sangath, my design studio, distills both the experiences of my ancestral home and of my work in Le Corbusier's studio in Paris. Its form and plan raise haunting questions about form and formlessness, duality and ambiguity. To reach the partially buried studio one has to pass through several meandering, open and enclosed passages in which natural elements such as sunlight, moonlight, water, flora, and fauna intermingle. The passage from one point to another highlights the connections between the man-made and the cosmic and provides a glimpse of the enigmatic and the immeasurable, the essential parameter of creation.

The word *gufa* (literally, "cave") means underground, dimly lit, and unfathomable space. Within the fluid space of the gufa, which has now become a natural *girbhagriha*, or "golden womb," one is able to discover previous births and reincarnations. Such unexpected experiences make one ask: Who am I? Where do I come from? What time is it? How much time do we have and whose time is it? Yet these questions become irrelevant as one delves deeper, as in a yogic trance. In the gufa, the past, present, and future fuse in a seamless continuum. There is no beginning and no end: in that space, time stands still.

BALKRISHNA DOSHI IS AN ARCHITECT AND EDUCATOR IN AHMEDABAD, INDIA. IN 1955 HE ESTABLISHED THE VASTU SHILPA FOUNDATION FOR STUDIES AND RESEARCH IN ENVIRONMENTAL DESIGN, LOW-COST HOUSING, AND CITY PLANNING.

D5

FREDRIC JAMESON Peter promised me an objection and an attack and I don't feel satisfied, so let me put words in his mouth. It looks to me from the outside that I was saying something like this: time becoming space. That means that time – historical time, experiential time, the future, and so forth – gets repressed into space, covered up by space, and then has to be somehow laboriously teased out. Now, what I understood him to be saying was that no, there was a kind of anytime that was available alongside space, inside certain kinds of space, and you could see it separately. My question is, what happens to this anytime when it does not have its privileged locus, when it does not have its privileged building that expresses it? Is it still around? Does it vanish and then reappear?

PETER EISENMAN Fred, I wasn't making an attack. I was trying to express, given what Ayse Erzan described, that we now have new means of understanding the relationship of space and time, even though that relationship has always existed. We now have new mechanisms – quantum mechanics, for one – that tell us about relationships of space and time that were never privileged for architects to consider. In other words, objects might have a time of their own, independent of experience, and therefore the understanding of these objects may not be through the experiencing subject. The understanding may be in some other way. They may have their own contingent relationship to the subject. This could occur in a building or in a city. We have to rethink what we assume to be, in a sense, a natural condition of time that was understood through subjective experience. We need to rethink how time is played out in the design of these experiences.

JAMESON So time has become space after all? That is to say, we're separate from that? It's going on in the object?

EISENMAN It's going on in the object.

AUDIENCE Peter, I'm having a little difficulty understanding how your Holocaust Memorial would not be sentimental, given that you followed a distinction that Marcel Proust made between two kinds of memory. That's what in philosophy today we call a typical binary opposition; that one sense of memory would not be without the other sense of memory. Moving too fast from one type of memory to the other type of memory is precisely what deconstruction, in particular Jacques Derrida, seems to be warning about. How do you respond? Do you see your work in these terms? I mean the very decision to build a Holocaust Memorial poses the possibility of being blind to oneself as part of the concept of sentimentality.

EISENMAN I don't believe that the construction of memorials or monuments always necessarily implies sentimentality. My argument here is that this is more of a warning about a future belief in rationality. In other words, if we believe in a system of order and logic to such an extent that it becomes excessive, it starts to create its own internal chaos, as we witnessed from Ayse's slides today. If it's sentimental to have a warning about a future belief in logic, so be it – then sentimentality can be used anywhere. Is it sentimental to build a house today? Is the nuclear family a sentimental idea? This was a very difficult project for us because I believe most Holocaust memorials, whether you go to Auschwitz or to Yad Vashem or wherever, have a sentimentality that becomes, for me, kitsch, and reduces the value of the memorial in face of the horrible nature of what it's remembering. We tried to create a separation between this idea of time, that is, the time of the experience of walking here, and the time of understanding what that was. There are no external references. There are no markings on these pillars; there is no order to these pillars; there is no reason for their size, shape, location, etc., other than the experience that one would have of them. If that's sentimental, then so be it.

MARK GOULTHORPE There are obviously many types of memory and they're privileged in different ways throughout history: active memory, passive memory, originary memories. All of the ways we've talked about memory thus far seem to be visually based. Throughout Western history, most modern philosophers suggest that vision and hearing have been the privileged senses, and therefore we've privileged memory related to vision and hearing, a metaphoric kind of memory. In this century, however, philosophers seem to be suggesting that the relationship of the senses to conceptual thought is shifting, and that we're moving away from a privileging of vision and hearing to a privileging of bodily senses. Derrida poignantly expressed that, in relation to a paradigm shift of technology from a scriptural sense to a computerized sense. Now, the memory of smell and taste and touch operates very, very differently than visual memory. Derrida's experimental writing begins to suggest ways of creating cognitive thought based on the other conceptual senses. It begins to suggest to me a completely different relationship with memory. I've found, these last three days, that although there are people beginning to experiment with new ways of creating spaces processionally — what Zaha did was the best and Greg Lynn is obviously releasing himself from his linear memorizing logic, visualizing logic into new modes of creativity — in the presentations themselves we keep returning to a kind of linear, temporalizing logic, a visual access to memory, and that's when the boredom sets in for me. There's very little experiment in the manner of presenting the projects, in talking about the creative process of the projects. There's a great deal of talk about the funky thing itself, but particularly in Peter's talk about memory I was left kind of bored by the narrative. If you're really going to talk about memory, why don't you begin to talk about it in a different sense or find other ways of communicating it?

EISENMAN I think it's very difficult to condense a series of ideas into 20 minutes. I could go through the process of these things but it would really bore most of the people in the audience — the diagrams upon diagrams that were made to reach a final conclusion. Now, the experience of that monument would be totally haptic, because you would have very little visual orientation. Your body would be compressed into a 92-centimeter space that would seem to narrow as the pillars got higher. The sound of your feet on the stones, the sound of your body moving in these spaces, would create a haptic experience that would be very little ordered by the optic. A lot of people said they wouldn't walk into this field — there is something problematic about it for them. At what point are you afraid to go any further? Doing a Holocaust memorial is probably the most difficult project we've ever done because the function is so problematic. How do you memorialize something which in itself is so horrific that it defies any kind of representation? I purposely chose this work to show the possibilities of disjuncting an experience related to an external event to an internal event that you couldn't understand, that is, as you experienced it, but I might not have been successful.

AUDIENCE I would like to raise a question of simulacra, what Ayse Erzan called the map that generates territory, which is very, very interesting. I want to connect this to the Bilbao museum of Frank Gehry, which we saw in Romi Khosla's presentation. We are told that the Bilbao museum was totally drawn by computer and then given to the factory, which, through the information it received from the computer, cast the metal pieces directly from what it was submitted. This means we are facing an architecture with no blueprints, an architecture that cannot be grasped as a picture, a sort of architectural immediacy where a total representational field seems to disappear. What are the ramifications of this? This issue of mapping on the computer makes possible what could not be mapped before, meaning that with a computer we have new geometries that we are now able to map and submit as information. This blurs the more essential issue of architecture's medium. What is the medium of architecture in our present day? I'm not thinking of Clement Greenberg's definition of medium, but medium as translation, the in-between condition when moving from one particular scale to another. Do we have a medium? Or is it all simulacra?

GREG LYNN I try not to be that anxious about the loss of certain kinds of techniques and effects and the advent of others because in fact the most elegant way of resolving a lot of issues in architecture is still a plan. I spend months lecturing my students not on how to use the software – that only takes two or three days – but how much easier it is if they would just draw a plan. When they're looking at these topological geometries and rendered space, they're completely befuddled and confused. I think a lot of the old techniques are still in place and the new techniques give us different kinds of opportunities. For me, as a designer, the most interesting temporal possibilities are how the design process now stretches into realms that couldn't have existed previously. It lets a lot of client and contractor issues stretch into what would have previously been design space. Typically you would tell a client they had to sign a piece of paper telling you how big each room is and what the budget was, but because dimensions are very flexible and elastic, before you ever sign that piece of paper you can start having discussions about modeling the space they want to be in and look at the space very diagrammatically. Where previously we would have been sitting around waiting for somebody to tell us what to do, now we're provoking certain kinds of spatial strategies. This gives me, as an architect, a real authority in a realm of design we wouldn't have had access to, and it lets us push clients much further than they'd ever be willing to get pushed. We can also stay fluid much longer, so if a client changes his or her mind during construction documents, the computer doesn't mind redimensioning the whole set of drawings. So design can be stretched into more diagrammatic, cultural, and economic and production realms.

AUDIENCE Greg, traffic in time and energy in a way becomes space in your drawings. Is it velocity, volume, driving, or walking? There are many components. Could you also consider energy? Heat, wind, sound, light, electricity? And are these things measurable, computable, or even sensible, or are they just inspirational or intuitive? And is your choice of materials – that is, concrete and aluminum instead of biomechanical systems – philosophically connected with time or durability? It all seems against natural things and natural phenomena – all concrete, very manufactured, and not portable.

LYNN I didn't really go into the H-2 House in depth. I talked about the traffic because it's the most public aspect of the building and because that's how most of the people will visit it. In fact, that building is generated out of the statistics of the traffic, the statistics our acoustical engineer gave us when he analyzed the interior space, and the planning of the mechanical engineer because it's all recovered heating and cooling. It's all powered with hydrogen energy, like the space shuttle, and all of the hydrogen energy constraints had to go into the design of the solar surface on the south facade, which was generated from the motion of the sun. All of these things were input at different times in the design process, and each one of those factors changed every single component of the building. So it wasn't as if we said, "Ok, on Monday we're gonna decide about the shape of the massing based on the highway data, and then on Wednesday we're gonna make another decision about the motion of the sun and we'll add something onto the surface." It's the same surface transforming subtly through the whole design process. To me, this is the issue of memory that's most interesting. The information gets built into the surfaces through their inflection and shape over time. We were constantly altering it, and in the end I think it has the aesthetic qualities it does because it's a surface with multiple interacting forces. Those kinds of surfaces have a quality that is highly differentiated and also highly continuous.

EISENMAN I would like to categorically say that I believe I'm the first architect to use titanium, and I used it because it is the only nonorganic material that will grow into the bone. A Swedish dentist discovered twenty years ago that the only way to make implants in the mouth was to use titanium, and my mouth is full of titanium, long before Frank Gehry ever dreamed of using it. Now, you would assume that that's a nonnatural material, but in terms of dentistry, titanium turns out to be the most natural material that you can use. We architects have to be flexible as to what we assume to be natural and nonnatural in the future.

ROMI KHOSLA There is a slightly more basic question about the nature of objects and time. Do objects or time exist outside of the senses? This is an eternal question. The Zen position is very clear: there are no objects outside the senses. In other words, objects exist in the senses. When you get to dealing with architecture in the realm of virtual reality, you are in fact getting closer to this question: does an object exist outside the senses? When you are dealing with architecture in virtual reality, you are getting closer to asking whether the creation of an object in virtual reality is part of your conditioning or if it's a stadium. If one starts looking at the conditioning process, then the nature of the object that you are going to be creating is going to begin to change. This process has shortened the time between imagining something and making an image of it. We know from the new particle physics that is emerging that when you are looking at a particle, the mere fact of looking at it changes its nature. When we start opening up this question of the nature of the observer, the nature of the designer and his conditioning of what object he is trying to create, we will get much closer to the Zen position, which is that the building does not exist outside the mind, and that you have to go much deeper into your sensibilities and into your memories and into how you are conditioned to create a completely new solution.

LYNN More and more, when people ask what kind of architecture these kinds of tools would generate, I say less and less capital **A** architecture. I think of myself as more of a subcontractor within a discipline of design than I do as a designer that knows every little nook and cranny in every single decision in every one of the projects. As a matter of fact, very early on I like people to start telling me what to do, and I've set my office up in such a way that there are always at least three of us telling each other what to do. What this does is diminish the role of the architect as a synthetic, authorial genius who oversees all components. I try to put a kind of schema or diagram into play and just keep it running, keep plugging information into it, because it ends up giving me things as an author that I wouldn't have come up with myself. There's always somebody making a decision about something, someone who has their own preconceptions and conditionings, but I think when you network it all together, you start to get things that are very unconditioned in that sense. It's a question of how you structure the design process.

AYSE ERZAN Architecture somehow has to stand somewhere between a preconceived design and function and meaning and this other extreme of letting this spatial-temporal pattern emerge of itself, so to speak. But if you go to this extreme of random or seemingly meaningless patterns, which also define a function that this building is also supposed to perform, define, and channel, then you are really faced with a very difficult question of meaning. One cannot really think of function as completely divorced from meaning. I was trying to come to terms with this when I was preparing my remarks. But I'm glad that you pointed this problem out, because I think this Holocaust Memorial is a most remarkable solution for this problem. It so happens that when you want to create very highly developed turbulence to study in the laboratory, you take a jet of water at very high speed and force it through a grid. Forcing this flow through a grid creates motion that's completely random, as random as you can get. It gives me goose-bumps to see how someone, without thinking of this, or perhaps thinking of this, has arrived at this solution in trying to build a monument to an event that would rather rule out attaching any meaning. For me, this was really the highlight of the conference.

AUDIENCE I have a question for Peter about the ethics of a Holocaust memorial. I want to stress that I am in no way arguing about not representing or not memorializing or forgetting the Holocaust, but it seems to me that when we put the Holocaust in its temporal context, that is to say, today, I have some hesitations or some doubts. Holocaust memory today seems to have started to act as a screen-memory, screening two things at two different levels. On the one hand, it is used as a political device to shift attention from many similar dreadful things going on all over the place. On the other hand, I hesitate to accept the arguments that the Holocaust is the telos of rationality, as your memorial also seems to represent. I am quite sympathetic with the reading of Adorno and Horkheimer, but they argue is that there was not enough rationality. The Holocaust created the power games like ethnic cleansing, the will to power, domination, etc., which are still with us and are reflected in our everyday life. How would your memorial relate to this? What are the critical strategies today that would shift the emerging fact that Holocaust memories are starting to act as a screen-memory?

EISENMAN I think it's a terrific question. There is a whole other issue about the relationship with power and form and monuments and how power uses these monuments to screen and repress other conditions. When we entered this competition, we had the choice of whether or not to enter. And the choice we made was, if they're going to do it, better that we take a shot at it than some of the other people, even though I have the same kinds of reservations about what it might do. What I was hoping was this: that fifty years from now, a person from Mars could land in Berlin and walk in this field, as opposed to walking in the Tiergarten or through the Brandenburg Gate or the Altes Museum, and be able to experience difference, and to be able to experience a haptic experience as opposed to one that deals with the eyes in relationship to some history that they know nothing about. I was hoping that some physical, visceral haptic experience would be alive fifty years from today, when we won't remember either who did the monument or maybe what it was about. Frankly, the interesting thing about monuments, and something I didn't say, is that very rarely does one remember what the Brandenburg Gate is memorializing. Who remembers what the Arc de Triomphe is memorializing? Who remembers what the Saint Louis Arch is memorializing? Monuments, as opposed to other buildings that have other connotations, lose their identity in relationship to the event and to the person who created them. Very rarely do monuments hold in their related history what they are about. They become symbolic of other events in the city. I would like to think that our monument will be a monument to its time and its place, as 1998 in Berlin, Germany. I have no psycho-social relationship to this thing other than the fact that I believe it will become an important urban artifact and, as such, have its own validity without its relationship to the screening of that event called the Holocaust.

HANS VAN DIJK I would like to go back to the tension, or the dichotomy, between the specific and the generic. In session three, Bernard Tschumi, who always finds an opportunity to have a discussion with Rem, said that Rem was studying generic processes and made very specific buildings. I felt the same about Winy Maas, whose rhetoric is that his buildings appear automatically from a kind of generic process, but when you visit them, they seem highly specific. Now in this session, Peter reintroduces the tension between the specific and the generic, and he reverses it in talking about his stadium design. He says, "I went just the other way around; I went from the specific to the generic because the design doesn't look like anything." This is something that he has liked to do for years, as a kind of result of his work, but what does it have to do with the specific and the generic? You may say it doesn't look like a stadium, which itself is not a specific but a generic thing, but because it doesn't look like anything we've known before, I think maybe it's one of the most specific stadiums we'll ever get.

LYNN There seems to be a particularly Dutch phenomenon, which could probably traced back to Rem and the competition for a house with no style, in which the generic is suddenly intersected with the banal. It's interesting that the generic has become thematic, but it's also become very muddled. I think you're asking about the banal, When Winy says, "We've looked at this datascape and it produced a form more beautiful than anything we could have ever imagined," that's a very strange and Dutch argument about the banal. You hear a lot of Dutch architects, Rem and Winy especially, say, "Well, we looked at this process where we really weren't designing, but, well, look — whaddaya-know, it produces an incredibly beautiful object." and I think that whole tension between design and the banal is really not about the generic. It's about style and it's about the fact that modernism is probably seen as the vernacular of Dutch architecture. So there's a real interest in making a beautiful, modern project into something vernacular and Dutch-banal. I want to resist that logic permeating all architectural culture. I'd pull that out of this discussion of the specific and the generic.

JALE ERZEN I want to ask both architects, where would you ideally like your design to stop? Or, how would you like to interact with the city? If you had the chance, how much would you expand it into the city? I ask this because we've just seen your objects placed in nowhere, with just some traffic and some idea.

EISENMAN I truly believe that a city full of my work would be awful. I have no desire to do a lot of buildings. What I do is not about creating a context but, as Greg said, about experimenting with critical strategies and values. It's like a poem. The poems of William Butler Yeats, I believe, had more to do with the Irish Rebellion than the guns and butter brought over from Liverpool. I would like to think that single buildings still have the power to act critically in a context, and therefore I do not desire to build a lot; I do not desire to leave traces. I'd like to see all of my buildings destroyed after thirty years so there would be room for all of the people out there to build.

LYNN It's funny, because I'm in a partnership where I play a very different kind of role than the other people, but I'm finding with the church under construction that building is actually one of the most overrated activities of architecture. Everyone told me that when the building went up, I'd be completely dazzled and surprised, and all these unforeseen things would come up, and it would be one of the more important experiences of my life. It started to sound a lot like a major life experience, but in fact I found it was actually fairly uninteresting. It's something I enjoy, but it doesn't become some special act that I feel like I've geared myself up for. Honestly, I enjoy much more having buildings provoke a discussion with people like Ayse.

EISENMAN There still have to be buildings.

LYNN Yeah, there have to be buildings, but I'm just saying it's one of the more overrated aspects of architecture.

EISENMAN But you still have to do it.

LYNN Yeah, I know! Fine! But the longevity of the building and its interaction with the city is not the place that I would put all of my energy. It's more about the next one than it is about worrying about the ones that are getting built.

AUDIENCE We've seen in many of the presentations a certain amount of criteria entering into the designs that is now more manageable because of computerized techniques. Don't you think that this presents a certain danger given that a certain set of criteria could actually have a certain effect in the final solution? Say that certain criteria have 70 percent of the effect; the actual priorities are lost. Isn't the architect still going to decide what the priorities should be? And when deciding this, what we see is not the set of criteria, etc., but his basic approach to architecture, in fact, his basic philosophy and basic ethics, no?

LYNN The people who write software for computers study people's behavior and consumerism. They'll figure out that someone will wait twenty seconds for a certain thing to happen on a computer. When the next generation of computers comes out and is ten times faster, the software designers write ten times more junk to clog them up because they know that we'll spend the same amount of time waiting for certain things to happen, and I think it's the same with architecture. If you give architecture more technology or more money or more time, what you do is you see us spending more time and more energy and more technology doing the same old things. Everybody at this table would stay on the edge of bankruptcy no matter what their fees or how many projects they have. That kind of stuff never changes, because in a certain way, if you approach architecture as research, you are always going to do that.

EISENMAN You are assuming that priorities are truths that are inflexible and valid for all time. I think we are finding at this conference that there is no such thing as a priori values or truths that are any more relevant today than they ever have been. We just have more techniques for opening things up. I believe that the sensibility of both client and architect today is far more open and willing to reevaluate priorities than ever before. The role of architecture in history has always been the critical reevaluation of those priorities that we assume to be norms at any one time and that are subject to change through the manipulation in architecture.

AUDIENCE After eight Any conferences, you must have some idea about what is going to happen in architecture in 2020. Do you have a forecast?

EISENMAN The Any conferences are precisely against deciding what the future is going to be; the whole premise is undecideability. The interesting question is, given that the thematic of undecideability seemed very relevant in 1990, when we end in the year 2000, will that same thematic seem relevant or will it have created new thematics simply because of its own ennui? Will that energy lack create new questions and new openings? Basically that's what we were setting out to do individually and collectively. I would like to think that these kinds of meetings are going to engender new sets of problems and issues for students and architects and clients that are totally unpredictable.

DEAR ANYTIME,

In a world in which avant-gardist attempts are rapidly institutionalized, think of a group of architects that has achieved success through "paper architecture" and ideas that challenged the existing norms. Since they can use the tools of the media more intensively in the information age, they have become acknowledged throughout the world more quickly than were their historical predecessors. Though the number of buildings these architects have built and the competitions they are invited to join has increased lately, they still want to preserve their self-image as the "neo-avant-garde" who produce ideas – not just buildings – to transcend existing predetermined notions of architecture. How, then, can one explain the fact that at the Anytime meeting in Ankara, most of these architects described their projects by artificially imposing the theme of "time" on their images, and some offered unrelated papers that seemed to have been presented elsewhere. Moreover, the Any organization itself was unenthusiastic about realizing some of its own claims, as we shall elaborate here. Perhaps one explanation would arise from critically rethinking the aim of the series of Any meetings. This does not mean that we prefer one type of approach to the other or that we build strict boundaries between them, but we would like to draw attention to some of the paradoxes that were at stake during Anytime.

It does not take much genius to realize that organizing and appearing in the Any meetings, whether or not there is a worldly subject to discuss or a problem that truly motivates a will-for-change, is one way for these architects to stay where they have arrived, that is, to retain their position at the "center" of the architectural media. Yet, when the majority of the participants remain indifferent to the problems that some members of the Any group have been defining for years, one should not be surprised if the sincerity of the whole event is received with some suspicion. Nonetheless, viewing the exhibition of some well-known professionals alongside the "young architects" was a rare chance to see the continuities and discontinuities between the two groups. The generosity each showed in donating their exhibition to the Association of Turkish Architects was also quite nice. However, some of us in the audience were struck by the ignorance of the Any group to the criticism that some speakers and audience members directed to the Any meetings in general and Anytime in particular. Only two among many, Ilhan Tekeli, who introduced the concept of "anyfication" and discussed the limits and paradoxes of such series of meetings, and Fredric Jameson, who remarked about the contradiction in searching for another "new" – "anynew" – as a consequence of an "anachronistic" discussion about "time," were particularly illuminating.

We would like to comment more on this "newness," which appeared like a dictum throughout the conference. The distinction between "old" and "new" architecture was explicitly voiced in the discussions by some participants. The "old" conventional notion of architecture was defined as the one which keeps public memories, for instance. The longing for newness may be understandable as a reaction against the nostalgia industry, but it should also be held suspect as a requisite for one to propagate and participate in capitalist society. It seems more than a coincidence that this myth of newness and amnesia becomes so strong in a meeting that needs to uphold itself within the context we have discussed above. We are not criticizing every "new" but the way "newness" becomes prescriptive. The definition of "new" architecture as the one which ignores collective memory is quite weak in explaining, for example, Daniel Libeskind's Berlin Jewish Museum or Peter Eisenman's Berlin Holocaust Memorial, both of which are an architectural expression of Holocaust memories in their own ways. On the other hand, Eisenman's definition of current public memorials as something which should embody living and changing memories, as opposed to nostalgia, was a nice, relevant, and not "new" idea. For example, as Eisenman would certainly remember, the definition of collective memory as a constant reconstruction itself, rather than a frozen past, was developed by Maurice Halbwachs in his book *On Collective Memory* as a critique of Bergson (the hero-philosopher of the Anytime meeting) in the 1940s. This should not necessarily mean that architecture is melancholic by definition, as Charles Jencks mentioned, either. Though architectural melancholy can be defined as freezing time and loving to remember a frozen past, architectural memory can still be presented with the metaphors of flowing time and life. Last but not least, in a context where the myth of newness, fast time, and amnesia has become status quo, memory itself can build one of the critical and resistant strategies, as Andreas Huyssen argues in his book, *Twilight Memories: Marking Time in a Culture of Amnesia.*

Multiculturalism was also voiced as one of the main ideals of the Any meetings by Cynthia Davidson in her closing remarks, as well as in her first introduction of the Any organization in Ankara in 1996. Yet this Any meeting was apathetic in realizing that claim. Throughout the meeting, multiculturality, which has a certain reciprocity with the critique of Eurocentrism, appeared to be paradoxical with the desire for any novelty. Newness itself is an obsession of the modernist conception of time, to which a challenge was attempted at the conference. With the rise of historical consciousness, an increased emphasis on concepts like development, progress, or newness had arrived. All of world history thus becomes judged in relation to criteria like "developing," catching up with the new, or staying behind. Therefore, time becomes perceived to be a single linear line; some societies are believed to be ahead on this line, some to be delayed and trying to catch up with the "new time." Such a single, linear time concept is antithetical to the ideal of "multiculturalism," which realizes the existence of multiple temporalities. The Anytime meeting in Ankara could have addressed this, but except for a few short moments, it missed the opportunity.

The discussion following Saskia Sassen's presentation was one of the rare moments when different spatial experiences met each other. For example, Jale Erzen's comment about the "time habits" of a Turkish bank to resist economic dematerialization, which was then interpreted by Sassen as an example of the frontier zone between the global and national projects, was one of the rare creative moments due to the encounter of different experiences of space. We would add one more point. Though Sassen brilliantly argued that the production process of late capitalism is bringing denationalization to many places, this has not been exactly the case in Turkey. As Tanil Bora discusses in his book *Milliyetciligin Kara Bahari* (*The Dark Resurrection of Nationalism*), being part of the late-capitalist world economy has brought another kind of nationalism to Turkey – one of the countries that has stayed out of the game for years. Being able to commodify products in the world market has reinforced the nationalist pride in this still peripheral country in more severe manners than imagined. There are many such examples that demonstrate different faces of the same process at work in many different places. Whether we like it or not, our value judgments about these processes need to take more than one place of this world into consideration. Gatherings like the Any meetings could be opportunities for such critical reevaluations.

Except for some brief moments, Anytime missed the opportunity for an intense encounter. The encounter of differences is entangled with productivity, and should intensify the opportunity for an other to emerge. Yet at this meeting, most of the speakers created the impression of a transplaced community that was only coincidentally in Ankara. It seemed as if the place were not important. Though randomly selecting the location of a meeting can be a conscious approach, being indifferent to the ideas in that place is inconsistent with Any's goal in making that detour. At the intellectual level, such an attitude resulted, unsurprisingly, in a kind of accumulation of information rather than in an effort to produce knowledge from that rare gathering or to be more responsive to the critical comments directed to the Any organization by eyes looking from "outside." The fact that Ugur Tanyeli's presentation, which was the only one to address the issue of different temporalities in different space contexts, was received with considerable disinterest can be noted as a more precise reason for our discouragement. The difference between the concepts of time determined by the mechanical and alla turcha clocks illustrates that the process of modernization was not the same in every space, and thus world history is not a single, linear line with some societies in front, some behind. Tanyeli's presentation could have also raised discussions about the consequences of these historical differences today.

Occasions like the Any meeting in Ankara are opportunities to test how much the voiced values such as multiculturality or the critique of (Euro)centrism are really at stake. We believe the actual event was not so willing to fulfill its claim. Our pessimism about this event and "optimism of the will" can be refuted by asking what more we could have expected.

Indeed, the fact that such meetings were not organized in "peripheral" countries a few years ago but now are can be regarded as hopeful enough. One might also ask, wouldn't an attempt to gather different space experiences without such "stars" be received with even less enthusiasm? Can this event, therefore, be regarded as a possible cunning twist on the power relations between places by using the tools that created those power relations? Though we agree that the participants seemed to refrain from acting like the "developed" who had come to bring "civilized" ideas and manners to the "underdeveloped," we still find it necessary to note that some time habits are too deeply rooted to be easily dropped. We don't want to generalize about all of the participants, but it seemed that the Anytime meeting was usually too much at the "center" to de-peripherize the "periphery."

The reception of the meeting in Turkey was equally problematic. Either it was downgraded by some intellectuals who didn't come to watch it, or it was celebrated by others as an event for "catching up with the new." On the one hand, there were students who publicly protested against the Any organization for its promotion strategies; on the other, there were "young Turks" who saw the social gatherings between the sessions as an opportunity to promote themselves. In a country where the majority of the architects have been chasing "Western stars" and legitimizing their ideas by referring to them for years, these are not surprising events, but they need reflection. The (we assume) ironic words of Suha Ozkan – "We [Turkish architects] don't copy immediately. We copy 10 years later. Now, we are waiting for the New Modernism to come and enlighten us. This conference may serve this purpose." – summarizes as a parody what we have been trying to say quite seriously. The entertainment decisions of the organizing committee in Turkey also misled the purpose of this meeting by isolating the lecturers and audience from one another, when their interaction should have been encouraged. For the sake of "hospitality" and providing meals for the participants, the mechanisms of border control were produced in space. For instance, the lecturers, their guests, organizers, and some selected people were marked by the colors of their name cards and by defining their lunch/coffee area in the foyer with strict boundaries. To add one more paradox to those we have been counting, the entrance to this area was controlled by a security officer. We were quite surprised to see that such mechanisms were built, given the Foucault-inspired literature that has become common in architecture, and to see how many of the scholars and architects – both guests and hosts – who criticize hierarchy, exclusiveness, foundationalism, etc., seemed quite content to live with these control mechanisms. As a result, the Anytime meeting reminded us of an "old" book with a twist: "Closed society and its friends."

Sincerely,
Esra Akcan and Sebnem Yalinay
Ankara

DEAR CYNTHIA,

As I write this letter at the end of March 1999, I remain very aware of the repercussions of the Anytime conference held in Ankara last June. The graphic identity of the conference, which was designed locally, drew inspiration from concentric waves emanating from a single source, a source perhaps as insignificant as a small drop of water. For me, the Anytime conference has had the same effect: the ideas and projects presented at the meetings, and the discussions that surrounded them, are still making waves in the architectural media. But unlike waves that gradually diminish in strength becoming mere echoes, the continuing discourse that has followed Anytime has become increasingly more profound, and still today reveals a growing impact on current thinking. Multidisciplinary plurality in the field of architecture has been at the core of architectural discourse following the global shake-up of intellectual and social values that began in 1968. At the Anytime meetings, multidisciplinary participation, exchange, and dialogue were unprecedented, not only for the international participants, but particularly for the "young Turks" who took part in the vibrant proceedings. Haluk Pamir was influential in identifying high-level contributions from the Turkish community. His inclusion of representatives of the younger generation of Turkish architects was both generous and courageous, and their reaction was one of excitement, enthusiasm, and commitment. I feel sure that the effect on them will generate work and discourse of real importance during the coming years. Anytime shook up architectural thinking in Turkey and seriously disturbed and challenged the status quo for the first time since the 1940s. In the press following the meetings, those from Turkey who had participated and contributed (Güven Sargin, Nur Yilmaz, Hasan Bülent Kahraman, Haldun Ertekin, Abdi Güzer, Jale Erzen, Aydan Balamir, Kadri Atabas, and Haluk Pamir) expressed positions with the long-range objective of transforming the norms of existing attitudes toward the intelligentsia in anticipation of radical changes in values, perceptions, and approaches. At the same time, distinguished members of the older generation of architects and scholars (Dogan Kuban, Aydin Boysan, and Cengiz Bektas) were not supportive and expressed cynicism as well as scepticism, as if their own fiefdoms of scholarship and practice had been invaded, and that new thinking would challenge and perhaps destroy all that they have cherished. While the former group was enthusiastic about the dynamism of the meetings and the potential to reactivate the idle, dormant architectural establishment and seek new syntheses, the latter group launched irresponsible attacks in the harshest language on every aspect of the meeting, seeking to deny its important and influential intellectual content. This dialectic is very healthy and very encouraging. It indicates the beginning of a debate that will bring thinking on architecture in Turkey to new and perhaps more creative levels. It also confirms the relevance of the graphic identity of the meetings, and clearly demonstrates the powerful, concentric, repercussive waves of new thought.

Suha Özkan

Geneva

GRAVITY'S TIME

1. In Ankara, the uprooted word.
2. In Istanbul, the image.
3. But here Thomas Pynchon's hymn resurfaces.
4. *There is a Hand to turn the time . . .*
5. From the Mamara Sea along the Golden Horn, from these warm waters, the dark outlines of the mosques of Byzantium advance, always bigger.
6. The archetype of the "Great Mother" inflates the immense domes built of pumice stone and bricks from the island of Rhodes, to hide time as the *ferege* hides the body of the woman.
7. Even as we are gliding with the wood, the stillness surrounds you as does the lightness of the *jasmac*.
8. And the eternal invades you with the flavors of Caucasus, the indelible perfume of Prometheus's torment.

1. The conference took place in Ankara.
2. But the first meeting took place in Istanbul, on an old and elegant wooden boat.
3,4. The author of *Gravity's Rainbow* closes the novel with a canticle that begins with these words. The ancient city of Constantinople appears like the "Asiatic hand" that overturns *the time* of modernity.
6. The "Great Mother" is the archetype of conservation, which opposes the "Father," the archetype of innovation, the project. The Hagia Sofia is built with these very light materials. In the Turkish tradition *ferege* is an ample tunic worn by the woman.
7. The wood, the boat by which we navigated the Bosphorus. The *jasmac* is the double veil that covers the head and face of the woman.
8. During the dinner that took place on the deck, we were served a Caucasian meat dish. It produced a sudden resurfacing of the myth of Prometheus (the god of *techné*) chained to the rocks, the chosen site for his divine punishment.

Renato Rizzi

Roveretto, Italy

DEAR CYNTHIA,

I realize that I cannot fulfill my promise of writing a detailed letter on Anytime. However, I would like to thank you, Peter, and Suha for introducing us to the very stimulating world of Any. The debate around the Any group and Anytime is still very much alive here in Turkey. The last four issues of *Mimarlik* (the journal of the Chamber of Turkish Architects) contained long articles still debating Anytime's contribution. Finally, I would like to repeat that I and my colleagues felt privileged to have such a provocative group of speakers with us.
Best Regards,
Haluk Pamir
Ankara
May 5, 1999

ROMI KHOSLA

DEAR CYNTHIA,

I liked the idea of holding your rather rarefied cross-Atlantic seance on the edge that divides Europe and Asia. The preconference boat sailed on that edge, along the easternmost coast of Europe as it went up the Bosphorus and returned along the western edge of Asia. I sat at the tail end of the boat with Arata Isozaki – remotely Asian. It was very interesting to feel and touch the sharp surface of the debate on modernism. I especially liked the process and proceedings of the Anytime Knights testing out their vows to modernism in the public realm. Turkey is just within tuning distance of Europe and North America, and it was clear that despite the crackling noises of terminologies, the audience was coming along just fine.

I must congratulate you for being able to assemble such a lively international event and orchestrate it through uncharted Turkish niceties almost without bumps.

I insist on sending you my carefully taken images. The project to capture all the key figures could not materialize, Zaha avoided the outdoors and the others seemed to have landed up directly at the conference. Arata seemed to me the remotest knight of the Garter, deep inside his context and made accessible to us through Akira Asada. My image of him is seen in the courtyard of Suleiman's Mosque, surrounded by enormous architecture.

I saw Fred Jameson defined within a stone framework, seemingly floating and yet oracle-like, telling us the narrative, guarding the doors of historical inevitability. The line between the shadow and sunlight beneath his feet places him in the cool shadows of academia.
Peter Eisenman, Charles Jencks and Michael Sorkin I saw and imagined separately and together, opening doors, rummaging in the patchy, stained landscape of architecture while continuously looking away, ahead, up there somewhere.

The conference was a rare moment for me as I met Rem Koolhaas and Bernard Tschumi after 25 years. Both of them seemed ripe now.

Historically, I believe the conference to be an important one at this critical time for modernism. It was so refreshing to see the advocacy of modernism conducted in such a relaxed manner that talked about defining modernism through seclusions rather than through charters and manifestos. With warm regards to you all.
Romi Khosla
New Delhi

DEAR CYNTHIA,

I was intrigued to be at Anytime, and found it stimulating and enjoyable. The mix of people surprised me, as did the ease of their interaction: there was a sort of gentleness to the entire event, which I liked. Predominantly American, perhaps, but quite European in its feel. The theme was vast, and everyone spaced out across it, I reckon, most speakers preferring a general overview to any specific claims. But there were moments (for me) of real insight, which I have taken away with me.

As a general tendency I noticed that macro-economics (indeed, commercialism in general) seemed to be figuring in architects' dialogue, which was curious to me, particularly as it comes in equal measure to the renewed call for a "critical" architecture. But the relation to "time" in this seemed only to be addressed by Saskia Sassen, who was attempting a critical assessment of economic tendency and areas where its changing process might have implications for architecture. Even then I took it that her definition of architecture was a relatively traditional one, which might itself require reassessment (she stressed repeatedly "building," which seemed limiting in light of the shift to the virtual practices of the financial markets she was highlighting). But we would do well, I think, to recognize the intractability of macro-economics at present, and the extreme difficulty of formulating a "critical" stance that might inform architectural production.

Koolhaas has perhaps opened this field to architects with his interest in demographics of all types, which is articulated frequently as an interest in the "generic" as the sort of commercial soup out of which we crawl in the tendency to the "specific." But I failed entirely to see it materialize in OMA's architecture, which remains highly specific. The Bordeaux House was about as specific as one might get, as was the embassy in Berlin, and seemed to confirm the disjunction between critical theory and practice – just an excellent house in response to a particular brief. Similarly, Winy Maas's use of illegal constraint as context to "allow" curious stuff to emerge is intelligent in its own way, but not what I'd call "critical" – just responsive, pertinent.

Eisenman came at it differently by frequently suggesting that the market is changing now and wants funky stuff (for the Monday Night Football blimp-shot, for instance). In this he comes perilously close to a fusion of critical discourse and simple marketing strategy, which is interesting or dangerous depending on how you look at it. Evidently, the work, which is consistent and compelling, is generated by a sort of "critical creativity," if one can call it that, but it is the point that this is left off that is interesting to me – the point at which it relaxes in tacit acceptance of blimp-shot logics!

The simple binary oppositions that kept popping up throughout the conference (Mau's cognitive/associative, Koolhaas' specific/generic, Eisenman's critical/commercial), as if the critical insights of deconstruction might simply be forgotten, were interesting for their failure to sustain themselves – their tendency to reverse at certain moments. Such that this *relaxation* of Eisenman – might one say, the ability to alternate between such oppositional states – I found perhaps the most interesting aspect to the conference. Simply the *time* that we're in, much more diffuse than we architects (consciously) allow!

Zaha's presentation was compelling in that she came at it in terms of process – the vague and fluid meandering of her imagination. This was very different from the kind of stricture of most of the others, where there's an IDEA that leads, that implies a temporal and linear sequence. Idea for her seems to emerge from a sensual cycle, or a series of sensual cycles, which presupposes a very different attitude toward creativity.

So, what of time? It seemed to me that almost everyone approached it in a quite abstract fashion, distant, conceptual. Which itself implies a certain temporalizing (visual) logic. Almost no one attempted to engage with it, except some of the young groups who seemed willing to take a few risks (in our hall – Zeynep Mennan, Can Bilsel), but who were not really heard. It was during Eisenman's discourse on memory that this was clarified for me, and suggested another way that the temporal debate may be framed.

There are many aspects of memory (active, passive, originary, etc.), which one might venture become emphasized differently throughout history according to shifts in conceptual thought. If the base of conceptual thought shifts – the "pattern of thinking" – it seems quite likely that memory, or our relation to memory, will also shift: it would be strange if our relation to memory were constant. I'm led (contra Jencks) to suggest that memory ain't what it used to be, or that the way memory figures in cultural activity alters continually. And with it, of course, our ability to narrativize events in any simple fashion (as he intends).

It seems evident that we are going through quite a radical paradigm shift as we pass from scriptural to electronic media: everyone (Jencks, Jameson, etc.) seems to "get" this, even if they don't feel comfortable trying to explain it – a kind of acceptance of McLuhan's suggestion that manuscript man, typographic man, and electronic man operated quite differently. Jencks, Jameson, and Tschumi all talked of narrative structure (J&J pro, T con), but what was more notable was that almost everyone adopted simple narrative structure in their presentations without exhibiting any awareness of it in terms of the cultural (temporal) expectations it implied.

For me, it's not that narrative is relevant or irrelevant, but simply that it presupposes a temporal attitude that might be looked at differently in an electronic age. Warhol's comment that "the moment narrative begins the boredom sets in," we might simply take as marking a shift in expectation – that the linear, visual-metaphoric logics that narrative seems to imply (as a gross generalization) are being eclipsed by other cultural tactics – that there's other forms of intelligence surfacing. One can "get" in this environment without necessarily "understanding," which seems to suggest a form of cultural *trauma* – a creative gap or absence. But frequently my experience is that the most vivid cultural moments are the ones that escape comprehension, not through banality but as a quite calculated play of expectation and effect. In the context of a discourse on time, it seemed strange that such effects were not highlighted, since this seems to impinge greatly on our day-to-day modes of practice and our structure of temporal comprehension.

The question might then be (without invoking astrophysics or space-time scientisms): how does one begin to address this absent cultural landscape in which the simple memorializing circuit of eye-ear is called into question? That seems to me architecture's most apparent temporal dilemma, which opens the entire field to speculation of effects: design process, reception, presentation, education, etc. The entire controlling schema!

One only has to listen to Tschumi to realize that one can operate coherently and intelligently even if one lacks the narrative gene! This despite the fact that the *effect* of his architecture, for me, falls well short of the nonnarrative intensity of the examples he sites (Joyce, etc.). To create highly charged event-space would seem to require not an ignorance of historic precedent (which he seemed to invoke) but a rigorous absenting.

Derrida has devoted much attention to all manner of temporal logic, and articulates the temporal (linear-causal) aspects of visual-aural privileging, which he suggests have dominated Western conceptual thought for centuries. If, as he conjectures, this privilege is compromised in numerous ways by electronic media, then current technical change raises profound questions for our patterns of (linear/causal) thought, and the metaphoricity that they imply. This is where I think critical thought might well apply itself in terms of temporality, in thinking through how all manner of temporality is implicated in terms of our patterns of reference, and in the structured, linear process we adopt in creating and comprehending cultural artifacts. We have privileged a quite direct and specific memory device to legitimate cultural reference, which may well no longer be effective as different cultural manners are adopted, as other patterns of thought and memory are stimulated into existence.

Derrida, of course, suggests that the bodily senses may well offer a more legitimate model on which to base conceptual thought in the computer age – senses which are not distant and idealizing, nor even capable of direct remembrance: they seem to need direct stimulation and then trigger wildly, almost metonymic rather than metaphoric, quite intense and trippy. This would seem to posit another way of comprehending the world – an intensity of lived experience rather than a distant and idealizing cultural memory filter. This suggestion is a powerful one, carrying enormous consequences for the temporal aspects of our familiar patterns of thought.

Throughout the conference there seemed virtually no experiment with the actual temporal rhythms of architectural practice, discourse, whatever. I've mentioned Zaha Hadid as offering what seems an atypical attitude to the linear creative process, one which made me think of Luce Irigaray's wonderful essay *Plato's Hystera*, which plucks the eyes out of Platonic rationality and forces it back into the cave, into the dark, fluid, cyclical meanderings of Mother Earth, so at odds with the (masculine, for Irigaray) clear light of day. Zaha's *Hystera* – now there's something challenging!

I found Greg Lynn's talk highly compelling in this sense, since his process begins to become one of differentiation, suspending determinacy in the matrix of the machine. As different factors impinge, so the fluid model adapts, the surfaces a sort of latent memory (of potential memory). This seems fascinating to me in that it almost reverses temporal logic. Erasing the trace that it remembers. And mindful of his compelling suggestion that old dogs chasing Frisbees need to know a bit of differential calculus, I'd add that our present compulsion might well be to create the architectural equivalent of a scarred-up old dog: which leaves us wondering, in a kind of narrative suspension, about the past that such traces mark absently!

It was a shame that there wasn't a summing-up session when everyone could let loose, or be put into narrow enough categories that would allow meaningful exchanges. I'd love to have seen Bruce Mau, for instance, articulating the various marketing strategies on display: who were the bottom feeders, who the factual obfuscators, etc.! That would have reversed a few positions!

Anyhow – it was fun and I thank you for it!
Mark Goulthorpe
Paris

JALE ERZEN

DEAR ANY,

For me, the Anytime conference was most
stimulating and reassuring at a time when I
was beginning to feel an urgent need to look
at art from new perspectives: e.g., science,
physics, new technologies, etc. It was reassuring, because I feel that art needs a new reality
intake, a shot in the arm, and it will come
from science. For me, it is fundamentally the
understanding of nature and the technologies
that facilitate art. This is reassuring for the next
SANART conference on Art and Science, which
will take place in Ankara in the year 2000.

What a treat it was to see Koolhaas's Bordeaux House, to see Isozaki's museum with
the Sun-Moon-Earth – a beautiful love triangle.
Eisenman's Holocaust Memorial reinforced
my conviction about the fact that meaning can
only come through form. Greg Lynn's architecture is cool and hot – poetry and precision.

I enjoyed – as all of us teaching people do –
talking about forms and their infinite implications, but I also at certain times felt a little
uncomfortable about too many words becoming amorphous. Is it that as the discourse gets
finer and sharper, the line that distinguishes
the rational from the esoteric becomes thin-
ner? Or is it that today's architects, with the
weight of the tons of architecture that have
accumulated over millennia, feel somewhat
guilty? May it also be that at the limit of his/
her powers every professional feels the need
to legitimize or rationalize or spiritualize his/
her production? Like Michelangelo pleading
guilty for his art. Many architectural texts talk
about architecture as if it were something
ephemeral. Regarding Lille, Koolhaas talks
about "refraining from architecture." Sassen
talks about dematerialization, others about
fluid architecture, about an architecture of
ruins, architecture of the end, etc. Certainly
they all say something true about the state
of architecture.

What shall we do with what is becoming
a Gargantuan fact – can we simply go on
ignoring architecture's immobile, heavy,
mostly ugly, aggressive, repetitious physical-
ity? It seems banal to talk about the negative,
yet, if not architects, who can bring about
change in the state of the building activity?
Jale N. Erzen
Ankara

JEAN-LOUIS COHEN

PARIS LETTER TO ANYTIME

Anytime I think of Ankara, I think of a city where civilizations have not only been layered since ancient
times, but have also been reinterpreted, at least in their
ornamental repertory, in the major structures built
since the national capital was moved there; a city
where architects were brought from Europe to help
create a Turkish identity with variable combinations of
traditional forms and modern aesthetic principles. In
the 1930s and 1940s the new capital had become a
sort of stage for the internecine, blood-spilling fights
of German architecture (Bruno Taut almost facing
Paul Bonatz on Atatürk Boulevard) as well as for the
worldwide competition between German and French
city-planning concepts.

Full of figurative, fictional energy and yet indicative
of an aspiration to values of modernity that are hardly
purely Turkish, in June 1998 this setting was only a distant backdrop for the discussions of temporality in
architecture, faithfully reproduced in the preceding
pages. Like the pervious ones, the conference was neither devoted to a nostalgia for a lost avant-garde, nor
to the delineation of an improbable future, but to fer-
tile conflicts between plural visions of current architecture. Most imported discourses remained unconta-
minated by their exposure to local expectations and
research.

Displacing these conflicts to Paris will confront
them with a very different city, also sedimentary, but
with a wider range of urban artifacts; a city where
architecture has developed amidst public interest, but
in an unexpectedly difficult relationship with intellectual culture. Many issues discussed in the previous
Any meetings, and in architecture at large in the past
twenty years, have been thought in a theoretical space
shaped by French structuralist and post-structuralist
discourse. Yet, one is struck by the resistance of French
architects to theory: one wonders if the denigration of
vision practiced by French intellectuals, and documented by Martin Jay, has not found its twin in what I
would call the denigration of theory by architects.

France develops yet another "*grand projet.*" But, unlike
the buildings, the Cité de l'Architecture et du Patri-
moine, scheduled to open in 2001/2002 in the Palais
de Chaillot, will be a facility where architecture would
be less *serving* than *served* as such, with the conjunction,
in a vast container, of a museum, an exhibition gallery,
a study center, and a stage open to debate. The invitation made by Cité team and the Institut Français d'Architecture to hold the Any mobile feast in Paris in June
1999 carries the promise of not letting a regrettable
denigration survive *Anymore*…
Jean-Louis Cohen
Paris